Praise for
The Facebook Era

"Shih clearly articulates the opportunity for businesses on the social Web, breaking it down into simple, actionable steps for companies to reach and connect with customers and prospects from around the world."

—Sheryl Sandberg, Chief Operating Officer, Facebook

"Looking to create a loyal ecosystem of customers, partners, and others online? Check out *The Facebook Era*, a timely compendium of tools, tips, and ideas to up your game—with authenticity."

—Keith Ferrazzi, author, *New York Times* #1 bestsellers, *Who's Got Your Back* and *Never Eat Alone*

"As Facebook grows to 500 million worldwide users and beyond, it's becoming increasingly clear that the social graph is transforming how business gets done. Executives and practitioners should read *The Facebook Era* and take its insights to work the next day."

—Justin Smith, founder, Inside Network; editor, Inside Facebook

"Social media has created a new world of transparency in business. Those who ignore it do so at their peril; this book tells you not just why but how you should change—or pay the consequences. It is a fundamental resource for anyone interested in the emerging discipline of 'digital influence.'"

—Miles Young, CEO, Ogilvy & Mather Worldwide

"This is one of the most comprehensive and useful books on the market for understanding how Facebook and Twitter are changing business and technology, regardless of your industry."

—Timothy Kasbe, CIO, Sears Holdings

"*The Facebook Era* is insightful, comprehensive, and practical, whether you are a marketer, a salesperson, or a user. Read it. And tell your friends (and weak ties) about it."

—Andrew Robertson, President and CEO, BBDO Worldwide, Inc.

The Facebook Era

Tapping Online Social Networks
to Market, Sell, and Innovate

Clara Shih

PRENTICE
HALL

Upper Saddle River, NJ • Boston • Indianapolis • San Francisco
New York • Toronto • Montreal • London • Munich • Paris • Madrid
Cape Town • Sydney • Tokyo • Singapore • Mexico City

The publisher offers excellent discounts on this book when ordered in quantity for bulk purchases or special sales, which may include electronic versions and/or custom covers and content particular to your business, training goals, marketing focus, and branding interests. For more information, please contact:

> U.S. Corporate and Government Sales
> (800) 382-3419
> corpsales@pearsontechgroup.com

For sales outside the United States, please contact:

> International Sales
> international@pearson.com

Visit us on the Web: informit.com/ph

Library of Congress Cataloging-in-Publication Data:

Shih, Clara Chung-wai.
  The facebook era : tapping online social networks to market, sell, and innovate / Clara Shih. — 2nd ed.
    p. cm.
  ISBN-13: 978-0-13-708512-5 (pbk. : alk. paper)
  ISBN-10: 0-13-708512-5
  1. Business enterprises—Computer networks. 2. Online social networks. 3. Facebook (Electronic resource) I. Title.
  HD30.37.S49 2011
  658.8'72—dc22
                            2010017030

ISBN-13: 978-0-137-08512-5
ISBN-10: 0-137-08512-5
Text printed in the United States on recycled paper at R.R. Donnelley in Crawfordsville, IN.
Third printing February 2011

Editor-in-Chief:
Mark Taub

Acquisitions Editor:
Trina MacDonald

Development Editor:
Michael Thurston

Managing Editor:
Kristy Hart

Project Editor:
Anne Goebel

Copy Editor:
Krista Hansing
Editorial Services, Inc.

Senior Indexer:
Cheryl Lenser

Proofreader:
Apostrophe Editing Services

Technical Reviewers:
Derek Overbey, Benjamin Schupak, Steven Sieck

Publishing Coordinator:
Olivia Basegio

Interior Designer:
Gloria Schurick

Cover Designer:
Anne Jones

To my parents, James and Sophia Shih;
my brother, Vic;
and my best friend, Daniel

Contents

Foreword

I've been a florist since 1976, when I opened my first retail flower shop in New York City. Today 1-800-FLOWERS.COM is a $700-million-dollar company selling flowers, confections, and gifts in more than 40 countries.

We are not in the technology industry. However, technology has always been a key to our success. Rather than fearing or avoiding new technologies, we have embraced them to continually redefine our industry, establish a competitive advantage, and, most importantly, make it easier for customers to do business with us. This has happened time and again, first with toll-free numbers, then with the Internet, and today with Facebook and mobile applications—what Clara calls the "social Web."

We were originally called 1-800-FLOWERS because I made a bet in 1986, the year toll-free numbers first became widely available, that customers would appreciate calling in more than having to come in person to place an order. People thought it was nuts then. But what retailer today *wouldn't* have an 800-number?

In 1991, we went online. At the time, a mere 4.5 million of Americans (fewer than 5%) were online and people still had to pay *by the minute* to surf the Web. I had a feeling, though, that this whole Internet thing would be big, and I wanted to make sure we were part of it. We started with online advertising, first on CompuServe and later on AOL. In 1995, when there were 25 million Internet users in America, we launched our first Web site and became 1-800-FLOWERS.COM. People thought it was nuts, again! But what retailer today *wouldn't* pay for online advertising and a Web site? In fact, the majority of our business now comes from the Internet.

So, what next? Well, you'd have to be nuts to ignore the 500 million active users on Facebook.

But it's more than just the numbers. Past technologies helped drive down costs, improve reach, and grow the business, but in the process we lost something very important: customer connection. I have missed the direct customer dialogue I had in our retail flower shops. The digital age has felt largely transactional in comparison.

This is why I feel even more excited about the Facebook Era than I did about toll-free numbers or the Internet. The social Web is about connecting with customers again—hearing their stories, and sharing in their joys and sorrows and the most important moments of their lives. It's about reopening the dialogue so that businesses can put customers back in the driver's seat and keep getting better.

I met Clara in Madrid last year after we gave back-to-back keynotes at a major business and technology conference. Her message struck a chord with me. The social Web is not just new technology—it is a cultural movement.

The Facebook Era is a powerful book about technology, culture, and business, written by one of the leading innovators in the field. Clara speaks and writes with passion because her conviction is deeply rooted in actual experience. In 2007, when most businesspeople thought Facebook was a passing college student fad, Clara conceived of and developed Faceconnector, the first business application on Facebook.

This book articulates in clear and simple terms the opportunity for businesses on the social Web. Clara presents a wealth of case studies, research data, best practices, and actionable steps, and writes in a style that everyone from the CEO to the summer intern will find enjoyable, invaluable, and immediately useful.

Whatever business you're in—whether you're selling flowers and gift baskets or cars and consulting—embrace the concepts and techniques in *The Facebook Era*. Use them to connect with your customers, and you will go far.

Jim McCann
Founder, Chairman, and CEO of 1-800-FLOWERS.COM

Acknowledgments

I am indebted to my editor, Trina MacDonald, who found me on Facebook, of all places; took a big chance on an unknown author; and then worked tirelessly to make the first edition a great success.

I thank the many tens of thousands of you from around the world who read the first edition of this book and engage in dialogue on social media business topics every day with me and one another. Special thanks to the most active contributors on our Facebook Page: Nadine Gerber, Samir Pandit, Todd Chaffee, Ernesto Bruscia, and Rich Liao. Though we have never met, your stories, questions, and comments inspired this second edition.

I would also like to thank:

Steve Garrity, my good friend and programming partner from college and, most recently, cofounder of Hearsay Labs. We started our company in summer 2009 to bring to life many of the concepts from this book.

The Hearsay Labs team, some of the most innovative and inspiring people (and best ping-pong players) I have ever known.

Sheryl Sandberg, Elliot Schrage, David Swain, and the Facebook team for their wonderful ongoing help and support.

The loving and gracious support of my family, especially Chiu Wu, Susan K. L. Mok, Patrick Mok, Peter Mok, Rich Mok, Otto Chan, and my grandmother, Lau Kim Ping, who has spent her life breaking glass ceilings, inventing her own rules, and making sure that I do the same.

My reviewers, Steve Sieck, Derek Overbey, and Ben Schupak, for keeping this manuscript honest and well balanced.

The individuals acknowledged in the first edition of this book, too numerous to list again here. The book's success has been a testament to your support, inspiration, and friendship.

Guest Contributors

One of the things I've enjoyed most about the last 18 months (since the first edition was published) has been the privilege of getting to know many of the innovators and thought leaders who are crafting the future of the social Web.

New to this edition, we are fortunate to hear from more than 30 guest experts whose thoughts, research findings, and best practices appear throughout the manuscript. I am extremely grateful to this group for their contributions to this book and to our field.

Here they are, followed by industry/academic affiliation and their Twitter or Facebook handle:

- Jennifer Aaker, Stanford Graduate School of Business (@aaker)
- Rohit Bhargava, Ogilvy Public Relations Worldwide (@rohitbhargava)
- Danah Boyd, Microsoft Research Labs (@zephoria)
- Ezra Callahan, Facebook (facebook.com/ezra)
- Amanda Cey, ABCey Events (@abceyevents)
- Daniel S. Chao, M.D. M.S. (@danielschao)
- Chris Cranis, Salesforce.com (@forceIUS)
- Guillaume du Gardier, Ferrero (@gdugardier)
- Frank Eliason, Comcast (@comcastcares)
- BJ Fogg, Stanford University (@bjfogg)
- Brady Forrest, Web 2.0 Expo (@brady)
- Joe Green, Causes (@causes)
- Paul Greenberg, The 56 Group (@pgreenbe)
- Gerhard Gschwandtner, *Selling Power Magazine* (@SellingPowerMag)
- Auren Hoffman, Rapleaf (@auren)
- Bernie Hogan, Oxford Internet Institute (@blurky)
- Daryll Johnson, EdBuzz (@darylljohnson)
- Tim Kendall, Facebook (@tkendall)
- Dave Kerpen, theKBuzz (@davekerpen)
- David King, Green Patch (@deekay)
- Charlene Li, Altimeter Group (@charleneli)
- Matt Mahan, Causes (@matthewmahan)
- Sarah Milstein, TechWeb (@SarahM)
- Jeremiah Owyang, Altimeter Group (@jowyang)

- Leah Pearlman, Facebook (facebook.com/leah)

- Natalie Petouhoff, Forrester Research (@drnatalie)

- Mikolaj Piskorski, Harvard Business School (@mpiskorski)

- Dan Schawbel, Personal Branding Blog (@DanSchawbel)

- Deb Schultz, Altimeter Group (@debs)

- Ann Smarty, Search & Social (@seosmarty)

- Ben Smith, Dunkin' Donuts (@bensmith32)

- Brian Solis, Futureworks (@briansolis)

- Gregg Spiridellis, JibJab (@jibjab_CEO)

- Don Tapscott, author (@dtapscott)

- Gentry Underwood, IDEO (@gentry)

- Ray Valdes, Gartner (@rayval)

- Kira Wampler, Intuit (@Kirasw)

- R Wang, Altimeter Group (@rwang0)

- Elizabeth Weil, Twitter (@elizabeth)

About the Author

Clara Shih created Faceconnector in 2007 (originally Faceforce), which integrates Facebook and Salesforce.com and was the first business application on Facebook. Clara is CEO and founder of Hearsay Labs—a provider of social CRM software that helps companies manage customer relationships and grow using Facebook, Twitter, and other social sites.

Previously, Clara was a marketing and alliances executive at salesforce.com, where she was responsible for the AppExchange and led the company's social media partnerships with Facebook and LinkedIn. She has also worked at Google and Microsoft in corporate strategy and software development. Clara holds B.S. and M.S. degrees in economics and computer science from Stanford and has a Master's degree in Internet studies from Oxford, where she studied as a United States Marshall Scholar. Clara has been quoted in *The New York Times, VentureBeat, The Economist, CRM Magazine,* and other global publications. She was named to *Fast Company*'s 2010 list of the Most Influential Women in Technology. Clara is a frequent keynote speaker at social media conferences around the world, including Web 2.0 Expo, Sales 2.0 Conference, Enterprise 2.0, Netgain, Social Ad Summit, AlwaysOn Innovation Summit, and the Social Networking Conference.

Clara's first book, *Using New Media* (International Academy of Education, 2005), was commissioned by UNESCO to help teachers, parents, and school administrators in developing countries use digital media to adopt best practices and distribute high-quality content and curriculum. Clara is an immigrant to the United States from Hong Kong and learned English as a second language. Clara blogs at http://thefacebookera.com/blog.

Introduction

"I am a firm believer in the people."
—Abraham Lincoln

This book is all about *you*. Neither the first edition nor this one would have been possible without your questions, contributions, and passion for the subject matter. I thank the many tens of thousands of you from around the world who read the first edition and engage in dialogue on social media business topics every day with me and with one another.

Similar to the Internet pioneers 15 years ago, *you* are the ones defining, shaping, and leading the Facebook Era. At a time when the business outlook still feels uncertain, *you* have stepped up to the plate with bold optimism, inspiring ideas, and a willingness to experiment, learn from mistakes, and share. Although in most cases we have never met, your stories, ideas, and comments have inspired this second edition and my new software company, Hearsay Labs.

After the first edition, many of you wrote to me saying, "Thanks for telling us about the incredible possibilities on Facebook for my business. Now please tell us what tools are out there to help us!" As it turns out, I couldn't recommend very many. So I left Salesforce.com, called an old friend and programming partner from college (Steve Garrity), and together we founded Hearsay Labs to help companies grow and manage customer relationships across Facebook, Twitter, LinkedIn, and other social sites.

Special thanks to the most active contributors on our Facebook Page: Jamie Parks, Joseph Ray Diosana, Olena Koval, Danni Aiken, Shannon Ng, Nadine Gerber, Samir Pandit, Todd Chaffee, Ernesto Bruscia, and Rich Liao. As the rest of you begin thinking about how to apply concepts from the book to your business, I encourage you to check out their ideas and contribute your own at:

- http://facebook.com/thefacebookera (I have set up discussion threads on each of the chapters. Please weigh in!)

- http://twitter.com/clarashih

What's New

Less than a year has passed, but the world has changed dramatically since *The Facebook Era* was first published. A goal of 200 million Facebook users sounded like a lot then, but more than 500 million people are on Facebook today. Back then, we had some ideas for what might work for businesses on social networking sites, but many of the case studies were admittedly half-baked. Everything was nascent.

This edition tells the rest of the story. By many measures, Facebook has "won." Twitter has become relevant (at least buzz worthy). LinkedIn has strong momentum. However, many of the other social networks in the last edition have all but disappeared or been forced to focus on narrow and specific niches, such as music in the case of MySpace or virtual worlds in the case of Hi5.

Today the social Web is filled with many more examples of innovative ways in which companies are successfully getting to know and support their customers, reach new audiences, and sell more stuff. We are finally beginning to understand and, in some cases, quantify the value of online social networks—whether for sales, marketing, customer service, innovation, collaboration, recruiting, or some other business function.

Few companies have completely mastered the social Web, but many are doing one or a few aspects really well. This book uncovers best practices, trade-offs, and pitfalls from leading companies across multiple segments and industries, and suggests how your business can take advantage of the social Web.

Social media is suddenly no longer a mystery. It is partly science that we can study, learn, and measure. This book teaches you how to do so. I've added new chapters based on your requests via Twitter and Facebook. I've largely rewritten the rest to reflect the many changes and innovations that have taken place during the past year:

- Each chapter now ends with a summary of takeaways and an actionable to-do list.

- We set up discussion threads for each chapter at http://tinyurl.com/facebookerachat for you to delve into specific concepts, share your own experiences, and learn from peers.

- The book contains more than two dozen case studies and examples to bring important concepts to life.

- Instead of talking about Facebook only, this edition also provides extensive coverage of both Twitter and LinkedIn.

- We have incorporated expert opinion sidebars from renowned social media authorities across the business, academic, and analyst communities, including Frank Eliason (director of customer service at Comcast, better known as @ComcastCares on Twitter), Mikolaj Piskorski (professor at Harvard Business School), and Charlene Li (bestselling author of *Groundswell* and *Open Leadership,* formerly at Forrester Research).

- We have added five new chapters, including ones on customer service (Chapter 5); innovation and collaboration (Chapter 7); ways to develop your Facebook Era plan and metrics (Chapter 9); advice for small business (Chapter 13); and advice for nonprofits, healthcare, education, and political campaigns (Chapter 14).

How It Started

It was spring 2007. Smoking indoors hadn't yet been outlawed, although this place might not have cared either way. These two older men, clearly regulars, sat in the back corner, with bare, lanky arms hanging out of their wifebeaters, a cigarette dangling out one side of their mouth and a toothpick out the other. They were gesturing animatedly, laughing, eating, smoking, and chattering away in loud Cantonese about this and that.

I tuned them out to focus on my steaming bowl of wonton soup. Just then, out of the corner of my ear, I heard them just barely: *"Blah blah blah Facebook."* I instantly sat up to listen. I had not been mistaken—these two men, slurping their congee at an anonymous diner tucked away in a corner of Hong Kong where foreigners never go, were talking about *Facebook*. Their children who were in college abroad had gotten them into it, and now they were hooked. I was floored. It was the moment I realized that if Facebook were not already mainstream, it would become so very soon.

I flew back to San Francisco the following week and attended the first Facebook "f8" developer conference, where they unveiled a new Web platform that would enable third-party software vendors to build applications for Facebook users. The product demonstrations were mind-blowing—new Facebook applications such as iLike for sharing music with friends, Slide for sharing photos, and so on.

Still, I felt like something was missing. Photos and SuperPoking are fun, but where were the business applications? At the time, I was working at Salesforce.com, which made its name developing customer relationship management (CRM) applications. But wasn't relationship management at the core of what Facebook was offering, albeit in a more fun, casual, and modern way?

That night, I went home and sketched an idea for bringing Facebook to business. As a product marketer, I had been spending a lot of time on sales calls and saw that the most successful reps established immediate rapport with their prospects and had the strongest personal relationships with customers. In my personal life, I saw Facebook help establish faster and better rapport with people I had just met, and help me maintain closer relationships with my friends.

Facebook, I realized, *is* CRM. So I decided to try something bold: Combine Facebook with Salesforce.com. With my friend Todd Perry's help, I developed Faceconnector, which pulls Facebook profile and friend information into Salesforce account, lead, and contact records. Instead of anonymous cold calling, sales reps and other business professionals could get to know the person behind the name and title, and even ask for warm introductions from mutual friends.

Fortunately, Todd and I weren't alone. Enterprise companies such as SAP, Oracle, and Microsoft evolved their products to include Twitter, Facebook, and other traditionally "consumer" social media. New companies emerged, such as Telligent, Lithium, and Jive, to build enterprise social technology from the ground up. The social CRM movement had begun.

Why You're Reading This Book

Social media is a disruptive force for business. Every customer and employee suddenly has a voice, and what they say matters. Companies have no choice but to become transparent, responsive, and collaborative, or else risk going out of business. Everything is changing around customer expectations, customer participation, and how companies are organized. Brands are being elevated or jeopardized overnight by a single customer's opinion that "goes viral." Next-generation products are no longer being conceived in the lab or executive boardroom; they're generated by customers themselves. Unquestionably, we are living and working in the Facebook Era.

As we saw with the Internet Era and the PC Era before it, mastering the Facebook Era has become the new competitive advantage for businesses. Just as when we had to learn how to Google and email 15 years ago, today we have to learn Facebook and other social technologies to be effective in our personal and professional lives. This book is meant to help you understand and successfully implement online social networking tactics and strategies for your company and career.

Perhaps these situations sound familiar:

- You know that your business needs to get on Twitter and Facebook, but you don't know where to begin or how to advance to the next stage.

- You use Facebook, LinkedIn, and Twitter in your personal life, but you aren't quite sure how it fits with your professional life.

- You want to hear how real companies are succeeding at sourcing and converting leads, engaging audiences, and transforming customers into evangelists on social networking sites.

- You understand that whether it's looking for a job, closing a deal, or advancing your career, a lot of it comes down to who you know in your social networks.

- Increasingly, you're being asked to do more with less, and you want to leverage the power of your networks, your colleagues' networks, and your customers' networks to get the job done better, faster, and cheaper.

500 Million and Counting

With more than 500 million people spending an astonishing 20 billion minutes per day logged in, social networking sites such as Facebook, Twitter, and LinkedIn are creating new norms around how we behave, share, and form relationships. And it's having a profound impact on just about every aspect of our lives.

As a businessperson, you *need* to be where your customers are, and customers are spending more time on social networking sites such as Facebook and Twitter. How will people use Twitter or Facebook to learn about or become engaged with your company and products?

What started (at least in Facebook's case) as a dorm room fad has blossomed into a cultural movement. More than a decade ago, the World Wide Web of information emerged, connecting us with news, content, and information. Today a World Wide Web of people is emerging, creating an online social graph of who is connected to whom and how. As with the Internet era before it, no aspect of society is untouched by these new technologies. From Iran's election to basketball player Shaquille O'Neil's million-plus following on Twitter, the rules are being rewritten across business, politics, and philanthropy alike.

With the lightning pace of technology, we are living in a very different world than just a few years ago. Today's college students don't use email except with "grownups" such as professors and potential employers—they send text messages, Facebook poke, and write on each other's Facebook Walls.

But it's not just college students. The largest and fastest-growing segment of Facebook and Twitter users are those aged 35–49. We are relying more on social networking sites as a primary means to communicate with friends and get the news. Newspapers, email, and traditional Web sites aren't going away (well, some would argue that they are), but certainly a new player is in town.

It's All About the People

Perhaps the social Web was inevitable. Technology shouldn't be—and was never meant to be—an end in and of itself. It is meaningful and valuable only where and when it serves people. Esoteric technology was the result of an immaturity of our systems and thinking. The social Web provides us with a new way to bring our identities and relationships to the forefront of technology and to make technology people-centric. This book started out about business and technology, but it's also about a paradigm shift in our sociology, culture, and humanity.

The future is anyone's guess, but we do know that business will never again be the same—whatever your industry; wherever you work; whether you are in sales, marketing, product development, recruiting, or another corporate function.

We were in a similar place of anticipation during the early days of the Internet. Then, as now, some companies jumped blindly onto the bandwagon, investing a tremendous amount of time, energy, and capital to implement technologies they did not understand, with no clear strategy and, ultimately, with little to show for it. Others dismissed the Internet as a fad and were gradually outcompeted by online businesses or companies that used the Web to achieve more efficient and effective sales, marketing, recruiting, product development, and operations. But the smart ones took notice and began preparing for what an Internet era might look like. They thought through the implications for their business, and they adapted and thrived. This book can help you be smart about online social networking so that this time around you, too, can adapt and thrive.

If it's true that we are separated at most by only six degrees, then you are not very far from any one of your customers or prospective customers. Read this book, and then go out and get them.

Welcome to the Facebook Era!

How to Use This Book

This book is structured into four parts:

Part I, "Why Social Networking Matters for Business" (Chapters 1–3), provides the bigger-picture framework and social implications from which we can develop a richer understanding and appreciation of social networking for business—what's happening, how it's changing our society and culture, and what we can learn and apply from past disruptive technologies.

Part II, "Social Networking Across Your Organization" (Chapters 4–8), takes a tour of five major functions in a company—sales, customer service, marketing, innovation, and recruiting—and explores how social networking technologies are affecting them.

Part III, "Step-by-Step Guide to Social Networking for Business" (Chapters 9–12), is a practical how-to guide on Facebook profiles, Facebook Pages, Twitter accounts, and social network ads.

Finally, Part IV, "Social Networking Strategy" (Chapter 13–16), is all about strategy and implementation. We discuss specific ways for companies of all sizes, including nonprofits and political campaigns, to best use the social Web to accomplish organizational objectives.

Part I: Why Social Networking Matters for Business

- Chapter 1, "The Fourth Revolution," talks about the social networking phenomenon in the context of the three digital revolutions before it: mainframe computing, the PC, and the Internet. It draws examples from Bloomingdale's department store and Starbucks to illustrate how past technology revolutions changed industry landscapes, and what business decisions helped these companies establish a competitive advantage. The chapter concludes with a brief history of social networking sites and a comparison of Facebook, Twitter, and LinkedIn.

- Chapter 2, "The New Social Norms," explores the changing expectations, behaviors, and etiquette that are emerging around sharing information on social network profiles. The chapter discusses personal branding, generational differences, and the concept of "transitive trust" and its role in purchase decisions.

- Chapter 3, "How Relationships and Social Capital Are Changing," discusses the concept of social capital, how social capital is used to achieve business goals, and how online social networks enhance our ability to accumulate and exercise social capital to achieve our personal and professional goals. This chapter explores how online interactions facilitate entrepreneurial networks, the crossover between offline and online networking, organizational flattening, and value creation from network effects.

Part II: Social Networking Across Your Organization

- Chapter 4, "Sales in the Facebook Era," speaks to the power of the online social graph for a sales cycle, from prospecting and the first call to receiving customer references, navigating customer organizations, and enabling sales teams to more easily collaborate. It features a case study on how Silicon Valley start-up Aster Data Systems has used employees' collective MySpace, Facebook, and LinkedIn networks to source leads and build personal relationships with customers.

- Chapter 5, "Customer Service in the Facebook Era," discusses new opportunities around crowdsourcing question and issue resolution with the customer community, ways to address negative feedback, and methods for harnessing customer support forum pages for search engine optimization. It features customer service experts Natalie Petouhoff of Forrester Research and Frank Eliason of Comcast.

- Chapter 6, "Marketing in the Facebook Era," talks about the breakthrough marketing techniques that online social networks make possible, including hypertargeting, enhanced ability to capture passive interest and conduct rapid testing and iteration on campaigns, social community engagement, and "automated" word-of-mouth marketing. It features multiple case studies, including national fast food restaurant Pizza Hut and start-up retailer Bonobos, demonstrating that large and small businesses are achieving marketing success with Facebook's new social advertising and engagement tools.

- Chapter 7, "Innovation and Collaboration in the Facebook Era," describes how the four stages of innovation—concept generation, prototyping, commercial implementation, and continual iteration—become more effective and efficient with social networking sites. This chapter features examples of how companies such as Experian are tapping into the wisdom of their customer communities on social networking sites to source new ideas and keep getting better. It features innovation experts Deb Schultz of Altimeter Group and Gentry Underwood from IDEO. Ezra Callahan and Leah Pearlman from Facebook also weigh in on how Facebook itself uses Facebook to innovate.

- Chapter 8, "Recruiting in the Facebook Era," applies these concepts to the ever-important task of identifying, hiring, and retaining employees. It features a short case study on how Joe, a Chicago-based headhunter, uses Facebook and LinkedIn to source new candidates, keep in touch with candidates who might not be ready to leave their current roles, and maintain personal relationships with successful placements. The chapter concludes with a short set of suggestions for job seekers on how best to use online social networking to find and land the right role at the right company.

Part III: Step-by-Step Guide to Social Networking for Business

- Chapter 9, "How To: Develop Your Facebook Era Plan and Metrics," walks through the tactical steps in defining and implementing a multistage social media strategy, including allocating resources and budgeting, organizing the team, and measuring. This chapter also introduces **social customer lifetime value,** a conceptual metric that I developed to give companies a starting point for calculating the return on their social initiatives.

- Chapter 10, "How To: Build and Manage Relationships on the Social Web," details how individuals can set up a social networking account and provides tips for creating effective profiles, establishing friend connections, organizing contacts, and managing different identities across your personal and professional contacts.

- Chapter 11, "How To: Engage Customers with Facebook Pages and Twitter," guides companies through the process of creating, managing, and facilitating successful customer communities on social networking sites. Featured examples include Ferrero, H&M, Coca-Cola, Sears, Newbury Comics, and Nestlé.

- Chapter 12, "How To: Advertise and Promote on the Social Web," is a step-by-step set of instructions on how to tactically execute and optimize hypertargeted ad campaigns on Facebook and LinkedIn using many of the social marketing techniques described in Chapter 6. This chapter includes tips on how to optimize your Facebook ad campaigns directly from Tim Kendall, who heads the ads team at Facebook.

Part IV: Social Networking Strategy

- Chapter 13, "Advice for Small Business," is geared toward small business owners and employees, sole proprietorships, and others who might not have someone assigned to look after a social media strategy (or, in many cases, any form of marketing support), and how these types of businesses should be using Facebook and Twitter.

- Chapter 14, "Advice for Nonprofits, Healthcare, Education, and Political Campaigns," has specific case studies and advice for charitable organizations, political candidates, and other groups whose constituents might include volunteers, donors, voters, aid recipients, and others who don't fit the traditional model of a for-profit customer.

- Chapter 15, "Corporate Governance, Strategy, and Implementation," speaks to the challenges, obstacles, and realities of implementing social networking technologies in a corporate setting. This chapter urges businesses to consider the risks around privacy, security, intellectual property, confidentiality, and brand misrepresentation, and the importance of partnering closely with legal and IT departments to put the right systems and policies in place to mitigate these risks.

- Chapter 16, "The Future of Social Business," explores the general trends emerging from the social Web: flatter organizations, greater collaboration across organizations, and a continued movement toward applications and experiences that are personalized, social, mobile, and real-time. Despite many unknowns and certainly more change, companies need to start thinking now about how social technologies will affect their business and take the necessary steps to adapt and thrive in the Facebook Era.

Why Social Networking Matters for Business

1

*"In the technology industry, people always overestimate
what you can do in one year and underestimate what you
can do in one decade."*
—Marc Benioff, founder and CEO, Salesforce.com

The Fourth Revolution

Approximately once a decade, a new technology platform emerges that
fundamentally changes the business landscape. In each case, regardless of
prior competitive dynamics, businesses that understand and appropriately
adopt the technology win, while those that fail to do so lose relevance. In
the 1970s, this was mainframe computing. In the 1980s, it was the PC. In the
1990s, it was the Internet. And today it is the **social Web** (see Figure 1.1).

The social Web revolution is already well underway. More than 750 million
people around the world are on social networking sites. And not only are
they signing up for accounts, but they are also logging in, spending more
than *20 billion minutes a day* on Facebook alone. More than half of Facebook
users log in at least once a day. That is a tremendous amount of attention
from a tremendous number of people. Many are using social networking
sites as their main entry point to the Web, choosing content based on what
appears in their Twitter stream and Facebook news feed. Facebook is the
new Internet portal.

The social Web is not just Facebook, of course—it also includes Twitter,
LinkedIn, MySpace, Renren in China, Mixi in Japan, Odnoklassniki in Russia,
and hundreds of others. I simply refer to the current state of the Internet as
"the Facebook Era" because Facebook is the largest social networking site
globally by an order of magnitude. Facebook recently even beat out Google
in becoming the most trafficked site on the Internet, according to Hitwise
and other sources.

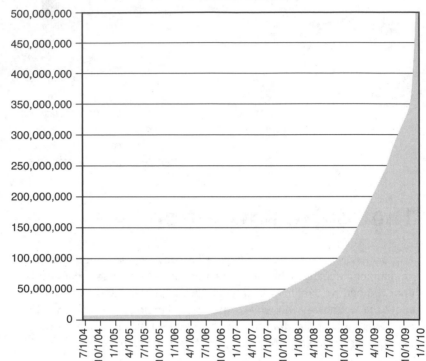

Figure 1.1
Facebook has had spectacular growth both in the United States and globally, recently topping 500 million users worldwide.

As you decide where to invest in building a presence, it's important to think about where your target audiences are spending time. Of the college students we surveyed for the first edition of this book, 94% said they do not use email on a regular basis. They prefer text messages and Facebook Wall posts. What happens when these cohorts of individuals graduate and become the people you are trying to hire, manage, and market to?

But not just college students use the social Web. More than 60% of Facebook users are older than 25. The largest increase in Facebook and Twitter users actually comes from users aged 35–49. And surprisingly, the fastest-growing audience on Facebook is women over 55, an impressive feat considering that this group traditionally tends to be techno-phobic. People are increasingly relying on social networking sites as a primary means to communicate with friends and get the news. As companies, we need to be where the customers are and communicate through the channels they prefer, and a growing number of people are preferring social networking sites.

Why? The social Web appeals to innate human desires for self-expression, human connection, and a sense of belonging. These desires are especially strong online. Before social networking sites, many users found the Internet overly vast, unnavigable, and anonymous. Social networking sites such as Facebook capture our pictures, feelings, and relationships, and make the Web feel human again.

In the following guest expert sidebar, Don Tapscott, best-selling author of 14 books on business and society, including *Wikinomics* and *Grown Up Digital,* offers some historical context on social networking and describes what's in store for the future.

Social Networking Has Been a Long Time Comin'

Don Tapscott

I remember my first job at Bell Northern Research in the late 1970s. I worked with a team of technologists and social scientists whose task was to understand what was then called "The Office of the Future." Our group was trying to understand how multifunction workstations connected to a vast network of networks would change the ways people communicated. At the time, only programmers used computers.

I was fortunate enough to collaborate with some of the pioneers of the digital age, such as Stanford Research Institute's Douglas Englebart. I'll never forget him showing me his "augmented knowledge workshop" complete with hypertext, collaboration tools, and a strange device he called a "mouse." One of the applications we created was something called "computer conferencing"—the forerunner to today's social networks. From the experience, I became convinced that collaborative computing would change the world.

But when I wrote a book on the topic in 1981, critics told me this idea of everyone using computers to communicate would never happen, giving a most bizarre reason—managers would never learn to type. No one could have predicted that not only would managers learn to type, but they would type with their thumbs.

The ideas of Englebart and other pioneers were ideas-in-waiting—waiting for a number of technological, social, economic, and demographic conditions to mature.

One of the developments these ideas were waiting for was Facebook. My son and daughter, whose email addresses ended in ".edu" at the time, gave me a demo. When I saw it, I knew this would change the world.

Flash forward a few years, and what we see today is nothing less than a social revolution. Social networks are becoming the new operating system for a business, changing the metabolism of work, innovation, customer interaction, and performance for the better.

The next step is social networks becoming a new mode of production. Anthony Williams and I discussed this in our book *Wikinomics,* and as evidence of the widespread interest in the topic, the book was the best-selling management book of 2007. Social networking is becoming social production. We're in the early days of profound changes to the deep structure and architecture of the corporation and most other institutions in society. Buckle up.

Don Tapscott (@dtapscott) is the best-selling author of 14 books on technology, business, and society, including the upcoming MacroWikinomics: Rebooting Business and the World *(Penguin Group, September 2010).*

Yes, definitely buckle up. This chapter provides important context for understanding the Facebook Era by looking at the technologies that led up to online social networking, comparing different social networking sites, and explaining the significance of social network platforms, including Facebook for Websites.

Today's Social Customer

In previous eras, the workplace prompted the adoption of new technologies. Online social networking is different. It is a movement that affects us personally first, professionally second. Most of us get on Facebook to connect with friends before thinking about using it for business purposes. In some cases, the lines blur between our personal and professional worlds: We befriend colleagues and customers, refer friends for jobs at our employer, and make business purchase decisions based on a friend's recommendation.

The role of the customer is changing, too. Customers used to be passive recipients, waiting for new products to come out or waiting on hold to speak to a call center rep. Today they are waiting no longer. Every customer and employee suddenly has a voice, and what they say matters. Whether companies like it (or even know about it), customers are demanding to become active participants across your business. They want to contribute new product and feature ideas, and receive an instantaneous response when something goes wrong. If you can win over this new breed of customers, they will become your volunteer sales force (spreading the gospel of your company to friends) and support staff (answering questions from other customers on Twitter).

Companies have no choice but to become transparent, responsive, and collaborative, or else risk going out of business. Everything is changing around customer expectations, customer participation, and how companies are organized. As we saw with the Internet, PC, and Mainframe Eras before it, mastering the Facebook Era has become the new competitive advantage for businesses. Just as ten years ago we had to learn how to Google and email, today we have to learn Facebook and other social technologies to be effective in our personal and professional lives.

Déjà Vu: What We Can Learn from the Internet Era

How things have changed in the 15 years since the Internet went online! The previous decade revolutionized how we live and work with the World Wide Web of information—linking Web pages, indexing content, and searching for information.

This decade, a World Wide Web of people has emerged—linking individuals, indexing the social network map of who is connected to whom and how, and delivering the right experience to the right person at the right time. The Internet Era connected all our machines and content pages. The current digital revolution is in capturing and using information about how we as individuals are connected. Metadata about Web pages, such as headings, keywords, and links, has been crucial for enabling us to manage and navigate an eruption of content on the Web. Similarly, metadata from the social Web about individuals—such as what networks they belong to, how we know them, and who we know in common—has become crucial for enabling us to manage many different kinds of relationships with large numbers of people. It took five years for the Internet to reach 350 million users. The same is true for Facebook.

Similar to how the Internet enabled businesses and individuals to access, consume, and manage far more information than previously possible, the social Web is enabling businesses and individuals to access and manage far more people and relationships than in the past to become more empowered and productive. In Chapter 3, "How Relationships and Social Capital Are Changing," we discuss the implications for personal networks, professional ties, and social capital.

But merely signing up for an account on Facebook won't revolutionize your business. Success requires patiently persevering, planning strategically, and applying the new technologies in the appropriate ways. We can learn a lot from studying how companies went through the sometimes painful process of adapting to the Internet Era a decade ago. The following sidebar walks through Bloomingdale's department store's attempt to get online. We can apply the same lessons Bloomingdale's learned about the Internet to how companies today approach opportunities on the social Web.

Internet Sales at Bloomingdale's Department Store, Take Two

In 1999, Federated Department Stores (FDS, now Macy's, Inc.), which owns Bloomingdale's, acquired e-commerce and online catalog company Fingerhut for $1.7 billion in what was seen as one of the most aggressive Internet plays in the industry. FDS planned to use Fingerhut's technology to create Bloomingdales.com, an online version of its Bloomingdale's By Mail paper catalog.

But just a few years later, they had very little to show. Customers did not see any benefit to shopping on the Web site, which was just an online replication of the print catalog. They were also not accustomed to making purchases on the Internet. Company executives decommissioned the e-commerce site, writing it off as a very expensive failure.

After a brief hiatus from Internet sales, Bloomingdales.com was reincarnated with a new approach that took advantage of the unique power and capabilities of the Internet. The new site was dynamic, engaging, and easy to search or browse in multiple different ways—by brand, size, genre, color, material, and price. Sophisticated online search marketing and email marketing campaigns now drive traffic and track each Web visit. All these were missing from the first version of the site and are simply not possible in a print catalog.

Now the fastest-growing part of the business, Bloomingdales.com has enabled the company to better engage its traditional customer base and reach new audiences while reducing costs. It has been so successful that Macy's, Inc., has decided to

continues…

discontinue the Bloomingdale's By Mail paper catalog, previously a hallmark of the company, to focus the direct-to-consumer strategy entirely online.

We can learn a few important lessons. First, even a technology revolution as powerful as the Internet (or now, Facebook) cannot in and of itself transform businesses. Success requires both a well-thought-out strategy and a market ready for the technology. Today people are finally ready and willing to buy online. Bloomingdale's uses sales data and customer segmentation to determine what merchandise to sell via which channel. Second, you gain from the new technology only if you use it to accomplish something that was not possible before. Merely posting a digital version of a static print catalog on its Web site was not transformative. But creating a new catalog experience with dynamic images, hyperlinks, and related item recommendations has paid off with real results.

What behaviors and interactions are your customers ready for and expecting from your company's social presence? In what new and creative ways will you engage them, instead of re-creating the same possibilities from the Internet Era inside the new social medium? The next chapters strive to help inspire answers to these questions.

The Evolution of Digital Media

Along with each digital revolution comes new forms of media. For example, look at how encyclopedias have evolved. In two decades, we have gone from heavy, leather-bound *World Book* volumes, to the Microsoft Encarta CD-ROM, to user-generated Wikipedia online, to the real-time messaging service Aardvark.im that connects people seeking information with knowledgeable experts in their network. Over time, new technologies are making it easier to deliver the right content in the right context at the right time while reaching larger audiences at a lower cost.

Mainframes digitized media, making it vastly more efficient and less expensive to store. Software on PCs has made it easy for anyone to create personalized digital content. The Internet has become a powerful distribution mechanism for media, which provides incentives for people to get involved in creating content and publishing their work. The result has been an information explosion.

During the last 15 years, we have been fighting a seemingly endless uphill battle against spam in our inboxes. When searching for information, we wade through pages of search results that are out of context. Annoying floating banners that are irrelevant to us block the screen showing the online article we are trying to read.

But all hope is not lost. The social Web might provide an opportunity to align what publishers and advertisers want to show with what users want to see. Technology companies have spent several years developing different ways of filtering the massive amount of information, such as content aggregation, search, and behavioral targeting. With the social Web, we can improve on this further by using friends, people who "like" our Facebook Page or @mention us, and people we follow as "social filters" for making sense of the vast amount of content on the Web.

Digital media is getting smarter. With technologies such as Facebook for Websites (explained later in the section on social network platforms), businesses are rethinking and redesigning the Web experiences they provide customers and prospects to become social, personalized, and real-time. Already, their efforts are paying off with improved engagement, sales, and loyalty.

Social Networking Versus Social Media

People often use the terms **social networking** and **social media** interchangeably. Social networking often facilitates many forms of social media, but a lot of social media also exists outside of social networking sites.

Social media (or user-generated content) includes blogs, wikis, voting, commenting, tagging, social bookmarking, photos, and video. Social media is all about content. People are secondary; they just happen to interact with the content by posting, commenting, tagging, voting, and so on.

Social networking sites turn the content-centric model on its head. Every social networking site has two components: profiles and connections. Facebook and LinkedIn, in particular, are all about *people* and *relationships.* Now most social networking sites also have features that also enable user participation such as tagging, commenting, voting (known as "liking" on Facebook), or posting photos. But on social networks, the content is secondary and temporary to the people.

The distinction between social networking and social media might seem trivial, but it's not. Even the most viral of videos on YouTube eventually falls out of favor. Content gets stale, but people never tire of seeing updates from friends and sharing about themselves. Social networking sites bring social media to life by enabling people to easily share media to entertain, inform, and connect with friends, customers, and others.

Facebook Versus Twitter and LinkedIn

People always ask if they should be on Facebook, Twitter, or LinkedIn—the top three social networking sites in North America. The answer is that it depends on what you are looking to get out of being on a social networking site. The answer might be that you need to be on all three, each for different reasons and perhaps with different levels of investment (see Figure 1.2).

This image is licensed under a Creative Commons Attribution-Share Alike 3.0 United States License.

Figure 1.2
Making friends in social media

At the risk of overgeneralizing, here are some factual and reputational differences of these top social networking sites.

Comparing Facebook, Twitter, and LinkedIn

Audience size and composition:

- With 500 million active members, **Facebook** is by far the largest global social networking site, in terms of both the number of users and time spent on the site. Facebook users span every age group and demographic, but the site is especially popular among college students and recent graduates. Facebook tends to be oriented toward personal friends and relationships, which presents both unique opportunities and challenges to businesses.

- **Twitter** has approximately 50 million users, although critics question how many are active or spammer accounts. Twitter strives to keep its service simple by limiting updates to 140 characters in length. It is heavily used by media and celebrity personalities but is going mainstream. Unlike the more enclosed environments on Facebook or LinkedIn, most messages on Twitter are public and searchable.

- **LinkedIn** focuses exclusively on business professionals. It has approximately 50 million members, mostly in the United States and Europe. Users tend to skew older, with an average age of 40. The site is used heavily for recruiting and business-to-business (B2B) business development. Users typically don't spend time engaging on the site, but instead log in occasionally to accept or initiate a connection request, search for people, or send a message.

How businesses typically engage:

- **Facebook** ads; Facebook applications; Facebook Business Pages (which are similar to Facebook profile pages for businesses and are used for sharing updates, special offers, video, photos, events, and applications).

- **Twitter** streams (sharing updates, special offers, and discounts or answering customer support questions).

- **LinkedIn** Pro and LinkedIn Recruiter enable enterprise-grade search and communication to individuals of a certain profile for recruiting or business development purposes; advertisting.

Best suited for:

- **Facebook**: Business-to-consumer (B2C); both big brands and SMB.

- **Twitter**: News and media companies; B2C; customer service.

- **LinkedIn**: Recruiting, B2B products and services.

Concerns:

- **Facebook**: Strict privacy policies limit access to people's data, and platform advanced programming interfaces (APIs) are constantly changing.

- **Twitter**: Spam.

- **LinkedIn**: Insufficient audience size and engagement.

How to determine business fit:

- Check your audience size on **Facebook**. Go to http://facebook.com/ads/create. Ignore all the instructions around creating an ad. Scroll down to Step 2 (where it says "targeting") and select criteria that best describes your target audiences. Near the bottom of Step 2, you will see an estimate from Facebook showing how many Facebook members fit the profile you specified. If it is a significant number (say, over 10% of your current or target customer base), then you should be on Facebook.

- Checking audience size and relevance on **Twitter** is less of a science. Go to http://search.twitter.com and search on your business name, competitors, and keywords relating to your business. If you get a sizable number of search results, then you should consider getting on Twitter.

- Check your audience size on **LinkedIn**. Go to www.linkedin.com/directads and fill out test data for Step 1. Under Step 2, specify audience category criteria and LinkedIn will display how many of its members fit your desired profile. If it is a significant number, then you might want to advertise on LinkedIn.

Why Facebook Won

As early as 1995, online social networking pioneers such as Classmates.com and SixDegrees.com introduced the notion of profile pages and friend connections. Next came Friendster, Orkut, MySpace, Bebo, and Hi5. These early social networking sites were tremendously popular, attracting tens of millions of users (or, in MySpace's case, more than 100 million users) but have largely disappeared from the scene or been forced into certain regions or niches.

Why did this happen? How did Facebook grow from a dorm room project to overtake MySpace and now dominate the social networking space by an order of magnitude? Two reasons: user trust and engagement.

First, Facebook's founders realized early on that people would log in only if the social networking site contained valuable information, and people would share valuable information only in an environment they trusted. During the last several years, the site introduced a number of features that have helped create a trusted environment on Facebook. Most of the other social networking sites don't have any of these features.

- **Email domain authentication**—Facebook doesn't allow you to join a college or employer network unless you can authenticate with an email address in that network. For example, to join the Harvard network, you have to sign up with an @harvard.edu email address. This makes it much harder for people to pretend to be someone they are not.

- **Real relationships**—From the beginning, Facebook was designed around real-world networks such as schools, employers, and other organizations. Facebook has always encouraged people to initiate and accept friend requests only from real people they actually know. In contrast, no such norms existed on Orkut or Friendster, so many people began accepting random friend requests from strangers. When strangers outnumbered friends on these sites, people no longer felt comfortable sharing personal information and stopped logging in.

- **Privacy settings**—Facebook also was the first to introduce privacy settings that enable users to categorize friends under lists and choose to share different amounts of information with different groups of people. Knowing that they can restrict others' access to all or certain parts of their profile gives Facebook users the confidence to share more about themselves.

- **Exclusiveness**—Initially, Facebook was available at Harvard only. Then it spread to other Ivy League schools. Its gradual expansion to other colleges and eventually to the public created a certain cachet of exclusiveness that made it seem more trusted and desirable. Adding only a few schools at a time also enabled Facebook to grow smoothly and predictably. In comparison, rapid growth on Friendster and Orkut often brought down those sites, turning off many of their users.

The final secret to Facebook's success has been keeping its users engaged on a continual basis. Its news feed, which broadcasts updates such as new photos and links posted, likes, comments, and event RSVPs, really set Facebook apart from the other social networking sites. Each person's news feed appears on his or her profile page, and a summary of feeds from all your friends appears on the home page when you first log in. It's ironic that the news feed, which has been instrumental to Facebook's longevity and has become a core feature of Internet applications today (including the basis for Twitter), was initially a huge source of controversy around privacy issues. In contrast, Friendster, Orkut, and Classmates.com fell out of popularity after the initial thrill of reconnecting with old friends wore off.

And what about the future of Facebook? At this point, all bets are on Facebook. In the social networking world, success begets more success. The more people are on a social networking site, the more people join. If all your friends and customers are on Facebook, you feel pressure to also be on Facebook to participate. You are less likely to join a different social network that contains fewer people and is therefore less valuable. Although Facebook might not be around forever, it seems likely to be here for quite some time.

Google Buzz

Just when we thought it was mostly down to Facebook, Twitter, and LinkedIn, Google has jumped into the race with Buzz, a new social sharing service for Gmail users. (It has approximately 176 million users worldwide, compared to 500 million Facebook users.) Google Buzz enables users to turn Gmail contacts into a social network and post status updates, photos, and links (similar to Facebook), but according to a one-way follower model (similar to Twitter).

Google Buzz is still a young technology, but it has potential. Google has a lot of smart people, a lot of resources, a lot of our data, and instant distribution to more than a billion users across its Web properties and applications. Buzz has three big areas of opportunity. First, Google could use email contacts as a more accurate and up-to-date implicit social graph, versus the Facebook/Twitter/LinkedIn social graphs that are all explicit. (Users must initiate and accept each connection.) Second, Google could leverage its breadth to weave a much richer social experience across a lot of applications including mobile, maps, search, email, YouTube, Picasa, and Google Reader. Thus far, the other social network ecosystems are not nearly as robust. Finally, Google could mesh multiple communication modes, including voice, chat, email, status updates, and documents or spreadsheets.

It's probably too early for most businesses to focus on Google Buzz (and a related technology, Google Wave), but I recommend keeping an eye out for developments.

Private Social Networks

Besides public, all-purpose social networking sites such as Facebook and Twitter, it is also worth discussing private social networks, such as those hosted on company Web sites or on Ning. Private networks tend to be affinity- or association-based networks instead of purely social networks in which people connect with the friends they choose.

Many larger organizations, in particular, have added community and networking capabilities to their Web sites to better engage visitors or improve search engine rankings. Certainly, this makes sense if at least one of the following is true:

❑   Your site offers something that people are willing to sign up and log in to obtain.

❑   You are able to drive a lot of traffic to your site.

❑   You want to remain exclusive instead of driving as much traffic as possible.

If you check all these boxes, then it probably makes sense for you to build your own online community, perhaps in addition to having a presence on Facebook and Twitter. You might consider using Facebook Platform's social plugins (described later in this chapter) to establish crossover points between your Web site and Facebook.

"Dogs are people, too," Del Monte's invitation-only online community for dog lovers, is a good example of a private network. By creating an exclusive environment for dog lovers to meet and discuss their passion for dogs, Del Monte has been able to effectively conduct market research and generate new ideas for their Snausages products while cultivating a loyal, passionate customer base. Other good examples include ESPN's fantasy football league Web site, Pampers' community for new mothers, and Groupon's Web site for daily deals.

A number of technology platforms on the market offer Web community and social networking features, including Lithium, Jive, Telligent, Pluck, KickApps, and Drupal, which is open source. The easiest private social networking service to get started with is Ning, which lets anyone create a social networking site in a few minutes, using point and click.

For example, John F. Kennedy High School in New Orleans, Louisiana, used Ning to create a comprehensive site for alumni, parents, and students featuring school news and events, the capability to connect with classmates and teachers, photos, videos, and fund-raising (see Figure 1.3). Thanks to Ning's Web tools and ready-made templates, high school administrators were able to get a site up and running in a fraction of the time. The school's private social network was especially important for the Kennedy community after Hurricane Katrina forced students to evacuate at the beginning of the 2005–2006 academic year. The site enabled parents and administrators to support one another, share information, and help facilitate transfers to other schools.

Figure 1.3

New Orleans, Louisiana–based John F. Kennedy High School's specialized social network community hosted on Ning

Other examples of organizations that have created Ning networks include The Epilepsy Foundation, *Essence Magazine,* and the Boston Chapter of the American Marketing Association. Today Ning hosts hundreds of thousands of specialized networks on its free, ad-supported version.

Should you create your own social network or go with Facebook Pages and Twitter? It's a trade-off. With your own network, you get to control the full experience and own the data, but you face the problem of getting traffic. With Facebook and Twitter, you can reach half a billion people, but you give up some control and risk getting lost in the crowd. Ultimately, the key questions are "Is your site compelling enough for people to visit and continually return to?" and "How much money and energy are you willing to invest to retain control?"

Social Network Platforms

The first online social networks were just Web sites. Today they are software platforms, which means that, in addition to the Web site Facebook creates and maintains, third-party software developers can build new applications that extend Facebook's functionality. Social networking platforms expose data, tools, and screen real estate to developers. We saw a similar phenomenon during the PC Era when Microsoft exposed its Windows platforms so that third-party developers such as Adobe, Lotus, and Frame Technology could create applications such as Photoshop, Lotus 1-2-3, and Framemaker. In an ideal scenario, the platform ecosystem is a win–win–win for everyone: *Users* have access to more functionality, *software developers* have access to data and users, and *the social network* becomes more interesting, valuable, sticky, and engaging.

The rise of YouTube is a good example of how this works. An important precursor to social platforms was the capability to embed YouTube videos on MySpace pages. Before MySpace, YouTube struggled to hit a tipping point and really take off. It had a small and scattered community of fans that used its video-sharing service as one-offs. Joining forces with MySpace changed everything. Overnight, YouTube found itself with a large global audience and infrastructure for word-of-mouth distribution. MySpace, in turn, saw its Web traffic go way up and its pages come to life with rich, multimedia video.

Facebook took this idea of embedded video further when it created the first social networking platform in May 2007 that enabled users to create any type of application (not just video) inside Facebook. Today Facebook has more than 500,000 platform applications (see the full list at http://facebook.com/apps). More than two-thirds of Facebook users have installed at least one platform application. Shortly after Facebook unveiled its platform, MySpace, Bebo, Hi5, Friendster, and eventually LinkedIn followed suit with their own platforms. Twitter is also famously easy to integrate with. Its application programming interface (API) has spawned a number of popular client and Web-based applications, including TweetDeck, Twitterholic, Digsby, Seesmic Desktop, and Twitpic (see the full list at http://oneforty.com). More than twice as many people interact with Twitter via a platform application than on Twitter.com.

Platform Applications

When social networking platforms emerged, most of the early applications were games. For example, companies such as Zynga, Playdom, and Playfish (acquired by Electronic Arts) have created applications that let Facebook users challenge friends to games such as math puzzles, trivia, or checkers. Many of the newest and most popular social games— such as FarmVille, Café World, Restaurant City, Mafia Wars, and Texas Hold 'Em—involve virtual goods in which players exchange real money for virtual items such as farm animals, restaurant equipment, and poker chips for use in games. Despite the fact that users can never exchange these virtual goods back to real money, people love social games. Games have become the most installed applications on Facebook. On Facebook alone, the virtual goods economy is expected to surpass half a billion dollars this year.

Whereas Facebook and Twitter's platforms are open to any developer to build applications, LinkedIn has restricted its platform to a handful of select partners. The most popular LinkedIn apps today are Slideshare (displays Slideshare presentations on user profiles), Amazon Reading List (enables users to share reading lists with networks and connections), and WordPress (enables users to display blog posts on their profiles).

But it's not just technology and games companies that are successfully building platform applications on social networking sites. Traditional businesses are also starting to explore the benefits of plugging into the online social graph with their own platform applications. Pizza Hut has developed an application that Facebook members can install on their profile page. Visitors to the page can order pizza delivery directly from within Facebook.

Another example comes from FamilyLink, a genealogy database company that provides ancestry-tracking tools to approximately 20,000 subscribers. FamilyLink developed a Facebook app, We're Related, that lets people indicate who they are related to on Facebook and create family tree visualizations. In less than two years, 18 million Facebook members have signed up for We're Related, enabling FamilyLink to promote its brand to a far greater audience than its original customer base.

Certainly for companies such as Pizza Hut and FamilyLink, Facebook applications have nicely complemented their marketing efforts. How might platform applications increase Facebook audience engagement for your business? Chapter 11, "How To: Engage Customers with Facebook Pages and Twitter," explains your options and helps you decide what makes the most sense for your company and goals.

Expanding the Social Web

So far, we have talked exclusively about applications that appear inside social networking sites. Some companies (especially small businesses) are ditching the idea of having a separate Web site and are using a combination of Facebook Pages and applications. Although these continue to grow in number, most applications and Web sites today are still not on Facebook. And sometimes it doesn't make sense for a particular application to live inside Facebook.

The Faceconnector application that Todd Perry and I developed, which integrates Facebook and Salesforce (actually created before Facebook Connect or Facebook for Websites), is one such example. Faceconnector pulls real-time Facebook profile and friend information into Salesforce. (Chapter 4, "Sales in the Facebook Era," talks more about how this application is used). Designing this application the other way (pulling Salesforce information into Facebook) might not be the best idea because that could expose highly confidential customer data to all your Facebook friends.

Facebook for Websites (also known as Facebook Connect and Facebook Open Graph) is a technology that enables companies to integrate Facebook data, stream, and login information with their own Web sites and applications. Visitors to Web sites that have implemented Facebook for Websites can log in to the site with single sign-on, using their Facebook username and password. They can view which of their Facebook friends have also visited or interacted with the site, or are currently logged in. And when visitors engage with the site, such as posting a comment or photo, they can choose to share this activity with friends on Facebook via the news feed.

Today nearly 100,000 Web sites and devices have implemented Facebook for Websites, including these most popular and interesting examples:

- **Eventbrite**—People registering for events can see which of their Facebook friends are also planning to attend.

- **Citysearch**—Web site visitors can filter by restaurant and nightlife reviews written by friends.

- **CNN The Forum**—People watching the streaming video feed of President Obama's inauguration on CNN.com could chat in real-time with their Facebook friends (see Figure 1.4).

- **Xbox Live**—Gamers can link their Facebook profile to their gamertag, update their Facebook status from within Xbox, and post gaming milestones to their Facebook news feed.

- **Virgin Airlines**—Flyers are able to see which Facebook friends are on the same flight and even send them a drink.

Figure 1.4
CNN.com's live coverage of President Obama's inauguration in January 2009, with Facebook for Websites social plugin (previously known as Facebook Connect and Facebook Open Graph) discussion widget

The major drawback of Facebook for Websites, of course, is that you become beholden to Facebook for interactions with and data about your Web site visitors. You are also giving Facebook visibility into these logins and interactions. This can be problematic for some companies that are accustomed to being able to capture and store more data about Web visitors, or that do not feel comfortable sharing site data with a third party such as Facebook.

But in many cases, the benefits of a frictionless login experience and vast distribution outweigh the inconvenience. There are five major components to Facebook for Websites:

- **Single sign-on**—You can can replace the registration process on your Web site with Facebook for Websites' single sign-on feature. Once a user logs into your site with his or her Facebook account, you can access their account information from Facebook. They are logged into your site as long as they are logged into Facebook (and vice versa). Behind the scenes, Facebook Platform uses the OAuth 2.0 protocol standard for authorizing users.

- **Social plugins**—Social plugins are embeddable social features that can be easily integrated onto any Web site with a single line of HTML. These plugins are hosted by Facebook and are therefore automatically personalized for any user visiting your site who is logged into Facebook, even if the user has not yet signed up for your site. Examples include the Like button, which enables users to post and associate with pages on your Web site back to their Facebook profile with one click, as well as the activity feed plugin and recommendations plugin.

- **Account registration data**—Facebook for Websites also provides easy access to basic account registration data which you would typically need to request via a sign-up form on your Web site, including name, email address, profile picture, and birthday. By using Facebook instead of a Web form, you can more easily ask a user for all of this information within a single dialog box and no typing required.

- **Server-side personalization**—When you have implemented Facebook for Websites single sign-on, Facebook makes it easy to personalize the content and experience on your Web site to each user who visits, such as referring to a user's friends when the user is on your site.

- **Analytics**—Facebook for Websites also provides detailed analytics about the demographics, sharing, and interactions of your users.

For example, when my friends and I built *The Facebook Era* Web site, we wanted to make it easy for people to interact with the site without having to sign up for yet another account. Implementing Facebook for Websites social plugins dramatically reduced the barrier to engagement for Web site visitors and still allowed me visibility into who was engaging with the content (see Figure 1.5).

Figure 1.5
Facebook for Websites discussion widget on The Facebook Era *Web site*

Even Second Cup, the largest coffee retailer in Canada, offers Facebook single sign-on as an authentication option to access free Wi-Fi in its stores (see Figure 1.6).

Figure 1.6
Facebook for Websites single sign-on login option to access free Wi-Fi in a Second Cup coffee shop location

In the following guest expert sidebar, entrepreneur Gregg Spiridellis explains why he chose to implement Facebook single sign-on as the primary login mechanism for his popular site.

Why JibJab Connects to Facebook for Websites

Gregg Spiridellis

JibJab was founded back in the digital dark ages—1999. Huddled around our blueberry iMacs, we put low-cost production software in the hands of great artists and set about distributing our work to a worldwide audience on the Web.

We had only email-based viral tools available back then, including the capability to send to a friend and sign up for our newsletter. It took us eight years to reach 1.5 million registered users. It took us only five months to achieve that milestone using Facebook single sign-on. How did we do it? We identified four ways to leverage Facebook's data and tools to enhance our user experience:

1. **Publishing**—Facebook for Websites is the most powerful way to get your audience to share your content. Presenting users a list of their friends, as opposed to presenting an email form field, reduces the friction of having to remember email addresses.

2. **Sign-on**—We subordinated our direct registration system in favor of Facebook. Why? Because a Facebook for Websites user comes with an audience of 130 friends, whereas a directly registered user comes with zero.

3. **Media access**—JibJab's Starring You product enables users to upload photos and put themselves and friends into personalized videos. Users previously needed to have a photo on their computer. Today users can access their own photos and also friends' photos on Facebook from within our product. Less friction in finding the right photo of the right person leads to more engagement and makes for an awesome customer experience.

4. **Data**—Facebook for Websites offers a treasure trove of user data. The question you need to ask yourself is, which data enriches your product experience? At JibJab, the answer was easy: friends' birthdays. The ability to show users which of their friends is having a birthday is an opportunity for us to create user-specific intent which that greatly increases the likelihood that someone will send a card or become a customer.

Facebook for Websites does come with some risks, as is the case when you are dependent on someone else's platform. When Facebook is slow, so are you. When it changes its APIs (which it does often) you have to divert engineering resources to maintaining products instead of building new products. For JibJab, the rewards of our Facebook for Websites integration have far outweighed these costs.

Gregg Spiridellis (@jibjab) is cofounder and CEO of JibJab Media.

A Promising New Era

We have come a long way since the heyday of mainframe computing, even since the early days of the Internet 15 years ago. On Facebook, Twitter, and LinkedIn, companies have many exciting new opportunities today to meaningfully engage with customers, prospects, partners, and employees in ways that simply weren't possible before the social Web. Facebook applications and Facebook for Websites applications enrich Facebook Pages and company Web sites with rich functionality, social context, and easy ways to engage audiences.

The Web used to be isolated and anonymous. Now it is social and personalized. Facebook and other social networking sites seem to have figured out the Holy Grail every business has been seeking to replicate online with their customers—trust and engagement.

Once again, we are this decade at the cusp of a massive paradigm shift. We are moving from technology-centric applications to people-centric applications. We are improving the World Wide Web of information with a World Wide Web of people and relationships. The social Web is enabling a fundamentally new Web experience that enables us to bring our online identities and friends with us to whatever site or application we choose to visit on the Internet. It is the end of the anonymous Web, and it is already transforming the way we work, learn, and interact across every aspect of our lives.

< < < TAKEAWAYS

✓ "The Facebook Era" refers not just to Facebook, but also Twitter, LinkedIn, MySpace, Renren in China, Mixi in Japan, Odnoklassniki in Russia, and hundreds of others around the world.

✓ In the Facebook Era, companies have no choice but to become transparent, responsive, and collaborative, or else risk going out of business.

✓ Facebook, Twitter, and LinkedIn enable us to use friends as "social filters" for navigating the incredible amount of content on the Web.

✓ Private social networks such as Ning might make sense when your site has a compelling enough offer that people are willing to create an account, you are able to drive substantial traffic to your site, or you purposely want to remain exclusive.

✓ Facebook quickly differentiated itself from its predecessors by focusing on status updates and the user privacy model to build trust and engagement. Before you build a Facebook presence for your company, you need to build a Facebook presence for yourself and understand the dynamics of how people interact and engage on social networking sites.

> > > TIPS and TO DO's

❑ Decide which social networks you will invest in building a presence on, based on not only where your current customers are, but also where your target prospects like to spend time.

❑ Study existing Facebook for Websites such as Citysearch, Live Nation, and Eventbrite to understand how the technology works.

❑ Consider implementing Facebook for Websites on your own Web site (or a subset of your Web site) to increase user engagement and insights about your visitors.

❑ Think about how you can apply lessons learned from the Internet Era to the Facebook Era. For example, brainstorm with your team about what new Facebook and Twitter initiatives you can launch to take advantage of the unique capabilities of the social Web instead of just rehashing existing online efforts.

❑ Check out what applications are already available on Facebook (facebook.com/apps) and Twitter (oneforty.com) so you don't have to reinvent the wheel.

2

"People have really gotten comfortable not only sharing more information and different kinds, but more openly and with more people. [This is a] social norm that has evolved over time."
—Mark Zuckerberg

The New Social Norms

The social Web is drastically changing how we communicate. Social norms are being invented about what, how frequently, and with whom we share even the smallest details of our lives. This, in turn, is having a tremendous impact on our sociology—including our expectations, behavior, and relationships, both with one another and with organizations and brands.

The pace at which social networking sites are growing and the fact that one in three American adults uses Facebook mean that these changes are rippling through society in profound ways that will only become more pronounced in the years ahead. This chapter explores how online identity and sharing have changed as a result of online social networks, explains the new etiquette and expectations about these sites, and introduces an important new concept of **transitive trust** in purchase decisions.

Identity, Sharing, and Influence on the Social Web

At the root of this sociological transformation is the social network profile (such as your Facebook profile), which has become the universal template for online identity and sharing. For most people, being on a social networking site today means sharing more about themselves than they ever have before (or ever thought they would) through their profiles and status updates.

Perhaps because Facebook, in particular, feels like a secure and trusted environment, we are sharing (in some cases) with people we barely know everything from our age, political views, job title, employment history, and academic pedigree to hobbies, interests, favorite books and movies, relationship status, and sexual orientation (see Figure 2.1). Even the profile picture with which we choose to portray ourselves says a lot about how we view ourselves and would like others to view us. Is it formal or casual? Are we alone or with friends? Is it a photo of our dog, our child, or ourselves as a child?

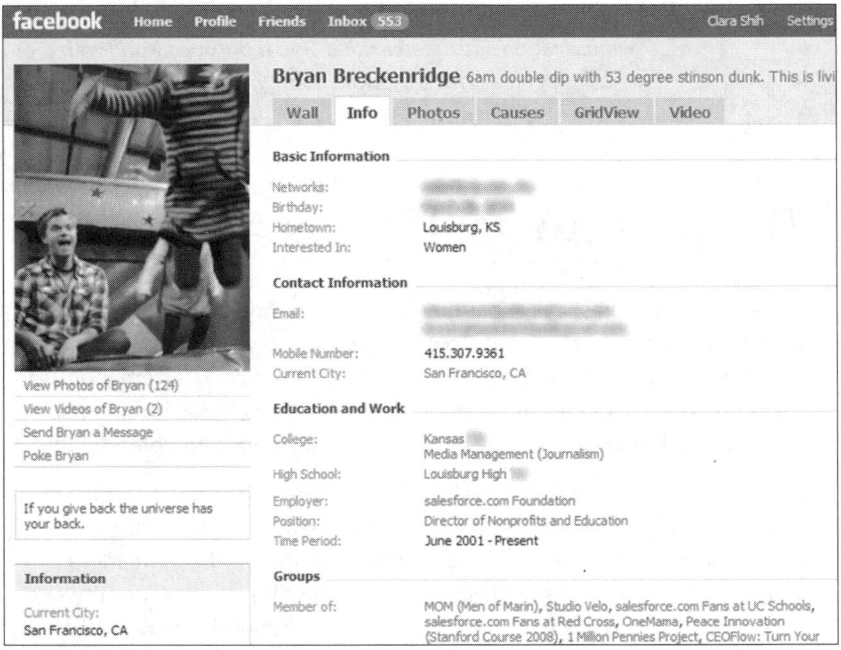

Figure 2.1
Thanks to the online identity template Facebook profiles provide, people are sharing more about themselves to more people than ever.

Before the Facebook Era, people didn't share openly like this. People didn't include their age, their kids' names, or that they were Republican in an email signature. It might have taken months or even years to discover someone's political views, religious preferences, and the breadth and depth of information that today is readily shared in a semipublic view on social networking sites. Most people today still do not have blogs, and those who do often keep highly personal information off the blog.

In addition to profiles, which are updated infrequently, real-time updates such as tweets and Facebook status messages help round out the picture of who someone is, through instantaneous snapshots of their thoughts, feelings, and interactions with others over time. On Facebook, a continuous stream of casual sharing is always happening in the background. But unlike the never-ending stream of news and content on the Internet,

Facebook updates feel relevant and personal because they are from people we know and presumably like. (If not, you can use the option to unfriend or mute updates from someone.)

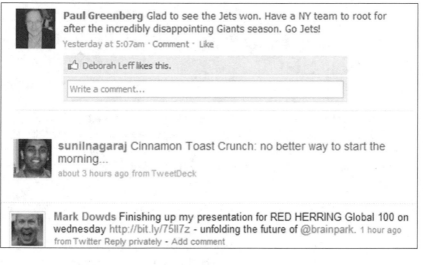

Figure 2.2
Facebook created a new social norm about sharing real-time updates (from top, status messages from Facebook, Twitter, and LinkedIn).

Today not only is it socially acceptable to share aspects of our identity on Facebook, Twitter, or LinkedIn, but it has become *expected* that we do so. Before interviewing a job candidate or after meeting someone new, in addition to "Googling" them, we now look them up on social networking sites to find out more. In fact, people's social network profiles on Facebook, Twitter, and LinkedIn often appear at the top of search results.

Facebook has become a sort of directory of everyone on the Internet, and although most people don't publicly share all their personal information, the majority feel comfortable with Facebook's default settings of sharing your name, profile picture, gender, current city, networks, list of friends, and Facebook Pages. Having this basic minimum profile is similar to declaring one's existence on the social Web.

As more communications, photos, and event invitations move onto Facebook, to not be on Facebook altogether is to risk being left behind, similar to the people in the last decade who refused to get online or buy a cellphone. Certainly, if you don't feel comfortable being on Facebook, you shouldn't do it. But recognize the trade-offs. And even if as an individual you don't want to share information on Facebook, you might still need to create and manage a Facebook presence for your business if that is where your customers and prospects are spending their time.

It's also interesting to think about how these norms and communication preferences vary by age group. In the following guest expert sidebar, Danah Boyd, a social media researcher at Microsoft Research and a Fellow at Harvard's Berkman Center for Internet and Society, provides a few tips on how to understand young people's use of social networking sites such as Facebook.

Understanding Young People on Social Networking Sites

Danah Boyd, Ph.D.

The social Web is most useful when it fits into people's lives and meshes with their needs, desires, goals, and mindset. The key to understanding what different demographics are doing with social media is to understand what's going on in their lives. Even a tool as ubiquitous as Facebook is being used differently across demographics, highlighting cultural and life-stage differences.

Keep in mind these four points when thinking about younger users' use of social media:

1. **Privacy is not dead.** Younger users recognize that social media enables them to be public, but this doesn't mean that they don't care about privacy. It's just that the equation has changed. It used to be private by default, public with effort; today it's public by default, private with effort.

2. **Not everyone wants to build an audience.** Plenty of narcissists exist—young and old—but not everyone is trying to broadcast their lives for all people across all space and all time to get attention. This might be the way of corporations and politicians, but it's not what most younger users are looking for. They primarily want intimacy with the folks they already know.

3. **Adults approach technology with preexisting expectations about how things "should" be.** Youth approach technology as though it's a given and learn to engage with it as they're learning to engage with the world around them. Their understandings of it reveal what makes sense for their life stage but without the baggage their parents have.

4. **It's made out of people.** Social media is, first and foremost, social; people use social media to communicate and connect. Sharing is a desirable by-product, but social interactions trump everything, especially for youth.

The underlying practices of today's youth are the same as in previous generations, but the technologies available to them today are different. As they grow older and change life stages, expect to see transitions in how they use technology. It might seem as if huge generational shifts are underway, but most of what is changing has to do with what happens when new technologies are available as people enter new life stages.

Danah Boyd (@zephoria) is a social media researcher at Microsoft Research and a fellow at Harvard's Berkman Center for Internet and Society.

Personal Branding

On a personal level, social network profiles have become an important new form of personal branding. On a business level, tremendous new opportunities exist for building corporate and product brand identity and using profile data to target messages to the right audiences.

Given the role of social networking sites in conveying our identity, profiles and status messages have become the new underpinnings of personal branding. For those we don't know very well, our profile is a quick introduction to who we are. For those we don't get to talk to very often, our profile is a quick summary of what's new.

Why does personal branding matter? Your personal brand is your reputation. Personal brand can shape how people treat you, how much they trust you, and, in our increasingly free-agent society, what jobs and opportunities you have access to.

It is a personal choice, of course, how much to share with whom—or even whether to be on social networking sites. That said, certain social norms are emerging about what most people seem comfortable with for themselves and expect of others on Facebook, Twitter, and LinkedIn.

Personal Norms on Social Networking Sites

What's Expected: Semi-publicness

- **Explanation**: We see a growing tendency toward greater publicness. People don't tend to share everything with everyone, but most are willing to share a subset of information publicly. This is especially true of younger cohorts of individuals who tend to have looser views on privacy.

- **Example**: Many people feel comfortable sharing a few pictures of their family, kids, and pets with coworkers. It enables them to be friendly without sharing too much or anything inappropriate.

What's Expected: Authenticity

- **Explanation**: People expect social network (especially Facebook) profiles to feel personal and authentic. Without sharing more than you feel comfortable, you can still let your personality shine through. Least appealing are profiles that feel dry and buttoned-up like a résumé, fake, or overly self-promotional and "salesy."

- **Example**: Even people with strict privacy settings can let their personality show without sharing any personal information by posting links to interesting articles or funny YouTube videos.

What's Expected: Updates

- **Explanation:** Think of a social network profile as your living online identity that you should keep up-to-date. Each time you update, your friends will see it in their news feed.

- **Example:** You don't need to update your status message ten times a day, but your connections will appreciate periodic news, photos, and musings.

Personal branding in the Facebook Era encompasses not only what we say about ourselves, but also what others say and imply about us based on their interactions on our profile (such as Facebook Wall posts and tagged photos, LinkedIn recommendations, and Twitter @mentions). Some of it we can manage with privacy settings, but a lot of it is beyond our control. Social media can affect an individual's personal brand just as it affects corporate brands (see Figure 2.3).

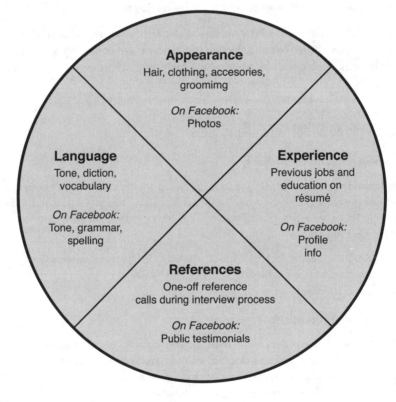

Figure 2.3

Four different elements of personal branding and how they manifest on social networking sites such as Facebook

Popular blogger Dan Schawbel provides a few tips on effective personal branding on the social Web.

Five Tips for Personal Branding on Social Networking Sites

Dan Schawbel

Personal branding, the process by which people market themselves as brands, is about creating a unique identity for yourself for career advancement. Social technologies have forced everyone in the world to become a marketer of their own brand. Consider these five essential personal branding tips:

1. **Discover your brand before you communicate it.** The first step in the personal branding process is to "discover your brand," because you need to identify what you want to stand for and your mission, values, brand attributes, and how you're differentiated in your industry. It's hard to reflect on what your strengths and long-term goals are, but without identifying them, you will end up rebranding yourself many times without a sense of purpose.

2. **Protect your brand by reserving your full name everywhere.** You need to own your digital property before someone else does. This includes your domain name (yourname.com) and your full name on social networks such as Facebook, Twitter, YouTube, and other social networks that are relevant to your brand. For instance, if you're a real estate agent, you should join Active Rain. Also, you can have more control over the Google search results for your name because all these networks rank high in Google.

3. **Set up a system where you can manage your online reputation.** To keep a pulse on your brand, you should set up a comprehensive Google alert (Google.com/alerts) for your name. This way, anytime your name is mentioned in a blog post or news article, you're aware of it. You should also use BackType.com for blog comment mentions, Facebook search, and BoardTracker.com for discussion forum mentions. If you neglect observing and responding to brand mentions, you risk negative word-of-mouth, which can travel very fast online.

4. **Choose a single picture, name, motto, and theme, and use it consistently.** As with a corporate brand, your brand needs to be consistent, which means you should have the same presence everywhere online and offline. Take one professional headshot of yourself and use it as your avatar on social networks, on your blog or Web site, on your business card, and other places where your name is mentioned. If your name is Matthew but you want to be called Matt, then use that name everywhere and don't change it. You can have a motto or tagline just like Nike or another brand, as long as you use it repeatedly. The same goes with your overall theme, including font, color, and style.

continues…

5. Publish content so people get a sense of your voice, not just a résumé.
A résumé isn't a differentiator anymore. Now you need an active voice online by publishing content. When you publish, it helps you to become more visible and credible and to connect with more people. Companies want people with fresh ideas and thinking, which is why participating online is so important these days.

Dan Schawbel (@danschawbel) is the founder of PersonalBrandingBlog.com and author of Me 2.0.

Chapter 10, "How To: Build and Manage Relationships on the Social Web," talks in greater length about how to create an effective profile and manage privacy settings.

Corporate Branding

For too long, mass market brands have broadcast what their ad agencies thought audiences wanted to hear but never took the time to listen. Brands became these large, intangible entities that no one could actually relate to. So people stopped trusting.

But just as individuals can shape their personal brand on social networking sites, companies can also take advantage of the trusted environment to better convey corporate identity, values, and initiatives, and win back the hearts and minds of their audiences. Research from Edelman, Forrester, and Nielsen shows that, for consumers, the most trusted source of information is now "people like me." The social Web takes this trust to the next level with "people I know."

Because of the identity profile and relationships, social networking sites feel personal. And they are breathing new life into corporate brand identities. Here, too, social norms are emerging about how people expect to interact with companies.

Corporate Norms on Social Networking Sites

What's Expected: Authenticity

- **Explanation**: Customers in the Facebook Era expect companies on social networking sites to feel personal and authentic. Many companies have achieved this by exposing the unedited voices and personalities of their customer-facing employees.

- **Example**: Dunkin' Dave tweets on behalf of Dunkin' Donuts and gives the company a human voice people can relate to. (See Chapter 6, "Marketing in the Facebook Era," for details and more examples of persona marketing on Facebook and Twitter.)

What's Expected: Transparency

- **Explanation:** Today's companies are rewarded for openness and transparency about business practices, community involvement, and shortcomings. Customers want to know about not only your business operations, but also those of your entire supply chain, to make sure your vendors and suppliers are embracing environmentally friendly practices, honoring child labor laws, and so on.

- **Example:** Peet's Coffee & Tea posts on its Facebook Page about community initiatives such as the San Francisco AIDS Walk, cycling competitions, holiday donation program, and updates on its Fair Trade Certified Coffee.

What's Expected: Engagement

- **Explanation:** Customers expect to have a voice and expect that what they say matters in how products are built, how complaints are addressed, and even what community initiatives companies are investing in. Facilitating customer engagement not only enhances corporate image, but it also creates additional opportunities to expose audiences to your brand and products . (Chapter 11, "How To: Engage Customers with Facebook Pages and Twitter," walks through how companies are using Twitter and Facebook Pages to provide audiences with plenty of opportunities to participate.)

- **Example:** Gap engages Facebook fans about style, seeding the conversation with tips from in-house style gurus and asking fans to suggest their own tips and favorite ensembles.

What's Expected: Real-time response

- **Explanation:** With the tremendous popularity of iPhones and BlackBerrys, people today are "always on" and want companies to keep up. The seething remark or video that "goes viral" could happen after business hours. Depending on your business, it might make sense to invest in around-the-clock monitoring and response.

- **Example:** TweetBeep sends almost real-time alerts whenever something is said about your business on Twitter, and a growing number of small businesses are using it to track and quickly respond to customer questions, issues, and comments.

What's Expected: Long-term view

- **Explanation:** Before the Facebook Era, many companies' digital marketing efforts were campaign-centric, optimizing for a particular transaction. It was all about click-through rates and conversion. In the Facebook Era, companies are on the hook to optimize for a longer-term view about customer relationships. The goal is to win customer loyalty in the form of Facebook fans, Twitter followers, and word-of-mouth instead of optimizing for click-through rates on a specific campaign.

- **Example:** Sears offers exclusive discounts to encourage people to "like" its Facebook Page. For Sears, the top goal is building a trusted customer relationship over the long haul instead of maximizing the profitability of a one-time transaction.

Mining Social Network Data

New norms about sharing personal information on social networking sites are also pro-viding companies with a wealth of audience data. Businesses are using this data to get a pulse on what people are saying, identify problematic issues, and reach precise audience segments with targeted ads:

- **Trending topics**—Smart companies are using the rich abundance of profile and status message data on the social Web to keep a pulse on what people are talking about and what matters. On Twitter, you can see trending topics or search on any keyword, phrase, or brand and find specific mentions at http://search.twitter.com.

- **Issues and complaints**—Companies are also using this same Twitter search tool to identify any issues or complaints that might arise about their product or service, and hopefully address the problem before it spirals out of control. Chapter 5, "Customer Service in the Facebook Era," elaborates on how social networking sites are changing the customer support process.

- **Hypertargeting**—Thanks to Facebook, people are sharing more about themselves online than ever. Everything individuals share about themselves on their profiles—including hometown, alma maters, jobs, and hobbies—can also be used by marketers and sales to "hypertarget" and personalize communications. Facebook and LinkedIn both have hypertargeting capabilities as part of their self-service advertising platforms that enable marketers to specify the profile attributes of people they want to view the ads being purchased. For example, if you are a manufacturer of golf clubs, you can choose to show your ads only to people who have specified on their social network profile that they like to golf. The idea is that as ads can become more tailored and rele-vant, conversion rates will go up. Chapter 6 goes into detail about how hypertargeting works.

The Importance of Being Customer-Centric

As a result of these new targeting possibilities and the ever-increasing amount of mar-keting messages to which each individual is exposed, buyers' expectations are rising. It has become harder than ever for companies to earn audience trust. Customers want to feel as if they are the ones who decide how and when a sales cycle begins. And when it does begin, they expect personalized interactions tailored to their specific needs. The days of "spray and pray" generic sales pitches and marketing messages are over.

Before an email campaign drop or sales call, marketers and sales have to do their home-work and truly become customer-centric in their approach, taking into account the prospect's industry, geography, company, role, and circumstances. Moreover, customers expect this level of personalized service across every interaction with your organization, from your Web site and emails, to the salesperson, to customer service.

Yet the customers of today not only expect a personalized experience, but also demand opportunities to engage, collaborate, and have a say in the products and services they consume. They expect to be heard, and they expect a response. Companies have always claimed to be customer-centric (or put another way, no company would say that it is not customer-centric), but too often in the past it was just lip service. Companies were drawn to the concept of being customer-centric, but when it came to implementation, no budget, metrics, or ownership existed. In the worst case, customer-centricity was abused as an excuse to further internal political agendas that actually had nothing to do with what customers wanted.

Things have changed. By giving customers a voice, social media is forcing companies to actually become customer-centric. Companies are being forced not only to listen to customers, but also to act and react based on what they say. To succeed, today's companies have to invest in rearchitecting their systems and processes around the customer. Internal agendas have to take a backseat to the customer experience.

The social Web is changing companies' interactions with their customers in four ways:

1. **Consistent experience**—Customers don't know or care about your organization's functional divides. They view your company as a single entity and expect to have a seamless and consistent experience whether they are dealing with your sales department or your customer support staff. For companies, this means much better coordination across departments, messaging alignment, and integrated systems.

2. **Ongoing feedback**—In the past, companies periodically held focus groups and surveys to collect customer feedback. Companies decided when to request feedback and what questions were asked. Today feedback is continuous, public, and on the customers' terms. Companies need to put in place new processes to listen on an ongoing basis and to come to terms with negative comments.

3. **Action and response**—Before, companies could do whatever they wanted with customer feedback and no one would know. Often they did nothing. In contrast, the public nature of the social Web pressures companies not only to respond, but also to respond quickly.

4. **Measurement and accountability**—External transparency has seemed to bring internal accountability. With the customer voice and companies' responses out in the open, a growing number of businesses are realizing the importance of ownership and accountability for listening, responding to, and measuring customer feedback.

Perhaps the biggest underlying change is reorienting organizational culture around customer-centricity. Chapter 15, "Corporate Governance, Strategy, and Implementation," talks about the practicalities and challenges behind culture change and other aspects of corporate governance and implementation.

Transitive Trust

Many prospects these days will refuse an unsolicited call or email, even with a perfectly tailored and customer-centric pitch. This is where the social Web can potentially help through something I call **transitive trust**. Consider this example of transitive trust: In trying to reach Graham, I discover that we both know Kelly. Because Kelly trusts me, and Graham trusts Kelly, Graham is more likely to "transitively" trust me if Kelly provides a warm introduction or I at least mention Kelly when reaching out to Graham. Not actually knowing me himself, Graham doesn't trust me as much as he trusts Kelly, but as someone trying to hire Graham, sell him something, or whatever the goal might be, I don't need him to trust me just yet. All I need is to get my foot in the door, and my product, service, or personality hopefully can do the rest. I just need a chance to be heard.

Transitive trust is not a new concept; in fact, it is how human beings have been making important decisions since the dawn of civilization. The challenge in the past was about discovery. I might have had to ask a lot of people before I found someone who knew Graham well enough to provide an introduction. Social networking sites bring transparency and efficiency to discovering mutual ties.

With a quick search on Facebook, I can immediately see all the friends Graham and I have in common and then use my best judgment to decide who to ask for an introduction—which will be a function of both how well I know the person and how well I think Graham knows the person (see Figure 2.4).

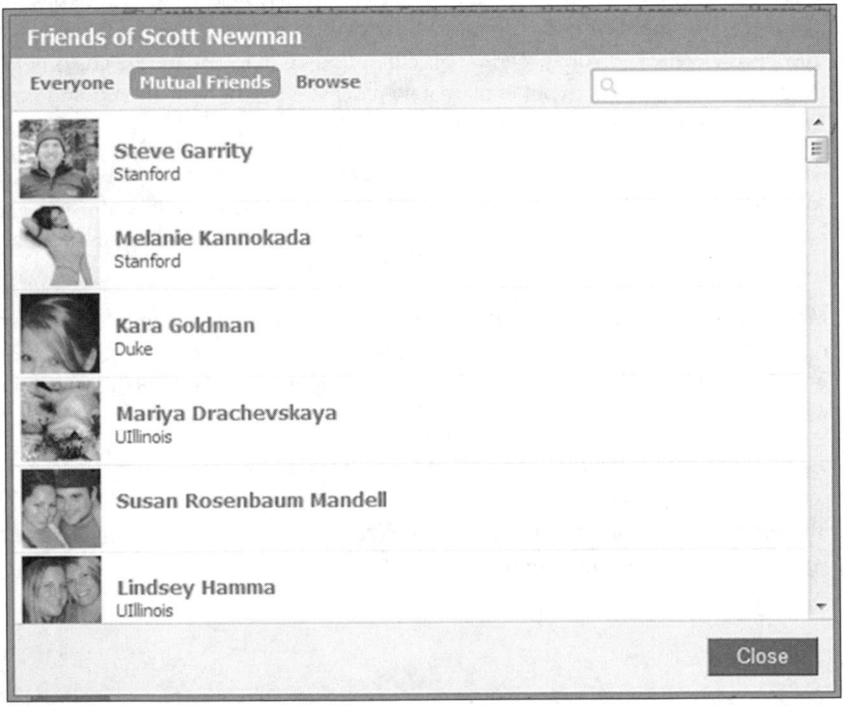

Figure 2.4
Facebook profiles include a list of mutual friends you have with the person.

On LinkedIn, the social network mapping is even more robust. I can see the path of people linking me to Graham, up to three degrees away (see Figure 2.5). Even if Graham and I have no direct connections in common, I could still play on transitive trust to improve my chances of reaching him, albeit via a few more hops.

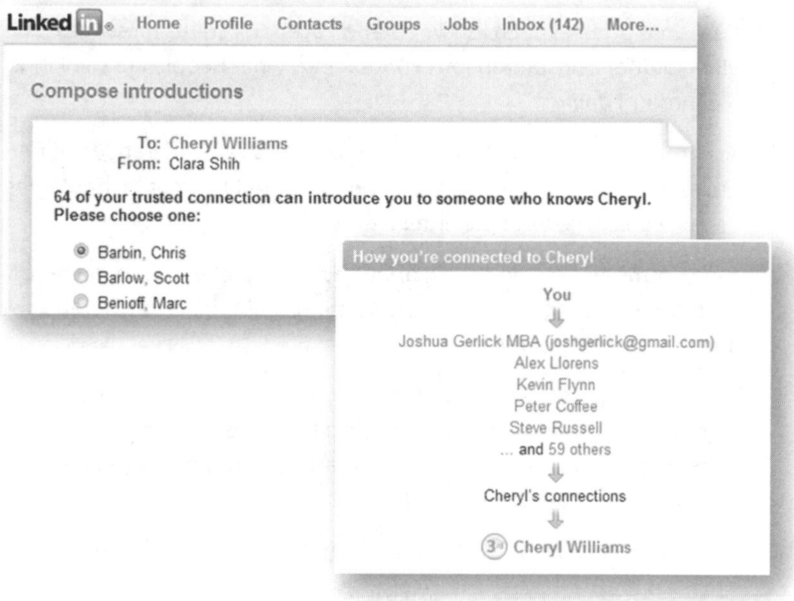

Figure 2.5
LinkedIn takes the transitive trust map of network connections out as far as three degrees and has built-in workflow for requesting introductions through mutual friends.

Transitive trust makes sense intuitively. Going through someone we know reduces risk on a rational level and feels more comfortable on an emotional one. For example, the Stanford University Alumni Association has found that, on average, alumni are more than four times as likely to donate when they are told that someone they know and like has also donated. Because of this remarkable return, Stanford has gone to great lengths to figure out how alumni are connected with one another. Transitive trust is also why direct employee referrals so often result in job candidate hires.

In Chapter 4, "Sales in the Facebook Era," we explore in depth how transitive trust is applied to a sales cycle. Chapter 6 describes how transitive trust can also be abstracted beyond people introductions to the marketing of products and services, also known as word-of-mouth.

< < < TAKEAWAYS

✓ The popularity of Facebook, combined with the importance of profiles in the Facebook experience, means that, on average, people are sharing far more about themselves than ever before.

✓ Real-time updates such as tweets and Facebook status messages provide additional instantaneous context into what people are thinking, feeling, and doing.

✓ According to social media researcher Danah Boyd, generational differences in social network usage can be attributed to what technologies are available when people enter a new life stage.

✓ New norms are also emerging about how people expect to interact with companies, including hypertargeting, real-time response, and personal, authentic interactions.

✓ Transitive trust is the concept that describes the transferred trust across mutual friends. It enables an increased response and success rate when companies and individuals are reaching out to prospective customers, job candidates, and business partners.

> > > TIPS and TO DO's

❑ Think about your personal brand and how you can reinforce it through a consistent name (such as a nickname), photo, bio, and voice on every social networking site where you have a presence.

❑ Establish a system for monitoring and responding to "brand mentions," both personally and of your company or product. Popular tools include Google Alerts, BackType, BoardTracker, and TweetBeep.

❑ Develop a process for responding to customer feedback, both in real time and with your product development and business operations. In the Facebook Era, companies have no choice but to become customer-centric.

❑ Use Facebook and LinkedIn search to find prospective customers, job candidates, and business partners—and tap into transitive trust from mutual connections to increase your response rate.

❑ Look at the social Web techniques employed by companies such as Dunkin' Donuts, Peet's Coffee & Tea, Gap, and Sears for examples of best practices in customer engagement.

3

"People who are members of online social networks are not so much networking as they are broadcasting their lives to an outer tier of acquaintances...."
—Lee Rainie, director of the Pew Internet and American Life Project

How Relationships and Social Capital Are Changing

The World Wide Web of information is about content. The World Wide Web of people—the social Web—is about people and relationships. By necessity, this book is equally about culture and sociology as it is about business and technology. Facebook and Twitter have played substantial roles in affecting the outcome of social movements, such as mobilizing volunteers for the earthquake in Haiti and helping facilitate the uprising in Iran. The social Web itself is a social movement, mobilizing Internet users every day in scarily efficient and far-reaching ways to engage with the people, organizations, and events they hold most dear.

Behind the scenes, social networking sites such as Facebook, Twitter, and LinkedIn have lowered the cost of staying in touch, so we are all staying in touch with more people. It's similar to when we went from in-person meetings to phone calls, and from phone calls to email. Each time, the cost of staying in touch went down, so our capacity to maintain relationships went up. We can call or telemarket to more people than we can see face-to-face on a regular basis. We can email or email-market to far more people than we can call on a regular basis. Today we can become Facebook friends, LinkedIn connections, and Twitter followers with far more people than we could visit, call, or email. Over time, thanks to new technologies, the average number of relationships each of us have is increasing. This is true for both businesses and individuals.

I AM TRYING TO
ADD MORE FRIENDS

Having bigger pools of people to draw from and ask favors of means we can all become more personally and professionally empowered to accomplish our goals and tasks. Equally important, understanding the concepts in this chapter can empower us to better help others.

This chapter talks about relationships in the social Web through the lens of social capital. It discusses how new modes of communication on Facebook, LinkedIn, and Twitter are expanding our weak-tie networks, supplementing offline networking, flattening organizational hierarchies, and creating a win–win situation from network effects for all network participants—that is, you, your customers, partners, and colleagues.

What Is Social Capital?

Individuals and organizations have two sources of competitive advantage: human capital and social capital. Human capital, which includes talent, intellect, charisma, and formal authority, is necessary for success but is often beyond an individual's direct control and is insufficient in most organizations. In contrast, social capital comes from our relationships. Robert Putnam, the Harvard political science professor who coined the term, defines **social capital** as the collective value of all social networks and the inclinations that arise from these networks to do things for each other. According to Putnam, we can measure social capital by the level of trust and reciprocity in a community or between individuals, and it is an essential component to building and maintaining organizations, communities, and even democracy.

More recent work on social capital has focused on the individual. Studies such as those by Deb Gruenfeld at the Stanford Graduate School of Business and Mikolaj Piskorski at Harvard Business School have shown that social capital is a powerful source of knowledge, ideas, opportunities, support, reputation, and visibility that is as influential as human capital (if not more so). Individuals with greater social capital close more deals, are better respected, and get higher-ranking jobs. In the Facebook Era, everyone's social capital increases. Online social networks offer greater access to social capital, empowering those who are well connected with private information, diverse skill sets, and others' energy and attention, and enabling everyone else to become better connected.

Early research already shows that bringing networks online makes people more capable and efficient at accumulating, managing, and exercising social capital. Consciously or unconsciously, people are using sites such as Facebook and LinkedIn as tools to maximize relationship social capital.

Sources of Social Capital on Social Networking Sites

Private Information and Conversation

- **Explanation**—Frequent and informal communications that occur on social networking sites, such as Twitter direct messages or Facebook messages, are an easy way to exchange or obtain private information. Emotional rapport built between individuals on social networking sites also carries into offline relationships, further increasing the likelihood of information exchange.

- **Example**—For those who need to work from home or are less able to join work events after hours (such as those needing to care for their children or the elderly), casual communications on social networking sites can help fill the gap in lost communication opportunities with the online equivalent of water-cooler conversations or chats over a beer.

Diverse Skill Sets

- **Explanation**—Hiring managers, recruiters, and others can easily search on LinkedIn or Facebook for member profiles that match desired skills and then either reach out directly or via mutual friends. Because online social connections are lower commitment and more abundant, chances are higher that someone in a friend-of-friends network fits the bill or at least knows someone who does.

- **Example**—With a quick search on social networking sites, someone seeking to hire a Java developer can reach a broader audience while being more targeted about which profiles of individuals to consider. The result is a bigger pipeline of more qualified candidates.

Others' Energy and Attention

- **Explanation**—The passive broadcast nature of information on social network profiles and status messages has made it socially acceptable for people to share more about themselves on a more frequent basis, enabling them to stay top of mind for friends and colleagues.

- **Example**—If you are waiting to hear back from a prospect or someone from whom you asked a favor, it's better for them to be passively reminded that they owe you an answer from seeing your update on a social networking site than for you to call or email to remind them.

Social capital is the currency of business interactions and relationships. This chapter provides an important conceptual framework about social capital that we repeatedly reference in subsequent chapters on social sales, marketing, product innovation, and recruiting. New modes of communication that social networking sites establish are encouraging weak-tie relationships, complementing offline networking efforts, and creating new social value for people who use these sites.

New Modes of Communication on the Social Web

Online social networking sites have invented new modes of communication such as Facebook pokes, Wall posts, and tweets that are easier and more casual than forms of communication in the past. The "transaction cost" of staying in touch has gone down, so it's now possible for each of us to maintain a greater number of more casual relationships. Although personalized, private messages still play an important role, new semi-public modes of communication such as photos, status messages, and pokes are creating efficient yet emotional ways for us to keep in touch.

In the past, we simply had to forego many relationships because we didn't have enough hours in the day to visit, call, or email someone on a semiperiodic basis. In the Facebook Era, our capacity for weak-tie relationships is almost unbounded. Ordinary people can keep in touch with everyone they have ever known or become Twitter "celebrities" with millions of followers.

Changing Expectations for How We Communicate

Over time, the expectations for how we communicate have changed as new technologies have emerged. It used to be common for friends or door-to-door salesmen to drop by unexpectedly. As people began to relocate and many living communities became less homogenous, phone calls gradually replaced surprise in-person visits as the norm for individuals and businesses to get in touch.

Then BlackBerrys and email came along and extended our workday to 24 hours, significantly cutting into our free time. One coping mechanism was to stop answering phone calls that interrupted us in real time and to move more toward email, which is asynchronous. For businesses, email marketing seemed like a godsend that enabled them to reach many individuals at a very low cost.

But the low cost of sending email has resulted in too much of it. Today, by default, many people treat emails from others they don't know as spam. Other people create separate accounts for the email lists they are on. They worry (and rightly so) that opting in to an email marketing list might mean being flooded with communications from the sender.

The World Wide Web of information is content overload—it is too much. The World Wide Web of people—the Facebook, LinkedIn, and Twitter online social graph—enables us to use transitive trust with friends and people we follow to filter out reliable, interesting, and relevant content, products, and individuals. As we discuss further in Chapter 6, "Marketing in the Facebook Era," Facebook Pages and Twitter accounts are a purely opt-in form of communications. People choose to "like" or follow a business, and they can just as easily choose to stop "liking" or following.

Privacy norms about communication are quite nuanced. People are less private than they were in the past, sharing a great amount of personal information openly on their Facebook profiles and tweets, and interacting with acquaintances. Conversely, people are much more guarded about who shows up at their home or calls on the telephone.

To be successful in communicating to their audience base, businesses need to adapt their communications to match what people want and expect.

Facebook: CRM for Individuals?

Social networking sites not only provide mechanisms for communicating, but they are also a useful contact management system. Facebook is similar to CRM (customer relationship management) for individuals—it is increasingly how many of us manage relationships across our personal and professional lives.

In the past, "keeping in touch" was hard work. After two people met—say, at a conference—staying in touch required one or both parties to actively communicate on a somewhat regular basis. Communication required time and planning.

In contrast, social networking sites are designed for passive communication. Facebook status messages, notifications, and upcoming birthdays remind us to keep in touch. It is fun and intuitive, visual, active, searchable, and self-updating:

- **Fun and intuitive**—Far from fitting the stereotype of traditional CRM databases as being boring and complicated, social networking sites bring games, multimedia, and intuitive design to managing contacts. A simple design and the help wizard that appears when you first register for sites such as Facebook enable people to start using these sites right away, reducing the barriers to joining the online social graph.

- **Visual**—The visual aspect of social networking sites is especially important. Most people in the world aren't very good at remembering names, especially when we have just met a large number of people during a short amount of time. After a party, conference, wedding, or the first day on a new job, profile pictures act as flash cards to help us put the face to the name and better remember people we meet. Seeing people's photos and videos from different aspects of their lives that they choose to share, such as pictures of their dog, also helps us get to know and understand them better.

- **Active**—Most databases are passive, in the sense that they wait for you to query them for specific kinds of data. Social networking sites go beyond passive data queries. Every time we log in to Facebook, we see News Feed updates—such as new status messages, profile pictures, friend connections, videos, gifts, and so on—about a different, random subset of our contacts. We are, in effect, reminded to think about people we know who might not otherwise have crossed our mind that day. Status messages, birthday and engagement announcements, and tweets are timely, proactive suggestions about whom we might want to reach out to and what we might want to say. Compared with before, communication with our contacts requires less work, planning, and remembering because we can count on social networking tools to tell us who, when, and what we want to communicate.

- **Searchable**—Social networking sites make it easy to find contacts within your network. Almost all the sites enable you to search and filter contacts based on various criteria of interest, such as name, employer, school, city, hobbies, gender, relationship status, and other profile information. This search functionality is useful both when you want to establish a new online connection and when you want to search from among your existing connections, such as finding which of your friends have a particular area of expertise.

- **Self-updating**—The advantage of social networking sites over traditional contact databases is that everyone is responsible for maintaining and updating his own profile. This means that information is more likely to be current and accurate.

The Power of Weak Ties

Although most people use Facebook and, to a lesser extent Twitter, to keep in touch with close friends and family members, these social networking sites make the greatest difference from the perspective of social capital with our weak-tie relationships. Weak ties include people you have just met, people you met only a few times, people you used to know, and friends of friends. Before Facebook, we would lose touch with most of these people. Now we stay in touch.

Interestingly, sociology research since the 1970s has shown that our weak ties carry the greatest amount of social capital. We are most often hiring, getting hired by, and closing deals not with our best friends and family members, but with acquaintances, friends of friends, and people we have just met. Weak ties also act as crucial bridges across clumps of people, providing an information advantage to network members.

For most people, social networks are characterized by few strong connections (such as with parents and best friends) and many weak connections. The exact number and type of connections vary by individual, but we all have a threshold beyond which we choose not to or simply are unable to maintain relationships. **Dunbar's number**, a cognitive limit to the number of people with whom one can maintain stable social relationships proposed by British anthropologist Robin Dunbar, has been approximated at 150. An interesting question being explored in today's research is whether social networking sites help increase Dunbar's number. Early data suggests no—that humans have a biological limit on the number of close relationships we can maintain. My theory is that social networks let us better manage *who* is in the inner circle and more fluidly adapt to new situations and circumstances.

In the following guest expert sidebar, Harvard Business School professor Mikolaj Piskorski shares compelling research about how social sites such as Facebook change interpersonal relationships and how companies can best position themselves to succeed in this environment.

Interpersonal Relationships and Facebook

Mikolaj Jan Piskorski

Popular press, bloggers, and certain academics often sound an alarm to warn us that the Internet, and online social networks in particular, make us lonely and estranged. Online social networks apparently make us focus on weak online relationships, which leads us to abandon our deeper and meaningful offline relationships.

The other view argues that online social networks make us more satisfied with our social lives by improving both strong and weak social relationships. Specifically, social sites such as Facebook and Twitter enable people to efficiently participate in the lives of loved ones, even when they are far away. They also help people sustain valuable acquaintance relationships that would otherwise disintegrate very quickly. Finally, online social networks make it easier to befriend people whom we could not otherwise easily find or approach in the offline world. With time, many of these new online relationships lead to meaningful offline relationships, which makes people happier.

Although both views have merit, and we can always find someone who has become either more isolated or more connected as a result of online media, it is useful to know what the numbers say. Overall, research supports the second point of view. The data shows that use of Facebook improves people's networks and their psychological well-being. Although social sites are excellent at helping maintain acquaintance relationships, the main source of user satisfaction with Facebook comes from helping people maintain and deepen offline contacts.

The Pew Internet and American Life Project, which involved more than 2,500 randomly chosen adult Americans, reported in 2009 that Internet users—and users of online social networks, in particular—end up having more diverse social networks. They are also more likely to discuss matters of high importance with people of another race or those who belong to another political party. These findings are great news for our society.

Research also shows profound implications for companies seeking to engage customers on the social Web. Many companies have attempted to engage customers on Facebook or Twitter only to find limited results. This is not very surprising: People go on these sites to connect with friends, not necessarily with businesses. But this does not mean that companies cannot get involved. On the contrary, business initiatives can be very successful, as a handful of companies are discovering.

But to become successful, companies need to change their mindset from trying to "friend" their customers to helping their customers build and improve relationships with other people. By facilitating these relationships, companies can then lower their marketing and operation costs, build brands, and increase willingness to pay for their products and services.

Mikolaj Piskorski (@mpiskorski) is an associate professor of strategy and Marvin Bower Fellow at Harvard Business School.

At their core, social networking sites are relationship tools that enable us to be both more aware and better able to engage with our outer networks. By reducing the cost of interaction and the cost of maintaining a relationship, sites such as Facebook and LinkedIn help increase our network capacity to include otherwise-foregone fringe relationships. As a result, we can capture more of the full value of our cumulative lifetime social network (see Figure 3.1).

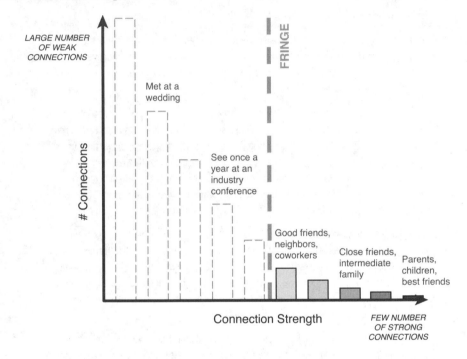

Figure 3.1
Social networking sites provide both low-touch communications and CRM-like features to help us maintain better relationships with more people, including weak ties.

Bernie Hogan and his colleagues at the Oxford Internet Institute have been collecting data on how offline networks manifest themselves online on social networking sites such as Facebook, which we summarized in the following guest expert sidebar. Their early findings suggest a high degree of overlap between people's Facebook networks and their offline networks, but the Facebook networks tend to be much bigger (because of the weak ties).

Comparing Facebook Friend Networks to Offline Personal Networks

Bernie Hogan

It is interesting to compare one's personal (offline) network and one's Facebook network. For this study, I use a hybrid of Hogan et al.'s (2007) and McCarty and Govindaramanujam's (2005) methods to determine personal networks. I first ask about groups the respondent belongs to, and then I ask about group members. I also have respondents start with a seed set of ties and work their way out toward other network members.

To give an example of this analysis, I have opted to use my own Facebook network, which I consider a pretty typical network.

As shown in Figure 3.2, the personal network has 27 nodes, whereas the Facebook network has 186, thereby representing a far larger number of nodes. A high amount of overlap exists between the two networks, as expected. The eight individuals who are in the personal network but not the Facebook network are primarily older individuals and several people who know of Facebook but have actively chosen not to participate. The dark squares represent the 19 (out of 27 total) personal network members on Facebook. The white squares represent the 186 Facebook network members—including 167 weak ties.

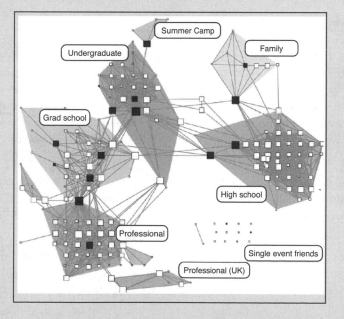

Figure 3.2
This is a rendering of Bernie Hogan's Facebook friendship network using NodeXL. The different shaded regions represent different real-world networks, including grad school, professional, and family.

Similar to a few hundred other networks I am currently analyzing, this one has some pretty tell-tale signs:

- **Dense pockets of connections with few links in between suggest a change in social context and often a change in geography.** When university students examine their networks, the two biggest clusters are high school and university, except those who grew up near the university—then the clusters are not as distinct. People who have lived in several areas for a long time tend to see multiple clear clusters. Family often represents a third, smaller cluster because the natural limit to the size of family is often smaller than the natural limit to who is "friendable" from other places.

- **Bridges are meaningful.** Two kinds of bridges generally exist between these clusters. The first bridge is just a coincidence: someone who happens to know people from your home-town and people from your current job. These bridges are characterized by few links between clusters. The second kind of bridge refers to people who have multiple relation-ships to several clusters. These are typically people whom you introduce to others. In this example network, you can see several people who appear to link across groups.

Dr. Bernie Hogan (@blurky) is a research fellow at the Oxford Internet Institute.

Relationship "Options"

Some of you might be wondering if it really counts as having a relationship with some-one if all you do is see pictures of their dog and "poke" them occasionally, and that's a fair point. Another way of thinking about weak ties on Facebook or Twitter is as relationship "options" that you have the capability but not the obligation to exercise down the road if it makes sense to invest more in that relationship. Instead of foregoing momentary rap-port shared with someone you met at a conference or on the plane, you can "file it away" for later.

The rationale is that, during a lifetime, you will build up a large and likely very valuable pool of weak-tie contacts for you to draw from when you are hiring, looking for a job, sell-ing a product, or accomplishing some other goal.

Twitter takes this even further by enabling one-sided relationships: Someone can follow you without you necessarily having to follow them back. It's not a bad idea to check out who has been following you, in case it's someone with whom you'd want to establish a mutual relationship or start interacting.

Discovering Which Relationships Are Valuable

In addition to increasing our relationship capacity, social networking sites provide impor-tant information that can help us better assess up front the potential relevance and value of a relationship. Instead of waiting for time or happenstance to reveal common ground, mutual friends, or overlapping interests, we can glean more of this information sooner from viewing profile information our new contacts have chosen to share. Having access to this information helps accelerate relationships by making us smarter about which relationships to invest in, prioritize, and potentially escalate from the fringe.

For example, it might never have come up during your brief conversation and business card exchange with the guy you met at a medical conference last month that he also plays soccer. If your league team is seeking another member, that new information could be enough for you to decide to become more than just fringe friends. You might have any number of reasons why you would actually want to stay in touch, but you might not have had a chance to discover this the first time you met—and without social networking, you might not have decided to stay in touch.

Online social networking gives serendipity extra chances. First, you are more likely to stay in touch with people you have just met because the bar for establishing an online social networking connection is lower compared with traditional relationships. Second, after you've established the connection, you are empowered with information to decide sooner whether this is a relationship worth pursuing. Information helps us qualify early and reduce false positives and false negatives: We waste less time on relationships that likely won't go anywhere, and we miss out less often on relationships that likely will go far.

Latent Value: When Options Come in Handy

Friend options come in handy when life circumstances change and new unmet needs emerge. If you are laid off, tap your social network to find a job. If you are moving or traveling to a new city, see who in your network is local and perhaps someone can show you the ins and outs. If you are starting a company, hire employees from your network. If you have a sudden need for advice or expertise, find answers and experts from your network.

For this reason, weak ties can carry immense latent value. Maybe that friendly gal who sat next to you on the flight to New York ends up introducing you years later to your new job or business partner. She might not have seemed "valuable" at the time you met, but she could become valuable later. Online social networking extends serendipity across time and circumstance.

Especially for younger generations of people who are starting to use Facebook at earlier ages, it provides interesting implications of having a database containing every person you have ever met. My friend's younger brother, Tyler, is a good example. Tyler is 13 (the minimum age for joining Facebook) and registered for an account several months ago. The first thing he did was search for all his elementary school classmates and add them as friends. If Tyler wants, he could be Facebook friends with these people forever. In fact, Tyler will be able to keep in touch with everyone he meets from now on, accumulating a lifetime of latent social capital. In 20 years, perhaps Tyler will find that his friend from kindergarten has become an important business partner.

Of course, Tyler might not want to stay in touch in every instance. (Who among us hasn't wanted to "start over" at some point?) When relationships or life circumstances change, it sometimes makes sense to reflect these changes in our online social networks. We have several options: adjusting privacy settings to limit what information is visible to a contact, "defriending" a contact, blocking a contact, or committing "Facebook suicide" (deactivating your account).

Supplementing Offline Networking with Online Interactions

One common objection to online social networking is that it sacrifices relationship quality for quantity. Although this might have been true of first-generation sites, it is becoming less the case as people become more sophisticated about the connections they accept and establish. As we discussed in Chapter 2, "The New Social Norms," interactions on social networking sites tend to augment instead of replace offline interactions. One of the reasons Facebook has been so successful compared with its predecessors is the focus on supporting offline networks instead of online-only relationships.

To test this assumption, I surveyed 100 of my own friends to ask whether they initiate or accept friend requests from strangers on social networking sites. A *stranger* is defined as someone whom you have never met in person. I tried to get representative coverage across different age groups, professions, and geographies, but admittedly many of my friends tend to reflect my own demographic. Also, this is not strictly an apples-to-apples comparison because not everyone I surveyed belongs to all four sites I asked about.

Still, the results are illuminating. Most (73%) had never received a friend request from a stranger on Facebook. Even among those who had, most had not accepted these requests. They either had clicked Ignore Request or simply had not responded (see Table 3.1). The results for LinkedIn follow a similar pattern.

Table 3.1   Survey of Friend Requests from Strangers

	Facebook	LinkedIn	Orkut	MySpace
Received friend request from a stranger	27%	34%	100%	100%
Accepted friend request from a stranger	5%	18%	66%	94%
Initiated friend request with a stranger	0%	7%	3%	47%

The respondents' experience on Orkut and MySpace was markedly different. Without exception, everyone had been solicited by a stranger. More tended to accept strangers' requests on MySpace than on Orkut. More people had also initiated friend requests with strangers on MySpace, presumably because it is common practice to befriend bands and celebrities on MySpace.

I dug a little deeper. Most people who had accepted requests from strangers said they had done so because the protocol for acceptance or rejection was not clear and they didn't want to appear rude. Many told me that after awhile, their Orkut networks degraded into largely random connections. Spam started drowning out interactions with real friends; as the site became less relevant, people stopped logging in and interacting, which made it even less relevant for their real friends who were on the site. Pretty soon, entire groups of friends stopped logging in.

Compared with Orkut or MySpace, Facebook and LinkedIn established a clear friend request protocol and culture of trust for their networks. Facebook did so through email-based identity confirmation (talked about in Chapter 1, "The Fourth Revolution") and online networks modeled off real offline networks. For example, when you join Facebook, one of the first things you must do is choose one or more networks to associate with. Your options include schools, employers, and other real offline networks that have real offline meaning and trust. LinkedIn took a different approach to establish protocol. By accepting a LinkedIn connection request, you implicitly agree to share your network and to professionally vouch for this person. Most people aren't willing to vouch for strangers, so they are more careful about accepting LinkedIn connection requests from strangers.

Even when people meet for the first time on Facebook or LinkedIn, they usually are friends of friends or at least belong to the same network. In the case of LinkedIn, a business objective is generally driving a connection that would result in a real offline relationship.

Far from signaling the end of traditional relationships, Facebook's success is a testament that nothing is stronger than in-person rapport. Protecting the quality of online networks and focusing them on supporting offline relationships keeps the Facebook experience relevant and valuable.

However, one interesting trend I did notice in the surveys is that teenagers are more willing to initiate and accept requests from strangers. As I investigated further, it became clear that this is because of competition over who has the most Facebook friends. Similarly, heavy gamers on Facebook have incentives for befriending strangers to gain virtual goods and points within various social games.

Fortunately, it is now possible on Facebook to classify and tag your relationships using Friend Lists, and to accordingly limit interaction and how much data is visible to each connection. For example, you could create a Never Met Friend List for strangers and hide all your photos, wall posts, and contact information for all connections on this list. Relationship tagging and tiering using Friend Lists can be extremely helpful in maintaining high-quality online networks. Chapter 10, "How To: Build and Manage Relationships on the Social Web," describes in detail how Friend Lists work.

With perhaps the exception of teens, we are seeing that online interactions tend to support instead of replace offline rapport, strengthening existing relationships and laying the groundwork for future relationships that you might not otherwise have enough context and capacity to pursue.

The Flattening Effect

It's interesting to think about how social capital from social networking sites affects organizations. The Internet democratized privileged access to information. Online social networking takes this further, democratizing privileged access to people.

Because fewer barriers exist, people are empowered to build social capital in more informal, entrepreneurial, and ad hoc ways. On most social networking sites, registration is open to anyone, and every member primarily starts on level footing. Sites such as Facebook were designed without hierarchy, so real-world social structures that are hierarchical don't translate well—they tend to flatten out. Take corporate communication, for example. Something the CEO says is more likely to spread across the company's informal word-of-mouth networks compared with something an entry-level worker says. But to Facebook, these statements look identical.

Imagine that the CEO posts a link on her profile to a news article annotated with her comments, and the entry-level employee does the same with a different article. Before Facebook, the CEO's comments would likely have propagated across the company and the employee's would not have. But on Facebook, both messages might have equal opportunity to propagate the company network. In the truly flat Facebook Era, entry-level workers potentially have the same opportunity as the CEO to have their voice heard.

Using online social networking, employees might also bypass traditional organizational hierarchy and boundaries to network directly with senior managers or colleagues in other departments, units, and geographies. Similar to how blogging democratized who had a voice on the Internet, someone who is active on Facebook and who posts interesting links and commentary might win visibility in the company in ways that would simply not have been possible before.

Creating New Value from Network Effects

Metcalfe's Law provides a good explanation behind the power and value of the online social graph. Originally used to describe telecommunications networks, it states that the value of a network increases exponentially with the number of members. This is because, for n members, roughly n^2 possible connections exist. Among these n^2 connections forms a social economy of mutual trust, favor, and contribution. Over time, as new members join, the value of each individual's network increases, as does the value of the overall social economy.

The Reciprocity Ring

I experienced Metcalfe's Law firsthand in spring 2008 during a somewhat contrived but nevertheless convincing offline experiment. It was the last day of a weeklong leadership course I was taking at the Stanford Graduate School of Business, and in our final session together, we created a reciprocity ring to demonstrate how social networking can create value for everyone who participates.

The first step was coming up with a request to put forth to the group. Each one of us wrote down our request and our name on a Post-it Note and placed it around a large circle that had been drawn on the whiteboard (see Figure 3.3).

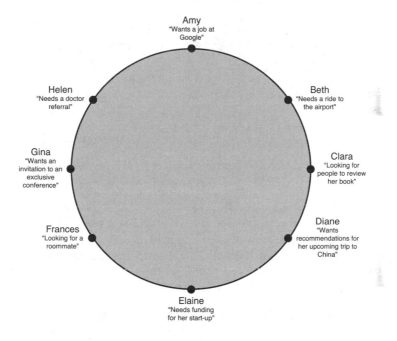

Figure 3.3
The first step in the reciprocity ring exercise was to write down your name and a request to put forth to the group, and then place these in a circle.

Next we were handed a pad of blank Post-it Notes and given ten minutes to survey the circle of requests. For each request where we could contribute, we wrote on a Post-it Note our name and how we might be able to help and placed it below the request on the whiteboard (see Figure 3.4).

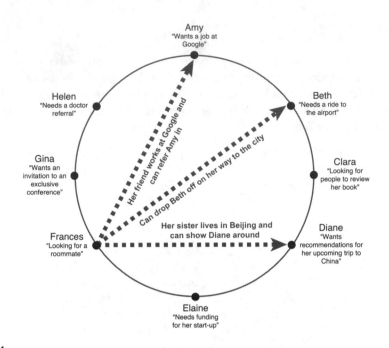

Figure 3.4
Each participant scanned the set of requests and volunteered to help where he or she could provide value.

The results were impressive. First, every request received help—and most requests received multiple offers of help (see Figure 3.5). Second, each one of us could contribute to at least one request—and most of us volunteered to help with multiple requests. However, it was most interesting that almost no one-to-one exchanges occurred. In the majority of cases, the person providing the favor to you was not the same person to whom you provided a favor.

For example, Elaine needs to find funding for her new start-up. Amy volunteered to help because she knows several of the partners at a venture capital firm. Amy, in turn, is looking for a job at Google. She receives help on this request, but not from Elaine. It is Frances, who receives help from Gina, who receives help from Elaine, who actually can help Amy. The reason this works is that the cost of helping is generally miniscule compared with the benefit of being helped. To Elaine, receiving an introduction to a venture capitalist is worth a lot because it could make or break her new start-up. But to Amy, providing the introduction is no big deal. It takes her just a few minutes to do so over email. In the end, new value is created for each individual and for the group collectively. Everyone wins.

Figure 3.5
Every request received help and every participant helped provided a favor, creating value for every-one in the group.

The Online Social Graph Reciprocity Ring

For the Stanford experiment to work, we all had to be at the same place at the same time for the same purpose. In real life, this is extremely rare. Offline, such explicit networking feels too utilitarian and contrived. And you would never physically assemble a large group of people for the purpose of asking each other favors. But in Facebook, Orkut, and LinkedIn, these large groups of people are already assembled and ready to be mobilized when you need a favor.

Social networking sites take the rapport we have established offline and bridge them into a system that you can call on in times of need. Online social networking extends the notion of the reciprocity ring across time, geography, and networks and is therefore capable of generating a tremendous amount of social capital for participants. Ultimately, efficiency gains from bringing technology to the intrinsically human activity of social networking create new, mutually beneficial value for individuals and to the collective community.

Lower Barriers to Engagement

Social networking sites might even be making it easier to ask for favors while making it harder to say no. Because interactions feel more casual on Facebook or LinkedIn, a lower bar is in place for when it is considered okay to make a request. Picking up the phone or visiting someone in person and asking for a favor puts the person on the spot and, therefore, carries a higher social cost. In contrast, sending someone a Facebook message is no big deal. By reducing the cost, social networking sites can make people feel more comfortable asking for favors.

What about being on the receiving end of a request? Even when they contain legitimate requests you should actually consider, emails and voicemails are easy to ignore or lose in the shuffle. These traditional forms of communication can feel impersonal in comparison.

At the risk of generalizing, similar requests made on Facebook might be harder to ignore because of the social pressure tied to them. Facebook messages do not come in isolation—you see the requestor's photo, profile, and who you know in common. The request feels personal, so you think twice before saying no. Especially if you have strong mutual ties or belong to the same networks (or the requestor belongs to a different network that has value to you), the social and mental cost of ignoring the request is higher. This ties back to the earlier discussion on how information on social networking sites helps people qualify the potential value of relationships earlier. If you receive a request on Facebook and can quickly identify that the requestor might be a valuable contact, it is much harder to ignore the request. If you received the same request on email, in our age of rampant spam, you might never give it a chance.

Because it feels more personal and more information exists about who is making the request, online social networking makes it both more casual and acceptable to ask for favors while making it harder to say no. As a result, more requests tend to get made and fulfilled, increasing the amount of social capital in circulation and overall value of the social economy. In a sense, social networking sites extend the notion of the reciprocity ring across time, geography, and networks. Therefore, they might have the potential to generate a tremendous amount of new value for everyone involved.

Of course, the easiest "favor" a company can ask for is any form of engagement, including a "like" or comment. In the following guest expert sidebar, Stanford University persuasion psychologist BJ Fogg explains why he believes Facebook is the most persuasive technology of all time.

Understanding the Power of Persuasion on Facebook

BJ Fogg, Ph.D.

Facebook is a landscape for persuasion, both for Facebook the company and for all of us who are on Facebook.

Facebook the company creates experiences that influence people to upload a profile picture, invite friends to join, comment on posts, and so on. In my lab at Stanford University, we've found more than 80 such behavior targets. When you do any of these, Facebook the company becomes more valuable.

But it's not just Facebook Inc. that sets out to persuade people. We, the users, are agents of influence. We use the features of Facebook to create groups and rally people to a cause. We post content hoping to provoke others to comment and engage with us. And on it goes.

Everything people do on Facebook is an act with intent. For example, imagine posting a photo every day and no one ever comments. You'd eventually stop posting. We *want* people to comment on our photos, posts, status updates, and so on, and each item of engagement makes Facebook the company more valuable.

Three factors combine to make Facebook the #1 persuasive technology of all time. First, people we know on Facebook—not brands or strangers—ask us to do things: Join this group or donate to this cause. Some of the requests are subtle, built into the interface: "Like" my photo. But still the messages are perceived to be requests from friends, not from a company.

Next, the flood of triggers that come to us when we use Facebook are actionable. I call these "hot triggers." And when you get a hot trigger on Facebook—accept my Friend invitation, watch my video, or play FarmVille—you can react immediately. As a result, behavior happens fast on Facebook, and it gives the Facebook experience a sense of energy, as if a party is always going on.

To explain the third factor of persuasive power, consider how different Facebook is from task-focused Web sites. If I go to Quicken.com, I'm on the site to pay bills. If I get a hot trigger to join a political group, I feel annoyed. It's distracting me from my goal. But on Facebook it's entirely different. Most of us use Facebook without any specific goal, and that means we're distractible. We want to be seduced away into something unexpected—that's what makes Facebook fun.

When you combine these three elements—friends as persuaders, hot triggers, and openness to distraction—you create an experience we've never seen before on a large scale. These three things enabled my Stanford students to engage 16 million people on Facebook with apps they created during my 10-week class.

BJ Fogg (@bjfogg and www.bjfogg.com) directs research and design at Stanford University's Persuasive Technology Lab.

< < < **TAKEAWAYS**

✓ Social capital is the collective value of all social networks and the incli-nations that arise from these networks to do things for each other. We can measure it by the level of trust and reciprocity in a community or between individuals.

✓ Unlike earlier social networking sites such as Orkut or Friendster, Facebook (and also LinkedIn and Twitter) is modeled off of people's real-world networks and relationships instead of encouraging people to connect with strangers.

✓ By making it possible to maintain relationships with a greater number of people, the social Web increases the average number of weak ties in our personal networks.

✓ Having a bigger pool of people to draw on for help increases our indi-vidual social capital when we are trying to accomplish personal and professional goals.

✓ Facebook is similar to CRM (customer relationship management) for individuals—it is increasingly how many people manage relationships across their personal and professional lives.

> > > **TIPS and TO DO's**

❏ Stay in touch with people you meet at conferences and events by con-necting with them on LinkedIn or Facebook, if appropriate.

❏ When you move to a new city or are traveling on a business trip and have extra time, search on social networking sites to see which of your friends and acquaintances you might want to reconnect with. On Facebook, you can browse friends by city.

❏ Understand the accepted etiquette on social networking sites, such as initiating or accepting friend requests only from people you know, and make sure your actions reflect the etiquette, especially when interact-ing with customers.

❏ Think about how you can help others based on the frustrations or requests they post on their status messages. Sometimes just liking or commenting on their post is greatly appreciated.

❏ Explore the mechanisms of persuasion on Facebook to increase audi-ence engagement and likelihood of response to your call-to-actions.

Social Networking Across Your Organization

4

"Sales IS social networking!"
—Geoffrey Moore, author, *Crossing the Chasm*

Sales in the Facebook Era

As anyone who has ever bought or sold something knows, selling is an intrinsically social activity based on mutual trust. Even in the case of commodity products and services, relationships can sometimes even trump price as the deciding factor in purchase decisions. Ultimately, people enjoy doing business with people they like and refuse to do business with people they don't trust.

A major result of the democratization of business described in earlier chapters has been unprecedented market competition. In today's business landscape, companies are faced with a greater number of competitors and savvier buyers empowered with information. More than ever, sales reps must take the longer-term view of their customer relationships instead of trying to maximize the value of a single transaction. With fewer unfair structural advantages for reps to count on, timely insights into customer needs and interpersonal communications in the sales process have become requirements for closing the deal. Online social networks are emerging as critical business tools to help facilitate these insights and communications.

In the first edition of this book, I described how the social Web changes each step of the sales cycle and how CRM systems should be updated to incorporate the new technology. Many of you contacted me on Facebook and at conferences, saying, "We don't just want to learn how to use Facebook—we want tools to do this!" Well, thank you for giving me the inspiration. I quit my day job at Salesforce.com and started a software company to build truly social CRM. My company, Hearsay Labs, provides social relationship management for companies to manage, socialize, and personalize customer interactions across Facebook, Twitter, and the social Web (see Figure 4.1).

A lot of the new depth and rich examples from this edition come directly from the tremendous learning and innovation we have developed with our customers in the last year. It's very exciting. We are breaking new territory with how people buy, sell, share, and make decisions in the Facebook Era. I know many of you out there are, too.

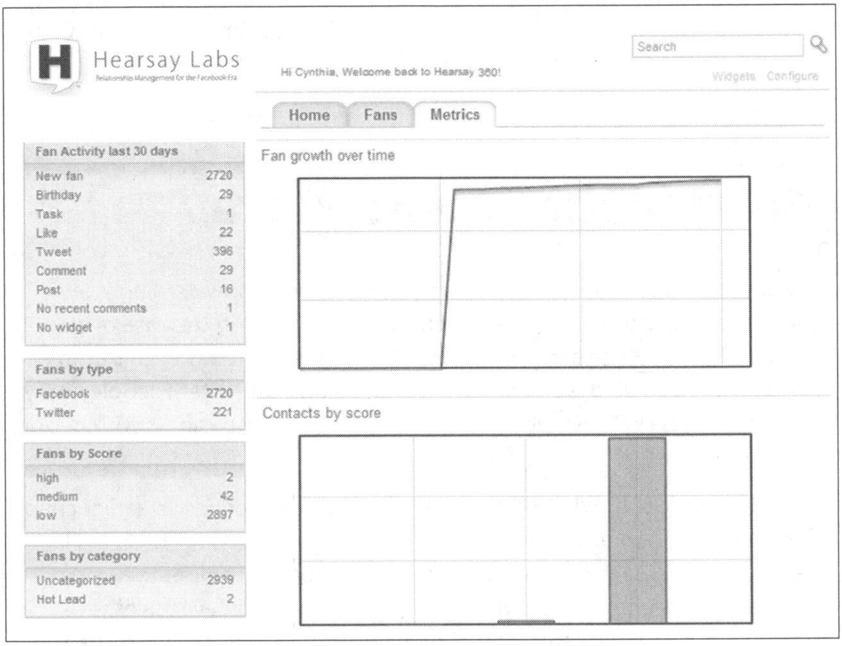

Figure 4.1

Hearsay 360 is a social CRM application. Inspired by feedback from the first edition, I started Hearsay Labs to help companies harness the social Web to reach new audiences, build better customer relationships, and achieve viral business growth.

This chapter walks through a typical sales cycle and discusses where it makes sense to leverage social networks to increase sales effectiveness. The chapter concludes with a short discussion on the implications for CRM and how the future of information contained in CRM will likely be bidirectional between companies and their customers. Chapter 10, "How To: Build and Manage Relationships on the Social Web," provides concrete instructions on how individuals can build and manage relationships on Facebook for sales or other activities.

Transforming the Sales Cycle

Sales reps can use online social networking to become more productive in two ways: to glean insights *about* customers and to engage in casual communications *with* customers. From the customer's perspective, the sales call has the potential to become more person- alized and relevant. It's no longer acceptable for reps to generically push every product and service. Today's reps are expected to have "done their homework" based on the infor- mation available on the Internet and on social networking sites. Customers, for their part, are responsible for managing and maintaining what information they choose to share with whom. Chapter 10 explains how to use Facebook privacy controls to manage online identities, and Chapter 15, "Corporate Governance, Strategy, and Implementation," speaks to more general issues and concerns about privacy and security.

Based on the sales deals I've been on, as well as interviews with other colleagues in sales, I have identified eight aspects of the sales cycle that stand to benefit from the online social graph: establishing credibility, prospecting, making the first call, navigating com- plex customer organizations, collaborating across sales teams, providing customer refer- ences, building and sustaining rapport, and ensuring ongoing customer success with post-sales support. These are also very much in line with the general techniques advo- cated by popular sales methodologies such as Miller–Heiman and Customer-Centric Selling. I describe the first seven in this chapter and devote the entire next chapter to customer service and support.

Before we delve into the sales cycle, let's call out some differences between B2B (business-to-business) and B2C (business-to-consumer) sales and discuss how these might affect social sales strategy.

B2B Versus B2C Sales

Selling to consumers, or business-to-consumer (B2C) sales, tends to be more straightfor- ward, transactional, and driven by product and marketing. Because of a lower price point and fewer people involved in making the purchase decision, B2C typically has a shorter sales cycle. For many items, especially those less than $100, it is usually more about mar- keting than about sales. Often no salesperson is involved. From an online social network- ing perspective, these goods and services can benefit from social merchandising, targeted advertising, and viral marketing tactics, which we discuss in Chapter 6, "Marketing in the Facebook Era."

As we go up in price and complexity, B2C begins to resemble business-to-business (B2B) sales. Especially when "intangibles" such as warranties, customer support, authenticity, and service quality factor into a sale, trust and relationships become critical differentia- tors (see Figure 4.2). B2B selling into organizations is often a multistep process involving multiple stakeholders and levels of decision making, resulting in a longer sales cycle. The upcoming sections on collaborating within a sales team and navigating customer organizations are directed especially at B2B sales. Finally, B2B deals tend to be custom transactions. These typically involve negotiation because of a higher markup and imprecise information about the value of the good or service being offered.

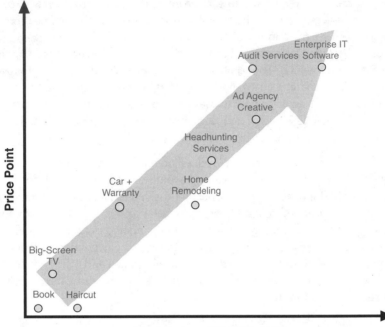

Credit: Timothy Chou, cofounder of Openwater Networks and lecturer at Stanford. He whiteboarded a similar concept for me in his office in June 2008.

Figure 4.2
Relationships and trust play a bigger role in purchase decisions of higher-priced items that are more difficult to value and require greater expertise to understand.

But why use a person-to-person tool such as Facebook for selling to an organization? The important point to keep in mind is that individuals are at the heart of any organization. Individual people, not entire companies, make purchase decisions. Transactions succeed or fail because of a few key individuals—your customer champion, executive decision maker, customer reference, sales rep, and product expert. By strengthening the bond and improving information flow among your internal deal team and with key customer stakeholders, social networking sites can help your company create a more productive selling machine.

In the following guest expert sidebar, veteran sales account executive Chris Cranis provides specific tips on how companies can use Facebook for B2B sales. Cranis has been a top sales rep at a number of B2B companies, including Ribbit (acquired by British Telecom) and Salesforce.com.

Five Tips for How Sales Reps Should Use Facebook

Chris Cranis

"The most valuable commodity I know of is information, pal."
—Gordon Gekko, *Wall Street* (1987)

The number one reason a sales rep should use Facebook for finding business is *research*. Sales reps can leverage this research in five ways:

1. **Research your prospect's company**—No better tool on the Web gives you as much insight into a prospect or customer. Facebook provides a global hub of information that you can use to understand the people you want to sell to. The information you gather is priceless when you talk to your prospect. The more you understand their business, the more your prospect will trust you and the ideas you are pitching.

2. **Research your prospect company's Groups and Facebook Business Pages**—Start by searching for Facebook Groups and Pages related to your prospect. If you are lucky enough to find one, join the Group or "like" the Page immediately. Scan the list of fans and read the wall posts, including recent announcements. Has the company posted anything recently that aligns with your product?

3. **Research your prospect's people**—After you "like" a Page, spend some time focused on other people who have also "liked" the Page. Many times you will notice that they are employees, ex-employees, vendors, partners, and the like. Knowing who else "likes" a Facebook Page is a great place to understand the marketing goals of your prospect or customer.

4. **Research your prospect's links**—When you join a company Page, often other members will post specific links redirecting you to other Web sites that provide incredible information for you to digest and understand their strategy. Visit each page and ask yourself a few questions, such as, "Why is this site important?" "How does this impact the overall business strategy or plan this company has set forth?"

5. **Research your prospect's ideas**—Facebook Pages provide you with amazing visibility into what your prospect's customers are saying and suggesting. Figure out what your prospect's customers are asking of your prospect and include that in your sales pitch.

Chris Cranis (@forceIUS) is a senior account executive at Salesforce.com.

Now let's walk through a typical sales cycle and talk about how the social Web changes each stage.

1. Establishing Credibility

First, sales reps need to establish credibility that they are competent and committed to delivering customer success. Traditionally, reps had to rely on the brand reputation of their company and products, and their Rolodex of customer relationships slowly built up over many years.

Following the personal branding discussion in Chapter 2, "The New Social Norms," sales reps and others today can accelerate the process of building trust by using social networking sites to convey qualifications. For example, a typical LinkedIn profile contains four types of information that would have been awkward or more difficult to provide in the past: public testimonials, list of connections, professional experience, and education pedigree. Similar to Amazon.com's customer reviews on books and Zagat's customer reviews on restaurants, social networking sites are becoming the *de facto* place for reviews on business professionals. If you have satisfied customers, it might not be a bad idea to ask them for public testimonials on LinkedIn or the Testimonials application on Facebook. Chapter 8, "Recruiting in the Facebook Era," goes into greater detail about LinkedIn recommendations in the context of job candidate references.

Bidirectional visibility helps foster mutual trust. With this information on hand (which you have chosen to share), prospective customers are empowered to "check you out" as a sales rep and hopefully gain confidence in your knowledge and competence in helping them find the right solution for their needs.

2. Prospecting

As we cover in the next chapter, marketing is responsible for generating leads en masse. But great salespeople are able to source their own leads, too. As Tupperware party hosts and Mary Kay beauty consultants have known for decades, sometimes your best prospective customers are right in front of you: friends, family, and acquaintances.

However, most people wouldn't feel entirely comfortable calling the list of contacts in their phone book. Fortunately, as we talked about in the previous chapter, online social networks have created a new set of interaction modes and relationship types, such as Facebook friends and LinkedIn connections, that make it less invasive, more comfortable, and easier to ask favors of your network.

Before social networking sites, it was both less efficient and less socially acceptable for sales reps to directly prospect into their networks. It was inefficient because they had no easy way to tell who among their contacts might be interested in their product. It was invasive because sales reps burned through social capital each time they tried selling to someone who was not interested.

In the Facebook Era, it is a different story. LinkedIn and Facebook (and Twitter, to a lesser extent) generally have employment information (location, employer, and role) for each contact. The sales rep can search on the exact profile of the ideal target prospect and qualify the lead earlier in the cycle. The sales call feels less invasive because the interaction feels more casual, and the pitch is targeted specifically to the prospective customer's profile. The following case study profiles how one company, Aster Data Systems, successfully sourced its initial wave of customers using social networking sites.

Social Graph Prospecting at Aster Data Systems

Aster Data Systems, a start-up software company located in Silicon Valley, has dramatically grown its business through creative use of LinkedIn. As a small start-up, Aster lacked brand recognition and did not have the budget for large marketing or advertising campaigns.

To source early customers, Aster instead tapped into the company's collective social network on LinkedIn, MySpace, and Facebook. Senior management asked all employees, not just sales reps, to tap their networks for potential prospects who had keywords such as "data warehousing" in their title or functional expertise.

In just a few months, the resourcefulness of this strategy has already begun to pay off. LinkedIn and other social networking sites are used to identify who among those contacts connected to Aster employees might be interested in the database product. Then a sales cycle is initiated through a combination of LinkedIn and traditional communication modes. Thanks to the power of the social graph, Aster has successfully signed on more than a dozen customers.

And it's not just immediate contacts. As Figure 4.3 shows, social networking sites also enable you to reach friends of friends and greater extended networks, expanding your addressable prospecting audience.

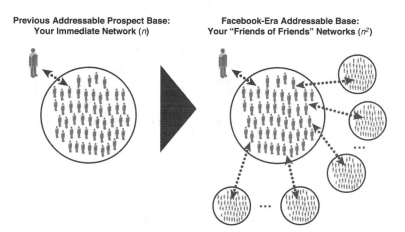

Figure 4.3
Using a service such as LinkedIn grows the prospect base from n contacts to n^2 or more contacts because of the "friends of friends" effect. This gets multiplied even further if more employees (including nonsales functions) tap their networks in this way.

To reach even broader audiences than your extended networks, LinkedIn Open Networkers (LIONs) have emerged as an interesting phenomenon, generally for those in sales, business development, and recruiting. Traditional social network philosophy says that people should invite and accept connection requests with only people they personally know. This approach is both what I generally advocate and what I found in surveying my friends about their usage of Facebook and LinkedIn, as we talked about in the previous chapter. However, some LinkedIn members view this as overly restrictive and have adopted a policy of accepting connection invitations from strangers (see Figure 4.4). These individuals are mostly sales professionals who have chosen to sacrifice network quality for quantity.

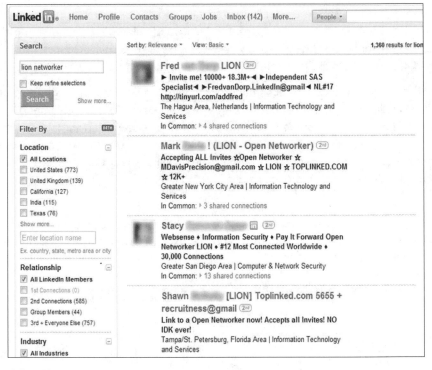

Figure 4.4
Some estimates suggest that LinkedIn alone has hundreds of thousands of open networkers who will accept a connection with anyone.

3. Making the First Call

Historically, most first calls don't have a high success rate. Prospective customers dread them because they are usually irrelevant and, therefore, can feel insincere and like a waste of time. The salesperson dreads them because the recipient is annoyed by the call.

In the Facebook Era, the first call looks very different. Sales reps can perform more lead qualification and preparation beforehand, saving both their time and the prospect's time.

Sales reps can learn the answers to many traditional discovery questions by poking around the prospect's social networking profile, such as his tenure at the company, key responsibilities and accomplishments, and past experience with solutions in your space, to name a few. Prospects are far more willing to take that first call if the pitch is tailored to their needs instead of just a generic push of every product and service. Data from the social networking sites enables sales reps to weed out prospects early. Or if they decide that the prospect might be a good fit, they can formulate the right introductory pitch and even involve mutual contacts who can serve as references. The basic expectation has become that salespeople have "done their homework" given the wealth of information available, and even the first call should reflect an initial level of effort.

The salespeople I interviewed said they are increasingly using LinkedIn for prospecting and making initial contact. They find that, surprisingly, the simplest emails solicit the most responses. Figure 4.5 shows a sample email one of my friends was kind enough to share. Tying back to the notion of bidirectional visibility, the sales rep in this example provides a link back to her own social networking profile so that the prospect can glean more information without sales pressure. The rep also calls out some commonality shared with the prospect (college alma mater, in this case) to differentiate herself and establish early rapport. Often profile data such as shared companies or industry experience, sports teams, hometowns, and fraternities and sororities are used to establish common ground and get one foot in the door. To prospects, the call feels less invasive because this is all information they have opted to share on public social networking sites, compared with the old model of marketing lists that might get bought or sold without their consent. This also ensures that the profile data and contact information reps are using are more accurate and up-to-date.

Subject: Quick question re: LinkedIn

I am looking at your LinkedIn profile right now and have a quick question for you.

My name is *Jane Sales* and I am on the *Prospective Customer X* account team here at *Vendor Y*. Check out my LinkedIn profile <u>here</u>. I see that you are a fellow *Arizona State* alum!

Let me know when you have a few minutes to discuss.

Thank you,

Jane Sales
Vendor Y
222-222-2222

Figure 4.5
A sample sales prospecting email sent to a social network contact. It's a good idea to keep initial contact short and simple and, if possible, find common ground to establish early interpersonal rapport.

Another great benefit of social networking sites is the capability for sales reps to see who they know in common with the prospect. Instead of a cold call, reps might consider requesting a warm introduction from a mutual friend or business colleague. The warm intro increases the chances that the reps will rise above the spam and at least get to make their initial pitch. Before social networking sites, even if mutual contacts existed, it was hard to know that they were there.

As we briefly discussed in the last chapter, Facebook is a rudimentary form of CRM. I created Faceconnector (originally Faceforce) in fall 2007 to help reps connect the dots between the leads they were getting and the *real people* behind the leads. Traditional leads are a name, title, and company. *People* are far more complex and interesting. They are defined not just by their current title and employer, but also by the rich set of past experiences that have collectively shaped who they are, their interests, their hobbies, where they're from, and who their friends are. People are getting more comfortable with sharing at least some of this information on their social networking profile. Faceconnector pulls real-time Facebook profile and friend information—such as schools attended, past employers, favorite books, interests, and friends in common—into Salesforce CRM so that reps viewing a lead or contact record inside Salesforce can see more than just the title and company (see Figure 4.6). They can begin to know the *person* and try to tailor a sales call that is more *personal* and relevant. They might even ask mutual friends for introductions.

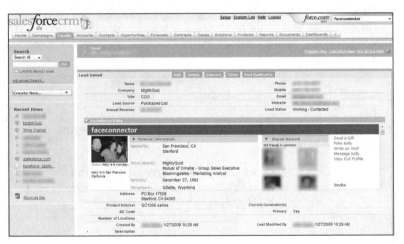

Figure 4.6
Faceconnector (originally Faceforce) pulls real-time Facebook profile and social graph data into Salesforce CRM account, contact, and lead records so that sales reps can tap into the insights of the online social graph to make their pitch more personal and relevant.

Of course, not every first call will result in a closed deal. The product might not be a good fit or the buyer might not have the necessary budget. Still, social and profile data from social networking sites can go a long way in increasing the first call success rate by enabling reps to qualify early, tailor their pitch, add a personal touch, and tap mutual contacts for references and introductions.

4. Navigating Complex Customer Organizations

In addition to helping facilitate one-on-one relationship building, you can use data from social networking sites at a high level for B2B deal strategy—that is, how to approach a deal, which individuals at the buyer you can connect with, and who has influence in the deal. Sales methodologies such as TAS, Miller–Heiman, and Solution Selling emphasize the importance of navigating customer organizations and identifying key decision makers. The online social graph contains powerful data to aid this exercise.

Online social networking sites reveal a wealth of information about people's title and role, status in the company, working relationship with other contacts, and decision-making status. One high-tech account executive who has successfully sold into many IT departments told me that whenever he gets a new contact, he immediately goes to LinkedIn to understand how the individual fits into the bigger picture. He's always on the lookout for a few subtle but critical pieces of information that greatly affect his strategy on a particular deal:

- **Political strength and tenure**—Almost always, people specify on their profiles how long they have been working at a company. If they are new, perhaps they have less political capital but more to prove, and therefore might be more open to bringing in a new vendor or way of doing things. You can usually also view their connections. Is the CIO connected to the CEO and CFO? Is she connected to her own IT directors? If not, this could be a sign that some internal politics might exist, and it could be a good opportunity to divide and conquer. On the other hand, if the CIO is seasoned and all her subordinates are new, that signals she might have greater say in the purchase decision. If many people in the company are connected and have publicly endorsed one another using LinkedIn recommendations, then it is likely a tight-knit organization that will require a different approach.

- **Likelihood of being a champion or roadblock**—Past experience, stated skills, and external connections provide valuable clues to whether someone could become a potential champion or roadblock to your deal. In this case, the account executive com-petes against Microsoft. He once came across a profile of an IT director at the prospec-tive buyer that showed this person had extensive experience implementing Microsoft solutions, had been certified in several Microsoft technologies, and had many LinkedIn connections to Microsoft employees, resellers, and consultants. This raised a red flag in the rep's mind, and, sure enough, this IT director became a big roadblock in the sale (which went through despite this). Similarly, someone who had been successfully using the account executive's product at previous companies is likely to be a champion. Your prospects want to do the right thing for their companies, but often this is in the context of what is the right thing for their careers and where their skill sets and comfort zones lie.

- **Organization structure**—The account executive also told me he always searches on company name to get a list of the prospective buyer's employees. Not only does this generate valuable contacts he might want to reach out to, but he can also glean infor-mation such as offices and subsidiaries, departments, titles, and how the company is organized. For example, the title of "vice president" might signal a powerful decision maker in one firm but be meaningless in another. One prospective buyer had 20 vice presidents out of 50 total employees! When you have a lay of the land, you can formulate the overall sales plan and start spending time winning over individual decision makers.

- **Commonality with deal team members**—Finally, this account executive recommends seeking commonalities not only between yourself and prospects, but also between other members of your account team and prospects. That way, you can strategically assign different people in your company to the various individuals at the prospective buyer to maximize rapport. For example, say a key technical executive at your prospect company is originally from Texas and graduated from Rice University. If you have a team of sales engineers and one happens to be a fellow Texan who also attended Rice, then that's the person you want to assign to this prospect. As we talked about in the previous section, shared personal experiences, even if they are small coincidences, can go a long way in establishing rapport and differentiating your deal. This extends beyond individual reps to entire sales teams.

Building on the previous chapter's discussion, social capital is the currency of influence in sales, too. Valuable information from social networking sites can arm reps with social capital for deals. Those with accurate maps of the social networks inside their prospective buyer know whom to talk to, are better known by others, know who gets along, and can use this knowledge to drive deal strategy and tactics.

5. Collaborating with Sales Team Members

Especially in B2B transactions, an entire sales team instead of one individual rep often works on a deal. In addition to the account executive, the team might include various product specialists, sales engineers, consultants, auditors, training staff, and others internal and external to the vendor company all working together to address a customer's needs in the sales cycle and close the deal.

In addition to collaborating to assign the right account team members to the right prospect, sales teams can use online social networking to communicate, collaborate, and coordinate across their different functions and to log individual interactions with prospect stakeholders. According to the reps I interviewed, if team members are geographically dispersed, the personal connections facilitated by social networking sites can be invaluable for establishing rapport and coordinating group effort.

Another important use of enterprise social networking is for discovering expertise within the selling organization. Especially in large vendor companies with vast product portfolios and high employee turnover, it is often a challenge for account reps to find the right product experts internally to involve in the deal.

Not only can online social networking help reps collaborate within deals, but it can also aid collaboration across deals (see Figure 4.7). Sales Rep A might find herself in a deal that is very similar along certain dimensions—such as industry, customer size, product interest, or competitors—to another deal that Sales Rep B worked on six months ago. Perhaps Rep B found certain customer references, product demonstrations, and collateral especially useful in closing the deal. Rep A can be much more productive if she can leverage the combined experience and expertise of Rep B and all the other reps in her company instead of reinventing the wheel.

Of course, reps don't—and shouldn't—provide deal information on public social networking sites. Instead, this informal deal collaboration is happening within enterprise systems such as CRM, wikis, and intranet sites. Chapter 7, "Innovation and Collaboration in the Facebook Era," discusses expertise discovery and internal collaboration in greater detail.

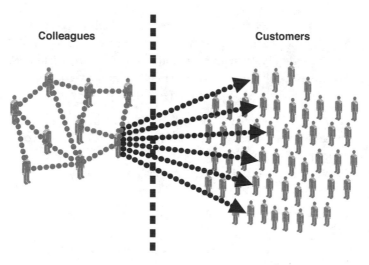

Figure 4.7
In addition to tapping social connections between sales reps and prospects, sales organizations can achieve greater productivity from collaborating within and across account teams. Internal social networking fosters collaborative coordination and collective wisdom.

6. Providing Social Customer References

Customer references are critical for establishing trust to close deals. Testimonials from existing customers provide the most convincing social validation of your product. Those customers have voted with their money and time.

Traditionally, salespeople track down references in the prospective buyer's region or industry to demonstrate competence serving the buyer's unique requirements. But in today's competitive environment, chances are good that other vendors have similar references. The online social graph provides valuable insight into who knows someone who can help set your references apart from the rest. Especially in situations in which you happen to be one of the lesser-known vendors, providing your prospect with references from *their* trusted friends and colleagues can be a powerful differentiator.

Why does this work? For any complex, noncommodity sale, an inherent degree of ambiguity exists in evaluating the product or service. Ultimately, differentiation means that a buyer is comparing apples to oranges and, at some point, needs to make a "leap-of-faith" decision in spite of the uncertainty. Customer references provide valuable information, both real and perceived, to mitigate this uncertainty. With social networking sites, it has become possible to take this further and find exactly which of your customers is connected with a prospective buyer. The following sidebar provides an example from medical sales.

The Power of Social References in Medical Sales

Rob is a top medical equipment sales rep, having achieved more than two times his sales quota each of the last five years. According to Rob, the biggest challenge in his job is getting and keeping doctors' attention during sales meetings. Having been in different types of sales before his current role in medical sales, Rob says physicians are an especially tough audience because they are constantly distracted by crises and typically have patients waiting to see them following his sales call.

Rob's secret to success? He relies on personal referrals from existing customers. He believes this has worked especially well for him because the medical community is a tight-knit group. People forge close friendships from medical school and residency, and develop professional contacts through conferences they are required periodically to attend.

These personal referrals used to happen on a one-off basis when an existing customer was willing to reach out to a friend. Social networking sites have made it more efficient for Rob to discover who knows whom. Instead of having to ask customers who they are willing to actively refer (often customers promise to make a referral and then forget), Rob goes on Facebook or LinkedIn to the prospect's profile page and views their mutual contacts. Sometimes these include some of Rob's existing customers. During sales meetings, Rob drops names. Rob says his prospects become instantly engaged, often recounting stories from medical school about the existing customer who is their friend. Rob's sales-win rate and average deal size have gone way up as a result of this valuable information from social networking sites.

Although medical professionals as a group have been slower to adopt social networking, younger generations of doctors are joining Facebook en masse, and even more seasoned physicians are seeing the value in keeping in touch with people they meet at conferences.

As we discussed in Chapter 2, trust is transitive, to a degree. Because Rob's customer trusts Rob (that's why he's a customer, after all) and Rob's prospect trusts his friend who is Rob's customer, Rob's prospect is more willing to trust Rob. Reps such as Rob are tapping the social capital of relationships between their prospects and their existing customers to help close the deal (see Figure 4.8). From the prospective buyer's perspective, she is getting a referral from a trusted colleague. This carries far more weight than an anonymous referral.

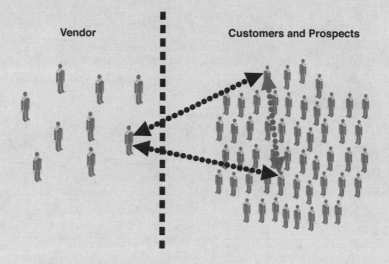

Figure 4.8
Customer references are more powerful when they come from someone the prospective buyer knows personally. Online social networking services enable sales reps to discover which of their existing customers might be connected to a prospective buyer.

7. Building and Sustaining Rapport

Because B2B sales cycles tend to take longer, reps often find themselves working multiple overlapping deals at once. As sales reps start new deals and shift focus from deal to deal, it is imperative they sustain rapport with prospects so that they can continue to make progress. Traditionally, this was difficult for most account executives to juggle.

Fortunately, Facebook can help. Casual interaction modes, such as Facebook pokes and messages, together with proactive updates in the form of News Feed alerts and Birthday Reminders (both described in Chapter 3, "How Relationships and Social Capital Are Changing") on social networking sites, help reps save time staying in touch with their portfolio of customer and prospect contacts.

One account executive I interviewed swears by a combination of CRM calendar alerts and Facebook. For contacts at all his key accounts, he sets monthly reminders in his company's CRM system to reach out and say hello. When a reminder pops up, he visits the person's profile on Facebook to find something interesting and personal to say, sometimes completely unrelated to the deal. For example, last month the Facebook status message of a prospect CEO indicated she was en route to Tokyo. The account executive sent a (virtual) Facebook gift of sushi along with recommendations of his two favorite restaurants in Tokyo. (Figure 4.9 gives you an idea of what this might look like.)

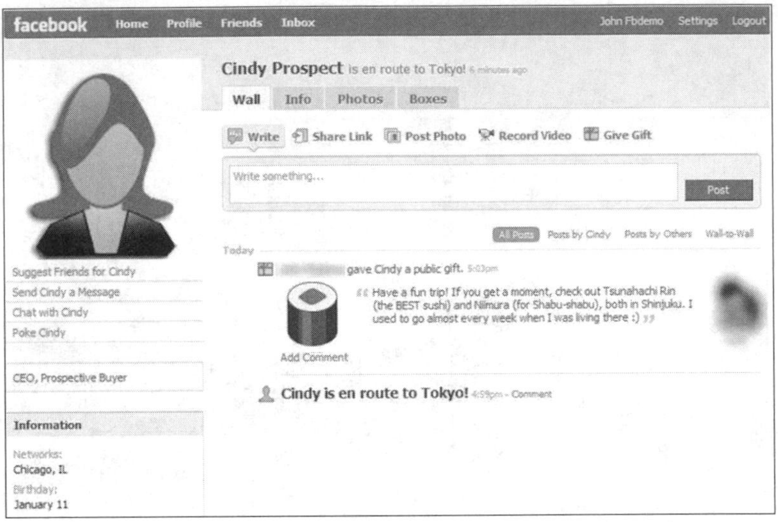

Figure 4.9
Playful, casual interaction on Facebook is an easy way for reps to stay in touch and sustain rapport with contacts. For example, an account rep might respond to this prospect's Facebook status message with a Facebook gift and Wall post.

Periodic casual communication enabled by social networking sites can also help keep leads warm when the timing is not right for a prospect. Company reorganizations, budget cutbacks, and other competing projects are all-too-common reasons deals get put on the back burner. Instead of walking away completely, reps can use online social networking to stay engaged without expending a lot of their time. Updates from social networking sites provide the perfect excuse to check in on prospects and remind them in a friendly way that you still exist, without being so explicitly pushy about closing the sale.

Sales Reps Need to Be Versatile Networkers

As we discussed in Chapter 3, the notion that weak ties are generally more valuable for business than strong ties is an oversimplification in sales. Success in B2B sales, in particular, demands a more nuanced view of social networks. Tuba Östüner from Cass Business School and David Godes from Harvard Business School did an excellent job of distilling these nuances in their 2006 *Harvard Business Review* article "Better Sales Networks."

We can gain new insights by revisiting the different stages in a typical sales cycle from the perspective of optimal network structures. The primary tasks required of a sales rep change, often significantly, at each stage in the sales cycle. The networks the sales rep utilizes to fulfill these tasks change, too. Different tasks require different kinds of networks:

- During sales prospecting, it holds true that entrepreneurial networks of weak ties are paramount for identifying and accessing opportunities. Therefore, LION networks are ideal during this initial stage.

- When it comes to winning buy-in across the prospect organization, the rep must focus on understanding the organizational map and who the key influencers are. As discussed earlier, a lot of this information can be gleaned from social networking sites, but ultimately, the rep needs to rely on one or a handful of internal customer champions. In terms of network structure, these relationships are characterized by clique networks of strong ties.

- Assembling the dream deal team is very much an exercise of internal networking at the rep's company. The rep needs internal entrepreneurial networks of strong ties with colleagues and solution partners to identify, mobilize, and coordinate the right resources for the account.

- Finally, customer references require external entrepreneurial networks of strong ties not only between account executive and existing customers, but also between existing customers and prospects.

If information matters, then "hole-rich" (that is, with sparse contacts) entrepreneurial networks are ideal; if consistency and coordination matter, dense networks are ideal. Salespeople need both types of networks to close a deal. Generally, the importance of strong ties increases as we advance in the sales process.

Reps can adopt several different strategies to accommodate the need for multiple network structures. One option is to create multiple profiles. For example, a rep might have two LinkedIn profiles: One is a LION profile for prospecting; the other is a higher-quality exclusive profile for valuable customer and prospect contacts only. A second option is to use different systems for different networks. For instance, a rep might maintain a LION profile on LinkedIn for sales prospecting, use Facebook for personal relationships with high-value customer contacts, and leverage Microsoft Sharepoint for networking and sharing with coworkers. Finally, a rep could use advanced identity- and relationship-management tools, such as Facebook Friend Lists, to segment contacts within a social networking system and treat different connection types differently. (Chapter 10 talks about how to do this.)

The following guest expert sidebar from Gerhard Gschwandtner, founder and publisher of the popular magazine *Selling Power,* showcases a few more examples and best practices on how to improve the sales process with social networking sites.

Improving the Sales Process with Social Networking Sites

Gerhard Gschwandtner

Social networking is no longer a social phenomenon; it has become an integral part of a company's sales and marketing strategy. A study released by Wetpaint and the Altimeter Group showed that companies with the highest level of social networking use for sales grew an average of 18% last year, and companies that used social networking the least declined by an average of 6%.

Consider these practical tips for improving the sales process with social networking techniques:

- **Creating trust and rapport**—Make it easy for your prospects to learn more about you on social networking sites. Action tip: On LinkedIn, you can drag and move the information categories on the left side to suit your needs. For example, if you are looking for a job, move your Experience and Education headings up front.

- **Making the first call**—Most salespeople try to schedule a call with their prospect. A sales manager of a software company recently came up with the idea to have the prospect make the first call to the salesperson. How? His team searches daily for tweets that contain their company name. Instead of connecting with the prospect directly, the manager set up a network of customers who are willing to tweet on the company's behalf. Recently, the company noticed a question on Twitter from Starbucks about its service. The rep emailed his closest customer contact in the same city: Microsoft. The Microsoft executive tweeted back to the Starbucks executive. The next day, they had lunch. After lunch, the prospect called the software company salesperson.

- **Navigating complex corporate organization structures**—The larger the company, the greater the information challenge. Let's say you want to sell to the head of research at IBM and you want to identify the top decision influencers. LinkedIn offers an advanced search capability that gives you access to IBM executives that work in eight research centers around the world. In this case, it is better to first visit the IBM Research Web site and click on People to find a list of program directors, scientists, and staff members by location. Then you can look up the contacts on LinkedIn.

Gerhard Gschwandtner (@SellingPowerMag) is the founder and publisher of Selling Power *magazine.*

Social CRM

Although many of the best salespeople are naturally instinctive relationship builders, certain sales methodologies have been proven in recent years to help the rest of us learn to emulate their success. Customer relationship management (CRM) attempts to capture the science of sales with software and processes to handle all of a company's interactions with its customers. Sales force automation, in particular, builds in processes such as forecasting, territory management, email templates, dashboards, activity management, and deal alerts so that managers have visibility and sales teams can be more productive. Online social networking adds another dimension of power to CRM by enriching critical sales practices with contextual information and relationship-building tools.

In many ways, traditional CRM has been an important precursor to many of today's social networking sites. At its most basic level, CRM is a fancy contact database. It is a one-way social networking tool that lets sales reps view "profiles" of their accounts, capture deal information, track performance, communicate with contacts, and share information internally with sales managers and other members of their account team.

The main difference with social networking sites such as LinkedIn and Facebook is that these offer bidirectional visibility and interaction. This transforms the sales dynamic into more of an even-sided partnership (see Table 4.1).

Table 4.1   Comparison of CRM and Modern Social Networking Site

	CRM ("One-Way Social Networking")	Social Networking Site
How are new connections established?	You can buy a marketing list, scan a trade show badge, or post a Web lead form.	Either party can initiate a connection, but the decision to connect on Facebook or LinkedIn must be mutual.
Where is the contact and personal information displayed?	It's displayed in the account, lead, and contact records	Social network profiles are the new CRM contact record.
Who are data, updates, and alerts shared with?	The sales team and the sales manager receive updates.	By default, updates are shared with friends and networks, but users can adjust privacy settings.
What communication mechanisms are used?	You can use email templates, notifications, and alerts.	People communicate via Facebook messages, Wall posts, and notes.
Who updates the data?	Sales reps or administrative assistants update the data.	Data is updated from the bottom up; everyone is responsible for updating their own information.

Already, many of the innovations from the social Web are making their way into CRM systems, as evidenced by recent integrations between existing software vendors and Facebook, LinkedIn, and Twitter. Next-generation social CRM (SCRM) tools, such as what we're building at Hearsay Labs, are incorporating even more Web 2.0–like interactions (see Figure 4.10). Other popular social CRM tools include Salesforce.com's Service Cloud (more on this in Chapter 5, "Customer Service in the Facebook Era"), SAP CRM's Twitter integration, and Microsoft Dynamics CRM "social networking accelerator" (see Figure 4.11). Oracle has a suite of social CRM applications too, but it's important to note the "social" aspects here are more around internal sales team collaboration (similar to Salesforce Chatter) rather than integration with customer-facing functionality on Facebook and Twitter.

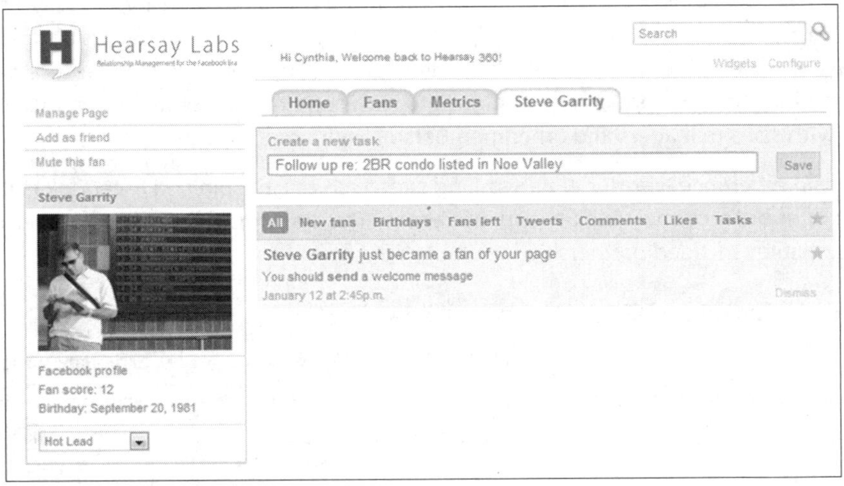

Figure 4.10
For many existing CRM applications, social integration is clearly an afterthought. We designed Hearsay 360 to incorporate the power and bidirectionality of Facebook, Twitter, and LinkedIn throughout the application experience.

By making the customer an active participant in CRM, SCRM helps companies not only benefit from more accurate data and better engagement, but also finally achieve a true 360-degree view of their customers across every touch point—whether it's on the phone, on Facebook, presales, mid-deal, post-sales, or beyond.

In the following sidebar, well-known CRM expert, author, and consultant Paul Greenberg weighs in on social CRM and how it encompasses far more than just social media.

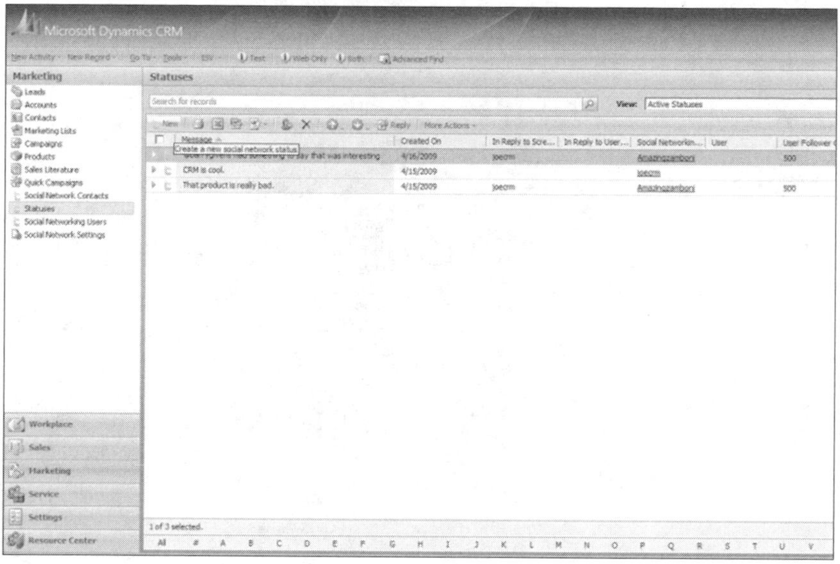

Figure 4.11
Microsoft Dynamics CRM recently introduced a social networking "accelerator" plug-in which pulls in social network status messages for contact records where a Twitter handle has been specified.

Social CRM Is *Not* Just Social Media

Paul Greenberg

A clear distinction exists between social CRM and social media. To understand the distinction, today's customer is a social customer who is demanding engagement far more frequently than ever. It's also a savvier customer—as Forrester Research revealed in 2009, more than 78% of all ages online are using social networks.

But this means a whole set of new requirements and tools for how a company will respond to the customer. I'm not saying to replace traditional customer relationship management: I'm saying extend it. One thing that remains the same regardless of this new customer is that businesses still have to run their operations, gather customer information, comply with government rules, and · make sure that they capture and use data.

CRM becomes social CRM (SCRM) when businesses respond to the social customer's ownership of the conversation that's going on outside the businesses' control.

I don't think I have to establish the increasing primacy of the customer activity going on in the social graph—that's done wonderfully throughout the book. The "conversation prism" developed by Brian Solis (shown in Figure 4.12) highlights the incredible array of channel *categories* where customers are talking about you outside your control.

continues...

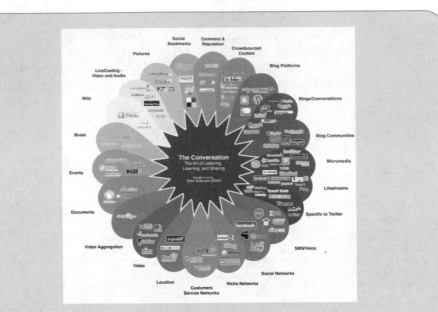

Figure 4.12

This is the "conversation prism," a map of conversations on the Social Web developed by Brian Solis, founder and principal of FutureWorks. (You'll hear from Solis in Chapter 6.)

SCRM as a strategy defines the parameters that companies have to consider when it comes to engaging the customers they need to engage—not manage them. That means finding out and then considering what the customers require for that engagement—what products, services, tools, and experience they need.

SCRM finds the channels customers are communicating on, tracks the communications, identifies those customers communicating, and captures the information that the conversations are providing.

The industry has adopted a somewhat awkward but working definition of social CRM:

CRM is a philosophy and a business strategy, supported by a technology platform, business rules, workflow, processes, and social characteristics, designed to engage the customer in a collaborative conversation to provide mutually beneficial value in a trusted and transparent business environment. It's the company's response to the customer's ownership of the conversation.

So much more than just social media, isn't it?

Paul Greenberg (@pgreenbe) is the author of CRM at the Speed of Light: Essential Customer Strategies for the 21st Century *(McGraw-Hill Osborne Media, 2009).*

< < < TAKEAWAYS

✓ The social Web is transformative in the sales process in two ways: First, reps can learn valuable information about customers and prospects. Second, social networking sites provide great opportunities for reps to engage in casual communications with and stay top of mind for customers.

✓ Facebook is valuable even in B2B sales because, ultimately, it is an individual or group of individuals who make the purchase decision. Facebook can help sales reps build better relationships with individuals, such as getting to know them on a personal level.

✓ Sales reps can build trust and credibility by conveying experience and qualifications through their social network profiles. The personal branding discussion from the previous chapter applies especially to outward-facing professionals such as sales.

✓ In the Facebook Era, much of the lead qualification process occurs before reps ever reach out to the prospect by using the information available on public social networking sites.

✓ In addition to explicit data such as role and company name, savvy reps can infer additional important information about prospect organizations from social networking sites, such as political strength and tenure, the likelihood of an individual to be a champion or a roadblock in your sales cycle, and organizational structure.

> > > TIPS and TO DO's

❏ Explore using advanced search on LinkedIn, Facebook, and Twitter to prospect for potential customers.

❏ Before you make the first call, check out your prospect's profile information and see if you have any common ground (such as your hometown or favorite baseball team) that you can use to start casual conversation, when appropriate.

❏ Use Facebook and Twitter to keep in touch with prospects and customers. Comment on and "like" their status messages, and wish them a happy birthday when it's their birthday. Do this only with prospects whom you feel would be receptive to this. (This is largely dependent on age.) Otherwise, it can be creepy.

❏ Make your next customer reference a "social customer reference"— that is, try to find an existing customer whom your prospect already knows and trusts.

❏ Per CRM expert Paul Greenberg's advice, integrate your social media strategy and CRM strategy. They go hand-in-hand. To stay competitive and to succeed, today's CRM *must* be social.

5

"Twitter gives companies the second chance they never had before to win back angry customers."
—Isaac Garcia, CEO, Central Desktop

Customer Service in the Facebook Era

Some people say that your company's relationship with a customer really begins after the deal closes. Certainly, we all know that it's far cheaper to retain an existing customer than to acquire a new one. But for many businesses, offering quality customer service is an expensive headache. Support calls are often wrought with negative emotions such as anger, annoyance, and impatience, and often for good reason. Customers are put on hold for longer than they can stand, they need to call back multiple times and repeat all the same information that they gave to the last agent, and sometimes they give up out of frustration.

But for these companies and their customers, Facebook, Twitter, and YouTube are turning customer service on its head. With the social Web, customers have a voice for the first time. They are speaking up, and other customers are not only listening, but also helping spread the word, as evidenced by the countless examples from United Airlines, Domino's Pizza, Comcast, and thousands of other organizations.

Social media adoption by businesses often *starts* with customer service because companies are discovering that customers are already complaining on Twitter and Facebook, and they have *no choice* but to react. Now that everyone has a voice, companies can no longer "get away" with providing bad service. I am certainly not suggesting that Twitter will replace your call center. But your communication channels with customers are expanding beyond the call center, traditional Web portal, email, and chat to include social media such as Facebook, Twitter, and social customer support communities.

Companies that master social customer service are finding not only tremendous cost savings, but also huge benefits to their brand and a reliable, low-cost conduit for feedback to continually improve their products, services, and operations. Whether companies like it, customers have been given a voice. If you choose to listen, you might be surprised at what you learn and find that your whole organization and value chain might be transformed. And that's not such a bad thing if it keeps your business relevant, makes your customers happy, and wins you more of them.

In this chapter, we talk about how the social Web is reorienting organizations to the customer experience, walk through the five steps to social customer service, and suggest how to quantify cost savings.

Thinking Holistically About the Customer Experience

The social Web is blurring the functional boundaries inside your company. It's no longer about marketing, sales, and customer support as separate departments with separate agendas. Customers view your company as a single entity. No matter who they are talking to at your company, customers expect a seamless experience that is consistent with your brand. The only agenda your company should have is your customers'.

Marketers and sales reps need to think about how to service customers. Customer service staff need to think about how to retain and up-sell customers. Most customers find it hard to love a brand if they hate the customer service. But if you help resolve their complaint quickly, chances are, you will have much better luck getting them to renew, upgrade, and evangelize to their friends.

More than ever, companies need to improve communications and collaboration across not only customer-facing functions, but also the entire company, such as accounting (how are your customers billed?), product development (is customer feedback driving new features?), and even purchasing (does your supply chain adhere to the ethical standards of your customer community?).

As part of this, companies must recognize that customer service is transforming from a reactionary function to a strategic cornerstone of the customer experience. In the following guest expert sidebar, Forrester Research senior analyst Natalie Petouhoff weighs in on the growing importance of the customer service function and why it needs to be more closely integrated with other departments in your organization.

Social Media Customer Service

Natalie Petouhoff, Ph.D.

Customer service is shifting not only its own paradigm in business, but also business itself. And although many people wouldn't necessarily see customer service as a change agent, the addition of social media has made it exactly that. Customer disdain, combined with a rapid rise in the adoption and use of social media by consumers, has formed a perfect storm that is rapidly driving change.

When companies blatantly ignore product or service issues, customers now can use the Internet as a medium to broadcast, very publicly, their frustration to millions. This has switched the balance of power from corporations to customers. And now the press is routinely taking up the cause, reporting on companies that provide good or poor customer service experiences. The risk of corporate reputations being ruined by poor customer service interactions has greatly increased as consumers have gained the capability to share their opinions directly with each other.

This perfect storm has forced companies to switch gears and reconsider not only the customer experience, but also social media as a serious enterprise business solution that is transforming customer service to reach the new goals of enhancing the customer experience and providing voice-of-the-customer data to transform other departments, such as marketing, sales, engineering, product development, and even operations.

Dr. Natalie Petouhoff (@drnatalie) is a senior analyst at Forrester Research who focuses on social customer service and CRM.

Keep in mind a few points about customer feedback:

- **Find value in constructive feedback**—Customer rants on Twitter aren't necessarily a bad thing. First, you can't do anything to prevent them. (And if you try, it will look really bad.) Second, the best way to improve is to listen to your customers.

- **Turn anger into loyalty**—If someone cares enough about your company to tweet about it, treat it as an opportunity to win that person back with excellent customer service. Before the social Web, angry customers complained to their friends and simply stopped buying your product or service before you ever had an opportunity to apologize, clarify, or right the wrong. In the Facebook Era, companies have a second chance to divert angry passion into fierce loyalty. Take anger over indifference any day, and rise to the occasion to get better.

- **Let employee personalities shine through**—As we discussed in Chapter 2, "The New Social Norms," social networking sites can help humanize companies. It's easy for customers to hate a stodgy corporation, especially 40 minutes into a support call when they still haven't been routed to a human to answer a simple question. It's much harder for customers to hate a friendly and helpful employee that you have chosen to make the face of your company's support page on Twitter. Comcast did this with Frank Eliason (@comcastcares), the senior director of customer care. You'll hear some thoughts from Eliason later in this chapter.

- **Respond quickly and with humility**—Because customer service issues and responses on social sites such as Twitter and Facebook are public and searchable, how quickly companies respond and what they say are now part of the company voice and brand—creating radical implications for cross-functional collaboration. For example, should your company require that customer service reps be PR-trained before handling issues on Twitter?

- **Tap into SEO benefits**—Search engines are indexing customer support dialogue on social networking sites and customer forum sites, which has a very substantial impact on search engine optimization (SEO). In fact, some companies I interviewed told me that their primary reason for investing in a Twitter presence or online customer support forum was for SEO benefits from user-generated content, not actual customer support.

In the following guest expert sidebar, Kira Wampler from Intuit discusses the value of sharing in addition to responding, highlighting the increasing overlap between marketing and customer service functions.

Intuit's "Care and Feeding" Approach

Kira Wampler

With online reviews being the second most trusted form of advertising according to Nielsen and with Twitter hitting its one billionth tweet, the way customers expect to interact with brands has fundamentally changed. It's not just new—it's a new normal.

For the online engagement team in Intuit's small business division, the new normal brings with it a mantra: "Be where customers are or beware." But with so many places to engage online, where should you focus a small team's efforts?

By analyzing what channels influence product purchases, researching where small business owners spend time online, and testing a variety of efforts in social channels, the Intuit team prioritized Amazon, Twitter, and Facebook as the key external social channels along with the Intuit Community—the team's home-grown site and the largest community of small business owners on the Web.

Intuit's small business division takes a "care and feeding" approach. On Twitter and Facebook, the team "cares" by responding to roughly 85% of product tweets and "feeds" by sharing relevant information about Intuit's small business events, grant opportunities, and articles to help small business owners grow.

Although the new normal might pose challenges, the rewards are high. Customers are more engaged and more successful with Intuit's small business products, and new customers see that Intuit actually cares about its customers.

Kira Wampler (@kirasw) is a group marketing manager at Intuit Small Business Group.

Five Steps to Successful Social Customer Service

Customer service organizations need to embrace five specific tactics: listen, embrace transparency, respond (and own up to mistakes), crowdsource, and care about your customers.

1. Listen

The most important step (which should also be the first thing you do) is to listen. Even if your company hasn't invested in building a presence on social networking sites, chances are good that if you have customers, someone somewhere is ranting or raving about your product and service, a competitive offering, or at least something related to what you offer. If you haven't already done so, take a few seconds to search on your company name at http://search.twitter.com, and you'll see what I mean.

In the Facebook Era, customers dictate where they want to be heard and, therefore, where you need to be to provide service and support. Research conducted by Natalie Petouhoff (whom you heard from earlier) and her team at Forrester shows that customers are increasingly turning to social channels instead of traditional call center channels because they can typically get a faster, higher-quality, and more empathetic response from the company, other customers, or both.

To automate monitoring on the social Web, use tools such as TweetBeep to set up notifications for brand mentions on Twitter and Google Alerts. Also consider free feed management tools such as Monitter, Seesmic, TweetDeck, or Hootsuite (see Figure 5.1) to easily manage and respond in-line to the continual stream of tweets about your company, your product, and related keywords that you specify.

Figure 5.1

Hootsuite and similar free tools let you simultaneously monitor (and respond to) multiple social feeds from one place. It's especially handy if you have multiple Twitter accounts or you are tracking multiple topics.

2. Embrace Transparency

Be open about sharing uncensored customer feedback because people will find it any-way. Instead of hiding customer discussions behind a user login or obscure Twitter han-dles, actively point prospects to your Twitter support page or public forum on your Web site and stream tweets onto your Web site. Let people see for themselves on their own terms the uncensored things your customers are saying about your company and how your company reacts and responds.

Akron Children's Hospital in Akron, Ohio, has built a presence across a comprehensive set of social sites, including Twitter, Facebook, LinkedIn, MySpace, and YouTube. The Web site not only links to discussions on social networking sites, but also actively educates and encourages the hospital's community members to explore these sites (see Figure 5.2).

Reprinted by permission

Figure 5.2
Akron Children's Hospital has built a presence across a comprehensive set of social sites, including Twitter, Facebook, MySpace, and YouTube.

3. Respond (and Own Up to Mistakes)

Handle negative feedback diplomatically. If it's factually incorrect, consider responding with a polite explanation. Sometimes it's best to do nothing and wait for someone from the community to speak up in your defense. It's less work for you, yet far more credible that way. Several companies got in big trouble with the public when it was discovered that they had created a fake online personality to defend or promote their business.

If someone offers constructive criticism or complains about something that is genuinely unfair or broken, acknowledge, apologize, and thank them. Then actually do something about it. If enough people complain about the same thing, it's probably worth listening to. People don't get mad at companies for making mistakes, but they do get mad when companies refuse to admit their mistakes. They get so mad that they write songs that go viral on YouTube, such as "United Breaks Guitars" (see Figure 5.3). Musician Dave Carroll wrote the song, which has received more than eight million views on YouTube, about his nightmare experience as he watched United Airlines' workers carelessly toss his guitar. Carroll decided to use the social Web after spending a year filing complaints, only to have United still refuse to take any responsibility.

Reprinted by permission

Figure 5.3
"United Breaks Guitars" has been a public relations nightmare for United Airlines and a clear example of how the Facebook Era is changing the rules of customer service.

Many customer support organizations struggle with the real-time nature of services such as Twitter. Customers tweet questions, issues, and complaints around the clock and often expect an immediate response. (Customers typically set a much lower bar for company-branded support forums.) So depending on how important of a channel Twitter is to your business and the volume of support inquiries you receive, you might need to significantly reorganize your support organization. For example, companies such as Zappos and Comcast began assigning dedicated support reps to focus on monitoring and responding to questions on Twitter. Other businesses have chosen to staff a handful of agents around the clock to respond to inbound Twitter complaints in real time for mission-critical issues or as a means of branding.

Admitting your mistakes scores you some points, but winning the hearts and minds of your customers requires action. Fix the issue someone found, deliver the new product someone suggested, and then tell everyone you did so and publicly thank the person who spoke up. This is how you create your biggest advocates who will stay with your company through thick and thin and rush to your defense whenever others criticize your company.

For this to work in practice, you need to create (or update) your business process for how customer feedback gets prioritized and implemented, likely by a different part of the company. This requires planning, cross-functional collaboration, and probably the use of some closed-loop project management tool.

Toyota made the courageous decision to do this when a defect was found in some of its cars (see Figure 5.4). It was a tough situation for any company to be in, but in light of what happened, Toyota did the right thing by widely acknowledging the defect in some of its cars and making sure every Toyota owner knew about the factory recall. The cliché works perfectly in this case: Actions speak louder than words.

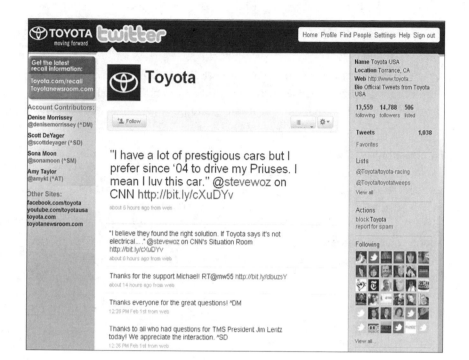

Figure 5.4

Not only did Toyota tweet about a defect (as painful as it must have been), but the company also placed a prominent red button on its Twitter page background, directing attention to the recall. Tweets from many customers suggest that people appreciated Toyota's transparency, sincerity, and action-oriented response.

The following case study, which summarizes analyses done by Forrester Research, profiles how European mobile retailer Carphone Warehouse is bringing customer service to the social Web.

Carphone Warehouse Uses Twitter to Transform Customer Experiences

Carphone Warehouse (CPW) is Europe's largest independent retailer of mobile phones and services, with more than 2,400 stores across nine countries. Because CPW's customers began posting comments about service issues on Twitter and blogs, CPW was faced with the decision of whether to engage on these social channels.

After deliberation, CPW customer service professionals decided to publicly acknowledge customer complaints on the social Web. Their strategy was to take a brave stance and change customer–company interactions by harnessing the power of social media to say "I'm sorry." This simple act of acknowledgment has

continues…

improved brand perception and transformed the customer experience by letting people feel heard and valued by the company.

CPW has found that Twitter offers a new opportunity to truly listen and engage in customer conversations, address customer complaints and feedback more quickly, proactively provide information to customers, and positively influence customer's opinions.

CPW also monitors RSS feeds on its brand and products. When customers post complaints or constructive feedback, CPW contacts the customer directly through traditional channels, such as email, to ask if the company can help resolve the situation. The customers often post a positive review about the help they have received from CPW (see Figure 5.5). Because customer complaints on the social Web are permanent, getting customers to update their original complaint helps CPW regain positive brand sentiment. Without this, the ongoing set of customers and prospects who see the post without the update might continue to have a negative impression of CPW.

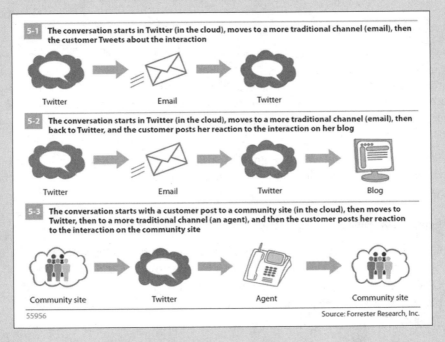

5-1 The conversation starts in Twitter (in the cloud), moves to a more traditional channel (email), then the customer Tweets about the interaction

Twitter   Email   Twitter

5-2 The conversation starts in Twitter (in the cloud), moves to a more traditional channel (email), then back to Twitter, and the customer posts her reaction to the interaction on her blog

Twitter   Email   Twitter   Blog

5-3 The conversation starts with a customer post to a community site (in the cloud), then moves to Twitter, then to a more traditional channel (an agent), and then the customer posts her reaction to the interaction on the community site

Community site   Twitter   Agent   Community site

55956   Source: Forrester Research, Inc.

Figure 5.5
This figure illustrates a few common scenarios of customer service transitioning between social and traditional channels.

4. Crowdsource

When your business has advocates, you can **crowdsource**—that is, outsource to your audience ("the crowd")—a surprising amount of your customer service to the community. You don't have to do anything special for this to happen. It happens automatically when your business has successfully cultivated fans and advocates through listening, embracing transparency, admitting mistakes, and taking action.

Companies are quickly realizing that it pays to encourage customers to talk to one another, troubleshoot for one another, and share tips and tricks in online forums across Facebook, Twitter, and company Web site forums. For example, a number of such customer self-support groups have sprung up on Facebook, often to companies' surprise and delight, as these groups greatly alleviate the burden on their call centers. It might seem crazy that people would be willing to volunteer their time to monitor your customer support channels and help others free of charge, but that is the power of customer loyalty. Many also derive either direct or indirect value from demonstrating their knowledge and being viewed as experts in the community.

In addition to your customer community, your employee community is a powerful and highly qualified source of ad hoc customer support. This makes obvious sense for brick-and-mortar retail store employees who invariably experience lulls in customer traffic at different times in the day. For example, Best Buy famously created Blue Shirt Nation, an employees-only social network where employees from stores across the country are recognized for answering technical, product, or other support questions. In addition to reducing company support costs, this has had the added benefit of improving employee engagement and loyalty—employees no longer feel bored and unmotivated when fewer customers are in the store.

And not only will you cut support costs and improve engagement, but also the quality of your customer service could potentially reach new levels because customer and employee support volunteers are driven by the most powerful motivator of all, which money cannot buy: *passion*. The key is to invest in developing the right policies and training for employees, which (unlike customers) could be perceived or even held legally liable as speaking on behalf of the company. The right amount of policy to introduce is enough to safeguard against lawsuits and bad PR if an employee makes a false product claim or says something inappropriate, but not so much that employees are scared of participating. One potential option is to have trained customer support staff review employee-generated content. Another option might simply be to update the terms of service of your online support forum to indemnify your company from any potential liability.

A lot of customer service exchange ends up taking place on Facebook and Twitter simply because that's where people are already spending time. However, in addition to these public channels, many companies are investing in custom online communities for social customer support from vendors such as Lithium. Lithium is a premium product with rich functionality, including blogs, a user-contributed knowledge base, live chat, and the capability to solicit and rank community ideas, which justifies the higher price (which is based on usage). In my opinion, it is the best solution for any company that receives a lot of technical questions in customer support, such as companies with a big ecommerce component or companies that are selling technology and telecom services. The following case study profiles how Best Buy uses Lithium to better engage with customers, effectively crowdsource to both customers and employees, and save millions of dollars annually.

How Best Buy Uses Lithium and Twitter to Save Millions Each Year

Three years ago, Best Buy began noticing a growing number of conversations taking place outside traditional support channels. Online community manager Gina Debogovich and her team quickly realized that customers were having these conversations regardless of whether the company was aware or involved.

Initially, Debogovich and her team scoured the blogosphere for negative mentions. When customers included their contact information, the team reached out privately in an attempt to right any wrongs. They hoped people would go back and update their previous blog post.

But few bloggers responded. So the team tried something radically different. Following a strategic overhaul, Debogovich and her team began tweeting responses and publicly responding on customers' blogs on behalf of Best Buy. They also created a custom Best Buy support community to consolidate consumer conversation on the Web. Instead of having customers go all over the blogosphere to post, the goal was to have customers go to these communities, which are run on Lithium's software behind the scenes.

On Best Buy's community, users can access blogs, product discussions, operating system discussions, carrier discussions, and news and FAQs.

Today Debogovich leads a team of 22 individuals, including 14 community connectors who engage with the blogosphere on behalf of Best Buy. Displaying a strong emphasis on transparency and personal connection, the community has a "Meet Our Moderators" page with profiles so that customers know exactly who is responding.

Anyone on the Best Buy team can sign up for a Twitter account to engage in greater dialogue with customers, and any employee in Best Buy retail stores can sign up for a Lithium community account to help answer questions online during lulls in store traffic.

With these developments, Best Buy estimates a return on investment (ROI) thus far of $5M annually—an impressive payoff for something customers are demanding of companies anyway.

The improvements are numerous. Last year, out of more than 70,000 conversations that took place on the community, Best Buy customer support was involved in just 5%. Other customers and Best Buy retail store employees responded to and resolved the rest.

GetSatisfaction is another popular customer support community application that companies such as Nike, Zappos, and Yola use. Pricing starts at $19 per month and increases as you add features such as integration with other support applications, customize the look and feel, and custom features. Compared to Lithium, it's a lot easier and faster to get up and running, but it has less functionality (see Figure 5.6).

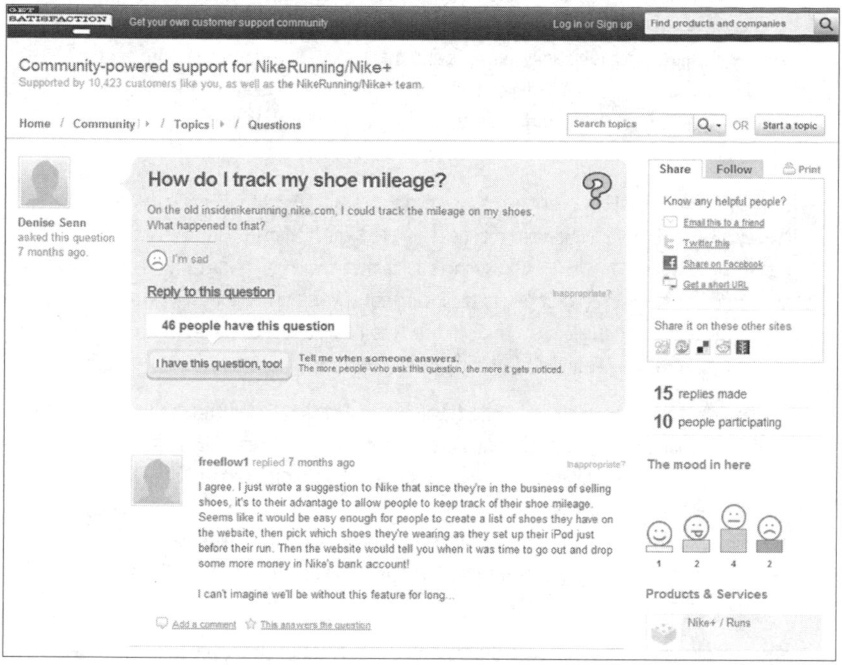

Reprinted by permission

Figure 5.6
GetSatisfaction is a popular community solution for crowdsourced customer support.

Many traditional customer support applications vendors, such as Helpstream, Salesforce.com, Parature, and RightNow, also offer Web portals as part of their solution, and almost everyone has integrated with Twitter. If you are a large enterprise organization and don't already have a case management tool with Twitter integration, another great option is CoTweet. It enables a social media administrator to assign incoming tweets to specific individuals and department queues for response instead of relying on employees to do so on a voluntary, ad hoc basis.

5. Care About Your Customers

In customer service and support, the issue customers are calling about can become secondary to their experience of interacting with the company. Customers want to feel listened to and valued by the companies they are providing business to. No one understands this better than the front lines of customer support, who are talking to customers every day. In the following guest expert sidebar, Frank Eliason of Comcast shares his personal story and thoughts on the importance of connecting with your customers.

Connecting with Your Customers

Frank Eliason

My name is Frank Eliason, and I am not a PR or marketing person, at least within the organizational sense. But as you have read in this chapter, the organization is changing. I am a simple customer service guy who has became known as @ComcastCares. I have worked in customer service for different organizations during the past 20 years. Throughout my career, I have seen dramatic changes, but none more dramatic than what social media is bringing to every customer service organization.

After years of service taking a back seat, social media is causing the customer to obtain the upper hand by owning the communications channel. Marketers and PR departments everywhere have been trying to work in the space, but customers don't always want to interact with those departments. And let's face the facts, marketers and PR are not always the best employees to have a dialogue with the customer. Dialogue with customers is something your customer service department excels at because they do it every day.

I have watched many companies start efforts within social media and fail. This happens for a variety of reasons, including not understanding the space, creating too many barriers (such as legal constraints), or pushing out information without participating in the dialogue. Other fears include being unsure of how it will scale. The scale question cracks me up because I remember hearing the same question about email. I also remember hearing a reluctance to personalize responses and hearing companies want the legal department to approve each email before it was sent. All this seems silly today.

When you care about your customers, they care about you, too. On July 26, 2008, I had to take the day off. It was a Saturday and the only day we could have a birthday party for our two-year old, Lily. It was the only day we could have the party because of scheduling, but it was with mixed emotions. I did not get into the specifics about why I was taking off, but, as I later found out, the community found out on their own. At some point, our customers Googled me and found out that it was also the anniversary of our other daughter's passing. When we finally got through the day, I looked through my normal Twitter search and saw the most amazing thing. Other customers (not employees) had started to respond to people with tweets such as "Let's let @ComcastCares have his day; can I help you?" or "@ComcastCares is not around today, but I had a similar problem and Frank had me do this ...."

Nothing is more powerful than connecting with your customers.

Frank Eliason (@ComcastCares) is the senior director of national customer service at Comcast.

Calculating Your Cost Savings

In addition to the benefit of improved customer service, you can calculate how much money your company has saved as a result of "going social." You can use a few direct and indirect ways to perform these calculations.

- **Cost savings from customers responding to other customers**—Count how many questions or issues the customer community addressed instead of your support staff. Automate this based on message threading and Twitter @replies to figure out who responded to whom. Then multiply this by your average cost of a support call (effectively, average call length times the average number of calls to resolution times a pro-rated customer support rep salary).

- **Multiplier effect from each customer solution being broadcast to everyone and made searchable**—Add a multiplier to account for people who would have contacted your call center had another customer not publicly responded with a solution to a similar question earlier. This is harder to determine precisely, but you can approximate it by the number of searches on a support community site that did not result in a question being asked (implying that the person searching found a satisfactory solution).

- **Savings from an improved knowledge base from community-generated content**—Solutions contributed by customer experts not only help in real time, but they also expand and improve the support knowledge base over time so that future portal or call center cases are resolved more quickly. One way to approximate the impact of community-driven knowledge base improvements is to track how often and which cases are resolved using customer-submitted solutions. Then compare average customer satisfaction and resolution time of those cases against similar cases in which a traditional solution was used.

- **Average case resolution time**—Compared to phone calls and even live chat, tweets (because of their 140-character limit) are short and to the point, forcing customers and support reps to eliminate banter and cut to the chase. Early data shows that this is drastically reducing the average time for case resolution for many support organizations that have added Twitter to their channel mix. To calculate your average case resolution time, have a team of reps go through at least a few dozen tweets (the more tweets, the more accurate your measurement) and respond to each. Divide the time they spent by the number of tweeted issues they resolved, and that is your approximate per-case resolution time. It is interesting to compare this to your average resolution times for other support channels such as phone or email.

< < < TAKEAWAYS

✓ Companies' social media adoption often starts in the customer service realm because people are complaining on public forums.

✓ Thanks to the strategic marketing and branding value of Twitter and Facebook, customer service is transforming from a reactionary function to a cornerstone of the customer experience.

✓ The five steps to successful customer service on the social Web are to listen, embrace transparency, respond and own up to mistakes, act, and crowdsource.

✓ Not only can you crowdsource questions and issue resolution to your customer community, but you can also tap into your employee community, especially if you are a brick-and-mortar business with retail employees who are not always fully occupied in the store.

✓ Customer rants on the social Web aren't always a bad thing. First, you can't do anything to prevent them. Second, you can probably learn a lot from what your customers have to say.

> > > **TIPS and TO DO's**

❑ Quantify your cost savings from investing in social channels for customer service. For example, you can approximate how much you avoided in call center costs based on the number of Twitter @replies answered.

❑ The first thing any company should do is to listen to what's already being said about the brand and products. I highly recommend that you add tools such as Monitter, TweetBeep, or custom integration into your existing CRM application for monitoring and responding.

❑ Think of ways your marketing and customer service teams can work together to provide customers with both "care" and "feeding." This potentially includes sharing a Twitter handle; running marketing campaigns based on customer feedback that was acted upon; and ensuring that marketers stay in touch with daily customer concerns, requests, and experiences.

❑ Let employee personalities shine through, especially in the customer support scenario. Your customers will be much more forgiving and less frustrated if they feel they are connecting to and being heard by a real human being, such as Frank Eliason of @ComcastCares.

❑ Have a policy and process in place so that you can respond quickly to issues that come up on Facebook or Twitter. Because everything is real time and searchable now, how quickly companies respond is becoming part of how their brand is perceived.

6

"Facebook advertising doesn't feel like advertising because it comes from your friends."
—Tim Kendall, director of monetization at Facebook

Marketing in the Facebook Era

Marketers need to be where the customers are, and, increasingly, customers are on social networking sites. This very moment, nearly a billion people (that is, most of the Internet population) around the world are logged on to a social networking site, updating their status, interacting with friends, interacting with companies, providing valuable information for you to understand them better, and learning about you in return (see Figure 6.1). Remarkably, the average Facebook user spends nearly a full hour per day on the site, according to official company data.

 Cindy Prospect Anyone know of a good realtor in Boston?
a few seconds ago 🔒 · Comment · Like

Figure 6.1
Social network profiles and status messages, such as this one on Facebook, are rich sources of information for companies to learn from customers, generate leads, and interact with fans.

Before launching into execution mode, marketers need to grasp how the social Web affects underlying audience dynamics. This chapter is about the new rules and strategies governing social network marketing, including hypertargeting, social word-of-mouth, and customer engagement, with a discussion at the end on challenges and limitations in this space. Chapters 11, "How To: Engage Customers with Facebook Pages and Twitter," and 12, "How To: Advertise and Promote on the Social Web," discuss the tactical ins and outs of Twitter, Facebook Pages, and Facebook ads, which are based off these principles.

The New Rules of Marketing

The same old marketing strategies don't work anymore—the medium has evolved. The marketplace for nearly every product or service is extremely crowded—it's never been harder for companies to differentiate their offerings. Meanwhile, in the wake of corporate scandals, product recalls, and the mortgage-backed securities crisis, consumer opinion has never been more skeptical of business. More than ever, people trust their friends the most. Social networks are emerging as a powerful new marketing channel for companies to hypertarget campaigns using profile information, engage community members by tapping into transitive trust within friend groups, and systematically cultivate word-of-mouth across their existing customer base.

Social network marketing requires a new strategy and tactics that take advantage of the unique features and capabilities of the social Web. Just as marketers had to learn email and Web marketing a decade ago, today they have to master Twitter and Facebook. Academic institutions such as Berkeley, Georgetown, Southern New Hampshire University, and dozens of others have begun offering courses and even entire degree programs focused on social media marketing. Companies of all sizes and industries are beginning to find utility in Facebook and Twitter across the marketing funnel (see Figure 6.2).

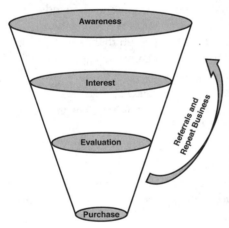

Awareness
-Word-of-mouth, including status messages and retweets, help you reach new audiences.
-Create a Facebook Page and Twitter account to establish your social network presence.
-Use a voice and creative that reflects your brand.
-Even being on Facebook and Twitter will positively influence your brand as being hip and with the times.

Interest
-Track social ad campaigns and analytics, including ad clickthrough rate, wall post clickthrough rate, page views, likes and comments, Twitter mentions, and retweets.

Evaluation
-Measure completed offers and events. (Use Facebook Events to keep in touch with attendees.)
-Keep track of your Facebook fan and Twitter follower count.

Purchase and Beyond
-Provide a commerce experience on your Facebook Page.
-Ask your fans for referrals and track them.
-Periodically survey and poll your customers.

Figure 6.2
You can use social networking sites such as Facebook and Twitter across the marketing funnel.

Why are social networks so effective for marketing? When people log on to a social networking site, they feel they are among friends. From status updates to birthday reminders, the content they see is tailored just for them. The highly personalized experience exudes trust.

Social network advertisers are, in effect, given access to a direct, customized portal for each individual audience member. The challenge has been that although advertisers might be catching their audience in a more trusting mind-set, social networking sites thus far have largely been about communication, not purchase intent. The question remains whether high context from friend and profile data will be able to overcome low purchase intent, or whether social networks will be able to successfully incorporate (or be incorporated into) high-intent online marketplaces, searches, and product comparison sites.

Hypertargeting

"Half the money I spend on advertising is wasted; the trouble is, I don't know which half."
—John Wanamaker, department store merchant

John Wanamaker's famous saying seems to ring as true today as it did 100 years ago. But especially as budgets are getting squeezed, more advertisers are saying that enough is enough. As tools and technologies for tracking campaigns have improved, we are seeing a fundamental shift in the online advertising industry toward performance marketing. With the exception, perhaps, of the biggest brands, advertisers increasingly are willing to pay for only hard-and-fast results.

Hypertargeting (also called **microtargeting**), the capability on social networking sites to target ads based on very specific criteria, is an important step toward precision marketing. Facebook and LinkedIn are leading the charge, with sophisticated targeting tools that enable advertisers to choose which individual profiles see their ads. Advertisers can target profiles based on filters such as location, gender, age, education, workplace, relationship status, relationship interests, and interest keywords. For example, a wedding planner might hypertarget only those whose relationship status is set to "engaged." Or a golf retail store in Carlsbad, California, might hypertarget men of a certain age who live within a 10-mile radius and have specified "golf" as one of their hobbies. But it's not just ads. On Facebook, Page admins can also target fan communications by location, age, and gender for updates, and location and language for Wall posts.

Hypertargeting is possible only because of what people share about themselves on social network profiles. Because of social pressure and a need for self-expression, most people reveal a lot about themselves. As we talked about in Chapter 2, "The New Social Norms," it's pretty standard for people to share gender, birthday, hometown, employer, college, and high school information, and it's not unusual to share relationship status, political views, religious beliefs, activities, interests, favorite music, TV shows, movies, and books. Companies can use all this information for hypertargeting. Even certain information, such as birth year, that is hidden based on privacy settings is fair game for ad-targeting purposes. (No personally identifiable info is ever shared with advertisers.)

Hypertargeting can be equally compelling for business-to-business (B2B) sales. Naturally, B2B decision makers have social networking profiles that can be targeted and advertised to. For many products and services, recommendations and referrals from trusted friends and colleagues are important factors in deciding whether to buy. For example, a software vendor might hypertarget ads to people whose job title contains the words *IT* or *CIO*. For even greater customization and precision, the hypertargeting criteria could specify the name of the company that the vendor is trying to sell to.

When done right, hypertargeting can improve ad conversions and reduce costs because it enables marketers to 1) show ads only to people most likely to buy, 2) tailor ad campaigns to specific audiences, 3) take advantage of better campaign data, and 4) cost-effectively reach so-called passive buyers, as detailed in the following sections.

1. Don't Waste Ads on People Who Will Never Buy

Before social network marketing, advertisers had no choice but to show ads to everyone who visited a Web page they sponsored or searched on a keyword they bought. Advertisers couldn't turn on ads for some people and turn them off for others. This was less efficient for both search marketing and display ads because some (at times, substantial) portion of the ads that they purchased were invariably shown to and wasted on the wrong audience—people who weren't the right age, gender, or religion, or didn't have the right occupation, marital status, or stated interests to likely demand the product. With hypertargeting, advertisers can remove audience segments from their campaigns who are unlikely to buy or have a lower probability of buying (which equates to a lower ad return on investment [ROI]) and focus on probable buyers.

Hypertargeting Golfers

Let's revisit the earlier example about reaching male golfers ages 40–55 in California. Previously, advertisers had no direct way to access this group. They had to access by proxy, either with brand advertising in men's golf publications or search advertising from California IP addresses on the keyword "golf." In either case, the targeting might be incomplete, imprecise, and potentially expensive. Some ads were wasted and demand was left on the table (see the upcoming section "Cost-Effectively Reach Passive Buyers") because advertisers couldn't limit who actually saw the ad.

As Figure 6.3 shows, social network hypertargeting lets advertisers minimize the number of wasted ads by targeting only the intended audience segment. Social network ads make it possible to specify who gets shown an ad.

In this example, advertisers would not show nongolfers the ad because they don't fit the hypertargeting criteria. Likely, nongolfers would be grateful to have been spared from an ad that's irrelevant to them. But to golf enthusiasts living near San Diego, the ad would be highly relevant. Ads that are targeted and relevant don't feel like spam, and they are much more likely to convert viewers into customers.

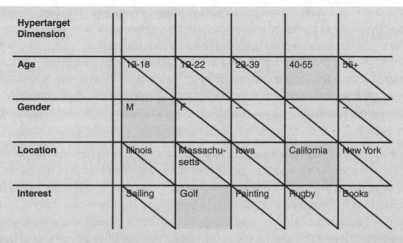

Hypertarget Dimension					
Age	13-18	19-22	23-39	40-55	56+
Gender	M	F	-	-	-
Location	Illinois	Massachu-setts	Iowa	California	New York
Interest	Sailing	Golf	Painting	Rugby	Books

Figure 6.3

It's hard to capture the full power of hypertargeting in this two-dimensional figure, but it illustrates the basic idea. Hypertargeting lets advertisers specify an audience profile—in this case, men in California ages 40–55 who mention "golf" in their profile. No ads are wasted on anyone who does not fit all these criteria.

Even brand advertisers who want to reach everyone should segment audiences and pay more to advertise to higher-value segments. Both Facebook and LinkedIn sell ads via CPC (cost-per-click) or CPM (cost-per-thousand impressions) auctions, similar to most search marketing models. As a marketer, you want to bid more per view or click for audience segments that have a higher likelihood of becoming customers.

2. Tailor Ad Campaigns to Specific Audiences

Not only can advertisers cut out undesirable audience segments in their campaigns, but they can also further segment among the people they do want to target and tailor which ads are shown to whom.

Before hypertargeting, advertisers had little choice but to show the same ad to everyone. If different ads were shown, it was usually done randomly. Hypertargeting makes it possible to run very specific ad campaigns; advertisers can customize ad copy for the exact segment of individuals they are targeting. Better-tailored, more specific ads result in higher click-through rates and, ultimately, increased returns on advertising dollars spent.

Social network hypertargeting provides a new capability to "think global, act local." Advertisers can use what they know about a particular hypersegment to make ads feel more personal. Advertisers know the exact demographic and psychographic—that is, self-ascribed preferences—attributes of the audience because the consumers have chosen the hypertargeting criteria. This enables advertisers to make their ads less about the generic features of their product and more about what's important to the people viewing the ad.

Bonobos, an online retailer of men's pants, uses hypertargeting to "act local." Its ads on Facebook hypertarget audience segments based on gender, age, and stated interest in a sports team. Bonobos' marketers use knowledge about sports team colors to determine which pant color to promote, and they tailor their ad copy accordingly. For example, men age 18 and older in the United States who have "Red Sox" in their profile are shown the ad in Figure 6.4. As you can see, the main message of the ad is not about Bonobos pants. It's about being a loyal fan and looking good when you attend a Boston Red Sox game at Fenway Park.

Ads such as this one have done well because Bonobos is able to tap into the positive feelings and emotional connection sports fans have with their teams to sell pants. Instead of showing the same ad to every male sports fan age 18 and older in the United States, Bonobos hypersegments its audience by college and hometown sports teams and then displays customized ad copy and the right pant color to each audience segment. The result is higher click-throughs and more sales. The case study at the end of this section goes more in-depth into Bonobos' success with advertising on Facebook.

Figure 6.4
Bonobos' ads on Facebook have done well because they appeal specifically to the hypersegment. For example, this ad targets Boston Red Sox fans.

3. Take Advantage of Better Audience Data

Hypertargeting also enables greater iterating precision because campaign performance is broken down by audience segment. If an ad campaign fails, did it fail for everyone or only certain audience segments? Which audience segments resulted in the highest click-through rates and conversions? Advertisers can now get very granular about whom they're showing what ads to, can continually test new ads, and can experiment with different ways of slicing and dicing their audience. Are males more responsive than females to an ad? Are these ads not working on people under age 20? What if the image and wording of the ad are altered? Hypertargeting gives advertisers more levers to test and optimize: location, gender, age, education, workplace, relationship status, relationship interests, and interest keywords.

Instead of having to optimize campaigns globally across all audience segments collectively, marketers can hypersegment, test, and iterate to optimize for each individual segment. Bonobos would develop different ads if it had to show everyone the same ad instead of being able to tailor ads for each segment. If advertisers are underperforming with a particular audience segment, they can focus on testing new messages with that segment, or even cut the segment from their campaigns, without affecting strategy elsewhere. This results in more optimal performance across the entire portfolio of campaigns—and no more weakest links.

Companies such as Bonobos are not only getting valuable feedback about ad campaigns, but they are also able to quickly learn which audiences are demanding their products and services. Demographic and psychographic information on social networking sites is helping companies better understand who their customers are beyond traditional purchase history information and prioritize limited resources across audience segments. Are high school students in the Midwest fanatical about clicking on your ads and buying your product? You could inadvertently have tapped into a bigger trend. Why not jump on the opportunity and concentrate your marketing efforts on this niche where you are seeing the greatest return?

The implications of these campaign insights reach far beyond marketing. Companies can use these insights to drive the overall strategy of the business, including decisions about research and development, sales, and operations—such as what kind of products to develop, which products to push through which channels, and where to locate inventory.

4. Cost-Effectively Reach Passive Buyers

Search advertising is effective because it catches people at the moment they are ready to buy. They have high intent, and the timing is right. But investing in search advertising alone can be expensive and can leave money on the table. It's expensive because everyone else also wants to access a high-intent audience; for some keywords such as "real estate" and "casino," advertisers have bid up prices to $50 *per click*. Yet money is left on the table because search advertising captures only a small portion of the total number of people you might want to advertise to.

Companies can realize value in showing ads to "passive buyers"—that is, people who aren't proactively seeking out your product but who might be interested in buying it if they are encouraged. An offline example of passive buyers is people at the grocery store who make impulse purchases in the checkout aisle—such as gum, magazines, or gift cards. People might not have gone to the store expressly to buy a soda, but seeing the item (especially on sale) makes them realize they want it.

Especially for new, niche, or unknown products, search advertising might not make sense because your target audience probably doesn't know that the product exists and, therefore, doesn't know to search for it. Hypertargeted ads such as the one in Figure 6.5 can be an effective way to tap into latent demand in your target audience segments.

Figure 6.5
Little-known products such as this custom Stanford diploma frame are not good candidates for Google AdWords because most people might not even know to search for them. However, they can be a great fit for hypertargeted ads, such as this one for Stanford alumni.

How do companies reach passive buyers? Display ads reach everyone, including passive buyers, but they are usually even more expensive than search advertising. There is less inventory because they tend to occupy dedicated ad slots. Because they don't utilize targeting, display ads tend to overshoot (reaching audience segments for whom your product is irrelevant), resulting in wasted ad spend.

Not only are some impressions wasted on people unlikely to buy (similar to search advertising, described in the previous section), but these ads also suffer from low audience intent. It's a double whammy. For example, a small start-up company such as Bonobos might not be able to afford display ads because too few people would find the ads relevant enough to click on. Traditionally, it made sense for only big brands to adopt the "spray-and-pray" approach of display ads. Fewer of their ads are wasted because they might appeal to a greater percentage of people viewing them.

But even the big-brand advertisers are demanding greater precision and better results. For them and other advertisers, hypertargeting might offer a cost-effective way to reach passive buyers and capture latent interest. By layering key demographic and psychographic filters that correspond to their ideal customer profile, social network advertisers can capture latent demand without wasting ads on the wrong audience segments. They can access passive buyers without spending a fortune (see Figure 6.6).

This doesn't imply that social network advertising will displace search engine marketing or display ads. On the contrary, the online social graph is already being used to make these models better. Facebook, LinkedIn, and MySpace all offer hypertargeted display advertising. It's reasonable to expect that social networks will also try to incorporate search marketing sometime in the near future.

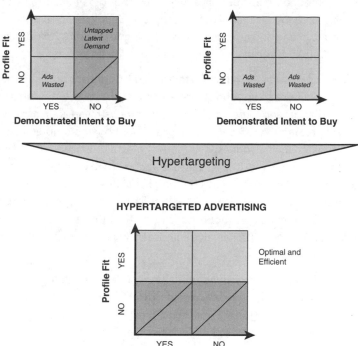

Figure 6.6

Hypertargeting enables advertising precision that can uncover latent interest from passive buyers and minimize wasted ad impressions. The result is a more optimal and better-performing ad campaign.

The following case study describes how Bonobos has used hypertargeting on Facebook to achieve impressive sales results.

Bonobos' Success with Hypertargeting on Facebook

Bonobos is an innovative men's clothing company started by two MBA students at the Stanford Graduate School of Business. Bonobos specializes in fashionable men's pants in colorful styles that are available only online through its Web store. As a start-up company, Bonobos lacked brand awareness and distribution. But creative campaigns run through Facebook ads helped Bonobos overcome these hurdles and achieve a $2 million sales run rate less than one year after launching the company. According to CEO Andy Dunn, Facebook ads were the only form of advertising that was cost-efficient when Bonobos was just starting out.

continues…

Facebook's targeting capabilities have given Bonobos greater control over ad development and optimization. By hypertargeting very specific audience segments by geography, college, and interests, the marketing team is able to quickly tailor, test, and optimize advertising messages while improving traction in new markets.

For example, July is summer in the Northern Hemisphere but winter in the Southern Hemisphere, so Bonobos targeted ads for shorts to American and European audiences and targeted ads for pants to Australian audiences. Another successful hypertargeted campaign previously mentioned promoted colored pants to fans that match their favorite sports team's colors. For example, Bonobos shows ads for Nantucket red pants (the "Capertons") to Facebook profiles in the Boston regional network who have "Red Sox" in their list of interests, and shows ads for orange pants ("Orange Crush") to profiles in the Clemson University network. Hypertargeting has enabled Bonobos to expand the brand's relevance and sphere of influence by relating to prospective customers in personal ways that are important to them.

The flexibility to start ad campaigns at any time of day has enabled Bonobos to successfully launch timely promotions that drive higher click-through rates and immediate sales. Returning to the sports team example, one time-sensitive ad strategy that worked particularly well was featuring pants that were "perfect for attending baseball games" as the baseball season was about to begin. Hypertargeted ads and timed ads have driven as much as 10% of Bonobos' site traffic volume.

Social Distribution and Word-of-Mouth

Hypertargeting is a tremendous innovation, but it becomes even more powerful when you combine it with social distribution. Especially in today's crowded marketplace—the average American is exposed to more than 3,000 advertising messages *each day*—social distribution from customer to customer instead of from vendor to customer is, by far, the most affordable and effective way for brands to stand out. Successful companies today don't market *to* people. They market *between* people.

In Chapter 2, we talked about transitive trust. Not only is trust transitive—so are brand attention, enthusiasm, and loyalty. Customer X pays attention to and likes your product. Prospect Y pays attention to and likes Customer X. Suddenly, without you really having a say, you might find that Prospect Y also pays attention to and likes your product. Although these dynamics have existed all along, it was much harder and less efficient to convey brand affinity before the Facebook Era. Social network updates such as tweets and News Feed updates provide ideal channels to let people discover and engage. Because people *choose* whom to friend and follow on Facebook and Twitter, these sites are ideal platforms for word-of-mouth. Trust is inherent in the social graph of friend and follower relationships.

"Going viral" is the Holy Grail of marketing. The exciting news for marketers is that social sites seem to facilitate virality by making it easier for people to share content and experiences they love.

David King is an entrepreneur who is passionate about using digital media and the social Web for positive change in the world. In 2007, he began working on a project that led him to found Green Patch, Inc., which grew to be one of the largest social gaming companies on Facebook before Playdom acquired it. (Lil) Green Patch is one of the most viral games of all time. In the following guest expert sidebar, King gives some valuable advice on how to "go viral" by designing for social distribution.

Viral Design Lessons from the Social Gaming Industry

David King

Our (Lil) Green Patch game has touched more than 25 million users who tend to their virtual gardens, with a large number playing the game several times a day. Users send their friends plants, buy virtual good decorations, and tend to the (Lil) Green Patches that belong to friends.

The (Lil) Green Patch game uses positive actions in the virtual world to make a real impact in the world around us. We started a movement that raised more than $250,000 for The Nature Conservancy's Adopt an Acre program to help save the rainforest on the Osa Peninsula of Costa Rica.

How did we touch so many people without investing in a marketing budget? It all comes down to virality. (Lil) Green Patch was primarily designed to be a viral experience. It was a decision that we debated about and reached agreement on early in the process. The (Lil) Green Patch game is practically impossible to play alone. Without your friends, you have a (Lil) Green Patch, but you have no plants to grow in it, no friend gardens to tend, and no ways to earn coins quickly. It's a very boring game without friends involved.

The (Lil) Green Patch game has a simple message: Join with your friends to help change the world. The simplicity and collaborative aspect makes the social design compelling to users. When designing social software, it's fundamental that the social interactions be the core of the design and the primary use of the software.

When designing social software, think about what the social graph enables. Can you instantly show interesting information about friends who are using the software so that the goodwill that users have toward friends enhances the quality of the first-time user experience of your product? Imagine beginning to use a new piece of software and finding that you already have 15 friends using it and you can see interesting things that they're doing. Can you provide simple calls-to-action at meaningful and relevant touch points where users will want to either share a great experience or include additional friends to see how their information looks in your application? This is the path to virality.

David King (@deekay) is the founder of (Lil) Green Patch.

Lower Barriers to Sharing

Marketers have always known that recommendations and referrals from friends are powerful influencers in purchase decisions (see Figure 6.7). This means that your existing customers are valuable because they have the highest success rate for converting new customers. For marketers, social networking sites provide easy ways to broadcast recommendations to your existing customer base.

Level of Trust in Advertising Tactics/Media According to Internet Users Worldwide, April 2009 (% of respondents)				
	Trust completely	Trust somewhat	Don't trust much	Don't trust at all
Recommendations from people I know	34%	56%	9%	1%
Brand Websites	13%	57%	26%	5%
Consumer opinions posted online	13%	57%	25%	5%
Editorial content such as a newspaper article	10%	59%	27%	4%
Brand sponsorships	9%	54%	31%	6%
Ads on TV	8%	53%	33%	6%
Ads in newspapers	7%	54%	34%	5%
Ads in magazines	6%	53%	36%	6%
Ads on radio	6%	49%	38%	7%
Billboards and other outdoor advertising	5%	49%	39%	6%
E-mails I signed up for	7%	48%	37%	8%
Ads before movies	5%	47%	41%	7%
Ads served in search engine results	4%	37%	48%	11%
Online video ads	3%	34%	51%	11%
Online banner ads	3%	30%	51%	16%
Text ads on mobile phones	2%	22%	47%	29%
Source: Nielsen Online, "Nielsen Global Online Consumer Survey," July 2009				
105653				www.eMarketer.com

Figure 6.7

An eMarketer study in 2009 showed that "recommendations from people I know" is by far the most trusted source of information. A more recent survey by Edelman suggests that, perhaps because of social media fatigue, consumers are trusting friends less. Marketers must determine who is a good friend versus a weak tie.

Before social networking sites, word-of-mouth marketing required people to be proactive about sharing and was pretty inefficient. People had to really love your product and also have the time to craft and deliver a message about it. A high bar was in place for what kinds of products got talked about—most products weren't so lucky. Even when people did talk about your product, they might not have told very many people, to avoid the risk of annoying friends.

In contrast, real-time updates on the social Web have made word-of-mouth marketing easy and automatic. Every time people on Facebook update a status message, write on a Wall, send or receive a gift, RSVP for an event, make a comment, "like" a Page, or play a branded game, *their friends find out*.

When done right, marketers can tap into this effect to magnify the return on their campaigns and engagement initiatives. For every person marketers successfully engage on a social networking site, potentially dozens more can become engaged. The barriers to sharing have been lowered, so marketers of products and services that previously were not well suited for word-of-mouth marketing are suddenly finding that this method is driving significant growth.

Imagine that Ally "likes" (formerly known as becoming a fan of) Human Rights First, a nonprofit international human rights organization. Ally's friends are instantly notified on their News Feed that she has "liked" Human Rights First, and they are also able to "like" the Page with one click in-line without leaving the News Feed page (see Figure 6.8).

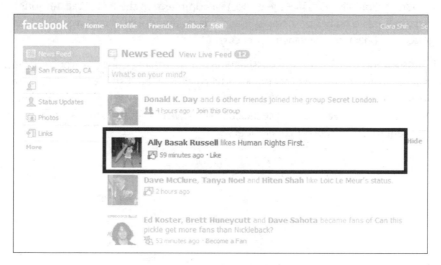

Figure 6.8
Ally's friends receive a notification in their Facebook News Feed that she "likes" the Facebook Page for Human Rights First (a nonprofit organization).

Anyone who visits Ally's profile will see this also (see Figure 6.9). Without doing anything extra, Ally has become a word-of-mouth marketer for Human Rights First. Similarly, your customers do not have to proactively endorse your game, product, or organization. Facebook automatically broadcasts their affinities and decisions. Initially, these automatic behaviors were a shock for many users, but as we discussed in Chapter 2, activity feeds have become a largely accepted, and even wanted, feature of social applications.

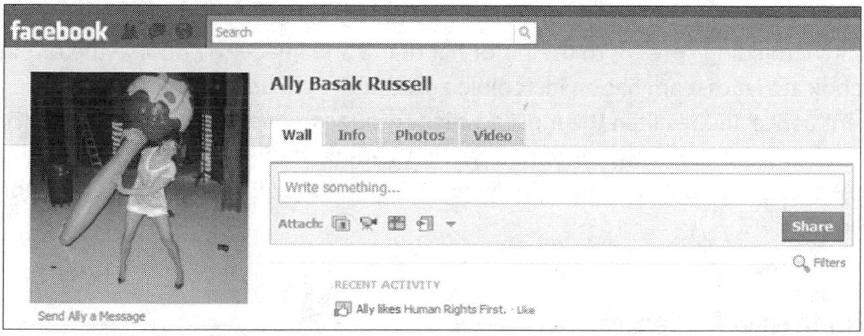

Figure 6.9
Anyone who views Ally's profile will also see that she has just "liked" Human Rights First.

Social Ads

In the previous example, Human Rights First benefited from free word-of-mouth advertising when Ally "liked" the Page, but the effect was temporary. Ally's friends get notified only when she initially "likes" a Page or posts a comment on the Page Wall. Although the *updates* are passive on her part, News Feed updates about Ally and Humans Rights First are generated only when new activity occurs.

Social ads extend the life of these passive word-of-mouth messages by "reusing" fan information in ads. Essentially, Facebook's advertising system uses Facebook Page fans as endorsers in the ad (see Figure 6.10). By associating an ad with a friend, brands can, in effect, tap into transitive trust and social capital between friends to win attention and engagement from new audience members.

Figure 6.10
Social ads on Facebook, such as this one that I created for The Facebook Era *Business Page, mention any friends of the person viewing the ad who have already "liked" the Page. The idea is that people are more likely to click on an ad for something one of their friends likes.*

From the perspective of Facebook users, every time someone "likes" a Page, that person is implicitly providing consent to use his or her name and image to endorse the brand. The Facebook analytics team has an incredible amount of data about which users have the most influence and result in the most ad click-throughs. For example, they found that endorsements from women carry more weight with men. The advertising system incorporates a lot of this data to determine which of a Facebook Page's fans to use to endorse to whom.

Reaching New Audiences

Even companies flush with cash find it extremely difficult to enter new markets. Not only can it be prohibitively expensive, but it's also full of many unknowns, such as which new market is the best one to go after.

Word-of-mouth that happens across social networks can often help companies "accidentally" discover new audiences and fan bases. By tapping the existing connections between individuals that cut across different homogeneous networks, such as region (see Figure 6.11), age, and industry, companies can extend their spheres of influence to new, sometimes unexpected markets and reach new pockets of people.

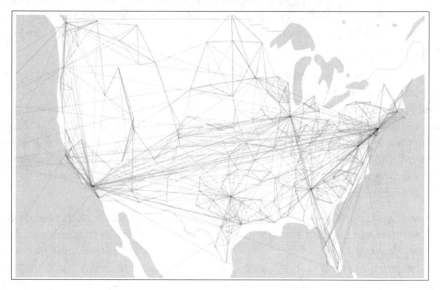

Figure 6.11
Ex–Apple engineer Pete Warden has done groundbreaking analyses and visualizations of Facebook connections across different cross-sections, including regional networks. As this visualization shows, although the majority of friend connections exist within regions, a substantial number of connections also bridge disparate regions.

For example, Barack Obama's 2008 presidential campaign used Facebook to recruit unlikely supporters among low-wage, blue-collar workers in Harrison County, Indiana—historically, a very Republican region of the country. At the time, Obama's TV ads didn't seem to be effective. Many campaign staffers wanted to write off this part of the state entirely. But Obama supporters elsewhere who had ties to people living in Harrison County started using Facebook to rally the locals around Obama's cause. Before long, a contingent of Harrison County residents were helping lead national phone-banking efforts and contributing to the campaign. Obama narrowly won Indiana in the general election.

Social Shopping and Recommendations

As business on the social Web matures, friend actions and recommendations are reaching beyond brand awareness and pervading the shopping experience itself. Shopping is an inherently social activity—we ask some friends how we look in a pair of jeans and other friends which camera to buy. Review sites such as Amazon, Yelp, and Epinions have been tremendously helpful. But what consumers want now goes beyond recommendations from strangers; they want recommendations from friends, and often a different set of friends for different items. (For example, you might ask a different person about the jeans than you would about the digital camera.)

Although we are likely still a few years away from social shopping becoming mainstream, exciting developments are already taking shape, both as Facebook commerce applications and as Facebook for Websites integrations on shopping sites. I don't go into exhaustive detail here—because that's beyond the scope of this book and also because I don't have much to share, given how nascent social commerce is—but I can share some early examples.

One of the Facebook commerce applications that has been around the longest comes from Pizza Hut, which we introduced in Chapter 1, "The Fourth Revolution." It enables you to order pizza without leaving Facebook. You even have the option to have the app post a News Feed update to your friends about your order. It's not perfect—you still have to sign up for a login with Pizza Hut and type in your address—but it's likely the direction we are headed. Especially as Facebook begins privately storing more physical addresses of its users, the shopping, ordering, and delivery experience will become even smoother and more common.

Don't worry, you don't have to build everything on your own from scratch. An easy way for retailers to start creating a shopping experience on Facebook is to go with ecommerce and payment vendors such as Payvment and Alvenda. Facebook itself has developed a payments system that enables people to buy Facebook "credits" using a credit card, and then to spend the credits on applications that are using Facebook's payment system, including Facebook gifts. Currently, Facebook charges 30% of revenue for use of its payment system (similar to what Apple's AppStore does).

Another option is to do what Best Buy has done: Bring your product catalog onto Facebook so people can browse, share with their friends, and make the decision to purchase within a social environment—and then the moment they are ready to buy, open a window to your existing ecommerce flow. This is certainly a lot easier than re-creating the entire shopping experience end-to-end within Facebook, but it still provides benefits of a social shopping experience.

No matter how successful Facebook continues to be, many commerce transactions and shopping experiences will continue to take place off Facebook. Implementing Facebook for Websites (introduced at the end of Chapter 1) on external commerce sites enables companies to bring the social experience to shopping (versus the previous examples, in which companies are bringing shopping to the social experience). For example, flyers on Virgin America can log in with their Facebook credentials to seek and book the same flights as their friends.

Many people think that the ultimate social shopping experience would emerge if Amazon or eBay integrated with Facebook for Websites. Groupon has done this, and it has experienced phenomenal growth. Groupon strikes volume deals with local businesses, such as spas, restaurants, and shows. Members can purchase gift cards and tickets at a steep discount, and they have built-in incentives to invite their friends to do the same, given the social nature of many of these activities, such as going out to dinner or visiting the zoo.

Promoting Events

The social Web is also extremely powerful for events. One of my favorite examples is Live Nation (which also owns Ticketmaster) implementing Facebook for Websites on its Web site. Concertgoers can log in to the site with Facebook credentials to discover which concerts their friends are going to. The Live Stream widget (get it from http://facebook.com/facebook-widgets) then enables Facebook users to connect, share, and post updates in real time on their Facebook Page or external Web site that has implemented Facebook for Websites.

In the conference world, Web 2.0 Expo is one of the most successful technology events in the industry, drawing thousands of people from around the world each year to its shows in San Francisco and New York. It features the latest Web 2.0 business models, development paradigms, and design strategies. In the following guest expert sidebar, Expo chair Brady Forrest shares some practical advice on how to promote events on the social Web.

Promoting Events on Facebook and Twitter

Brady Forrest

The events business is all about community. If your communities leave or forget you, then you are out of business. You have to consider each of their needs and give them something that makes them want to be at an event instead of just reading about it later. You can use Twitter and Facebook to help with this before, during, and after the event using these tips:

- **Be there**—You need to be present on social media networks. Create a Twitter account and Facebook Page for the event that people can follow or fan. Use Twitter's List feature to put all the accounts into one place.

- **Create connections**—The number one reason people go to events is to meet people—so help them do this. If you're looking for a new employee, use Twitter and Facebook to spread the word. If you're going down the street for drinks, let others know. Doing so will make the event more memorable, useful, and, ultimately, well regarded.

- **Promote your attendees**—If someone shares an insight that they learned at the conference, help them spread it. Suddenly more people will start sharing their thoughts on the event with the hope that they'll be recognized (and you should retweet some of those, too). Use the Twitter Lists feature to create groups of attendees.

- **Share the event (and make it easy for attendees to do so, too)**—Talk about the event. Write about the event beforehand. Announce when you sign up speakers. Offer discounts. Give people a reason to pay attention to you before the event happens. Then during the event, you want to be the news source. You want people who aren't there to be curious about what is happening *now* and what *will* happen. You want attendees to know the coolest thing that is happening right now. If you've done your job right, the attendees know the hashtags and are doing half the work for you.

- **Don't stop**—Your social media accounts should be staffed year-round. You should all use the same hashtags, and you should make sure your attendees know what they are.

Brady Forrest (@brady) is the cochair of Web 2.0 Expo and cocreator of Ignite.

Engagement Is King

In addition to hypertargeting and social distribution, marketing is shifting from being tactical and transaction-oriented to more strategic and embedded in experience.

Marketing for the Long Term

Before the Facebook Era, online marketing was about optimizing for the transaction— that is, open rates, click-throughs, and conversions. We did this because we had to—no other data was available.

The social Web has changed all this. For the first time, companies can capture not just the customer transaction, but also the *customer relationship*. Through fans and followers, organizations can now confidently invest in "upper funnel" activities—that is, driving more casual interest in their products and services without pressuring the commitment of a purchase transaction. Relationship marketing in the Facebook Era lets companies take a longer-term view of the business, optimizing for lifetime relationships and loyalty tomorrow instead of a single transaction today.

The most successful companies on the social Web are not constantly pushing their products and promotions; instead, they are investing in building their sphere of influence in their business area. In the following sidebar, marketing and branding expert Brian Solis explains the value of engaging audiences with content.

In Social Media, Brands Become Media

Brian Solis

One of the greatest challenges new media champions encounter today is not the willingness of a brand to engage, but its capability to *create*. When blueprinting a social media strategy, enthusiasm and support usually diminish when faced with the dedication of the resources and commitment required to produce regular and engaging content.

The democratization of publishing and the equalization of influence enable us to create and connect with a wider reach. Everything starts with a mission and is fortified by the content we create. Therefore, we not only become our media—through production and engagement—but we can become influential.

Although establishing a presence is elementary, captivating audiences is artful. In the near future, brands and organizations will create new roles or augment existing roles for editors and publishers to create timely, relevant, and captivating content on all social media channels. This work is in addition to the other reactive and proactive social media campaigns that are already in progress. A strategic editorial calendar should blend video, audio, imagery, text, updates, and other social objects and networks to reach, inspire, and galvanize communities.

As media, brands earn prominence and, hopefully, influence as rewards for contributing meaningful content. On Twitter, brands can earn legions of loyal and responsive followers. They, in turn, become brand advocates and ambassadors, extending the messages, mission, and purpose of the brand to their followers as well. On Facebook, brands can cultivate vibrant and dedicated communities in which interaction inspires increased responses—each reverberating across new social graphs. On Ustream and YouTube, we can earn global audiences of viewers who tune in to watch our programming and interact with brand representatives in a live community that spills into other social networks. And, of course, our blog is more important than we might realize. Through our posts, we can establish a strong alliance of subscribers who hope to learn new things and participate in the discussion of a brand's future.

We now have the capability to earn noteworthy, equal, and, in some cases, greater influence than those authorities we've relied on to help us reach greater audiences and communities. As influence is equalized, our capability to earn presence and relationships is derived from how we program, manage, and participate across the social Web. In essence, brands of tomorrow will become media.

Brian Solis (@briansolis) is the principal of FutureWorks and the author of Engage: The Complete Guide for Brands and Businesses to Build, Cultivate, and Measure Success in the New Web *(Wiley, 2010).*

Embedded Marketing and Appvertising

Companies are also discovering that it's often more effective to engage people with applications instead of trying to get them to click on ads, which can be distracting. This embedded marketing strategy on social networking sites is similar to product placement in a TV show versus advertising during the commercial break.

The idea is that people are more likely to engage when your message is embedded in the context of what they are already doing—such as reading their News Feed, playing a game, or socializing with a friend. Otherwise, it can be pretty disruptive for people to stop what they're doing, click on an ad that loads up your Web site, and read your landing page. This is why most people don't usually click on ads. When your ad shows up, they were in the middle of doing something else. So they tune it out, similar to switching channels or fast-forwarding through a TV commercial.

Compared to other social networking sites, Facebook has the most developed set of options for embedded marketing. Facebook itself offers what it calls engagement ads for brand advertisers to reach people on the Facebook home page. These are interactive ad units for people to "like" something on Facebook (refer to Figure 6.10), view and comment on videos, respond to polls, send sponsored virtual gifts, or RSVP for events without having to leave the Web page. We discuss these engagement ads in Chapter 12, "How To: Advertise and Promote on the Social Web."

Minimum campaign spending thresholds (around $50,000) on Facebook engagement ads generally preclude everybody but the big-brand advertisers from taking part. Advertising, sponsorship, or branding of Facebook platform applications, or **appvertising**, is another form of embedded marketing that is open potentially to anyone. If Facebook engagement ads are similar to product placement, then appvertising is similar to creating your own TV show and experience. (Note that I don't cover Twitter or LinkedIn here because you can't really embed applications inside the Twitter experience, and only a handful of select approved partners are able to do so on LinkedIn.)

Apps tend to be more active and engaging than ad clicks and impressions, but they also take a lot more work to put together. As a marketer, you have three options when it comes to platform apps: build it yourself, commission someone to build it for you, or sponsor an existing app.

- **Build it yourself**—This is likely the hardest option for most companies, unless you have a staff of developers on hand. But depending on your budget and requirements, you might not have a choice but to try it yourself. Companies such as Sprout and Transpond have developed fantastic point-and-click app-development platforms that make it a lot easier (see Figure 6.12).

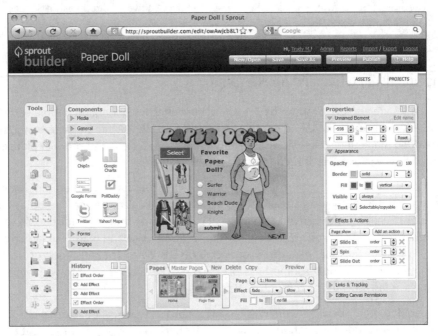

Reprinted by permission

Figure 6.12
Sprout Builder is a Photoshop-like environment for developing interactive widgets and applications.

- **Commission a custom application**—A growing number of digital agencies now provide custom Facebook app-development services. Dedicated Facebook app-development companies, such as Context Optional, Buddy Media, and All Widgets, provide custom-branded application-building services. For example, Microsoft commissioned Context Optional to change brand perception and drive awareness for its most recent version of Microsoft Office. The resulting application was Office Poke!, a play off Facebook pokes that enables users to throw staplers, steal chairs, and, of course, upgrade their machine to Office 2007 (see Figure 6.13). Office Poke! resulted in more than 4 million branded pokes sent in the first 60 days of the campaign.

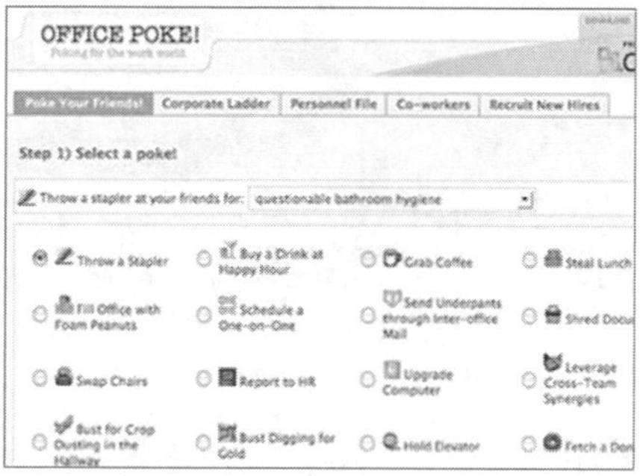

Figure 6.13

Facebook app-development company Context Optional created this custom Office Poke! application for Microsoft.

- **Sponsor an existing app**—Despite some successes with custom-developed applications, most companies are finding it difficult to know which apps will take off and are unwilling to spend the time and money on something that might fail. Instead, marketers are choosing to sponsor apps that are already successful. Marketers work directly with application developers to sponsor or advertise an app, or they advertise on ad networks such as Adknowledge and Rocketfuel that serve ads to these applications. For example, American Family Insurance decided to sponsor a popular Facebook application, FamilyLink, that has nearly 18 million monthly active users, instead of trying to build its own application (see Figure 6.14).

Reprinted by permission

Figure 6.14

American Family Insurance sponsors FamilyLink pages such as this one that enables people to organize and celebrate important milestones of a new baby, new home, or graduation. American Family Insurance provides site content about family safety, home maintenance, and family protection.

Early in the Facebook Era, a number of companies, including Offerpal and Super Rewards, developed platforms for creating special offers. For example, Facebook users could receive special status or points for use in games by filling out lead-generation offers, such as signing up for a trial of Netflix to get $49,280 in virtual Texas HoldEm poker chips (see Figure 6.15). Although this was a good deal for users (they opted in to do this), advertisers soon realized that these leads were not very good. People filling out the offer form had no interest in Netflix—they just wanted to get some more poker chips for free. After a searing blog post by Michael Arrington of TechCrunch in fall 2009 about social gaming lead-generation scams, a number of these companies have taken a step back and pledged to rethink their special offers.

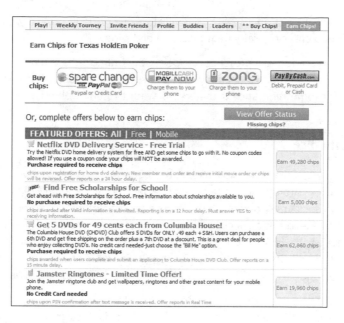

Figure 6.15
Before November 2009, Zynga's Texas HoldEm Poker app let players earn virtual poker chips by completing special offers from sponsors such as Netflix, Free Scholarships for School, Columbia House DVD Club, and Jamster Ringtones. The problem was that people weren't actually interested in these products—they just wanted more poker chips.

Challenges and Limitations

We are still in the early days of social network marketing. Tremendous opportunities and possibilities exist, but so do serious challenges and limitations. Yes, Facebook advertising is precise, personal, and social—but so what? Some progress has been made, but poor brand fit, poor performance, social network fatigue, adjacency to questionable content, and negative buzz are real problems that need to be considered and addressed.

Poor Brand Fit

In many situations, social network marketing doesn't make sense because people don't want to broadcast their affinity for your product. Success often depends on two factors: the product and the site demographic.

Certain product and brand categories—such as sports, recreation, politics, movies, books, food, clothing, and celebrities—are ideal because they evoke passion and individuals use them to express themselves. Products that might be less exciting, more commoditized, embarrassing, and either too personal or too impersonal—such as laundry detergent, medication, and office supplies—are generally less of a good fit. Similarly, luxury items such as high-end cars or jewelry might feel like bragging.

As a company considering a presence on social networking sites, the best thing you can do is to guide your brand in a direction that is exciting but credible. Position your product to stand for something, and customers will want to stand behind it.

Poor Performance

Ad performance on Facebook and LinkedIn has been pretty bad—on average, one-tenth or less of the click-through rate on search ads. However, average CPM bids tend to be much lower on social networking sites. No one has completely figured out how to overcome low purchase intent on social networking sites. I expect that this will change over time. First, Facebook will probably add more search and ecommerce functionality. Second, a logical next step would be for Facebook for Websites to provide AdSense-like social ad syndication to partner sites, including search, shopping, and ecommerce sites.

In the meantime, the best advice is to start small and simple, and set realistic expectations. Just as slapping up a Web site and buying AdWords doesn't automatically transform businesses into a success, effective social network marketing requires strategy, testing, and iteration. Chapter 12 goes into detail on how to optimize click-throughs and conversions with social network ads.

Social Network Fatigue

One concern about social network marketing is that people are starting to tire of Facebook and Twitter, similar to how they tired of Friendster. Only time will tell whether people continue to sign up and log in after the novelty wears off.

Fatigue is also occurring with social ads. Some social network members are already beginning to complain that the sites feel too commercial. One danger is that people could get turned off if their experience on social networking sites becomes too inundated with ads and stops being about them and their friends. The social networks will need to balance pursuing monetization efforts against keeping people happy and engaged.

This concern was a large motivation behind Facebook's decision to create Business Pages and, more recently, Community Pages that are distinct from individual profiles. Having this clear distinction enables Facebook to create separate privacy models for individuals versus organizational entities, and also lets individuals keep these two worlds separate whenever and however they want.

Adjacency to Questionable Content

One challenge advertisers face with any type of social media is adjacent placement to questionable user-generated content, such as a sexually explicit MySpace profile page. For example, a brand might not want to be associated with a particular political group or controversial celebrity.

The social networks are starting to explore ways to give advertisers more control over where their ads appear. For example, Facebook enables advertisers in the United Kingdom to opt out of ad placement next to all Facebook Groups.

Negative Buzz

The risk in empowering users to define and spread brand messages is that these messages might not always be positive, and brands might have very little control over the aftermath. Many believe the 2005 movie *King Kong* failed to meet expectations at the box office because negative word-of-mouth that it was "too long, too loud, and overdone" caused many people to not even give it a chance. The Segway scooter is another example of a product that generated a lot of buzz from word-of-mouth, but it was mostly negative. A reputation of being "funny looking" and "dangerous on sidewalks" did not help sales.

People are having brand conversations whether you are even aware of them. It's better to try to facilitate where it makes sense, reward and provide channels for your advocates, and address feedback from the community than to not do anything.

In our age of information and transparency, people will talk about your product. The only difference when these conversations occur on social networking sites is that brands gain visibility and have the chance to respond. Instead of turning a blind eye, companies should welcome and respond to feedback from the community. Ultimately, this is real and valuable feedback that could improve your product or service in ways you might never have considered.

<<< TAKEAWAYS

✓ Many social networking sites now offer hypertargeting, the capability for companies to target ads and messages to people based on their profile information.

✓ Hypertargeted ads that are about the friends, places, and issues important to your target customer are far more effective than ads about your company.

✓ With hypertargeting, you don't have to be a big-brand advertiser with a multimillion-dollar budget to capture latent demand. By honing in on key audience segments with highly tailored messaging, companies of any size can cost-effectively run brand campaigns.

✓ When someone becomes a fan or follower, you've won over not only that person, but potentially also a subset of that person's friends and followers.

✓ The biggest challenges to Facebook marketing are poor brand fit, poor performance, social network fatigue, adjacency to questionable content, and negative buzz.

>>> TIPS and TO DO's

❑ Tailor your ad copy based on the hypertargeting criteria you select in the campaign, as companies like Bonobos have done in appealing to sports fans with their clothing ads.

❑ Bid different CPC or CPM based on audience value, including expected customer lifetime value and empirical conversion rates.

❑ If you are looking to maximize campaign reach, consider sponsoring or advertising within an already-popular application that a third party has created.

❑ If you are looking to maximize engagement within your existing base, consider building your own custom application and make it available on your Facebook Page.

❑ Use hypertargeting as a cheap way to test receptiveness of new markets to your products and services.

7

"Social networking is becoming social innovation. A new mode of invention and production is in the making."
—Don Tapscott, coauthor of *Wikinomics*

Innovation and Collaboration in the Facebook Era

Innovation—the introduction of a new and useful method, process, product, or service—is the lifeblood of business and, indeed, of civilization. Innovation comes in many forms. This chapter focuses on product innovation, although you can apply the ideas presented here to other kinds of innovation.

Roughly speaking, the innovation process has four stages: generating concepts, prototyping, commercial implementation, and continual iteration (see Figure 7.1). Although these stages aren't clear cut or sequential, they have guided most innovations in history.

Every stage is an intensely social process among inventors, collaborators, customers, business partners, critics, and others. It's no wonder that product innovation is starting to move onto social networking sites. Companies previously had a one-sided relationship with customers. Product managers had very little information to work from, so product development mostly followed a "build it and hope they come" mentality, which is costly and high risk.

The social Web has changed the relationship between companies and customers from one-sided to a partnership. Social innovation takes the guesswork out of new product development because customers can tell companies exactly what is important. Armed with information about customers and what they want, companies can feel more empowered to go after new features and new markets. Because their ideas are heard, customers feel more accountable for providing input and more grateful when that input is incorporated into the design of new products. It's a win–win for companies and their customers.

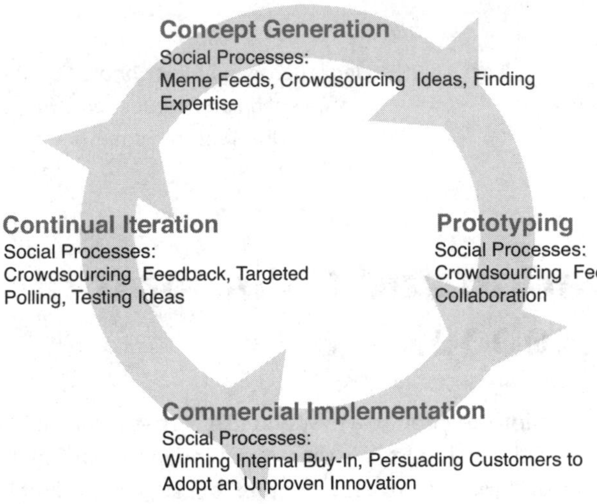

Concept Generation
Social Processes:
Meme Feeds, Crowdsourcing Ideas, Finding Expertise

Continual Iteration
Social Processes:
Crowdsourcing Feedback, Targeted Polling, Testing Ideas

Prototyping
Social Processes:
Crowdsourcing Feedback, Collaboration

Commercial Implementation
Social Processes:
Winning Internal Buy-In, Persuading Customers to Adopt an Unproven Innovation

Figure 7.1
The cycle of innovation typically follows four stages, each containing multiple social processes: concept generation, prototyping, commercial implementation, and continual iteration.

Concept Generation

The first stage in innovation involves creatively brainstorming new ideas and then formulating those ideas into concepts. Traditionally, designated people within the company—usually product managers or research labs—created the ideas. The company generally drives the approach from the top down instead of from the bottom up (from the customer and employee base). Because of a lack of time or the right tools, customer input tends to be more serendipitous than systematic and typically ends up heavily biased toward feedback from the largest, most vocal customers.

The social Web reverses this traditional approach. By closely connecting product managers with internal and external communities in real time, the online social graph facilitates three important bottom-up processes in concept generation: inspiration, ideation, and expertise discovery.

Getting Inspired from Social Memes

Sometimes all it takes to come up with a killer concept is a little inspiration. Talking to customers is a good way to get inspired. It could be an article that someone forwarded to you, something you saw in a movie, or an interesting tidbit you overheard in the hallway that reminds you of something, makes you think about something new, or helps you see things in a new light.

At the heart of these ideas, thoughts, and tidbits that inspire us are **memes,** a term Richard Dawkins coined in his 1976 book, *The Selfish Gene,* to describe the unit of information representing a basic idea that can be transferred from one individual to another. Dawkins applied evolutionary principles about how viruses propagate and mutate to explain the spread of ideas and cultural phenomena.

How can product managers expose themselves to the right amount of the right memes to become inspired without feeling overwhelmed?

It's important to have access to both external and internal meme streams. For external memes, people use tweets and Facebook status messages to share what they're thinking about, what they're doing, how they're doing, and other memes. It is a blank slate: *"Jill is …"*—Jill can type whatever she wants, and it will be broadcast to her network. Twitter and Facebook feeds have generally done a good job of helping people "digest" the stream of memes that continually flows from friends. By investing in building diverse networks of contacts on social networking sites that cut across different homogeneous groups, product managers can increase the chances that they will be exposed to radically new thinking.

Product managers can also use Twitter search to see trending topics or get a pulse on what *people* are saying about something in particular. For example, I periodically search on "The Facebook Era" at http://search.twitter.com to find out what is being said about this book. It's been a great source of ideas and inspiration (see Figure 7.2). Popular free applications such as Hootsuite, TweetDeck, and Seesmic let you save Twitter searches on the keywords, phrases, and hashtags that you want to track over time.

External memes are generally good at helping product managers identify problems. Internal memes are often good at helping them find solutions. Your colleagues are probably thinking about the same or similar problems (often from a slightly different angle) and how to solve them—and your colleagues share your goal of making the company successful. Memes spread every day in meetings, at the water cooler, and in emails that get forwarded to certain distribution lists. Unfortunately, with everything else going on in an organization, the capability for memes to be transmitted isn't as great as it should be. Especially as organizations get bigger, it becomes increasingly difficult to share memes. One reason start-up companies are so effective at getting inspired and coming up with new concepts is that it's easier to brainstorm and share thoughts with the whole team.

Figure 7.2
This figure shows my saved Twitter searches inside Hootsuite. Comments, articles, and musings from my Twitter followers, people that I follow, hashtags that I follow, and people who mention the book or my name. These searches have been an invaluable source of ideas, inspiration, and feedback in writing this book.

Not everyone has something breakthrough to say all the time, so rarely is having everyone hang out at the water cooler efficient or feasible. Nor does everyone care about what everyone else has to say, so emailing the entire company every time someone has an idea is too distracting and disruptive.

Yammer and Socialcast are meme-broadcast tools for individual company networks. Both are similar to Twitter for business. Yammer, in particular, aims to make organizations more productive through the exchange of short, frequently updated answers to one simple question: "What are you working on?" Any employee who has a working email address in the company's domain can join and start posting on the company's Yammer page. Colleagues can then discuss ideas, ask questions, post news, and share links.

Unlike an email blast, Yammer is noninvasive. It provides what Leisa Reichelt and others call **ambient intimacy** within organizations. Employees visit Yammer when they have a free moment and have something to say or want to see what other people are saying. Unlike on Facebook or Twitter, all the memes are related to work and are visible only to other employees. Some of the memes might be silly or not readily applicable. But at a minimum, they enable employees to feel better connected to their coworkers and might provide just the right meme for them to make progress on an idea (see Figure 7.3).

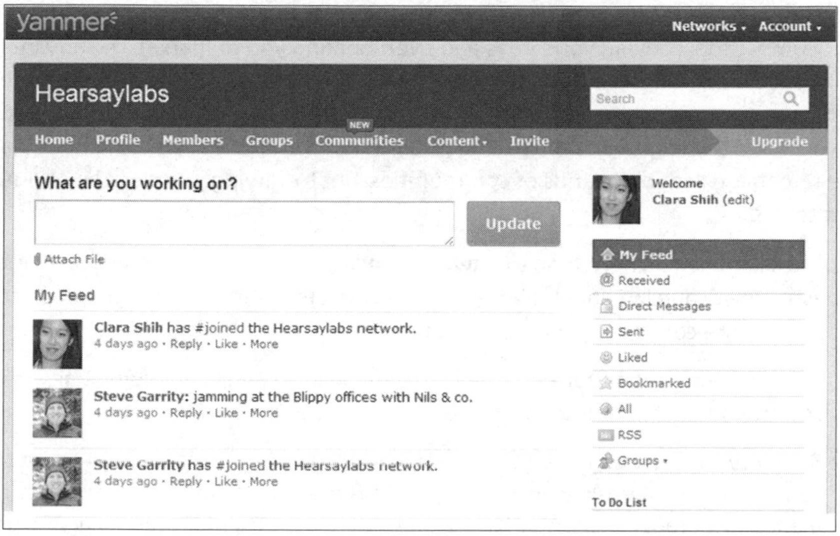

Figure 7.3
Yammer is a status-broadcasting tool that enables employees of the same company to answer and view colleagues' answers to a simple question: "What are you working on?" This is Hearsay Labs' Yammer page.

Status updates are getting incorporated everywhere. Following Yammer's cue, a number of enterprise-sharing and collaboration applications have started to add status updates as a feature. Among these are Microsoft SharePoint, IBM Lotus Connections, ThoughtFarmer, and Salesforce Chatter.

Through status messages and serendipity, the social Web extends the water-cooler effect across geographic regions and time zones. It helps promote a sense of inclusiveness to everyone in your organization and helps working mothers, employees at satellite offices, and others who must work remotely to be at less of a disadvantage in contributing to innovation and engaging with the rest of the company.

Crowdsourcing Ideation

Inspiration is good, but ideas are even more valuable when they are more concrete and actionable. We introduced the notion of *crowdsourcing* in Chapter 5, "Customer Service in the Facebook Era," in the context of customer support. Product managers can also use crowdsourcing techniques to generate ideas from the community for product development.

Depending on the product and competitive situation, it might make sense to engage with internal communities, external communities, or both. The advantage of internal communities is that your colleagues are often the people with the greatest expertise about your product or service because they live, work, and think about it every day.

Internal communities also provide a confidentiality advantage if you are concerned about competitors copying your ideas and even beating you to market. The advantages of external communities are that customers and partners can bring new, often more realistic perspectives about your product, and they will feel more engaged, grateful, and loyal that you value their input and are willing to be transparent. In many situations, it makes sense to engage with both kinds of communities, but to varying degrees and about different topics.

Few product managers have time to interact regularly with every customer on a one-to-one basis. Crowdsourcing enables one-to-many conversations between the product manager and the community through these steps:

1. **Establish an ideation forum**—The product manager or an online community manager sets up a forum for ideas to be solicited, generated, and collected.

2. **Seed the conversation**—To get things going, the product manager might need to post some initial ideas or ask open-ended questions that get community members to participate. Some product managers have even launched contests for user-generated product ideas to achieve greater commitment and a better response (see Figure 7.4).

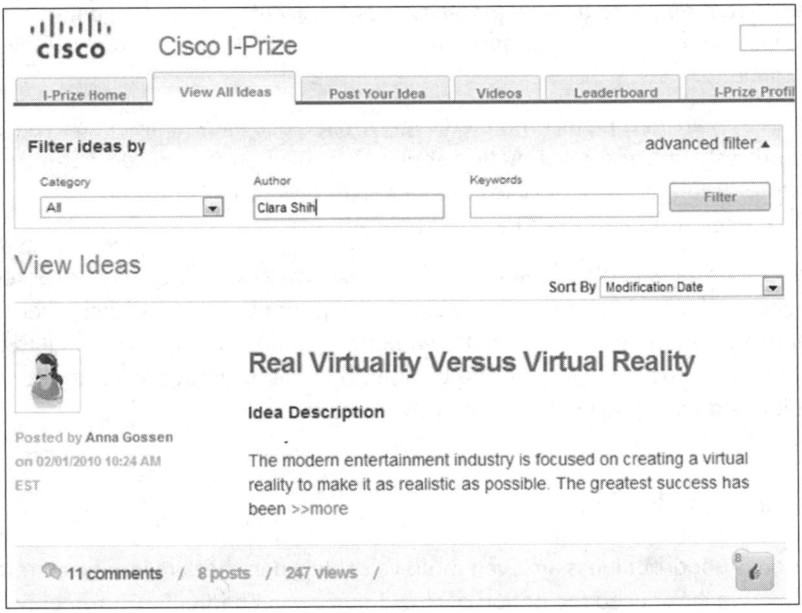

Courtesy of Cisco Systems, Inc.

Figure 7.4
Cisco has issued its second-annual I-Prize Contest to solicit ideas for the Cisco "next billion-dollar business." Entrepreneurs from around the world can log in, submit ideas, vote, and collaborate with Cisco product managers and executives. I-Prize runs on the Spigit social ideation platform.

3. **Encourage customers to interact with one another**—Product managers can motivate and encourage participation by setting up a strong system of trust, identity, and recognition. Lithium's communities, in particular, have a lot of gamelike features that create incentives for participation. A lot of the best ideas will come out of this process of customers sharing their ideas and opinions with one another while the product manager is in the backseat listening and facilitating.

4. **Act on results**—When a good idea is suggested, the product manager might want to intervene and ask the community to develop it further. When it is sufficiently developed, it might be time to take the idea back to internal teams and start prototyping, periodically sharing updates with the community.

5. **Reach out to key contributors**—In most communities, a small number of members are the most active and vocal with their ideas and opinions—the classic 80/20 Rule. Product managers should engage in more in-depth conversations with these individuals to dig deeper and gain even more insights.

As powerful as social network communities are for encouraging customer brand conversations, they can also be a lot of work to manage when used for ideation. Unlike marketing, involving customers in the innovation process is not just about making them feel engaged. A concrete end goal exists to find the best ideas and act on them. Often the hardest part is making sense of the tremendous number of ideas that can be generated. It really is like finding a needle in a haystack.

Tools are being developed to help product managers aggregate, summarize, analyze, and prioritize community feedback. The most popular tools are UserVoice, Spigit (see Figure 7.4), Brightidea, and Salesforce Ideas. For example, UserVoice ideation communities provide an end-to-end system to capture comments, track bugs, and manage new feature requests. The capability to create widget instances of a UserVoice community helps further permeate these ideation opportunities across different Web properties, including blogs and Facebook Pages.

Ideation communities have evolved during the last couple years. First, to prevent or minimize duplicate ideas on most of these sites, a search is run against any new idea being submitted to make sure it doesn't already exist (or overlap too substantially with an existing idea). Second, most sites have the capability to create structured categories for classifying different ideas.

Especially for larger, geographically dispersed organizations, social ideation tools provide a great solution for internal collaboration. Experian, a global financial information services company headquartered in Dublin, has found great results managing the employee ideation pipeline using Brightidea. With a large number of offices spread across the globe, including more than 20 locations in the United States alone, the company (and many other companies in similar situations) faced a difficult communication and coordination challenge. Experian transitioned its employee idea submission process from spreadsheets to Brightidea. A year after deploying Brightidea, Experian launched 100 new products, including a major product, ChoiceScore, that originated from an employee idea. In addition to the revenue impact, employee engagement has boosted morale, productivity, and retention.

Online communities have been around for some time and are starting to become essential tools for ideation. What makes social network ideation of the last few years different? One reason is the strong online identity component we talked about in Chapter 2, "The New Social Norms." People feel more engaged in providing ideas because it helps them build their credibility and personal brand. Another reason is the rising popularity of community voting on idea sites, inspired by sites such as Digg.

In the following guest expert sidebar, IDEO designer Gentry Underwood helps us understand the new paradigm of crowdsourced innovation and design emerging on the social Web.

The Social Design Process

Gentry Underwood

The term *open innovation* is all the rage lately, in no small part because of the success of paradigm-shifting experiments in design and problem solving by companies such as Innocentive, Netflix, and 99designs. The idea is attractive because these platforms open the innovation process to a vast crowd of talent who can compete for the chance to produce a winning design. And although it's still the early days for crowdsourced creativity, we already know quite a bit about what works, what doesn't, and how social networking is changing the face of innovation:

- **From who you know to who's the best**—Historically, analog social networking has limited innovation. Searching for creative help has meant pinging your network and hoping to find someone with the right skills and availability. This talent hunting is tedious and inefficient, and is similar to fishing in an oil drum.

  Most open innovation networks reverse this problem by throwing out a challenge to the crowd and letting designers compete for the work by doing it up front, winner take all. But the contest model can get you only so far. The best designers often shy away from such models because the risk is too high that they won't get paid. And many innovation problems aren't well suited for a contest-type deliverable. In the long run, tapping much larger digital social networks will replace using analog ones. Searching for people based on what they're good at, what they know, and who they've worked with has never been easier. And we're only getting started.

- **From vague and intangible to operational and well defined**—Working with broader networks of talent often means working across distances and in numbers previously thought impossible. And although no substitute exists for a handful of creative people sitting in a room together and using every wall as a shared display, remote collaboration technologies get better every day.

When working with others remotely, the "brief"—that is, the definition of the problem that needs to be solved and any known constraints of a solution—has to be extremely clear, with lots of specific and well-defined milestones along the way. Therefore, the best innovators in a social networking age are the ones who are capable of expressing themselves clearly and breaking down problems into specific, executable chunks.

• **From the designer-as-aristocrat to everyone-as-designer**—One of the most exciting results of the changes we're seeing in innovation is how they open the process of design to anyone who wants to partake. Ultimately, design is a *way,* a method of solving problems and creating what previously didn't exist. Such creativity is a uniquely human trait, not one that's unique to certain humans. Just as social media tears down traditional publication models for a long tail of anyone-as-publisher, modern technology is tearing down the traditional model of elite designer.

If you want to be a designer, it comes down to how good you are at solving certain kinds of problems creatively and who knows about your particular skill. Historically, that might have meant hoping and dreaming that you got famous enough for traditional media to immortalize you and spread your name around the world; now all you have to do is find the right networks and express yourself within them.

Social networking has turned many undervalued savants into respected niche geniuses with enough work to keep them full and happy. The long tail applies to people, too.

Gentry Underwood (@gentry) is director of knowledge sharing at IDEO.

Finding Answers and Expertise

Beyond inspiration and ideation, concept generation requires finding the right expertise within your company to finish baking half-baked concepts. Product managers often have a general sense for what areas they want to focus on or what problems to solve, but they don't know where to begin or how to make progress on an abstract concept.

Traditionally, people have relied on tacit, anecdotal knowledge about who knows what and who used to work where to track down internal expertise. However, this is extremely difficult in organizations that are larger, that are geographically dispersed, or that have high employee turnover—the trend most companies are headed in. Also, the needed expertise often lies across organizational and functional boundaries where tacit knowledge and regular communication links are weakest.

On Facebook and especially LinkedIn, member profiles typically include past employers and roles, projects, and areas of interest and expertise. Using these social networking sites enables product managers to tap not only among their direct connections and coworkers, but also among friends of friends and extended networks.

How does it work? At the most basic level, you can perform a search for people on social networking sites. LinkedIn enables you to search based on name, title, location, and keywords. Facebook lets you search based on location, workplace, and school.

In addition to finding people, you can find answers. LinkedIn Answers is a free service that enables members of LinkedIn to ask and answer professional questions of their networks. For example, people in my network have posted these recent questions:

- *"Attention Flash Developers: What books do you recommend for learning ActionScript? I'm currently using Flash 8."*

- *"Are you aware of company policies that address quota relief for sales reps on maternity leave?"*

- *"Are there any CPC ad marketplaces or aggregators (not tags or feeds)?"*

Community members are motivated to provide answers because it builds up their expertise reputation on LinkedIn, which comes in handy if they are looking for a new job or project (see Figure 7.5). If they know you personally, answering your question also builds their social capital with you. You can ask certain questions privately to select members of your network if the question involves sensitive or confidential information, and you can publicly ask other questions when the more "social" aspect encourages reputation-building responses from the community-at-large.

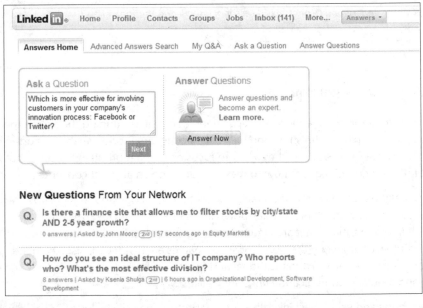

Figure 7.5
LinkedIn Answers enables LinkedIn community members to post professional questions to their networks. People who answer questions can build their reputation by earning points for expertise in the question's category.

In addition to encouraging employees to use public social networking sites to track down external expertise, companies are beginning to invest in internal knowledge and expertise management tools, such as Connectbeam and IBM Lotus Connections.

Connectbeam builds expertise profiles on every employee based on projects they have worked on, articles they have bookmarked, and information they have posted to enterprise wikis, blogs, and other systems. Product managers can use Connectbeam to search for subject matter experts in the company. In addition, Connectbeam proactively recommends colleagues with whom to network based on similar expertise, projects, and interests (see Figure 7.6).

Online social networking is helping product managers be more efficient and effective at locating the internal and external resources needed to make progress on their ideas. In particular, expertise-discovery solutions such as Connectbeam help minimize redundant efforts within companies and enable product managers to leverage past related work done in a particular area of interest.

Figure 7.6
Connectbeam is a popular enterprise social networking solution that specializes in expertise discovery.

Prototyping

Prototyping—that is, the rapid development, testing, and iteration of products before a commercial version is created and released to the mass market—is a critical step in the innovation process. In many ways, prototyping largely consists of concept generation and iteration, which are covered in separate sections in this chapter. Prototyping also requires collaboration and feedback channels.

Collaboration

Successful collaboration is built on trust and mutual commitment. As we discussed in Chapter 3, "How Relationships and Social Capital Are Changing," social networking sites enable individuals to build better rapport and, therefore, can contribute to a more trusting and satisfying team environment. In particular, three aspects of online social networking make it ideally suited for supporting collaborative prototyping efforts: casual communication and interaction modes for establishing rapport; the capability to connect with individuals outside your networks, including different organizations and geographies; and the capability to find functional experts and view the expertise of collaboration team members.

In addition to the informal collaboration that takes place on public social networking sites such as Facebook and LinkedIn, a number of software companies have emerged in the last few years that provide enterprise collaborative productivity tools and intranets. Pioneers in this space include Lotus Connections (as mentioned earlier), Trampoline Systems (more focused on sales collaboration), ThoughtFarmer, Small World Labs, and Socialtext (see Figure 7.7). Most of these offer some combination of the following features to help employees work better together: enterprise wikis, blogs, social networks, employee directories, calendars, tag browsing, feeds, document collaboration, employee learning and training, and messaging.

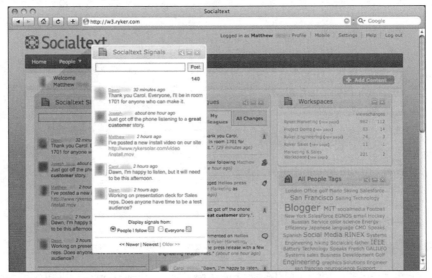

Reprinted by permission

Figure 7.7
Socialtext provides a suite of "enterprise 2.0" internal collaboration tools, including private, Twitter-like microblogging (shown here), social networking, blogs, wikis, and dashboards.

In the following guest expert sidebar, innovation expert Deb Schultz gives us valuable advice on how to facilitate collaborative innovation in the community.

Successful Collaboration on the Social Web

Deborah Schultz

"If you're not failing every now and again, it's a sign you're not doing anything very innovative."

—The "great philosopher" Woody Allen

Innovative ideas often appear when we least expect them. I am often asked, how do you create an environment where innovation can flourish? To catalyze collaboration and innovation, certain elements need to be in place whether you are working within a social network or in an internal enterprise peer group. Most important, the environment must believe that failure is indeed learning. Consider these five tips on how to start collaborating on the social Web:

1.   **Build a foundation of trust**—Without trust, no one wants to collaborate or share ideas—whether online or offline. A community of co-collaboration with customers is very different than an internal employee community because the motivations for participation are very different. Understanding the motivations of members and communicating program benefits, roles, and purpose sets a tone of trust from the outset to drive collaboration.

2.   **Start small, be choiceful**—Collaboration is an art and a skill. If you are new to connecting with customers or employees, start small to build up your "social muscles." Put up a forum and ask for feedback on an existing feature, or proactively email a small group of loyal customers and ask them whether they might be interested in collaborating in the future.

3.   **Iteration trumps perfection**—Don't try to craft a perfect program behind closed doors that you will unleash to the world. Realize that collaboration and innovation are, by nature, iterative and a bit messy and involve give-and-take. You might design a program to do A and then gather feedback from customers who really think that B is much more important. Be open to change and be listening for the gems that pop up when you least expect them.

4.   **Understand the culture and norms of the community you are joining**—If you are connecting to an existing community, spend some time there, be part of the community, and add value. Get to understand the raison d'être of the community before you pounce in as a business or individual. If you join or create a Facebook Page, get to know the people there and the cultural norms that emerge. Only then can you add value to the group.

5.   **Focus on people and relationships**—You are now in an ongoing relationship with a community. When collaborating online, the most important resource you can put in place is the right people to engage with your community. If you build it, they will *not* come. Every successful online community has a human being in there connecting people and ideas and catalyzing action. I call this person the **tummler**—the role is part host, part connector, part rabble-rouser, and part moderator. Tummlers are more than merely community managers (you cannot manage community); they are the social fabric of the space—the people who build trust, forge connections, and weave among the nodes in the network to bring out the best in others.

Deborah Schultz (@debs) is a cofounder and partner, leading innovation and design at Altimeter Group.

Feedback Channels

The act of prototyping also demands continual feedback from internal and external parties. Sometimes it might make sense to solicit feedback from the "masses" through crowdsourced ideation communities, as described in the previous section. But that typically requires significant lead time and is overkill for prototyping. Obtaining frequent, high-quality feedback from an important few stakeholders is often more helpful.

Backboard (recently acquired by Box.net) is a useful social feedback tool that helps people do just this. Backboard enables prototypers to invite feedback and approval on documents, images, and presentations from their LinkedIn, Gmail, and Yahoo! contacts. Reviewers can mark up files to provide feedback using a combination of drawing and text comments (see Figure 7.8). They can also view one another's suggestions and approve different versions of files.

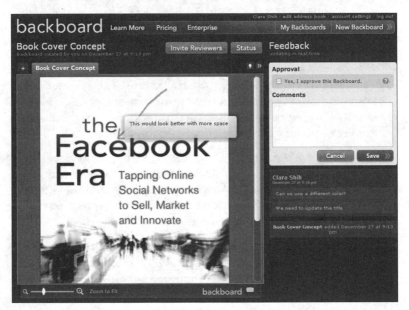

Figure 7.8
Backboard is an innovative social feedback tool for documents, images, and presentations. Product managers and others use Backboard for obtaining frequent, high-quality feedback on concept prototypes. You can try it at http://getbackboard.com.

Commercial Implementation

An important distinction between innovation and invention is that innovation is the successful practical deployment of an idea or invention. That is, innovation is about execution as much as anything else. Having a good idea and prototype is necessary, but not enough.

Execution is a very social process. Successful execution requires both internal buy-in from colleagues and executives, and external buy-in from customers, partners, and others. Online social networking can help.

Winning Internal Buy-In

Before focusing on your product's go-to-market plan, you have to win over the right stakeholders and decision makers internally. Support from colleagues and executives is essential for mobilizing the necessary resources to build the product, secure sufficient levels of marketing investment for the product, and persuade sales reps to talk about the product with customers.

Many of the concepts from Chapter 3 about building social capital are applicable for winning internal buy-in. By cultivating strong and diverse entrepreneurial networks across different departments in your company, you will be better positioned to ask for help, feedback, and support. The flattening effect of online social networks discussed previously means that wherever you are in the organizational hierarchy, executives and decision makers might be more accessible to you than in offline networking situations.

Using communication tools such as Twitter, Yammer, or Socialcast, as described in the earlier section, you can broadcast updates about your project and do some internal marketing about your initiative. People can't support something if they don't know about it or don't understand it. This stage of the innovation cycle when you have a solid prototype is an ideal time to engage people broadly across the organization and solicit additional feedback and support.

Finally, nothing provides more compelling evidence to make the case for a new product than demonstrated customer demand. The crowdsourcing techniques discussed earlier, such as ideation communities on Facebook, can provide reliable customer data to back up your internal pitch. Have customers been receptive to the product concept? Was it their idea to begin with? Has the idea received a lot of votes, comments, and attention? Product managers should collect this feedback, both in aggregate and as a few anecdotal examples, and socialize it within the organization.

In the following guest expert sidebar, Ezra Callahan and Leah Pearlman share how Facebook itself uses Facebook to build a collaborative culture of sharing, brainstorming, and employee bonding.

How Facebook Uses Facebook to Drive Collaboration

Ezra Callahan and Leah Pearlman

Here at Facebook (the company), we use Facebook (the product) in much the same way as our users—perhaps a bit more actively, on average, but not fundamentally different in nature. We upload photos from our vacations. We write notes about our lives. We share the big news of our day.

We congratulate each other on engagements and babies. We support each other through marathons and fundraisers. We friend one another's spouses and roommates. The ubiquity with which we share our lives with one another has several profound impacts on our work environment and the success of the business.

As we connect on a personal level, deeper professional relationships inevitably develop. These personal connections lead to increased patience, cooperation, and empathy—qualities that we believe lead to effective collaboration.

This openness also has a special effect on the relationship between employees and employer: It breeds mutual respect and trust. Employees engage in honest conversations, open feedback, and more collaborative decision making.

Open and efficient communication leads to a lot of idea sharing from diverse perspectives. Facebook (the product) is designed to help popular content—the good ideas—gather support and generate calls to action. Real change results from this process, which is evident in the many ways that Facebook has already had an impact on the world. Facebook (the company) is a microcosm of this very chain of events. Using privacy settings, employees can casually brainstorm new ideas with each other through the site itself. Good ideas gather support, which broadens the distribution among others in the company. Without any formal process, the great ideas reach the relevant development teams with a lot of creative and diverse thought already invested.

Facebook does not fit the mold of what one would usually think of as an "enterprise tool." Yet it proves to be an incredibly powerful means of building energy and loyalty within a company, surfacing great ideas, and promoting an openness that drives collaboration, efficiency, and success.

Ezra Callahan and Leah Pearlman work on internal communications at Facebook.

Winning Over the Market

In previous chapters, we discussed social sales and marketing techniques for winning over customers. This is especially critical for innovative products and services that might not yet have customer trust, proven success, and widespread demand.

The diffusion of innovation theory offers a good way for thinking about how online social networking affects the commercial success of a new product. In his 1962 book *The Diffusion of Innovations,* Everett Rogers describes how innovation spreads through members of a society following an *S*-curve—initially with a few early adopters, followed by the majority, until the innovation becomes mainstream. By facilitating communication across vast networks, social networking sites accelerate the rate of diffusion for a product, as shown in Figure 7.9.

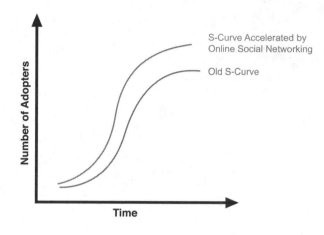

Figure 7.9
Social networking sites accelerate the traditional S-curve of innovation diffusion, enabling more people to adopt new products more quickly.

Diffusion research looks at the factors that might accelerate, increase, or decrease the chances that members of a culture will adopt a new idea or product. According to Rogers, innovation diffusion from an individual's perspective occurs through five stages: knowledge, persuasion, decision, implementation, and confirmation. Online social networking changes each of these stages:

1. **Knowledge or exposure**—To accept an innovation, people first need to know about it. The passive word-of-mouth broadcasts that occur on social networking sites, such as Facebook News Feeds, encourage the diffusion of information through a trusted medium that people have opted into (see Figure 7.10).

Figure 7.10
Product managers can follow Twitter accounts and join Facebook Groups, such as this one that I moderate, to discover content and contacts relating to the product and in peripheral knowledge areas. Twitter followers and Facebook Group members receive updates in their stream.

2. **Persuasion**—Next, individuals must be persuaded about the value and validity of the innovation. Social proof and transitive trust play an important role: Because Person X endorses the innovation and Person Y trusts Person X, Person Y is more likely to become persuaded in favor of the innovation. Customers are more likely to be persuaded of an innovation (or to at least try a new product) if they were involved in its development. Internal corporate stakeholders are more likely to be persuaded to pursue development of a new product if the customer community has voted it up. It's hard to argue with customer data.

3. **Decision**—Individuals then need to make a decision to adopt or reject an innovation. Social networking sites help in a few ways. First, they can help advertisers create a sense of urgency and force a decision with time-sensitive campaigns (introduced in the previous chapter). Displaying a timely offer that is associated with a real-world event with an expiration date might accelerate an individual's decision of whether to accept an innovation. Second, for people who aren't ready to decide, social networking sites can help prolong the decision to give the innovation more chances to be accepted. For example, feed stories—including information and products—linger instead of disappearing right away and are searchable, as shown in Figure 7.11. Finally, ideation tools provide opportunities for customers to provide feedback on what's missing or not quite right so that the company has a second chance to make the innovation better until customers decide to accept the new product.

Figure 7.11
Public voting and commenting, such as on Dell's IdeaStorm community, provides valuable social proof and transitive trust to encourage participation and support.

4. **Implementation**—At this point, individuals must carry through with setting up and actually using the innovation. As we talked about in Chapter 5, social network communities help connect novice adopters with others (both employees and expert customer users) who might be more experienced with the product and be able to offer help and guidance. The encouragement and support from people you know both accelerates implementation and increases the likelihood of success.

5. **Confirmation**—Finally, individuals evaluate the results of an innovation they have chosen to adopt. Here again, it might be useful and more enjoyable to reflect on your experience in the context of a social network community instead of in isolation. Which of your friends also adopted this innovation? What are their thoughts and reactions, and how do they compare with yours? Customer evangelists can publicly sing your product's praises via Twitter or by "liking" your product's Facebook Page.

Continual Iteration

After you've implemented your idea and released the product to market, your ongoing success depends on your capability to continually respond to customer feedback and iterate. This is especially crucial if you have launched a radical new product, you have a radical new take on an existing product, or you are addressing a new market.

Feedback

Similar to the concept-generation stage, it can be highly efficient to crowdsource feedback from social network communities. After all, feedback is just another form of ideation focused specifically on how to improve existing products. As a product manager, feedback might automatically come to you through these forums you have set up. Otherwise, it's a good idea to solicit qualitative feedback by moderating these forums, asking open-ended questions, and even offering real or virtual rewards for participation. if needed.

Companies can also establish systematic feedback channels by using Facebook survey applications or posting links to online surveys on their Facebook Page. Feedback from Twitter and this book's Facebook Page was instrumental in the writing of the second edition.

Case Study: Driving Development of *The Facebook Era,* Second Edition from Feedback on Facebook

When I sat down in January to begin work on this edition of the book, I looked to readers on Facebook and Twitter, in addition to Amazon reviews, for feedback and inspiration. I collected ideas using these methods:

- **Polls**—Polls are a good way to get quick data and decide among a few clearly defined alternatives. When we were trying to decide on the subtitle for this edition, I posted a poll to make it easier for people to weigh in (and then tweeted it to get even more people involved). The next section talks more about polls.

- **Ad test**—To collect more objective evidence beyond the poll, we ran a small ad campaign on the different subtitle options and compared the click-through rate. In our case, the click data confirmed the poll data. This edition's subtitle is the result of the polls and ads.

- **Status updates**—Compared to polls, tweets and Facebook status updates are more free form. As shown in Figure 7.12, I asked a general question to readers, "Any suggestions, special requests, or new direction you want me to take?" and received a variety of responses, many of which I have incorporated into the book. For example, the ideas to include new chapters on small business and customer service, more industry-specific examples, and a discussion of Facebook versus Google all came from open feedback on Facebook and Twitter.

- **Private messages**—During the last year and a half, I've received a number of Facebook messages and Twitter direct messages. I've read them all. Many of you asked for nonprofit and political campaign coverage, which inspired the new chapter in this book.

The Facebook Era, by Clara Shih It's official: I am working on The Facebook Era 2nd Edition! :) Any suggestions, special requests, or new direction you want me to take?
5,918 Impressions · 0.64% Feedback

December 17, 2009 at 7:52am · Comment · Like

👍 Helen Todd, Jeff Conkey, Koichiro Tsukamoto and 17 others like this.

Scott Newman I think the first edition really laid the ground work for those new to the game and I think that part should remain. However, I also think some industry specific examples would really help so people can see exactly how others are implementing the classic and newest aspects of Facebook into their business plan.

Shawn King Since alot of attention has been given to existing companies converting their marketing efforts to social media, why not discuss cases of startups using FB to create a brand from the ground up and the results of thereof.
December 17, 2009 at 2:31pm · Delete · Report

Todd Chaffee Shawn, I second that. Would love to see companies that are using ONLY SM for marketing. Much like the Internet itself created web-only companies like Amazon and Google.
December 18, 2009 at 1:40pm · Delete · Report

Helen Todd I'm a big fan of The Facebook Era and can't wait to see the 2nd edition! There's definitely more that can be delved into from the standpoint of using Facebook for marketing purposes whether for a small business or a big corporation. Now there are many more case studies since your first edition to draw on. I'd also touch on Facebook Connect and Mobile and the implications of the popularity of these two aspects of the platform. Some other suggestions to include:

-Facebook vs. Google for online dominance (long are the days of Myspace being a serious competitor)
-A closer look at Insights for fan pages and what companies, non-profits and individuals can learn from them
-Real-time search (including Twitter) and the implications for SEO and businesses wanting to be found online...

See More
January 11 at 12:30pm · Delete · Report

Figure 7.12
I relied heavily on Facebook Page status messages to quickly post questions and get answers on what I should change and add to this edition of the book. A big thank-you to everyone who weighed in.

Polls

Polls are an easy way to conduct simple market research or get customer feedback on specific product decisions. When products are already available, product managers often find themselves faced with decisions of whether to offer slight variations on the product, such as offering it in different colors, adding or subtracting functionality to create premium and basic versions, and providing a children's version. These kinds of "either/or" and multiple-choice questions are perfect for polls. Almost every online social network enables community managers to incorporate polls (see Figure 7.13).

The Facebook Era, by Clara Shih Social Networking Poll:

Which social network has been most effective for your marketing efforts?
1.: Facebook
2.: Twitter
3.: LinkedIn
4.: I have not seen much value yet

5,727 Impressions · 0.09% Feedback

February 23 at 8:31am via Poll Daddy Polls · Comment · Like · Vote In This Poll

2 people like this.

Stephanie ____ Clara is amazing. She is my FB buddy. Her book is awesome.
February 23 at 8:50am · Delete · Report

The Facebook Era, by Clara Shih Thanks, Stephanie! The readers are pretty awesome too :-)
February 23 at 3:41pm · Delete

JunE ____ Facebook is most effective when I reach out 2 ppl within my network.
February 23 at 4:18pm · Delete · Report

Write a comment...

Figure 7.13
Polls such as this one posted to the book's Facebook Page can be a good way of periodically engaging the community about questions and trends that everyone might find interesting.

Transforming Customers into Partners

Online social networking tools can help product managers transform customers into true participant–partners. In the Facebook Era, companies and customers are able to achieve a new level of conversation that is bidirectional and extends across product development, sales, marketing, and customer support. Thanks to the social graph, not only are customers encouraged to engage with your company, but they are also motivated to engage with their friends and colleagues about your company—contributing to your sales, marketing, support, and product innovation efforts.

<<< TAKEAWAYS

✓ Each of the four stages of innovation (concept generation, prototyping, commercial implementation, and continual iteration) is a highly social process involving multiple actors.

✓ A combination of internal (such as those shared on sites like Yammer) and external memes (such as those shared on sites like Twitter) is important to fully stimulate the creative process.

✓ Increasingly, companies are crowdsourcing the ideation process to communities of customers and communities of employees.

✓ Internal collaboration and networking tools such as Connectbeam, Lotus Connections, and Salesforce Chatter enable employees to locate internal expertise.

✓ Collaboration tools are not only good for ideation, but they are also very valuable in generating awareness and support for new products, especially if they originated from community ideas.

>>> TIPS and TO DO's

❑ Build a culture of trust and collaboration by establishing clear ground rules and goals, and then recognizing and rewarding participants.

❑ Encourage product managers and R&D staff to sign up for Yammer and Twitter to monitor and be inspired by conversations, sentiments, and ideas in their field of work.

❑ Consider building a crowdsourced ideation community to track market demand for proposed features and generate new ideas.

❑ Use contests and prizes as incentives for community members to contribute high-quality ideas.

❑ Train remote innovation teams on better communication skills so they can express themselves clearly and break down problems into specific pieces for different individuals to solve.

"Friends of our employees are more likely to have the same characteristics our employees do—hard-working, smart—so they've gone through a natural filter."
—Ed Scanlan, chief executive of Total Attorneys

Recruiting in the Facebook Era

It's hard to find good people, and it's only getting harder with time. Even with the recent periods of economic recession, people are complaining about "the war for talent" and "looming talent shortages" for highly skilled labor. To make things even more challenging for employers, people today are switching jobs more often, creating sometimes very sudden staffing gaps that can disrupt company growth and productivity—after all, backfilling key positions can take time.

As the competition for talent grows, recruiting is becoming an even more vital function, and recruiters who understand how to tap the social Web will be at a disproportionate advantage. Most people find jobs through someone they know and accept job offers from people they trust. Recruiting through social networking sites takes advantage of these facts and makes matching job opportunities and candidates a faster and more efficient process.

I have experienced this firsthand at Hearsay Labs while trying to find great software engineers and other talent. I never imagined, that as the CEO of a company, more than 90% of my time would be dedicated to recruiting. But that's exactly what happened as soon as we raised venture capital and got our first set of customer orders. Suddenly, it came time to deliver, and we needed to hire people fast without compromising quality. Our personal and extended networks on LinkedIn and Facebook were invaluable in helping us get through this period and continue to grow. The concepts, tips, and tactics in this chapter come from my own experience and from interviewing dozens of in-house recruiters, free-agent recruiters, and hiring managers from companies large and small.

In many ways, recruiting resembles a sales cycle. The recruiter is "selling" the employer, role, and job opportunity. She has to generate leads and pipeline, and manage candidates through a qualification process that hopefully results in some percentage of successful hires. As in sales, recruiters and hiring managers need to take a longer-term view that even if a candidate is not ready to close today, it is worthwhile to maintain that relationship for tomorrow or for referrals.

But compared with selling a product or service, people on the receiving end of a recruiting call are generally more open to learning about job opportunities. Because of the fixed supply of good jobs, the ratio of jobs to job seekers is typically low. In contrast, product advertisements and sales pitches greatly outnumber interested buyers. Recruiting is also more personal. Job decisions can determine people's livelihoods and how they spend most of their waking hours. They can be life-changing. This means that interpersonal rapport between recruiters and candidates is even more important than in sales, and that online social networking tools can potentially be even more transformational in human resources.

This chapter explains how recruiting and human resources can use social networking sites. First, let's compare LinkedIn, Facebook, and Twitter in terms of recruiting.

Which Social Network Is Best for Recruiting?

Should you use Facebook, Twitter, LinkedIn, or business-oriented social networking sites such as Doostang or Ryze to recruit new employees? A recent survey of recruiters across the United States revealed that 80% of employers are already using or planning to use social networking sites to identify and attract job candidates this year. Depending on your industry, what types of jobs you recruit for, and where you are in the recruiting cycle, one or a combination of these online social networks might make the most sense. The default rule of thumb for many recruiters is to focus on LinkedIn only, but you might miss out on a big opportunity to reach people who either aren't on LinkedIn or aren't as open to communications on LinkedIn. This largely depends on your audience demographics and preferences. Great recruiters go where the candidates are—and, increasingly, this is not only on LinkedIn, but also on Facebook and Twitter.

LinkedIn

Used by more than 95% of white-collar employers in the United States, LinkedIn is by far the most established professionally oriented network and has already become a standard recruiting tool in many industries. Launched in 2003, LinkedIn now has more than 50 million business professionals among its membership across 150 different industries. Member profiles are akin to a living version of a résumé, which is ideal for recruiters seeking up-to-date information about a candidate. LinkedIn is good for posting jobs, requesting candidate referrals, and making contact when it's explicitly related to a concrete business objective.

The biggest challenge of using LinkedIn is that it can feel impersonal and undifferentiated, especially for highly sought-after candidates who are contacted often by recruiters. To help improve chances of getting a reply, some recruiters use LinkedIn to generate a list of candidates and then use other means—including Facebook, phone, and email—to actually reach out to the candidates.

Facebook

Used by 59% of U.S. white-collar employers, Facebook is emerging as a popular recruiting tool because of its extensive reach to 500 million people around the world—more than an order of magnitude larger than either LinkedIn or Twitter. Certainly, for any positions geared toward college grads, MBAs, or other Gen-Y hires, Facebook is a must. Recruiters also like Facebook (generally used in addition to LinkedIn) because it feels more personal and can more effectively build relationships with candidates over time, whereas LinkedIn or Twitter can feel more transactional.

Hundreds of recruiting applications have been built for Facebook, but most have fewer than several hundred monthly active users. The problem is that these applications are hard to find among the jumble in the Facebook Application Directory. Candidates must install the applications, which means recruiters typically will not reach passive candidates. The most popular application is Jobvite's Work With Us, which has approximately 5,000 monthly active users (see Figure 8.1) and uses a different approach. Instead of targeting candidates directly, Work With Us is meant for existing employees at a company to help refer candidates from their networks of Facebook friends, presumably motivated by referral bonuses, social goodwill, and enjoyment from working with friends.

Figure 8.1
Recruiting site Jobvite has one of the more popular job applications on Facebook. Work With Us is available only to employees of companies using Jobvite, and it enables those employees to easily refer their Facebook friends for job openings at their company.

The more common way to recruit on Facebook is to use the same techniques on how to market and sell products that we talked about in Chapters 4, "Sales in the Facebook Era," and 6, "Marketing in the Facebook Era," to market and sell job opportunities. You can apply these marketing and sales techniques to recruiting on Facebook:

- **Hypertargeting**—Recruiters can target job advertisements based on candidates' profile information, such as location, current and past roles and employers, and interests.

- **Social word-of-mouth**—HR can create a Facebook Group community for employees to discuss topics (nothing confidential, of course). The group appears on employee profiles, and any new activity appears on their News Feed and is visible to everyone in their networks.

- **Transitive trust**—When recruiters are trying to reach a candidate, they can improve their chances of a positive response by going through a mutual friend. Because the candidate trusts the friend, and the mutual friend trusts the recruiter, the candidate is more likely to transitively trust the recruiter and at least be willing to hear about the job opportunity.

- **Relationship building**—People might not be ready to switch jobs when a recruiter first reaches out. Facebook can be a low-cost but effective way to stay in touch with candidates until they are ready to move from their current employment.

For example, hypertargeting is ideal for recruiters who are generally seeking a very specific set of skills and work experience, education, and location. Starbucks Coffee Company is one employer that uses Facebook ads to recruit new employees (see Figure 8.2).

Figure 8.2
Starbucks used this recruiting ad on Facebook. An increasing number of employers are using hypertargeted Facebook ads to source job candidates based on profile criteria such as age, college, work experience, and location.

Twitter

Approximately 42% of U.S. recruiters surveyed have tried using Twitter for recruiting, with mixed but mostly positive results. Twitter is especially popular for finding contractors, generally by tweeting or searching on hashtags that describe the role or skills you are seeking—for example, "Looking for a good #web #designer in #Chicago."

Twitter can also be very effective at finding thought leaders in a given space who might be good candidates for your marketing and communications team, particularly if you are seeking a social media manager or community manager. Because most Twitter users have public profiles, you can easily see who is tweeting about which subjects most often, who is getting retweeted most often, and the full history of any user's tweets. If someone is good about tweeting regularly, has interesting things to say, and has a strong following, that person could likely do the same on behalf of your company. Hiring managers for these kinds of positions might source candidates from more traditional routes, but they often check Twitter, Facebook, and blog accounts as part of candidate due diligence in the hiring decision process.

Depending on the audience you are seeking, it might make sense to invest in a combination of these networks (see Table 8.1). In the following sections, we talk about candidate sourcing, reference checks, branding and reputation, and how recruiters can keep in touch with a greater number of candidates.

Table 8.1 Advantages of Different Social Networks for Recruiting

LinkedIn	Facebook	Twitter
Large and concentrated audience of highly skilled and educated business professionals	Feeling of personal connection with photos and friends	Capability to publicly broadcast opportunities to a large number of users
Rich tools for searching on key candidate criteria and reaching out (paid version)	Capability to reach almost any high school or college student	Capability to generate especially effective results for temp or contract workers, such as design talent
Up-to-date contact and experience information on passive candidates	Significantly greater reach than either LinkedIn or Twitter	Capability to view public stream of tweets by candidates as one gauge of their style and favorite topics
Capability to read public testimonials for candidates and view mutual friends to ask for references from sources you trust	Capability to search for prospective candidates by location, school, and workplace	Capability to easily search by topics and hashtags to identify the most vocal thought leaders as potential job candidates

Sourcing and Screening Candidates

Hundreds of millions of the best-educated, most qualified job candidates have joined social networking sites such as LinkedIn and Facebook. Increasingly, smart recruiters are also joining these sites to connect with these individuals and cultivate lasting relationships.

Why do social networking sites attract top candidates? One reason could be that high-achieving professionals become successful because they are savvier with technology and are better networkers. These individuals are more likely to periodically reevaluate their careers and seek out, or at least be open to, new opportunities for career advancement.

In the past, a big problem with job boards was outdated résumés, sometimes making it hard to even get in touch with candidates if they moved, got a new phone number, and so on. Social network profiles have the benefit of being self-maintained, living documents. Social pressure motivates you to keep your profile up-to-date. Social network profiles go even further than traditional résumés to make the recruiter's job easier, such as showing who you know in common, testimonials from colleagues, and profile search. Recruiters and hiring managers have access to more information than ever before to find and then qualify candidates earlier in the cycle, resulting in less wasted time if the employer and the candidate aren't a good fit.

Two kinds of candidates exist: Active candidates are proactively seeking a job, and passive candidates are usually currently employed but still might be open to hearing about new opportunities.

Active Candidates

Increasingly, people who are actively seeking jobs are looking to LinkedIn and Facebook. A typical scenario is for people to discover job openings from company Web sites, alumni communications, or even Craigslist, and then to use social networking sites to see how people they know could connect them to these jobs. The other scenario involves people searching directly on LinkedIn for job openings.

We all know that the easiest way to get hired is through someone we know who already works at the company. The job search is a big investment that requires a lot of time; today's job seeker doesn't want to waste time on long-shot job opportunities. Applying for jobs within her social network is the best way to maximize the odds of getting hired while having greater visibility and influence in the process.

For recruiters, this means two things. First, list your jobs listed on social networks. By filling out a few basic fields, recruiters can post jobs to their networks for free on Doostang, and for a small fee on LinkedIn. Ask hiring managers and other employees to help spread the word about these jobs to their networks. Second, use the information and public references about candidates on their social network profiles as an initial screening step.

Passive Candidates

Social networking sites are great for finding active candidates, but they are even more powerful for discovering passive candidates. Many of your greatest potential hires might not be actively looking because they are happily employed. These passive job candidates don't post their résumés on Monster or CareerBuilder, but they do sign up for LinkedIn and Facebook. Why? Because their friends and colleagues are there.

Social networking sites have drastically expanded the talent pool we can recruit from by including passive candidates who previously were hard to reach. Instead of waiting for candidates to come to you, you can proactively reach out to your ideal candidate profile. Using advanced profile search, recruiters can specify very precise criteria based on information such as past employers, roles, projects, education level, location, and relevant skills and experience to find potential candidates in their network.

LinkedIn Recruiter, shown in Figure 8.3, is a premium service that enables paying subscribers to search by title, company, or keywords across all LinkedIn members, not just people in their network. It also includes collaboration tools to enable recruiting teams to group candidates into folders and tag them with comments.

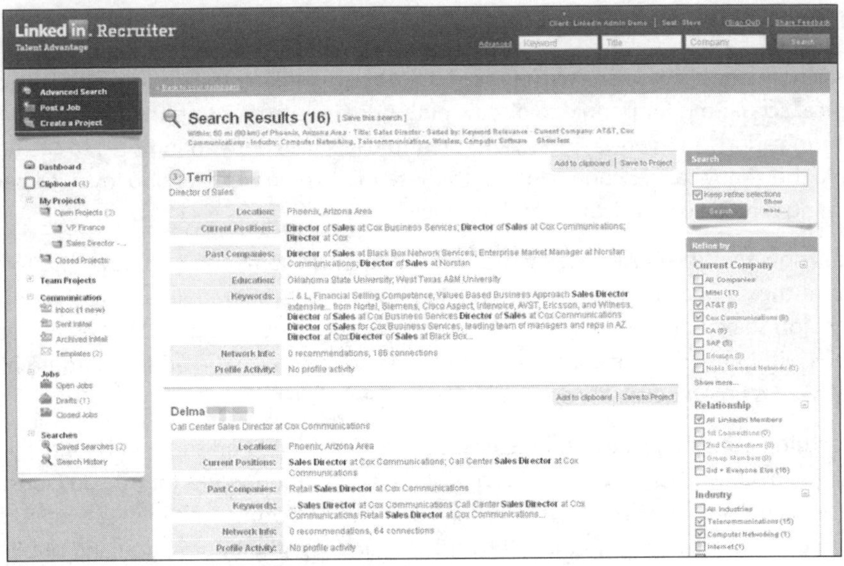

Figure 8.3
LinkedIn Recruiter is a premium corporate recruiting service that helps recruiters identify, contact, and manage passive job candidates.

College and MBA Recruiting on Facebook

Just about every high school, college, and graduate student today is on Facebook. It's the best way to reach that demographic. What remains to be seen is whether this younger generation will also join LinkedIn as they reach post-graduation working age.

Recruiters are using Facebook more often to provide information about prospective employers, promote campus information sessions, connect with student groups, stay in touch with interns, and even perform due diligence on prospective applicants. Many college recruiting teams are setting up Facebook Pages instead of Web sites to provide company information and foster communities of recruiters, employee alumni (current company employees who are alumni of the school), interns, and prospective applicants. (See Chapter 11, "How To: Engage Customers with Facebook Pages and Twitter," for how to set up and manage a Facebook Page.)

Recruiters use Facebook Events to promote information sessions, campus talks, and other recruiting events. Events can be associated with Facebook Pages, enabling people who have "liked" a Page to receive updates when event details change or new events are posted. For example, P&G created a Facebook Page for its recruiting efforts at the University of Dayton (see Figure 8.4). The page describes job opportunities at the company, invites students to attend an upcoming "Meet and Greet P&G Engineers" session, and introduces a current P&G employee who recently graduated from the university, encouraging interested students to get in touch.

Figure 8.4
Facebook Page for P&G recruiting at the University of Dayton

Similar to the word-of-mouth marketing scenarios described in Chapter 6, "Marketing in the Facebook Era," enthusiasm and awareness about employers spread across friend groups on Facebook. When prospective applicants look at your Facebook Event page, they can see which of their friends are also planning to attend. When students RSVP for a recruiting event or "like" your recruiting page, their friends are notified via News Feed. As mentioned previously, employers can amplify the effects by sponsoring social ad campaigns hypertargeted to the right campus and majors. Recruiters can time in-person events and ad campaigns with the recruiting season or school calendar, such as offering a study break during midterm exam week or placing an ad for résumés submissions a few weeks before on-campus interviews.

Another effective, low-cost strategy that college recruiters use is engaging with campus student groups. Most student organizations have a Facebook Group that lists their officers. Recruiters or employee alumni can send a Facebook message to these individuals to say hello and perhaps offer to sponsor or speak at an upcoming meeting. Afterward, the company can follow up with group members by posting the slides presented, related links, and speaker contact information to the group.

Many employers offer summer internships or co-op programs to provide students with an opportunity to work at the company before graduation. Facebook is a great way for recruiters and hiring managers to stay in touch after the program ends. By keeping these students engaged with the company, recruiters not only increase the chances they will join full-time after graduation, but they can also treat students as campus ambassadors to find additional candidates. The second-to-last section in this chapter goes into greater detail on using social networks to keep in touch.

Finally, recruiters and hiring managers are using Facebook, MySpace, and Twitter to check out prospective applicants. Is the candidate's profile consistent with how she has presented herself in interviews and on her résumés? Does this person seem friendly and well balanced, or is her profile blatantly inappropriate and unprofessional? Obviously, recruiters need to balance privacy and due diligence. The last section of this chapter gives advice to candidates on what information to share, when to restrict profile access, and how to manage social network identities.

Referrals from Extended Networks

As we discussed in Chapter 4, social networking sites enable people to reach far beyond just their immediate networks. For recruiters, the capability to find and contact candidates among friends of friends and greater extended networks dramatically expands the pool of trusted talent.

LinkedIn, in particular, lets recruiters reach *the extended networks of their extended networks*. Instead of asking only *N* people in their extended network whether they would be interested in a job, recruiters can ask those *N* people if they *know* anyone who might be interested in the job (see Figure 8.5), potentially reaching *exponentially more* people. Recruiters can further expand their network reach by joining a LION network, which we introduced in Chapter 4 in the context of sales prospecting.

Figure 8.5
This request for referral was sent to me from a LinkedIn connection. LinkedIn enables recruiters to tap extended networks not only for interested applicants, but also for referrals of interested applicants. This has a multiplying effect on how many people within the trusted network they are able to reach.

Jobvite, the company mentioned earlier in this chapter that developed a popular Facebook recruiting application, has a full solution that helps companies create and distribute job posts via their employees on Facebook, LinkedIn, and Twitter.

Because of the high costs of recruiting and the near-universal tendency for many of the best candidates to come through existing employees, many employers offer some form of referral. Motivated by the referral bonus or wanting to help the company find more good people, employees can access Jobvite from either the Web site or the Facebook application mentioned earlier, kicking off a matching process that compares the company's job listings to the profiles of the employees' Facebook friends. As we talked about earlier, most social network profiles contain relevant information for recruiting, such as interests, location, former employers, associations, role, and title. The Work With Us application recommends the matches found between job postings and potential candidates for referral to the employee. The employee can then decide whether to actually submit the referral.

Say an employee, John, refers his friend Kelly for a business development role at his company. The next time Kelly logs in to Facebook, she will receive a notification that John referred her for this position. Behind the scenes, John's company can track where candidate referrals come from, and if Kelly eventually gets hired, it can ensure that John receives his referral bonus.

LinkedIn recently added a similar feature that matches profile information to job titles and descriptions (see Figure 8.6). LinkedIn's feature goes even further in suggesting not only first-degree connections, but also friends of friends.

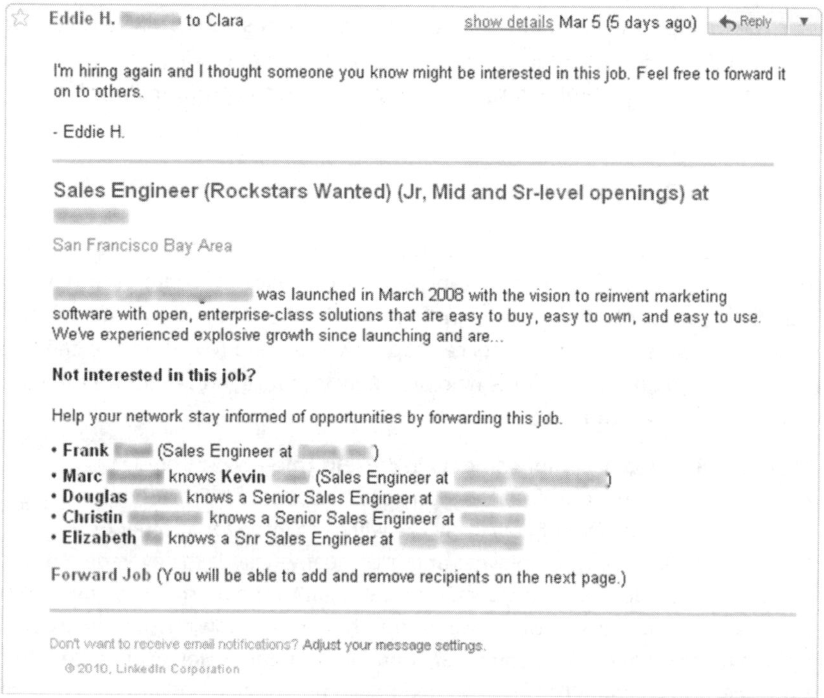

Figure 8.6

A popular feature of LinkedIn is the capability to email job opportunities to your network. LinkedIn enhanced this feature by automatically suggesting to recipients who in their network and extended networks might be a good fit for a job opportunity based on profile keyword matching to the job description.

Targeting Specialized Networks

Social network communities and affinity groups are another great source of talent, particularly if you are looking for candidates of a certain background. Hundreds of thousands of Facebook groups and LinkedIn groups exist, based on company employees and alumni, roles, industries, conferences, and trade associations—for example, the Northeast Black Law Students Association group on Facebook, the Healthcare Management Engineers group on LinkedIn, and the Women Business Owners group on Ryze.

Sometimes membership and access to these groups are restricted, but they are generally relaxed. Several recruiters I spoke to for this chapter told me that they have never been denied membership in one of these groups when they tried to join. After joining, recruiters can post messages, view members, and reach out to specific group members.

For example, my friend is on the diversity recruiting team at a large engineering company in Ohio. One of the first places he goes to find candidates is the Society of Women Engineers group on LinkedIn. He has brought dozens of welcome job opportunities to the group and successfully hired four group members last year. Every few months, he checks on the group to see who has joined and browses member profiles to look for potential candidates. His advice is to take extra precaution to respect the group's posting policies and to try to send highly targeted and personalized communication.

Reading Between the Lines

Aside from obviously important information that recruiters usually look at—such as experience, education, and current title and employer—a lot of subtle information on social network profiles can be very insightful and valuable. By reading between the lines and "doing their homework," recruiters can tap powerful data to determine candidate fit, opportunistically go after candidates who are likely unhappy, and increase the odds of closing the deal with a candidate:

- **Tenure and stated accomplishments in current role**—Most people specify job tenure on their social network profiles. How long a candidate has been at her current employer is an important indicator of how likely she will be to leave for another opportunity. Based on profiles of past employees at this company, what is the average tenure of an employee? How does this person's tenure compare? If the person is relatively new (there less than one year), with few accomplishments to show, the timing probably isn't right to try to recruit this person for an immediate opening. However, you might find someone whose tenure has far exceeded the company average, with a lot of accomplishments but perhaps not a proportional number of promotions. This person might be more open to persuasion that another opportunity could be better for career advancement.

- **Organizational structure**—As most recruiters know, titles can vary significantly among companies. Just as sales reps need to understand their prospective buyer organizations, recruiters can benefit from understanding the organizational structure of the existing employers of people they are trying to recruit. As we talked about in Chapter 4, poking around on social networking sites can yield valuable information about which departments have the best people and what titles really mean.

- **Mass exodus from a particular company**—Occasionally, companies make poor decisions. Some go out of business, and others flounder and stagnate. Their employees are the people closest to this information, and sometimes recruiters see a voluntary or involuntary exodus of people from a particular company. In LinkedIn, you can see this activity in the Network Updates section of the home page. In Facebook, this activity is broadcast via the News Feed feature. For example, when I logged in to Facebook last month, I saw three updates from my network saying "so and so has left her job at Company X." If I were a recruiter, now might be a good time to tap Company X's employee pool.

- **Commonality with you**—As in sales, shared personal experience between the candidate and recruiter, such as the same hometown or alma mater, can help establish personal rapport. Especially if you are an independent headhunter not affiliated with a particular employer, this rapport can help differentiate you as someone the candidate remembers, likes, and trusts with finding career opportunities.

- **Commonality with company employees**—It's common practice when recruiters are trying to close a candidate on a job offer to introduce that person to employees and executives at the company. These individuals can offer different perspectives on the employer and help persuade the candidate. Recruiters can take this to the next level by looking for commonalities between company employees and the candidate, to strategically pair up people and maximize those conversations. We can repurpose a prior example from Chapter 4 to illustrate this point. Perhaps the candidate you are trying to win over is originally from Texas and graduated from Rice University. Among the executives in your company, one is also a Texan and attended Rice. Instead of a random employee, this employee is likely one of the people you want on the phone helping to close this candidate. Deciding whether to accept a job is a very personal and emotional decision, and tapping shared experiences—even if they are small coincidences—can make a big difference.

Candidate References

The shortcoming of traditional candidate references is that the candidate provides them, and any rational candidate will disclose only favorable references. As a result, recruiters might be getting a biased view of the candidate. The openness and transparency of the social Web solves this information asymmetry problem; by publicly exposing candidates' work history and which individuals candidates are linked to, social networking sites create strong incentives for candidates to tell the truth on their profile (because everyone can see what they write) and provide recruiters with an easier way of finding independent references who might be more objective than candidate-supplied references.

More Objective References

The online social graph can make reference checking more independent and objective. Instead of asking the candidate to supply references, a recruiter can go to LinkedIn and find them. The recruiter might want to browse the candidate's LinkedIn contacts, including mutual connections, or search for profiles of people who have overlapping tenure with the candidate at a previous employer.

For example, when we are considering candidates at Hearsay Labs, we always do a search on LinkedIn and Twitter to find mutual contacts. We call the mutual contact (or contacts) whom we trust will give us the most objective view of the candidates.

More Accountable Information

Another type of candidate reference comes in the form of professional testimonials on social networking sites. For example, LinkedIn members can publicly recommend another member. The testimonial becomes part of the member's profile (see Figure 8.7).

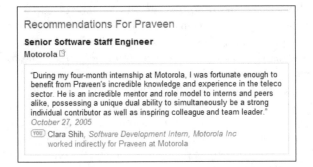

Figure 8.7
Profile recommendations on LinkedIn tend to carry more weight because they are public testimonials that other members can scrutinize.

LinkedIn recommendations are public and last forever unless the members remove them from their profile. Because it's a public and permanent record, people tend to think twice before providing an endorsement that they'll be accountable for. Providing a testimonial on a social networking site is a much higher commitment than a reference phone call that is private and transient.

The social Web introduces a new level of transparency and accountability to these endorsements that private reference checks in the past might not have supplied. In addition to LinkedIn endorsements, the Facebook application Testimonials offers a similar professional testimonial capability.

Employer and Recruiter Reputation

Online social networking is powerful because it's a two-way street. Not only can recruiters and hiring managers perform due diligence on candidates, but candidates can also research the hiring manager and other employees, see who they might know who works there, and reach out to learn more. In the competitive landscape for top talent, companies can use social networking to brand themselves as desirable employers and recruiters can use social networking to establish credibility.

Marketing Your Company as a Desirable Employer

With employees switching jobs more often, it's more important than ever for companies to establish their brand as a desirable employer. As we described in the earlier section on college recruiting, some companies are using Facebook Pages and hypertargeted ads to achieve this objective.

Employee testimonials can be another important resource for providing social proof that the company provides a fun, diverse, stimulating work environment. Some companies have seen great results from asking select employees to blog about their experience working there. Others encourage employees to be engaged in recruiting communities and make themselves available to share their experiences or answer questions. Many of the techniques we covered in Chapter 6 for marketing products also apply to marketing your company as an employer.

Establishing Your Credibility as a Recruiter

Especially for independent recruiters or head-hunting firms not affiliated with one particular employer, public recommendations on LinkedIn from successfully placed candidates are a great way to highlight your track record and establish credibility.

In addition to public testimonials, recruiters can use online social networks to see if they and the candidates have any mutual contacts. As in the sales example, the recruiter could ask these mutual contacts to provide references for both the candidate and the recruiter.

Transitive trust happens at two levels for job candidates:

1. **Trust in the employer**—Friend X works for Employer Y. Candidate Z trusts and respects Friend X, so Candidate Z is more likely to trust that Employer Y is good. Otherwise, his friend would not be working there.

2. **Trust in the recruiter**—Friend X went through Recruiter M and landed a good job that she is very happy with. Candidate Z trusts Friend X and sees that she is happy, so he is more likely to believe that Recruiter M is qualified.

Because finding a job is so personal and emotional, transitive trust plays an even bigger role in recruiting than in sales. In most cases, no single job is "perfect" or "best," and an inherent level of uncertainty surrounds any opportunity. Until the candidate actually starts working there, she won't have full information about what her experience will really be like. At a certain point, she needs to make a "leap-of-faith" decision based on trust that this is the right job. Employee references, especially from friends the candidate knows and respects, provide the best information for mitigating the uncertainty.

Keeping in Touch

Despite their greatest efforts, occasionally even the best recruiters aren't able to close a candidate. The timing isn't right, the candidate decided to go with another opportunity, a personal emergency is preventing the candidate from relocating—multiple reasons could exist. Before social networking sites, it was easy to lose touch with candidates— even those with whom recruiters invested months and even years.

As we first talked about in Chapter 3, "How Relationships and Social Capital Are Changing," and then explored further in the context of sales in Chapter 4, one of the most valuable aspects of online social networking is the capability to maintain more weak ties. For recruiters, this means being able to keep in touch with candidates regardless of whether they were successfully placed.

Recruiters can then revisit those candidates later when new opportunities emerge. Recruiters can also further capitalize on those relationships by tapping those candidates' friend networks for additional talent.

Why would candidates want to keep in touch? As we talked about at the beginning of this chapter, most people view recruiting as more mutually beneficial than sales calls. They want to keep their options open in case something happens with their current job or something better comes along. Maintaining relationships with recruiters, especially low-effort weak ties, buys them privileged access to new career opportunities in the future. So more often than not, assuming that the working relationship was positive, we see candidates accept LinkedIn invitations and Facebook friend requests from their recruiters.

Making the Most of Successful Placements

A successful candidate job placement is just the beginning of a relationship. Candidates who have been successfully placed feel the most indebted and grateful. These individuals can become a recruiter's greatest allies and advocates. Good recruiters depend on trust and rapport from past placements for future placements, introductions, and referrals to other candidates. They might even get employment and contracting opportunities to recruit at the company who hired the candidate.

One recruiter I interviewed who specializes in placing industrial designers said that because of the high turnover in her industry, nearly half of her placements have been repeat placements. During the last decade, she has built up a network of artists and

designers who look to her every time they are ready to pursue a new full-time or contractor opportunity.

Keeping Lines of Communication Open with Nonplacements

Nonplacements can be equally important for a recruiter to stay connected to and continually grow her network. The capability to easily keep in touch on Facebook and LinkedIn
means that recruiters can take a longer-term view on candidates and not feel as if they
have wasted any time, even if things don't work out the first time around.

According to the same design-industry recruiter, she views every rejection as an opportunity to place the candidate in the future and ask for referrals. Many candidates feel a
slight sense of guilt when they turn down an offer and are eager to help by referring
other candidates. Usually the designers with whom she works know a large number of
other designers socially or from school or work.

The following case study profiles another recruiter, Joe, who uses LinkedIn and Facebook
to cultivate long-term relationships with younger Gen-Y candidates. (Incidentally, I found
and contacted Joe on LinkedIn.)

Financial Services Recruiting in Chicago

Joe is one of the top financial services recruiters in Chicago. During the last five
years, Joe and his staff have helped place hundreds of recent MBAs and banking
analysts with two to three years of experience into associate-level roles in banking,
real estate, private equity, and venture capital. As a free agent, Joe's success
depends on his capability to network with both employers and candidates. Joe
separates his candidate network into three categories: candidates he has successfully placed, candidates he will successfully place in the future, and people he has
just met.

1. **Successful placements**—Joe maintains close relationships with his top
   placements because they often become repeat job candidates, and eventually even clients who employ his recruiting services. With or without online
   social networks, Joe invests heavily in these relationships, checking in at least
   once a month and catching up during lunch or dinner once a quarter.
   Especially in working with candidates who are mostly in their mid- or late
   twenties, Joe can use casual interaction mechanisms on Facebook to be
   more playful and make these relationships feel less businesslike. He sends
   virtual Facebook gifts for birthdays and other milestones. Joe pokes, bites
   (with the Zombies application), and shares photos of his newborn son with
   his top recruits. Far from replacing quality face-to-face interactions, Facebook
   enriches Joe's relationships with this top-tier network with more casual but
   also more frequent and personal interaction.

continues…

2. **Candidates he is still working to place**—Generally, Joe's relationships with "candidates in progress" tend to remain more professional. Most communication occurs through more traditional means, such as phone or email. Joe prefers to prove his capability as a competent recruiter before trying to establish more personal relationships with people. However, if a candidate drops out of the process because another opportunity emerges that was not sourced through Joe, he adds the candidate to his LinkedIn and Facebook networks to maintain the relationship. Joe benefits from having instant access to the individual's social network to find additional talent, and potentially working to place this individual in the future.

3. **People he has just met**—For new candidates that Joe has just met or interacted with only once or twice, chance and timing (a combination of the candidate's immediate availability and Joe's pipeline) used to determine whether he made an effort to stay in touch. With online social networking, the cost of establishing the connection is so low that there's almost no downside to doing so. Joe might or might not ultimately end up working with a particular candidate, but with each connection, he receives a free option—but not obligation—to reach out in the future.

In every case, online social networking has enriched the reach and perpetual value of Joe's network. Perhaps it's the secret to his success.

Alumni Networks

Company alumni are another powerful but often overlooked source of talent and new business opportunity. No matter how great the working relationship is between employer and employee, people eventually move on. It's disappointing for employers, but it can also be seen as an opportunity.

Despite choosing to move on, most corporate alumni view former employers in a positive light. After all, they did choose to work at the company for some period of time. Company recruiters can often rely on these alumni just as they might rely on current employees for referrals and access to their LinkedIn or Facebook contacts. With such heavy competition in the market for top talent, companies should not overlook the very people they invested in so heavily and who likely still feel loyal to their former employer.

In addition, retirees are proving to be an unexpected, indispensable source of talent for many American employers. The rising wave of baby boomer retirements has left some employers suddenly short-staffed, particularly in areas requiring deep domain knowledge where newer hires aren't as able to contribute because of their lack of experience. As the following case study shows, some companies, such as Dow Chemical, are using online social networking to reengage retirees to help fill the gap.

In addition to the recruiting angle, company alumni are a great source of new business opportunities, such as forming potential partnerships and generating leads for prospective customers. Alumni know their former employer's product or service better than anyone else and are likely to be an advocate in their new role. Consulting firms such as McKinsey & Company know this and are providing updates on where alumni end up and actively engaging them in everything from conference speaking engagements to recruiting events.

My Dow Network

To address sudden workforce gaps from a wave of retiring boomers, Midland, Michigan–based Dow Chemical Company turned to online social networking. Using corporate social networking software from SelectMinds, Dow created My Dow Network, an online community for Dow alumni, retirees, and current employees. Anyone with a Dow employee ID number from the last seven years can register for the site.

My Dow Network has taken off, boasting thousands of members several months after launching. People are signing up to network with current and former colleagues, renew old friendships, stay abreast of the latest developments within Dow, and explore new full-time and contractor opportunities. Dow benefits from staying connected to its cumulative talent pool, tapping special skills and knowledge from experienced alumni, facilitating knowledge transfer across different generations of employees, and fostering a more inclusive, diverse work environment.

From new moms who take time off to retirees with domain expertise, most alumni are grateful and enthusiastic about the opportunity to reconnect and reengage. According to retiree Jeff Schatzer, "One of the great losses of retirement is the severance of ties that had such meaning. [My Dow Network] is one way to reestablish those ties. After three years of retirement, it's heartwarming to know that people think of me, that they have a comment for me, or that they want to share some news with me."

Not surprisingly, alumni who have returned to Dow as consultants or employees are proving to be more affordable to hire and train, more productive, and less likely to leave for another company.

Advice for Candidates

For someone who wants a job or wants to keep a job, the need for social networking has never been greater. The tenure for C-level positions averages less than two years. New hires, especially at the top, are being asked to hit the ground running and produce quick results. With more jobs going overseas, fewer guarantees about employment, and rising competition for the top jobs, people need to take full advantage of online social networks to strategically and opportunistically develop their careers. Many of the concepts from Chapters 2–4 on personal brand, social capital, and social sales, respectively, apply to candidates trying to "sell" themselves for certain roles internal or external to their company.

For job seekers, social graph information available from searching and browsing on LinkedIn and Doostang can help line up informational interviews and uncover tacit information about prospective employers and what it's really like to work at a particular company. Job seekers can learn a great deal about interviewers, hiring managers, and prospective colleagues. Because online social networks enable people to maintain a greater number of weak-tie relationships, job seekers might discover in their expanded networks that they know people at the company where they want to work, and then use those relationships to get their foot in the door.

However, remember that it works both ways. It's becoming increasingly common for hiring managers and recruiters to perform due diligence on candidates via social networking sites. (They used to just Google candidates.) It is a good idea to keep Facebook, Friendster, and MySpace pages PG-13, if not G. If you must post photos from a bachelor party in Las Vegas, at least create different profile views and Friend Lists for professional contacts versus college fraternity brothers. Chapter 11 includes a more in-depth discussion on how to manage your professional identity on social networking sites.

Be Aware of Employee Poaching

The unprecedented access that online social networking provides is tremendously empowering for recruiters and job candidates, but it can be worrisome for employers. Poaching is not a new phenomenon. Employees of reputable firms are constantly being sought—these individuals are prescreened and know the company's best practices, so their experience is highly valued by others. Online social networking can be scary for employers because recruiters can be very systematic about their poaching.

Employers might want to be careful and make sure that employee communities on social networks are properly moderated and watched over carefully to prevent poachers from joining. Some companies have instituted internal policies listing what employees can disclose about the organization and their role in public forums, including social networking sites. Employers should remind employees that any company proprietary work, including sales deals with material financial consequences and not-yet-launched products, should not be shared on LinkedIn profiles.

Ultimately, employers should be aware that poaching is a reality and happens all the time. Second, have backfill plans ready to be mobilized in case a mission-critical role is suddenly left vacant. Most important, create a great workplace environment so that employees won't want to leave.

< < < TAKEAWAYS

✓ In many ways, recruiting resembles a sales cycle, so recruiters and hiring managers should brush up on selling techniques—such as the ones in Chapter 4.

✓ With employees switching jobs more often, recruiters and hiring managers need to take a longer-term view in building relationships with talented professionals. Even if someone isn't available today, it might be worthwhile to invest in that relationship when that person does become available in the future and for referrals.

✓ Most recruiters for professional positions are on LinkedIn, but a big opportunity remains to reach broader audiences on Facebook, especially those in college or graduate school.

✓ Most hires come through employees and their networks. In addition to offering a referral bonus, make it easy for employees to make the referral by using LinkedIn or Jobvite to suggest who in their network might be a good fit for a particular job.

✓ A growing number of companies are building explicit alumni networks for past employees who have moved on to other companies or to retirement. Alumni have proven to be great sources for part-time or contract work and for referring new business opportunities.

> > > TIPS and TO DO's

❏ Especially if your work involves college and MBA recruiting, consider creating a Facebook Page to build community and enthusiasm for the company, and to connect school alums who are now employees with applicants at their alma mater.

❏ Take full advantage of the rich information on LinkedIn and Facebook profiles to decide whether someone is likely to be a good candidate before you even perform a phone screen.

❏ Join and participate in organization, alumni, and diversity groups on Facebook and LinkedIn as a means to find and engage large numbers of individuals who might fit your ideal candidate profile.

continues…

❑ During your due diligence process, don't just rely on references provided by the candidate, which are likely very positive. Search for mutual contacts on LinkedIn and others who might have worked with the candidate at previous employers to hear a more well-rounded and balanced set of perspectives.

❑ Be aware that other companies' recruiters are likely actively pursuing your best employees, and take the time to put a policy in place for what employees are and aren't allowed to disclose on their profiles. For example, sales reps shouldn't be allowed to put any confidential deal information on their LinkedIn profiles—especially if it's a highly competitive situation, a nondisclosure agreement has been signed with the customer, or you are a publicly traded company and the deal has material implications for your quarterly earnings.

III

Step-by-Step Guide to Social Networking for Business

9

How To: Develop Your Facebook Era Plan and Metrics

With the conceptual frameworks and functional application ideas from Parts I, "Why Social Networking Matters for Business," and II, "Social Networking Across Your Organization," behind us, the remaining chapters are an action-oriented guide on how to get started. First, we need to develop a Facebook Era plan for your company, which will be driven by your business goals and the customers' goals mapped against Facebook and Twitter's capabilities and your organization's resources.

Listening First

Before you dive into planning and execution mode, you should monitor and scan the social Web (and the Web more broadly) for what's *already* being said about your company, products, and brands. You likely already have fans and critics *somewhere*—perhaps on Facebook, Twitter, LinkedIn, Yelp, Amazon, YouTube, Google Buzz, or blogs.

Understanding *what* is being said about your company and *who* is saying it provides valuable context for setting your business objectives and subsequently developing your plan. For example, if people are expressing a lot of negative sentiment about your company on social networking sites, then one of your top social media goals should be to address negative comments and elevate your brand. On the other hand, if people love your brand and are creating viral videos, writing glowing reviews, and posting photos of themselves in your stores, your social media goals might be to recognize and promote these individuals across your social Web properties.

A common situation that many large brands face is that by the time they get serious about engaging on social networking sites, fans have already beat them to the punch and created unofficial Facebook Pages, Groups, and Twitter accounts. An example is Ferrero, the European chocolate maker whose products are popular and loved around the world. In 2008, Ferrero executives discovered that a zealous fan had created a Facebook Page for Ferrero Rocher, one of their most popular products. And not only had a Page been created—it had actually become one of the most popular Pages on Facebook, with more than 2.5 million people who "liked" the Page.

Similarly, Coca-Cola execs stumbled upon a Facebook Page for Coke started by two passionate fans and worked out a deal to co-manage the Page with the two individuals. (For liability reasons, Coca-Cola made sure it's the legal owner of the Page.) On Twitter, car-sharing company Zipcar has more than 30,000 followers but professes to largely be in "listen only" mode.

Without taking the time to research and listen first, brands might accidentally create redundant efforts or compete against their own fans. Instead, brands should, at a minimum, be monitoring and complementing or, in some cases, even working directly with grassroots efforts to best engage their community of fans.

To help separate official brand Pages from fan-created efforts, Facebook has introduced Community Pages to provide passionate customers with unofficial outlets for capturing the causes, topics, ideas, and brands they love.

Establishing the Business Objectives

As with any investment you might be considering for your business, you should always start by determining your strategy. What are your goals? These common objectives guide many of the early business forays into social networking sites:

- Conducting market research, such as identifying trends and recruiting early adopters for more in-depth focus groups
- Improving customer satisfaction by providing opportunities for engagement and for customers to help one another
- Promoting additional products and services to existing customers
- Expanding into new markets
- Encouraging word-of-mouth marketing
- Recruiting new employees
- Establishing or evolving your branding and positioning

Dig deeper. How would you ideally want your brand to be perceived? Which new audiences do you want to reach? Are they on Facebook, Twitter, or LinkedIn? Is your priority to up-sell existing customers or find new customers? Because of their expansive reach across different regions, age groups, and other segments, and their capability to target specific segments, social networking sites are a great place to test and expand to new markets. Think about not just where you are, but also where you want to go. Perhaps your business sees an opportunity to expand from adults to a children's offering, or a new region, industry vertical, or audience personality type.

Use the top two or three goals as the basis of your strategy and decision making. When creating the prioritized list, it might be useful to evaluate goals based not only on importance to your business, but also on whether social networking is uniquely capable to contribute to a goal. Your social media investment will evolve and adapt over time, but it's important to have a goal or set of goals, even if they change, so that you can justify the time and effort, mobilize internally, set expectations externally, and measure the return on your investment.

The following guest expert sidebar from R "Ray" Wang and Jeremiah Owyang of Altimeter Group summarizes common business-use cases for the social Web. This book has already covered most of these scenarios, so chapter references are also included at the end of each bullet for your convenience.

Social CRM Use Cases

R "Ray" Wang and Jeremiah Owyang

Customers continue to adopt social technologies at a blinding speed—yet organizations are unable to keep up. Why? Rapid adoption of social networking enables users to connect with individuals and communities who share mutual interests, increasingly leaving organizations out of the conversation. Companies need an organized approach using enterprise software that connects business units to the social web—giving them the opportunity to respond in near-real time and in a coordinated fashion.

Social CRM augments social networking to serve as a new channel within existing end-to-end CRM processes and investments. After months of study and interviews with over 100 organizations, Altimeter Group has identified 18 use cases for Social CRM, listed here:

- **Social customer insights**—*Social customer insights form the foundation for all social CRM initiatives.* The social Web delivers insights into the opinions about an organization's products and services that help companies achieve a credible marketing presence. (Chapter 15)

- **Social marketing insights**—*Listen before talking.* Marketers must listen to what consumers are already saying, identify top influencers, rank top conversations, prioritize top channels, identify velocity of discussion, and gauge the tone of topics. (Chapter 6)

continues...

- **Rapid social marketing response**—*Defending the brand.* To be successful, brands need to identify what's being said, the severity of the information, the influence of that person, and the context of previous interactions. (Chapter 6)

- **Social campaign tracking**—*Optimizing in flight.* Unlike traditional advertising, social marketing is constantly changing and requires constant attention and massaging. (Chapter 12)

- **Social event management**—*What happens in person goes social.* Marketers need a social strategy before, during, and after both online and physical events. (Chapter 6)

- **Social sales insights**—*Finding your prospects' and customers' watering holes.* To succeed, organizations must identify not only where their key prospects and customers interact, but also the key needs that a brand aims to fulfill. (Chapter 4)

- **Rapid social sales response**—*Catching a lead in midair.* Rapid social sales response monitors key channels for sales opportunities. Sales teams can target key buying communities and rapidly react to potential sales triggers. (Chapter 4)

- **Proactive social lead generation**—*Using peer-to-peer lead generation.* Proactive social lead generation reaches customers who want to be educated by the organization or its ambassadors. Referrals, online customer testimonials, and social recommendations are key for scale. (Chapter 4)

- **Social support insights**—*Realizing that social smoke means a social fire.* Social support insights provide organizations with the information needed to rank an individual's level of influence, determine friend or foe status, associate the relationship with the organization, and select an appropriate response channel. (Chapter 5)

- **Rapid social response**—*Discovering that real time isn't fast enough.* Despite the proliferation of channels, organizations must be able to triage support requests and customer feedback. (Chapter 5)

- **Peer-to-peer unpaid armies**—*Harnessing your advocates.* Smart organizations find ways to harness this collective expertise from customers and partners. (Chapter 7)

- **Innovation insights**—*Catching innovation trends right under your nose.* Organizations must capitalize on innovation trends that can range from product fixes and enhancement requests to feature and solution suggestions. The goal is to capture, organize, and prioritize ideas. (Chapter 7)

- **Crowdsourced R&D**—*Real-time innovation and feedback.* Crowdsourced R&D improves concept-to-delivery time frames. Customers, partners, and industry watchers can play a role to expedite requirements gathering, prototyping, and demo tests. (Chapter 7)

- **Collaboration insights**—Organizations must learn from different areas in the company to quickly respond to customers. (Chapter 7)

- **Enterprise collaboration**—*Not everything lives in SharePoint.* Departments must work together in a seamless way to get work done. Empower department and teams to work together across boundaries of functional fiefdoms through shared advanced programming interfaces (APIs) that often feed back into a centralized system. (Chapter 7)

- **Extended collaboration**—*Help me help you.* Extend collaboration to partners, channels, suppliers, and other stakeholders, providing a common collaboration tool for partners outside the firewall to interact and work with employees and other partners. (Chapter 7)

- **Seamless customer experience**—*Customers don't care what channel or department you work in.* Presenting a consistent face to customers improves their comfort and satisfaction. (Chapter 5)

- **VIP experience**—*Reward your best customers or lose them.* VIP experience delivers premium programs to top customers. The goal is to ensure that your most profitable customers remain loyal. (Chapter 11)

R "Ray" Wang (@rwang0) and Jeremiah Owyang (@jowyang) are partners at Altimeter Group.

Defining Your Metrics

After you've decided on goals, it's useful to create business metrics for these goals to help define what success means, determine the appropriate level of investment, and measure direct value to the business. For example, these are some common business metrics and targets from some of the companies I have worked with during the last two years:

- Identify X new trends.

- Recruit focus group of X early adopters age 14–18 to help us understand the teen market and design the next generation of our product.

- Improve customer satisfaction scores by X.

- Decrease customer support call center volume by X%.

- Increase existing customer average spending by $X this year.

- Acquire X new customers in a new region, such as Taiwan and Hong Kong.

- Achieve X responses to our word-of-mouth campaign and X% conversion rate into sales.

- Source X number of candidates for the recruiting department.

- Elevate company brand, as measured by a customer survey on how customers perceive our brand.

- Increase our net promoter score by X.

When you have your business metrics, determine which activity metrics correspond and begin tracking these. Consider these common social Web activity metrics:

- Number of fans and followers

- New fans and followers per week

- Facebook Page visits

- Number of brand mentions (positive and negative)

- Shared link click-through rate

- Mentions and retweets

- Number of fan posts, likes, and comments

- Ratio of new fans to fans who left

- Ratio of new followers to unfollows

- Ratio of fan activity to your activity

- Ratio of fan activity to fan number

Start with a modest level of investment and increase it as you see results. Set realistic goals and expectations. It probably took several iterations to arrive at your current Web site strategy. Coming up with an optimal social network strategy requires the same kind of learning by doing. Starting overly aggressively can set up companies for disappointment down the road and risk losing internal support for these initiatives.

Evolving Our Metrics

We shouldn't be using only old metrics to value these new initiatives. Just as we had to "invent" new measures such as cost-per-click in the Internet Era, we need to develop new measures to capture the nuances of the social Web. Last decade, Yahoo! Overture and Google AdWords transformed the marketing discipline with online transactional data. For the first time, we could see much richer data about each transaction across the marketing funnel, from page rank and page views to clicks and conversions. Search marketing trained us to become obsessed with optimizing click-through rates and conversions. We became narrowly focused on optimizing for a single transaction at a time because that's all the data that we had.

With the social Web, we are again gaining more insights—not about the transaction. but about the customer. Through Facebook personal profiles, Facebook Business Pages, Twitter, and behavioral ad targeting and retargeting (more on this in Chapter 12, "How To: Advertise and Promote on the Social Web"), companies are able to form and track actual *relationships* with customers on the Internet. And for the first time in online marketing, companies can take a longer-term view of the customer and optimize not for the click but for the lifetime relationship with a customer.

This is really big news—it means that companies need to be okay that any given online conversation might not click through to a sale today (gasp!) but will contribute to sales tomorrow.

Everyone on my book tour always asks about metrics and return on investment (ROI), so I've been thinking about this a lot. I don't claim to have figured out the magic bullet, but I have developed a new metric, **social customer lifetime value** (described in the next section). Many of the companies I have worked with are finding it useful in allocating their social media investment, prioritizing initiatives, and calculating ROI.

Social Customer Lifetime Value (sCLV)

Customer lifetime value (CLV) is a popular marketing metric that approximates the business "value" from a customer. Traditionally, it has been calculated as the net present value of future cash flows from a customer relationship—how much someone will spend on your products or services across his or her lifetime as a customer. As a business, you wouldn't want to spend more on marketing and selling to someone than their CLV minus the cost of goods sold, because then you would lose money.

CLV has been instrumental to the marketing discipline, but it is outdated. Traditional CLV assumes that people operate in a vacuum, which was perhaps more true before the Facebook Era. It's definitely not accurate on the social Web, which is about influence and crowdsourcing.

As we saw in Chapter 5, "Customer Service in the Facebook Era," a growing number of customer support questions are being answered *by other customers* on public social Web forums, such as Twitter and Facebook, instead of at the call center. As we talked about in Chapter 6, "Marketing in the Facebook Era," friends and colleagues are the strongest influencers of purchase decisions, which means that companies need to place even higher value on existing customers because they are your most credible salespeople. Finally, as we talked about in Chapter 7, "Innovation and Collaboration in the Facebook Era," some of the most successful and profitable products from companies now are originating from customers themselves on social ideation and voting.

I've combined these most valuable aspects of the social Web in developing a new way of thinking about CLV, which I call **social customer lifetime value (sCLV).**

$$\text{sCLV} = \text{CLV} + \text{Sales from word-of-mouth} + \text{Customer support savings} + \text{Product revenue from crowdsourced ideas}$$

Let's dig a little deeper into each of the components.

- **Sales from word-of-mouth**—This is roughly the size of your customer's contact network multiplied by your customer's level of influence among the network. For example, if your customer has a huge network but little influence, she might not materially affect your business. Same thing if she is highly influential but has a small network. But if the customer has a large network *and* high influence on friends and colleagues, then even if she doesn't directly spend a lot of money on your products and services, her sCLV could be extremely high and this is a relationship your company should invest in and cultivate. Practically speaking, word-of-mouth sales are often backed out from retweets and custom URLs that are shared via Facebook status messages.

- **Customer support savings**—This is calculated from the number of customer questions answered by a customer expert that didn't need to be answered by your support staff, and then multiplied by your average cost of answering a question.

- **Product revenue from crowdsourced ideas**—This is the dollar value of any new products that originated from a customer-suggested idea voted up by the community.

sCLV looks different for each company based on the business goals defined and initiatives pursued. For example, a company that uses Facebook and Twitter for customer support might want to focus on calculating that component in the formula. A business that creates a Facebook Page and Twitter account to rebrand itself as being more modern and technologically savvy might tweak this formula with a different component that represents brand value.

Mobilizing the Team

An important factor in developing your Facebook Era plan is the amount of available internal resources for social networking initiatives. If you have budget authority, this means reallocating from somewhere else to fund the additional heads, agency support, Facebook ad spending, or application development. If you don't have budget flexibility, this means reallocating your own time and priorities.

Most larger organizations that need to juggle several different social media goals are hiring someone new or having someone internally focus on social efforts. Some large consumer brands have a team of people (usually a combination of in-house and agency staff), each focusing on Facebook, Twitter, YouTube, or Yelp. The initial level of resources required depends on how much your company is being talked about across the social Web and whether it makes sense to respond. Not surprisingly, the most labor-intensive social media efforts I've seen are in customer service and customer care departments in which companies try to reply to every tweet or Facebook Wall post.

Another very likely scenario in bigger companies is that multiple departments or business units will want to create, manage, or otherwise be involved on Facebook or Twitter. Although social media thrives on grassroots leadership within companies, it's important that you establish executive consciousness and sponsorship of these programs. Individual business units and departments can own their social media strategy and execution, but you should create a companywide social media task force to make sure certain minimum standards are adhered to, such as brand and regulatory compliance. An informal cross-functional task force helps align incentives, best practices, resources, and vendor relationships across the company and realigns corporate incentives on the customer (more on this coming up in Chapter 15, "Corporate Governance, Strategy, and Implementation").

If you're a smaller or medium-sized business, it's unlikely that you will have the luxury of being able to dedicate an employee, much less a team of people, full-time to Facebook and Twitter initiatives. The default seems to be asking a marketing person to take it on, which can be a very good solution.

For larger organizations that are already working closely with PR or digital agencies, it can be tempting to outsource your social efforts. But outsourcing completely might mean missing out on a crucial opportunity to connect with customers. In the following guest expert sidebar, Ben Smith from Dunkin' Donuts explains how his team is approaching social initiatives and why they have decided to in-house the voice of the brand.

Stay Close to the Customer

Ben Smith

In recent years, many brands have realized that social media can be a cost-effective marketing and communications channel, and they have sought to define and implement a social strategy. Too often, these internal strategy sessions start with an internal debate about who should "own" social media. What department does it belong in? Is it marketing, PR, media, or customer service? We had some healthy debates about this but eventually agreed that the best approach for Dunkin' Donuts was a social engagement strategy that had a blend of PR, CRM, and media. It might sound cliché, but we believe that our customers are actually the ones who own these spaces, not us. And to effectively connect with them and engage in a meaningful way, every department needs a seat at the table.

Know your role. If everyone has a seat at the table, it's important for roles and responsibilities to be clear. At Dunkin', we have a multiagency approach to marketing. Although ideas are welcome from any agency partner, we've had success with our digital agency taking the lead on social strategy, creative, and technology initiatives; our PR agency being responsible for blogger outreach and word-of-mouth; and our advertising agency buying and planning any online media (such as Facebook ads).

Find your voice. The voice of the brand is something that should not be outsourced. It's important to remember that every tweet or post represents the brand, and it's critical that the conversation adds value and remains brand related. At Dunkin' Donuts, we are fortunate to have an internal resource (@DunkinDave) who is an ideal representative of our brand voice and personality. With more than two years of experience in our communications department, he knows what to say, what not to say, and who to go to if he needs more information. He is empowered to make the right decisions, respond in the moment, and speak on behalf of the brand.

In contrast, if an agency partner was responsible for this activity, client approvals would be necessary. It would be incredibly inefficient to run every tweet up the flagpole for approval. Not every brand will have an existing resource ready to take on this role, but if you can, I strongly recommend bringing this job in-house instead of outsourcing it.

Ben Smith (@bensmith32) is an interactive marketing manager at Dunkin' Donuts.

Another emerging trend is that some senior leaders in companies of all sizes are starting to personally embrace Facebook and Twitter. Prominent CXO tweeters and Facebookers include Richard Branson (Virgin Chairman), Bob Parsons (Go Daddy CEO), Jacqueline Novogratz (Acumen Fund CEO), Dave Kellogg (Mark Logic CEO), and Jonathan Schwartz (Sun Microsystems CEO). Despite their busy schedules, these company leaders realize the strategic brand value in listening to the customer firsthand and sharing their thoughts through an authentic personal voice.

Framing Your Strategy in Terms of the Customer

Your company's goals are important, but the foundation of all your strategies and tactics needs to come back to the customer. Why would they want to engage? What are their incentives, motivation, expectations, and thought processes? Generally, you can tap into one or a combination of these reasons:

- To express strong emotion. Perhaps they are overjoyed, overwhelmed, or frustrated. Your product has really been a positive or a negative in their life.

- To improve your product with constructive feedback.

- To associate themselves with what your brand stands for.

- To feel important in helping others answer questions.

- To benefit from selling peripheral goods and services, such as a vendor selling iPod cases on the iPod group page.

- To meet new people.

- To bond socially with friends through the experience of using your product.

At the end of this initial planning exercise, you should have a strategy that you are ready to execute:

- Prioritized list of objectives, including time frame, metrics, and targets

- Value you expect to bring to your business

- Level of resources you are willing to commit (you might even be able to calculate expected ROI)

- Means and frequency by which you will evaluate progress

- The person in your organization who will be responsible for carrying out this initiative

Getting Started on Facebook and Twitter

With a rough idea of your goals, metrics, and resources, and knowing things will evolve over time, you are now ready to get started on Facebook and Twitter. Companies use

Facebook and Twitter in several ways. One or more of these might make sense for your business, depending on the objectives you laid out:

- **Facebook personal profiles**—You might need to help your sales reps and hiring managers either create Facebook profiles or make sure their existing profiles reflect well on them and the company. Develop employee social media guidelines and provide training. Chapter 10, "How To: Build and Manage Relationships on the Social Web," walks through how to build and manage relationships on the social Web. *Time required: 1–2 hours plus periodic updates.*

- **Facebook Business Pages**—Facebook Pages are very similar to personal profiles, except that they are for a business. Facebook Pages are the logical first step for companies to create a presence on Facebook. Large companies with multiple products and audience segments might want to create separate Pages for each. Chapter 11, "How To: Engage Customers with Facebook Pages and Twitter," explains the ins and outs of building and maintaining a Facebook Page. *Time required: 1–2 hours to set up, plus periodic updates. You can have an agency create a Facebook Page for you for a few hundred dollars (I would pay no more than $1,000, but it also depends on how fancy you want to make your Page.)*

- **Facebook ads**—Facebook ads take advantage of hypertargeting and word-of-mouth to help market to existing fans and customers and to reach totally new audiences, as discussed in Chapter 6. Chapter 12 talks about how to generate interest, traffic, and leads with social advertising. *Time required: Several hours per campaign for setup and analysis. Most digital agencies now handle Facebook ads in addition to search marketing ads and take a percentage of ad spending as their cut.*

- **Facebook apps**—You can custom-develop or choose from tens of thousands of existing games, polls, contests, and other apps in the Facebook Application Directory to enhance your customer's experience on your Facebook Page or, more generally, extend the set of customer interactions with your company within the Facebook environment. *Time required: Weeks or months to develop or outsource a custom application (depending on complexity) or hours to sift through existing app offerings and then install them.*

- **Facebook for Websites**—As we introduced in Chapter 1, "The Fourth Revolution," Facebook for Websites enables you to integrate your Web sites and Web applications with Facebook's login system. *Time required: A few hours or days, depending on level of integration.*

- **Twitter**—Twitter is by far the simplest to set up. As with Facebook Pages, the key is to post high-value content on a consistent basis. *Time required: A few minutes to set up, followed by periodic updates.*

Before you actually dive in, you will likely need to consult your company lawyers, PR team, and IT department if you are at a large company. Hopefully, representatives from each of these areas are represented in your cross-functional task force. Chapter 15 delves into detailed corporate governance issues, but I recommend not getting bogged down early on. Test the waters with small grassroots initiatives before you get the whole organization involved.

In the following guest expert sidebar, social media agency CEO Dave Kerpen shares a few words of wisdom about common pitfalls to avoid when launching your Facebook Era plan.

Five Social Pitfalls to Avoid

Dave Kerpen

The social Web can help individuals and organizations grow and become more efficient in numerous ways. However, organizations have made mistakes and continue to make them as they try to harness new tools and sites to their advantage.

Avoid these five pitfalls:

1. **Jumping in too quickly**—Don't get started with social initiatives until you're ready to commit consistent time and resources to your efforts. Nothing is worse than a never-updated Facebook Page or Twitter community, what I call a "deserted island." Instead, reserve your usernames, monitor and listen to what your customers and prospects are talking about, and then join the conversation—when you're ready.

2. **Not having a defined strategy and objectives**—Building a Facebook Business Page or Twitter profile is not a strategy. Why are you doing a Facebook Page? Who is your specific target audience and how will you regularly engage them? What value will you provide to your community? What are your expectations for results and how will you measure them? Answer these questions (and more) before you get started and reexamine them along the way.

3. **Falling victim to "Shiny New Object Syndrome"**—It's easy to get excited about the latest, greatest tool—whether it's Twitter, Foursquare, or another new site that everyone's talking about. However, it's important to stay the course with your strategy and plan, and spend your time and resources where you know your customers are and will be.

4. **Selling too much**—Too many people and organizations jump onto Facebook or Twitter and immediately start making offers, sharing links to their sites, and showcasing their products or services. The social media sales cycle is much slower than a traditional sales cycle. It's listen, build, engage, grow, engage, and (soft) sell. You must be authentic and share value along the way. The leads and sales will come.

5. **Giving up too easily**—Because social media does involve relationship building and a longer sales cycle, it can be frustrating to put time, effort, and money into a venture that doesn't provide an immediate return. But as long as you're providing value, sharing great content, and targeting your audience well, your patience will be rewarded, sometimes in ways you hadn't even imagined.

Dave Kerpen (@davekerpen) is the CEO of theKbuzz, a social media and word-of-mouth marketing agency.

< < < TAKEAWAYS

✓ Your Facebook Era plan should be a function of your business goals, customer goals, budget and resources, and Facebook and Twitter capabilities.

✓ Just as we saw last decade with the Internet, new metrics will evolve and be developed for the social Web.

✓ Customer lifetime value (CLV) assumes that people operate in an isolated vacuum. sCLV tries to make the metric social by accounting for word-of-mouth, customer support cost savings, and new product sales.

✓ A handful of executives and entrepreneurs, not just the marketing team, are starting to embrace Facebook and Twitter as strategic conduits for communicating with employees, customers, and the public.

✓ Most companies are choosing to engage on the social Web in five ways: Facebook personal profiles, Facebook Pages, Facebook ads, Facebook apps, and Twitter.

> > > TIPS and TO DO's

❏ If you are at a larger company, assemble a cross-functional social media council.

❏ Develop simple social media guidelines for employees.

❏ Update and introduce training to include mention of Facebook and Twitter.

❏ Create new business metrics and definitions of success based on your social media objectives and realistic expectations.

❏ Before you start using Facebook or Twitter for your company, try using it in your personal life to get a feel for how it works.

How To: Build and Manage Relationships on the Social Web

As we talked about in Chapter 3, "How Relationships and Social Capital Are Changing," social networking sites are great contact databases for us to manage relationships across our personal and professional lives. Whether we are selling a product, looking for a job, looking to hire, or pursuing a different business goal, having a larger pool of contacts to draw from for help increases our likelihood of success. And not only will we become more successful, but building real and meaningful relationships with colleagues, customers, and business partners outside of work can also make our jobs more enjoyable and personally fulfilling.

Before you think about creating a Facebook presence for your business, you need to build a Facebook presence for yourself. This chapter is about how to set up and then optimize your personal Facebook profile to balance your professional identity, set the proper levels of privacy, interact with customers and colleagues, and ultimately support meaningful and fulfilling business relationships. If you master person-to-person interaction dynamics on Facebook, you can put yourself in your customers' shoes when they are interacting on Facebook. If you are already an expert Facebook and LinkedIn user and have mastered the personal profile, you can skip ahead to Chapter 11, "How To: Engage Customers with Facebook Pages and Twitter."

Personal Versus Professional Identity

We all carry multiple identities. We might be a sales executive or engineer by day, but we have equally important identities as fathers, sisters, classmates, church leaders, customers, and so on. Privacy settings on Facebook,

LinkedIn, and Twitter enable us to segment our audiences, similar to how companies segment their audiences, and to be our authentic selves with each audience.

In certain professions—such as psychiatrists, social workers, government workers, military intelligence, and school teachers—anonymity is preferred and is even a matter of personal safety in some cases. For these types of individuals, I recommend putting Facebook on the strictest privacy settings, which prevents your profile from showing up in any search results on Facebook or Google (see Figure 10.1). Celebrities might want to also hide their personal profiles from search results, but also create a separate public Facebook Page for fans. (See the next chapter for how to do this.) LinkedIn similarly enables you to specify what information you share on a "public" profile (indexed by search engines outside of LinkedIn); the visibility of your status messages; and whether you are open to receiving messages, invitations, and InMails (LinkedIn's paid system for unsolicited inbound messages and requests) from other LinkedIn members. On Twitter, you can't prevent anyone from @replying to you, but you can limit who gets to see your tweets by making your profile private. The following sections focus on Facebook because that's where many people are sharing the most information.

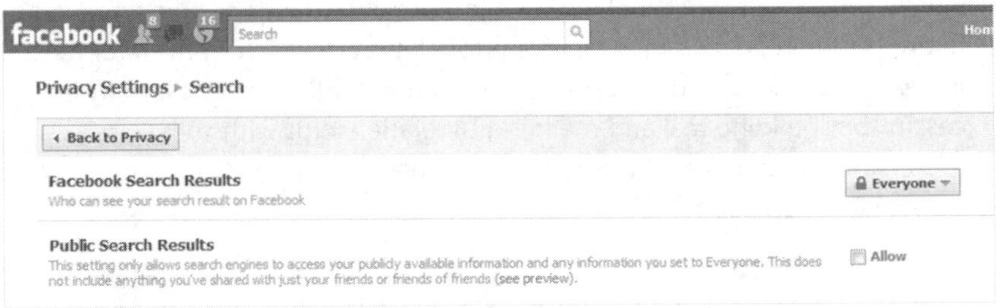

Figure 10.1
Under Privacy Settings, Search, you can specify whether you want your profile to show up in search results on Facebook and on search engines such as Yahoo! or Google.

Segmenting Your Audience

Using Friend Lists on Facebook, you can create custom profile views for different groups of friends. Friend Lists help you organize and manage relationships in three ways. First, they provide context of how you know someone. Especially for weak-tie relationships, it's helpful to have reminders of how you met someone. Second, Friend Lists enable you to customize what information you share (your personal brand) with each group. So you might share your job history, blog posts, and a handful of photos of your newborn with coworkers, but reserve the Vegas bachelor party pictures and full baby photo album for college friends. Third, you can use Friend Lists as distribution lists when you are sending a Facebook message (although you are restricted to a maximum of 20 recipients at a time) or inviting entire Friend Lists of people to a Facebook Event.

You can define new Friend Lists either when you are adding a new friend or by clicking on Create New List under the Accounts, Edit Friends tab (see Figure 10.2). Friend Lists are similar to tags because you can categorize a Facebook friend under multiple lists.

You decide how to define your lists, including how granular to make them, but a good rule of thumb is to have between two and five lists. If you have fewer than two, either you probably are sharing information with some people you shouldn't be or you aren't sharing enough with others. If you have more than five, it becomes confusing to remember and manage. For example, I previously had 12 Friend Lists, but I recently consolidated them to these 5:

- Hearsay Labs customers

- College friends

- Coworkers

- People I met at a conference

- People who read my book

You aren't being two-faced by exposing different parts of your identity to different groups of people. We all juggle multiple facets of our lives, and before Friend Lists, it was hard to reflect these differences online. It is not appropriate, relevant, feasible, or considerate to share everything with everyone. Just as you have boundaries in real life between work and play, family and acquaintances, and adults and children, it's natural to want to also set boundaries in our online social networks. Think of it as tagging your relationships or creating different folders for the different people in your life.

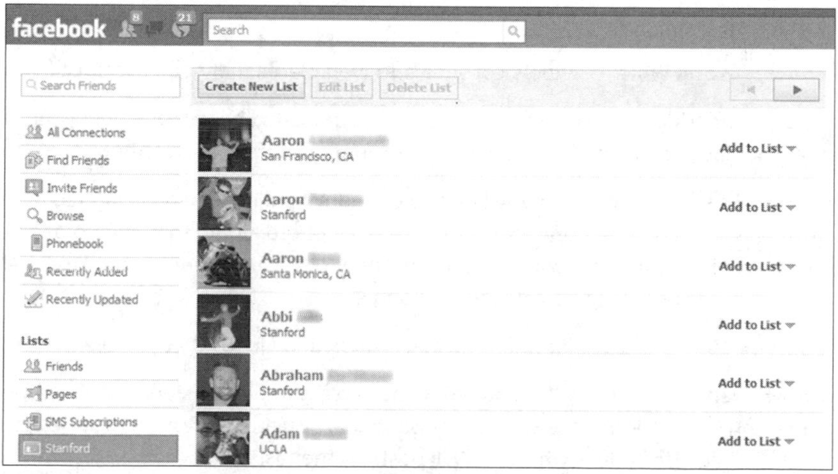

Figure 10.2
To define, view, and manage Friend Lists, click on the Accounts drop-down box and select Edit Friends. After you create a new Friend List, you can associate any of your contacts with the list.

Setting Your Privacy

Now that you have defined your Friend Lists, you can decide which list sees what infor-mation (see Figure 10.3). What you share with whom should depend not only on what *you* upload to Facebook, but also on what *others* are adding to Facebook and tagging you in. For example, even if you haven't uploaded any photos to Facebook, it's very possi-ble that your friends have uploaded photos and tagged you in them. Unless you explic-itly tell Facebook otherwise, these photos will be visible to anyone in your network (such as Facebook friends and others who went to your school or who work at the same place you do). Similarly, your friends can tag you in videos, write on your Wall, and send you Facebook gifts, which all appear publicly on your profile by default.

In early 2009, Facebook redesigned its privacy settings so that 1) your profile pictures, 2) mutual friends, and 3) Facebook Pages that you have "liked" are viewable to everyone (unless you choose to not appear in search results). The remaining information was classi-fied into 11 categories, and you can specify who has visibility to each category:

1. **About Me**—A description you write about yourself on your profile.

2. **Personal Info**—Activities, interests, and favorite music, TV shows, movies, books, and quotation.

3. **Birthday**—Birth date and year.

4. **Religious and Political Views**—Your stated preferences, if any, regarding politics and religion.

5. **Family and Relationship**—Family members, relationship status (including who you are in a relationship with), what you're interested in (gender), and what you're looking for (what kind of relationship).

6. **Education and Work**—Schools, colleges, and workplaces that you have specified.

7. **Photos and Videos of Me**—Photos and videos, uploaded by you or any of your friends, that you have been tagged in. You can always untag yourself in any photo or video.

8. **Photo Albums**—Photos that you have uploaded, regardless of who is tagged in them. You can specify different privacy settings for each photo album that you upload (for example, you might share your company party photos with everyone but limit your family holiday photos to personal friends only).

9. **Posts by Me**—Status updates, links, notes, photos, and videos that you post.

10. **Allow Friends to Post on My Wall**—Who has access to post links, notes, photos, and videos on your Wall, or have a status message that you are referenced in appear on your Wall. You can also control who sees Wall posts by friends.

11. **Comments on Posts**—Who has permission to comment on posts that you create.

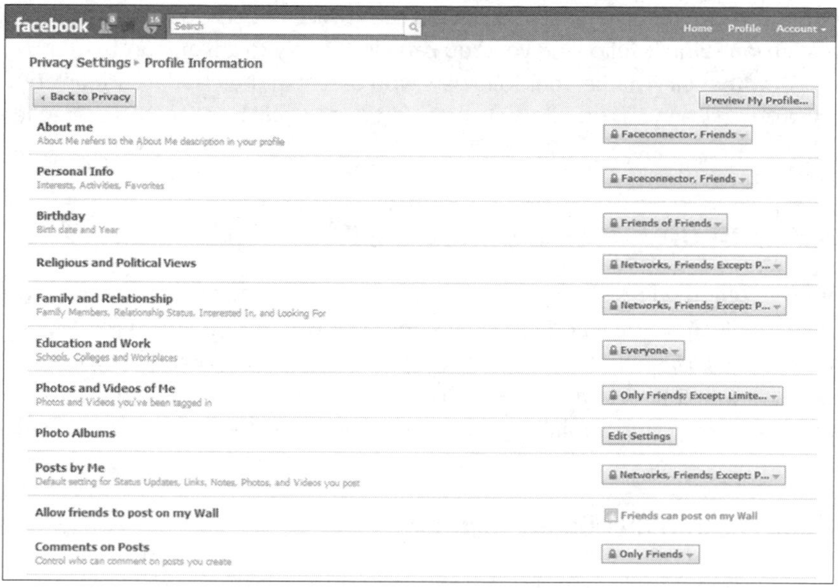

Figure 10.3
Facebook maintains 11 categories of content and information. You can specify privacy controls for each category. By default, your information is visible to your networks only, including friends of friends.

Facebook privacy controls even extend to people on Facebook who aren't your friends. You can choose to expose certain information to My Networks and Friends, Friends of Friends, or Only Friends (see Figure 10.4). For example, you might not want to share your profile with everyone on Facebook, but you might feel comfortable sharing with anyone from your alma mater or other network. Privacy settings are important for business professionals interested in social networking. By strategically sharing some personal information, such as a photo of their newborn, and hiding other information that is unprofessional or otherwise too personal, people can show a softer side and build rapport with colleagues while supporting their corporate image and personal reputation.

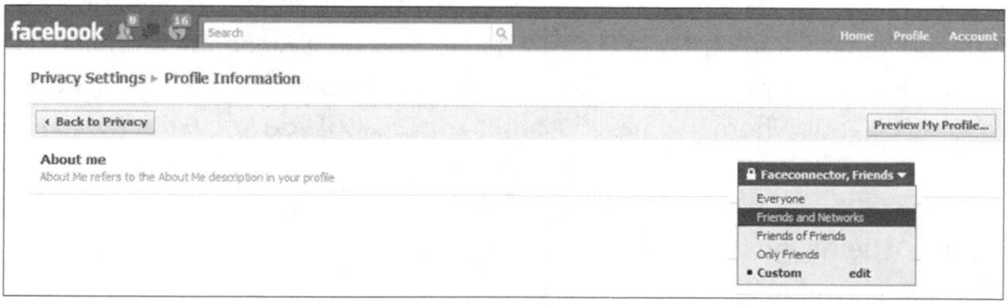

Figure 10.4
Facebook has sophisticated privacy settings, even enabling you to specify visibility and access for people who aren't your immediate friends.

Twitter has less functionality to segment who sees which tweets. You can privately direct-message anyone who is following you. You can also @reply to anyone on Twitter by starting a tweet with their @name. Your followers won't see it in their update stream, but anyone who clicks on your profile showing tweet history will be able to see @replies.

Interacting on Facebook and Twitter

After you are set up on Facebook, get in the practice of logging in at least once a week to keep your profile up-to-date and see what's going on with your friends. (The average Facebooker spends 55 minutes a day logged in.) As the number of friends you have increases and your interaction history with each friend grows, your experience on Facebook will become more fulfilling. This is also true for Twitter.

Breathing Life into Your Online Identity

Your online identity is a dynamic living entity that changes and refreshes as you and those around you share thoughts, blog posts, pictures, tweets, and other updates. On a pragmatic level, it's an efficient way to broadcast to everyone who cares (and who you also want to care about) when you move to a new city, change jobs, get a new cellphone number, or start a new hobby. The more active you are on Facebook, the more frequently your updates will show up on your friends' News Feed. The more you tweet, the more your tweets will appear to your followers. It's not a bad way to stay top-of-mind for people who are important to you, but you should also be careful not to overdo it and annoy people with a narcissistic frequency of status updates (see Table 10.1 at the end of the chapter).

When to Initiate or Accept a Friend Request

Because everyone uses Facebook differently, has different privacy thresholds, and might be using nuanced privacy controls with Friend Lists, it's hard to generally define when it's acceptable to initiate or accept friend requests. However, the Facebook friend is emerging as a new kind of more casual relationship, and it is becoming perfectly acceptable to add people as friends whom you have just met, especially if you know people in common. If you aren't feeling confident about making a request, one good way to test the waters is to send the individual a short, casual Facebook message, then gauge based on the response whether he or she would want to stay in touch—better yet, that person might initiate a friend request with you.

What if someone you don't really know requests to be your friend? You have three options: reject, confirm, or don't respond. Not responding can be a polite way of rejecting a request. The requestor is effectively put on hold. If he sees you on someone else's Friend

List or searches for you, he sees a "Friend Requested" message from Facebook and can't take action until you have rejected or confirmed the request. If you reject ("ignore request" in Facebook lingo) someone, he won't get actively notified, but if he ever sees you on someone else's Friend List or searches for you, he will be able to request you as a friend again. The final option is to confirm the request but then put that person on a "Limited Profile" or other custom Friend List with restricted capability to view and interact with your profile. For any update that appears on your News Feed or Wall, you can also choose to hide all updates from that specific individual if he is annoying you by posting too much or posting things that you don't find relevant.

As we discussed in Chapter 3, one of the benefits of Facebook is being able to capture weak-tie relationships so that we can build larger pools of people to draw on for help later. But it's ultimately a personal decision of how much you feel comfortable sharing with others.

In Twitter, it's less nuanced. You can follow anyone with a public profile, and anyone except people who you explicitly "block" can follow you if your profile is public.

Keeping in Touch

Frequent, high-touch interaction—such as making phone calls, sending a letter, hanging out, instant messaging, or even sending email—are not only time consuming and difficult to sustain across many friends, but they also require a base level of rapport to feel socially acceptable. For example, if you don't know someone very well, sending them a birthday card or suggesting dinner might feel out of place. Facebook and Twitter open up the world of casual interaction with communication modes that are easy, playful, and spontaneous. The most popular interactions are Facebook Wall posts, messages, pokes, gifts, and tweets. But a number of third-party-developed applications and games built on the Facebook platform have also become popular ways to socialize on Facebook.

The social Web facilitates casual interactions and weak-tie relationships through notifications, friend classification, and communication modes. First, Facebook provides visibility into what's happening with your friends, and provides reasons to get in touch with them using notifications and reminders:

- **Friend visualizations and reminders**—Every time you refresh your profile page or your home screen, or view your Friends tab, a different set of friends is shown. During a site visit, you are reminded of and updated with news from just a few Facebook friends, but across multiple visits you eventually get coverage from all your friends with lightweight, nonintrusive reminders and visualizations. If a particular name, profile picture, or status message piques your curiosity, you can click through to that person's profile page for a more detailed update. These notifications don't feel intrusive because you see only a few at a time, and because Facebook (instead of an individual) passively broadcasts them to you.

- **Birthday reminders**—The home page displays your list of friends who have birthdays today or in the next few days. You can then click through to wish them a happy birthday with a Facebook message, Facebook Wall post, or Facebook gift.

- **Status and incentives to encourage interaction**—Your number of friends, public Wall posts, gifts received, and comments made about you are all displayed on your profile. They serve as reinforcements and incentives to publicly pronounce your fondness for others by writing on their Wall, giving them gifts, and making comments about their photos and notes. Your friends feel compelled to return the favor in the future.

Second, both Facebook and Twitter offer different ways to categorize friends so that you remember how you met, you can easily look them up later, and you can tailor what information about you is visible to them:

- **Lists**—Although Facebook initially offered predefined categories only, users wanted more control and granularity over classifying their connections. In response, Facebook introduced Friend Lists to help users organize their networks. Friend Lists not only help users remember, search, and filter connections, but they also limit who gets to see what information on your profile. Twitter similarly enables you to create lists of people you follow. The main difference is that your Twitter lists are public (whereas your Facebook Friend Lists are private) and people can choose to follow your lists (that is, everyone on a list that you have created).

- **Search and filtering by school or employer network, city, or Friend List**—On Facebook, you can sort and search for friends based on school or employer networks, based on geographic location, or by Friend List. This capability is useful in a variety of situations. For example, if you are moving to a new city, you can search for all connections that belong to the network in that city and you potentially have a great starting point for looking for jobs, friends, and an apartment. Another example could be a fundraiser that you are organizing for your alumni association. Instead of notifying your entire network on Facebook, you might want to target just your friends from school. On Twitter, you can search for people or organizations.

When you have both a motive to communicate and a method for finding whom you want to communicate with, Facebook and Twitter offer several ways to interact with your friends:

- **Facebook messages**—As we talked about in Chapter 3, our communications arsenal has evolved to become more casual and inclusive—from in-person visits to letters, telegraphs, phone calls, email, and instant messaging. Facebook messages are the next step in this evolution. It's standard to omit the opening greeting and closing signature and use incomplete sentences, abbreviations, all lowercase letters, and so on because expectations are lower. Messages are especially well suited for fringe relationships that you don't want to escalate too early with an email or phone call—it might feel too formal, premature, uncomfortable, or inappropriate, as if you are overstepping social bounds. Messages are also great for reaching out to strangers, especially those in your network, because people are more likely to reply if they see that you know people in common and can get to know you (or at least something about you) through your picture and profile information. The automatic linking of the message to your profile also saves you from having to introduce and explain yourself in the message; you can just cut to the chase. On college campuses across America, Facebook messages are the preferred means of communication. I was told in surveys that email is reserved for "grown-ups," such as parents, professors, and prospective employers.

- **Facebook Wall posts**—One of the most interesting features of Facebook are Wall posts—publicly broadcast messages that appear not only on the recipient's profile Wall page, but also via the News Feed and Mini-Feeds. Wall posts are most commonly used for congratulating, wishing a happy birthday, and sharing other news, although some people enjoy publicly announcing everything they have to say.

- **Facebook pokes**—(See Figure 10.5.) What is a Facebook poke? Is it friendly, romantic, or funny? I don't think anyone really knows. The mystery makes it fun and playful. It's an easy way to call attention to yourself or let friends know you are thinking about them without the stress of needing to say something or expecting a reply.

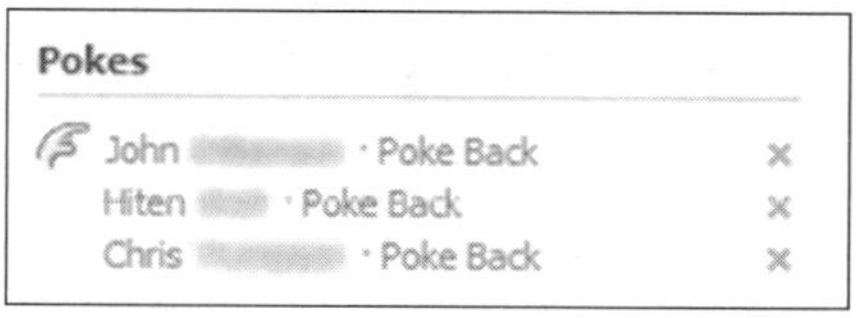

Pokes

John ▨▨▨ · Poke Back		✕
Hiten ▨▨ · Poke Back		✕
Chris ▨▨▨ · Poke Back		✕

Figure 10.5

No one really knows what a Facebook poke means, which makes it fun. Generally, it's a casual, playful way to interact with someone without saying anything. Facebook etiquette is to poke back or to respond with a Facebook message or Wall post.

- **Likes and comments**—(See Figure 10.6.) Users can comment on any Facebook news item, which drastically increases the opportunities for engagement. For example, you might want to comment if a friend posts a photo, updates a status message, changes relationship status to Engaged, or joins a group.

Figure 10.6

Likes and comments are easy, fast ways to engage with Facebook friends. Most people "like" and comment in-line on posts that appear on the home page News Feed instead of going to the author's Facebook Page.

- **Games and other social apps**—(See Figure 10.7.) When you don't have anything to say, Facebook games and other social apps come to the rescue. In addition to the standard interaction options that Facebook offers, other companies have developed social applications on top of the Facebook platform that enable users to do things such as throw virtual sheep, send virtual cupcakes, give a virtual hug, and play Scrabble with their Facebook friends.

- **@replies**—@replies are public messages mentioning another Twitter user. If you start your tweet with @name, the message is directed at and appears only to the person. (It doesn't show up in your followers' feeds.)

- **Twitter direct messages**—Direct messages (DMs) are private messages that you can send to people on Twitter who are following you.

These three components—visibility and notification, capability to organize connections, and casual ways to interact—have come together to define an entirely new class of relationship. In addition to our close ties, Facebook friends, Twitter followers, and those we follow on Twitter can encompass all the weak-tie relationships we have over time and across different aspects of our lives so that we have a larger pool of people to count on.

Figure 10.7

In addition to Facebook messages, gifts, Wall posts, and pokes, a number of platform apps and games have emerged that enable people to playfully interact with their friends on Facebook. Jeffrey Hoffman-Yip's application, Send Cupcakes, is a prime example. It enables users to send premade cupcakes or to design their own and send them to friends.

It is good Facebook Era etiquette to send a message, Facebook gift, song, cupcake, or tweet, or at least write well wishes on the Wall, for birthdays, engagements, weddings, and baby arrivals. The continual stream of feeds such as posted links and updated status messages also provides frequent opportunities to interact in authentic, meaningful ways.

In the following guest expert sidebar, Elizabeth Weil from Twitter shares her insider perspective on how to build business relationships using Twitter.

Building Business Relationships on Twitter

Elizabeth Weil

Here at Twitter, we use Twitter a lot to communicate both with one another as well as our customers and partners. Here are a few tried and true tips from us on how to build relationships, 140 characters at a time:

- **Embrace Twitter's real-time nature**—Messages on Twitter are short, quick, and capable of reaching people wherever they are. That combination makes it an instantaneous medium and a compelling tool for businesses. Use Twitter to ask questions of your followers, float ideas by potential customers, and network with other attendees when you're at an event.

continues...

- **Grow conversations**—Twitter enables you to provide a voice for your business. Use your tweets to grow conversations and build relationships—build trust, respond to customers' questions, provide information about product improvements, and give behind-the-scenes looks through photos or descriptions of what goes on at your business. Also, gauge the pace at which you tweet. Keep your audience engaged but not overwhelmed.

- **Reward your customers**—Twitter enables you to be creative. Experiment with providing exclusive Twitter deals or coupons to your followers. Some businesses provide early looks at new products or announce sales. Providing relevant, interesting, and timely information or announcements can also be a reward for your audience.

- **Monitor your brand**—Twitter enables you to watch what people are saying about you and your brand all over the world. Use this form of communication to listen to what people are saying about your products and services. Provide stellar customer service by messaging people who have questions or concerns. Also, use Twitter's retweet functionality to echo what others say about your brand (such as to highlight positive feedback).

- **Tweet on the go and always be in touch**—You can access Twitter anywhere: from your mobile phone, on the Web, with a desktop client, or integrated onto your Web site with @anywhere. Be there for your customers, partners, and employees, and experiment with new ways to use Twitter.

Elizabeth Bailey Weil (@elizabeth) works in corporate and business development at Twitter.

Networking on the Social Web

As we discussed briefly in Chapter 3, social Web interactions are great for building casual rapport, but they are most powerful when used in conjunction with offline networking efforts, such as due diligence and networking at conferences. During the last decade, it has become an expected part of the due diligence process to search on Google for anyone you are considering as a job candidate, business partner, hiring manager, and so on. Today it's also becoming standard practice to look up people on Facebook and Twitter. Through the tone and content on users' profiles, status messages, and tweet history, you can quickly figure out what makes them tick. The context is invaluable for learning who they really are and then establishing common ground, rapport, and trust. Even if the person's Facebook privacy settings prevent you from seeing the full profile, you can often at least see aspects of the profile, such as mutual friends and which Facebook Pages someone "likes."

Twitter and Facebook are also ideal for networking at conferences and other professional events. If the organizers have created a Facebook Event for RSVPs, usually you can browse the list of invitees (see Figure 10.8). Many event organizers create hashtags well before the event so that attendees can start mingling and seeding content suggestions. Maybe someone you have been wanting to meet will be there, or you come across others with whom you want to network. You could tweet at or send a Facebook message before the conference to introduce yourself and arrange a meeting. Similarly, you can use Facebook and Twitter to follow up and start to form a closer relationship with someone you met at the conference. Your photo and professional information will help people remember who you are and the context in which you met. Your other information that you decide to share, perhaps where you are from and photos of your children or your history of tweets, will help people get to know you better.

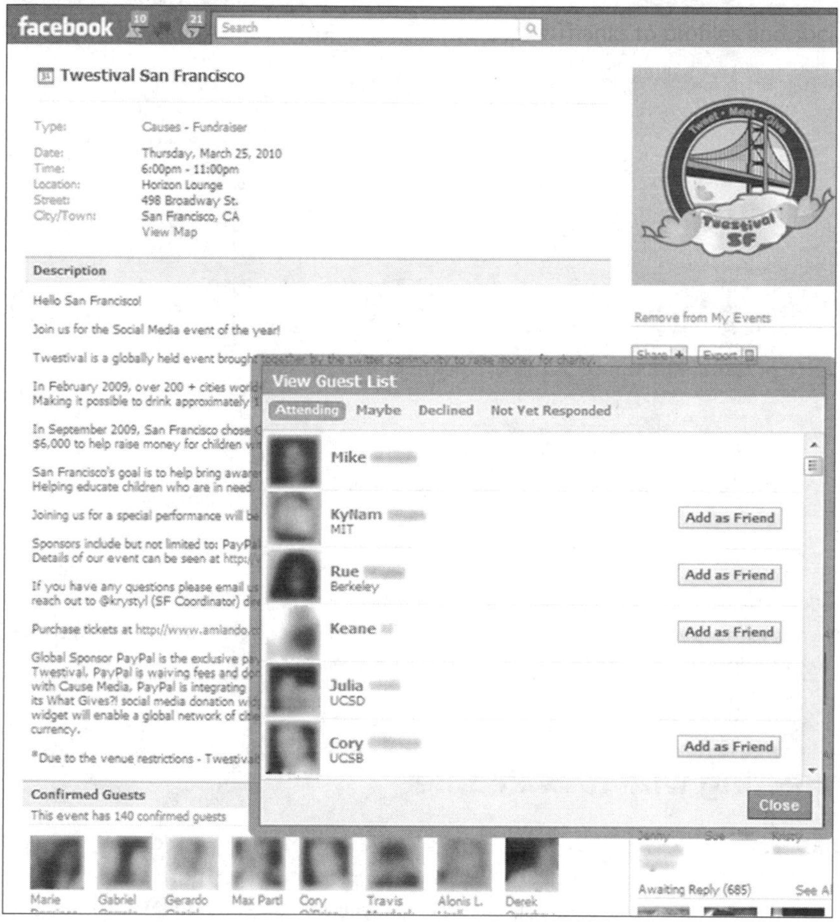

Figure 10.8
Facebook Event RSVPs are an easy way to check out and network with other attendees before, during, and after an event such as a conference.

In addition, you can join Facebook networks that correspond to your real-life networks, such as a workplace or school, to meet or reconnect with more likeminded people (see Figure 10.9). This can be a good way of quickly finding people you know so that you can make friend requests without searching on individual names. It is also helpful for getting to know more people in your company or school, especially those whom you might not normally run into while at work. Workplace or school (high school, college, or university) networks require email addresses from that domain. For example, to join the Hearsay Labs network on Facebook, I have to provide my work email address that ends in @hearsaylabs.com. Facebook sends me a verification email to that address. When I click on the link inside the email, it validates that I work at Hearsay Labs, and Facebook enables me to access the other members in the network.

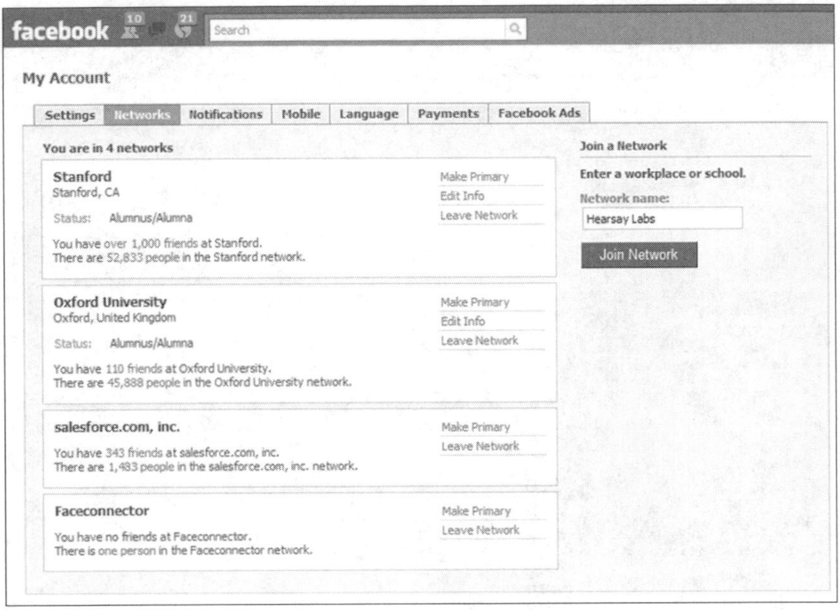

Figure 10.9
Specify your school and workplace networks by going to Account, Account Settings, Networks. You need to verify with an email address in the network's domain.

Connecting with New People

Being able to connect with new people, through either reaching out directly or requesting an introduction from a mutual friend, makes Facebook even more powerful. In the offline world, it's difficult to cold-call or email people out of the blue and expect that they'll respond. In contrast, Facebook and LinkedIn provide plenty of context about the person reaching out to us, and we can quickly see mutual contacts and decide whether this is someone we want to be in touch with.

If you're asking for an introduction, social networks also make it really easy to see exactly how you're connected to someone. For example, LinkedIn shows up to three degrees of separation and has a mechanism for requesting introductions that get forwarded by mutual contacts until you reach the desired person (see Figure 10.10). However, many people find it more effective to use LinkedIn to find how you are connected, but then ask for an introduction using a different means than LinkedIn, such as via email or Facebook.

LinkedIn can sometimes feel utilitarian and impersonal, but I do know that the site is changing this with new features such as profile pictures. Explore which method works better for you.

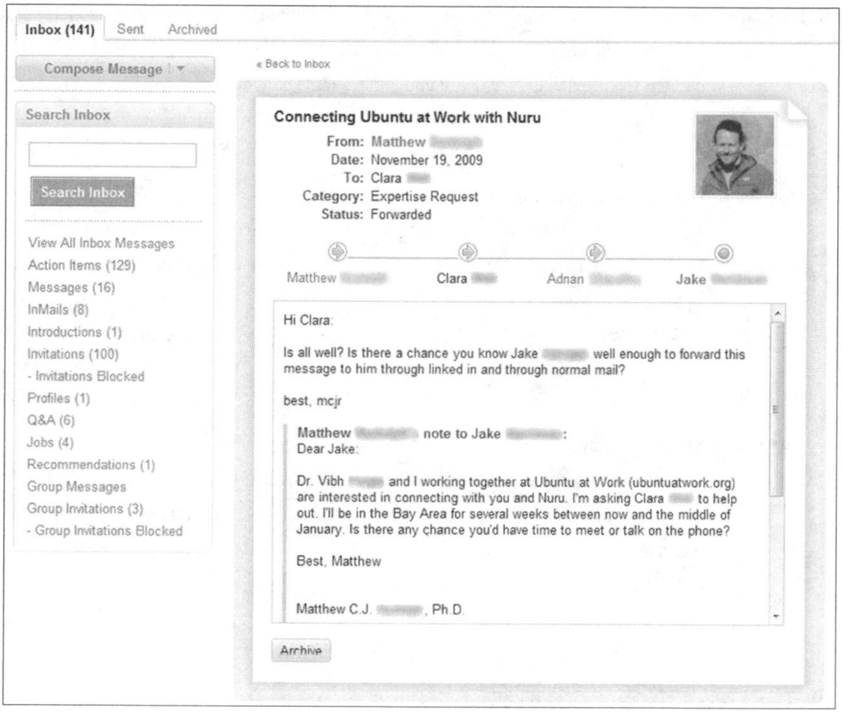

Figure 10.10
LinkedIn has a built-in mechanism for requesting and forwarding introductions.

Your job is also made easier when others ask you for introductions. Instead of needing to explain who someone is, you can assume that the person you are introducing to will be able to click through and check out the profile of the person you are introducing and also be able to see mutual contacts.

As we discussed in Chapter 3, the cost of doing someone a favor (such as providing an intro) is a lot less than the value the person feels, so we can replicate many of the benefits of the reciprocity ring. LinkedIn and Facebook lower the barriers to asking and receiving favors, and are especially well suited for introductions. When you have established a solid network and have begun to build relationships and social capital on the social Web, it will become an invaluable tool for you to find prospective customers, business partners, employees, consultants, and hiring managers, and to help your friends do the same. Table 10.1 summarizes the social network etiquette discussed in this chapter.

Table 10.1 Social Network Etiquette

	Facebook	Twitter	LinkedIn
Tone and professionalism	Casual and authentic. Use privacy settings to block colleagues and business partners from anything that is too personal.	Concise and authentic. Be consistent in what kinds of info you post. Little profile information is available about tweeters, so you really are what you tweet.	Professional and authentic. All contacts are business contacts.
Update frequency	At most a few times a day. Many people who link their Facebook status messages to Twitter inadvertently annoy their friends.	Up to dozens of times per day is okay.	At least once a week, but not very important because most LinkedIn users don't log in very often or for very long. So even if you link to Twitter or update a lot, you will likely not be at risk of annoying people.
Privacy settings	Very sophisticated controls enable you to customize privacy for 11 categories of information, including age, interests, posts, and photos. You can't hide your profile picture, mutual friends, or Facebook Pages that you have "liked."	Most people enable their Twitter stream to be publicly viewable, but some professionals create a separate personal account in private mode and each follower must be approved.	Privacy controls are limited to topics such as status messages and list of connections because people generally don't share that much personal information on LinkedIn.
Friend connections	Generally accept or initiate friend requests with only people you actually know, but it's also possible to network with new individuals with whom you might have mutual contacts and business to discuss.	You are free to follow anyone with a public Twitter account, and anyone can follow you. You can use a tool such as Nutshell Mail to track new followers and people who have unfollowed you.	Generally accept or initiate friend requests only with people you actually know from a professional context, but it's also possible to network with new individuals with whom you might have mutual contacts and business to discuss.
Watch out for	Beware hacked accounts of your friends that might ask you to click on a spam link or wire money.	Because anyone can @reply to you, be careful of spam accounts that @reply your spam links.	Overly aggressive sales or recruiters sometimes add as many people possible and can "pollute" your network, especially when they start reaching out to your contacts.

< < < **TAKEAWAYS**

✓ Before you build a Facebook or Twitter presence for your company, you need to build a presence for yourself and understand the dynamics of how people interact and engage on social networking sites.

✓ We all carry multiple identities across our personal and professional lives, relationships, and reputation. Friend Lists and privacy settings can help replicate these identities online and ensure that we are sharing the right information with the right people.

✓ Privacy settings are important even if you don't share much on your profile. For example, your friends could post photos and tag you in them.

✓ Facebook enables you to control who sees your information for everything except your profile picture, mutual friends, and Facebook Pages that you have "liked"—that information is always public.

✓ Social network profiles provide instant context when reaching out to someone new or providing an introduction, so the introduction itself requires less explanation.

> > > **TIPS and TO DO's**

❑ Most people don't need to create a total separation between their personal and professional identities. Consider sharing some personal information, such as pictures of your dog and favorite books, with business contacts. It helps with relationship building and makes work interactions more fun for both of you.

❑ Be consistent in how frequently you update your profile with status messages, photos, and links. Updates help you stay top-of-mind with your friends and contacts.

❑ Browse Facebook Event attendee lists and event hashtags to network with people before, during, and after events such as a conference.

❑ Information on social network profiles can help accelerate relationships. When you meet someone new, in addition to searching on Google, look up that person on Facebook, Twitter, and LinkedIn to get to know him or her better and decide more quickly whether this is someone you want to interact with and do business with.

❑ Use a combination of Facebook Wall posts, messages, posts, likes, comments, pokes, games, and tweets to send birthday or congratulatory wishes and easily stay in touch with friends.

11

How To: Engage Customers with Facebook Pages and Twitter

A Facebook Page (also known as Business Page or Fan Page) is like a Facebook profile for your business. In fact, Pages have many of the same components as personal profiles, including a profile picture, a descriptive blurb, photos and videos, messaging, and a Wall (see Figure 11.1). But instead of "friending," people can "like" a Facebook Page. Facebook Pages also offer far richer analytics about who your fans are and how this trends over time.

1. Page Picture
Image to represent your business.

2. Quick Info
Address, phone, and hours.

3. Fan List
Instead of friends, business pages have fans (that is, people who "like" the Page)

4. Custom Applications
Companies like Hearsay Labs offer widgets like lead capture, surveys, and polls you can customize and display on your Page.

5. Page Wall
Place to engage fans with updates, tips, contests, and special offers.

Anything you post appears to fans in their home page News Feed.

Figure 11.1
The components of a Facebook Page are pretty similar to those of a personal profile.

For large organizations and brands, Facebook Pages and Twitter can be important extensions to an existing web strategy for engaging existing audiences and reaching new audiences. For small businesses, Facebook Pages easily link to Twitter and provide a nice separation between your business and your personal life. Of the more than three million active Pages on Facebook, more than half have been created by small and local businesses. More than 20 million people "like" Pages every day.

This chapter starts with an overview of Twitter and Facebook Pages, including cost and benefits. We then walk through how to set up a Page and cover best practices for getting more people to "like" your Page, maximizing engagement, and deciding what to post. Finally, we talk about how to build social network communities to achieve your objectives, while taking into consideration existing brand conversations. The keys to success include appropriate use of persona marketing, seamless integration with other web initiatives such as blogs and Web sites, and creative techniques to differentiate your business and keep people coming back.

This chapter focuses mainly on Facebook Pages instead of Groups, although many of the concepts here also apply to Groups. I recommend Pages over Groups for most business use cases, but for the sake of completeness, the following guest expert sidebar from blogger Ann Smarty explains the differences between Facebook Pages and Facebook Groups.

Facebook Group Versus Facebook Business Page: Which Is Better?

Ann Smarty

Facebook Pages and Facebook Groups have two major differences:

- Unlike Groups, Pages are publicly visible (even to people who aren't on Facebook) and are indexed by search engines. This can be important for reach and reputation management, for example.

- Unlike Pages, Groups allow any member to send out "bulk invites," which means you can easily invite all your friends to join the Group. With Pages, you are forced to invite people individually. Therefore, groups can be more conducive to viral marketing because any group member can send out bulk invites to all his or her friends.

Beyond these high-level differences, Table 11.1 provides a detailed comparison of features.

Table 11.1   Comparing Features of Facebook Pages and Facebook Groups

Key Feature	Facebook Page	Facebook Group
"Ugly" URLs	No	Yes
Discussion hosting	Yes	Yes

Key Feature	Facebook Page	Facebook Group
Discussion wall and discussion forum	Yes	Yes
Extra applications added	Yes	No
Messaging to all members	Yes (via updates)	Yes (via personal messages)
Visitor statistics	Yes (via Page Insights)	No
Video and photo public exchange	Yes	Yes
"Related" event creation and invitation	Yes	No
Promotion with social ads	Yes	No

To conclude, Pages are generally better for a *long-term relationship* with your fans, readers, or customers. Groups are generally better for *hosting an active discussion* and attracting quick attention.

Ann Smarty (@seosmarty) is director of media at Search & Social.

Overview of Twitter and Facebook Pages

A Facebook Page is your company's home base on Facebook. For big brands and companies with significant Web traffic, it doesn't make sense to switch everything over to Facebook Pages. Instead, these organizations can use Facebook for Websites (discussed in Chapter 1, "The Fourth Revolution") to bring aspects of Facebook Pages, such as fans, interactive widgets, and News Feed, to existing Web properties. Having a Facebook Page to supplement these efforts might not be a bad idea, however, because linking from Facebook to your corporate site has tremendous SEO benefits.

For small businesses and other companies that struggle with generating traffic, Facebook Pages are definitely the way to go. A growing number of small businesses and sole proprietorships are ditching traditional Web sites altogether and using Facebook Pages as their Web site. Companies that do not have an SEO expert in-house or resources to easily update a Web site are realizing that it is far simpler and more effective to go where the customers are instead of expecting customers to come to them. But not only is Facebook better at generating traffic initially—Facebook is also better at getting people to come back again and again. Hitwise conducted a study in March 2010 comparing repeat traffic for the top five print and broadcast media sites (see Figure 11.2). Facebook helped generate 77% repeat visitors, compared to just 64% from Google News, which represents an increase of more than 20% in repeat visitors.

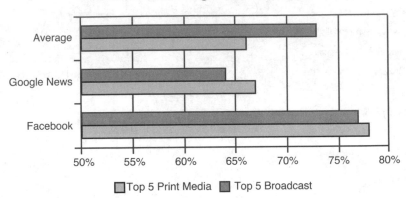

Hitwise US: Returning Visitor Rate. Week to 3/6/10

Top 5 Print Media   Top 5 Broadcast

Reprinted by permission of Experian Hitwise

Figure 11.2
Consider these results of the March 2010 Hitwise study comparing repeat visitors to top media sites originating from Facebook versus Google News.

Tweeting or updating a Facebook Page is as easy as posting a link with descriptive text—you don't have to go through a Web programmer or fancy content-management system. Finally, Twitter and Facebook Pages have all the word-of-mouth benefits inherent to the Social Web, so the right campaigns can trigger a ripple effect across friend groups.

Your Opt-In Fan Base

Twitter and Facebook Pages are the ultimate opt-in marketing channel. Everyone who "likes" or follows your business has actively chosen to do so. Having elected to receive your company's updates and communications, these individuals are likely some of your hottest leads and most valuable customers. Cultivate those relationships!

Because of the many page views from people spending so much time on Facebook, average click-through rates for social network ads remain pretty low compared to search marketing ads (see next chapter for more detail). However, click-through rates for Facebook Pages tend to be much higher than even in search marketing—as high as 9% to 10%, in a recent study by Vitrue. When they "like" your Page, people are explicitly opting in to your updates, so, of course they are more likely to click.

Companies have also recognized the power of Twitter and Facebook Pages for creating a following behind different subsets of product offerings. The most famous example is that Dell Computer sold more than $3 million in damaged or refurbished inventory through its @DellOutlet Twitter account. Dell found a loyal following of individuals on Twitter who were willing and happy to find deals through this channel without eating into its main, higher-profit business selling full-priced products on the Dell.com Web site.

Benefits of Twitter and Facebook Pages

In addition to potentially replacing your existing Web site, Facebook Pages offer a good opportunity to really learn from your customers; encourage customers to help other customers; and promote products, services, and messages to people who are already likely to be interested. Of the different ways your company can get on Facebook (see Table 11.2), I recommend starting with Facebook Pages so that you have a place to drive people once they click on an ad or if they have interacted with your application and now want to learn more.

Table 11.2   The Three Ways to Build Your Company's Facebook Presence

	Facebook Pages	Facebook Ads (See Chapter 12)	Facebook Apps
What it's best for	Building a community of existing customer advocates, retaining customers, building loyalty, and up-selling/cross-selling.	Hypertargeting specific audience profiles for branding or initiating a call to action to drive traffic, generate leads, or recruit fans.	Encouraging brand engagement and word-of-mouth app invitations.
Cost and commitment	Free to set up but requires commitment to ongoing updates and response to be successful.	CPC or CPM bids, similar to the Google AdWords model. Can specify budget and campaign start/stop dates.	Significant upfront cost of development. Few "go viral," but those that do can reach a lot of people very quickly.
Best practices	Offer exclusive promotions to encourage fans but reuse creative assets from the Web. Create separate pages for different audiences and languages.	Drive existing customers to your Facebook Page. Drive prospective customers to a custom landing page on your Web site that tracks the lead source as Facebook.	To reduce risk and time to launch, many brands temporarily sponsor an already-popular app for a specific campaign instead of building their own app.
How to get started	Go to http://facebook.com/create.php and seed your fan base with friends, family, and employees, to provide early critical mass.	Go to http://facebook.com/ads. Start with a test campaign using less hypertargeting criteria and gradually narrow it to your highest-converting segments.	Identify app ideas consistent with your brand. Build apps on your own, outsource development, or sponsor. Check out http://developer.facebook.com.

Depending on how much audience overlap you have between Facebook and Twitter (and how well staffed you are in your organization), it may make sense to link your Twitter account to your Facebook Page so that any posts such as status updates, links, and photos get automatically tweeted out. After you set up your Facebook Page, you will see an option inside Facebook that enables you to add your Twitter account. This is how I manage my Facebook Page (http://thefacebookera.com) and Twitter account (http://twitter.com/clarashih), and it has been a convenient way to have a consistent voice. Typically, I post once per day on my Facebook Page and tweet an additional two to three times. Conversely, a Twitter application on Facebook Platform lets you autopublish any tweets as Facebook status messages.

Cost and Commitment of Facebook Pages

Facebook Pages are free to get started—the true cost comes from the time required to maintain your Page on a regular basis. How much time do you need to spend to have a productive Facebook Page? It depends—you can find examples of successful Pages at both ends of the spectrum.

As we introduced in Chapter 9, "How To: Develop Your Facebook Era Plan and Metrics," Ferrero executives in 2008 discovered that passionate fans had created a Facebook Page for Ferrero Rocher that had millions of fans (see Figure 11.3). Instead of demanding that this Page be taken down (which would be a big mistake, as some other brands have discovered), Ferrero decided to go into listening and learning mode. The company realized that people around the world are extremely passionate about its chocolates and that taking a backseat on this Facebook Page was actually *more* effective at building authentic community. Over time, the social media team is slowly getting more involved and now is in a much better position to do so because the company has been really listening to its customers. You hear more from Ferrero executive Guillaume du Gardier later in this chapter. To help distinguish official brand Pages from fan-led efforts, Facebook has since introduced Community Pages to provide loyal customer advocates with a way to create unofficial communities about the products and brands they love.

Figure 11.3
The cost of and time commitment to this Facebook Page has been minimal for Ferrero because the Page is completely fan driven.

On the other end of the spectrum are Facebook Pages such as H&M, a popular global clothing retailer headquartered in Sweden. With over two million people who "like" the Page, the H&M Facebook Page gets updated daily with special deals, news, and contests; it averages more than ten new posts and comments a day (see Figure 11.4). High levels of audience engagement are involved here, and each company post generates several hundred (and sometimes thousands of) likes and comments. The Page has a number of custom tabs and applications, such as polls, discussions, and spotlights on the season's fashions and featured designers. This Page is clearly the work of one or more individuals who devote a significant amount of time (if not all their time) to Facebook for the company.

Figure 11.4

H&M has a very successful Facebook Page that the company actively manages; it posts multiple times throughout the day and responds to a percentage of fan posts.

Whether you take a backseat or post ten times a day, the important point is to be consistent. Don't post five times a day for two weeks straight and then not post again for six months. Start small and decide what you can and want to commit to, and then slowly add more. When you have fans and are posting regularly, try to gauge the significance of Facebook or Twitter to your business relative to your other online and offline customer channels, and use that to determine future levels of commitment and investment.

Setting Up Your Facebook Page

Okay, let's roll up our sleeves and get tactical. Setting up your Facebook Page will take anywhere between 15 minutes and an hour, depending on how familiar you already are with the Facebook screens. The way Facebook is currently set up requires you to sign in to your personal account to create a Facebook Page for your business. If you are a brand or larger organization, make sure you create redundancy and add multiple members of your team as admins on the Facebook Page, in case the person who created the Page leaves the company. Unfortunately, it is not currently possible to remove the person who created the Page as an admin. (Facebook might get mad at me for saying this, but some companies also create fake personal accounts whose login and password remain at the company, to avoid this issue of being tied to one individual's account.)

Step 1: Choose a Business Category and Name.

Go to http://facebook.com/pages/create.php and select a business category, such as Brand, Product, or Organization; or perhaps Food and Beverage (see Figure 11.5). Don't worry if you don't find an exact match for your business type. For example, if you are an insurance agent, Local, Banking and Financial Service should be close enough.

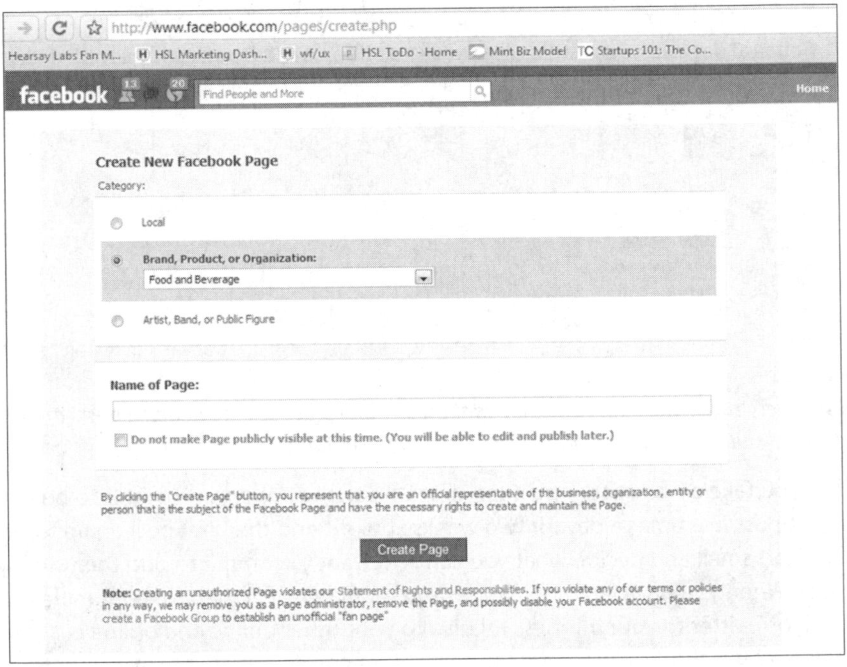

Figure 11.5
The first step in creating a Facebook Page is to choose a business category and Page name.

When it comes to naming your Page, be concise but specific! If you are a local business, specify where you operate. Good example: Kevin M. J. Fox | Mercedes Benz Manhattan—Park Avenue. Bad examples: Mercedes Benz (unless you are the corporate brand rep), MB

Manhattan (people might not know what "MB" stands for), Mercedes Benz Manhattan (not ideal if there are multiple Benz dealerships in Manhattan or if this page is for a specific salesperson), Kevin M. J. Fox | Mercedes Benz Manhattan—Park Avenue, New York, New York (way too long). Keep in mind that although it's important to be specific, it is mentally and visually overwhelming for people to keep track of overly long titles. Also, your Page name will precede each Wall post, and if it's too long, it might be distracting.

As for the check box to keep your Page private, unless you have a reason to keep your Page secret for a later launch date or don't think you'll have time to finish setting up the Page today, leave it unchecked. You can always change this later under Page Settings.

If you are a national brand with multiple franchises, come up with a naming convention (and business type) for your subsidiaries—say, Brand X—City, State; or Brand Y (Zip Code). Newbury Comics does an excellent job of giving each of regional store a unique identity while remaining consistent with the corporate brand. The company's social media marketing manager created a simple naming convention for stores that is also reflected in the Facebook Page profile picture (see Figure 11.6). The branding gives each store a unique identity while still conforming to the overall Newbury Comics brand.

Reprinted by permission

Figure 11.6
From left to right, these are the Facebook Pages for Newbury Comics brand, Newbury Comics Portland store, and Newbury Comics Buckland Hills store. Each has its own identity while supporting the overall brand identity.

Take the time to decide on the right business type and Page name, because you can't change either of these properties after you finish with this process. (You have to delete the Page and start over if you find a misspelling or other error.)

Step 2: Add Business Information.

The next step is to customize your Facebook Page with information about your business, such as a profile picture, blurb box, business address, and telephone number (see Figure 11.7). Choose a profile picture that best sums up your business. Choose one that looks catchy, appears professional, and is a high enough resolution not to appear grainy. The ideal image dimensions are 200 pixels wide by up to 600 pixels high.

Facebook has different default custom fields for the Page, depending on which business category you selected in the first step. For example, local retail businesses will be asked to enter store hours, whereas store hours don't really make sense for a brand or celebrity.

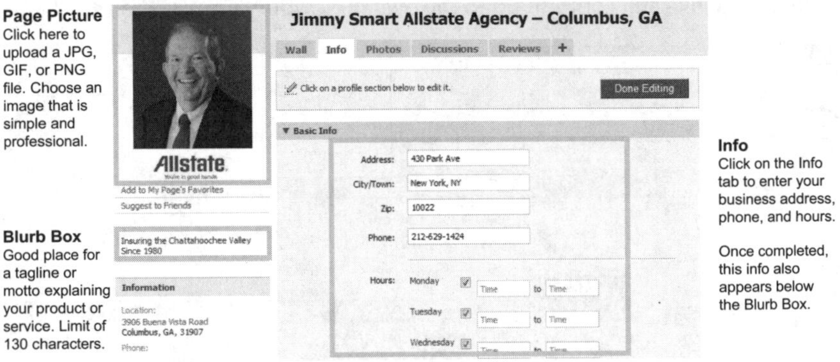

Figure 11.7
The next step in creating your Facebook Page is to enter your business information. Facebook asks you to provide different kinds of info, depending on the business type you specified in step 1.

Step 3: Configure Page Settings.

Click the Edit Page link under the profile picture on your Facebook Page to start configuring how your Page looks and behaves (see Figure 11.8).

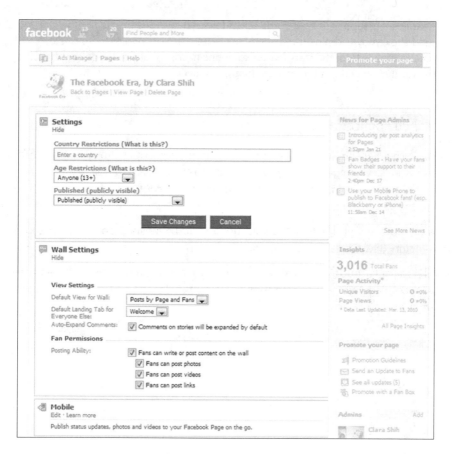

Figure 11.8
The final step in creating your Facebook Page is to configure settings for what appears on your Page and who has access to modify the Page.

You may customize four configurations:

- **Settings**—You may specify the country or countries where your business operates, to limit visibility of your Page. If your product has certain age restrictions, such as cigarettes or alcohol, by law, you have to specify a minimum age to view your Page. If you are working on a series of changes to the Page or getting ready for a product launch, this is where you can turn public visibility of your Page on and off.

- **Wall Settings**—Unless you have a huge issue with spam, I recommend changing the first drop-down box (Default View for Wall) to Posts by Page and Fans so that your Page is more interactive and is not dominated by your brand's voice. This is also where you can specify the landing tab someone sees when coming to your Page (by default, this is the Wall tab), whether comments are expanded by default, and fan permissions.

- **Mobile**—Click on the Mobile settings to see how to use SMS and email updates to your Page Wall.

- **Admins**—Last but not least, if you scroll down, you will see on the right where you can add and remove admins. It is a good idea to have at least two or more trusted employees as admins from the start, in case someone needs to take a sick day or abruptly leaves the job without time for a smooth handover.

Step 4: Add Applications.

By default, your Facebook Page comes with standard Page applications such as Photos and Discussions, which generally appear as tabs. To reorder tabs, go back to the Page itself; if you are an admin, you can drag and drop tabs (except Wall and Info, which are fixed) to the desired location.

You can remove any of the default applications. To add new apps, go to the Facebook App Directory (www.facebook.com/apps/directory.php).

Several popular Facebook applications providers exist. For example, Hearsay Labs develops Facebook Page widgets to help companies capture leads (see Figure 11.9), increase fans, and run promotions.

Figure 11.9

Interest and lead capture widget from Hearsay Labs, customized and embedded on a hotel's Facebook Page. Available at http://hearsaylabs.com/fbsignup.

Other popular Facebook application providers include Wildfire (specializing in sweepstakes), Involver (specializing in big brands and celebrities), and Context Optional and Buddy Media (both providing custom application development for big brands). The trade-off, of course, is that going custom creates a differentiated experience on your Facebook Page but costs more ($10,000–$20,000 or more, depending on how much functionality you want).

If you have your own Web development resources, you will likely want to install the Static FBML (Facebook Markup Language) application provided by Facebook. Facebook Page Wall posts don't support HTML or customization beyond changing image and text previews on links. Static FBML lets you customize your Page by inserting a tab or widget that renders HTML or FBML so that you can display custom fonts, images, video, Flash, and any other elements you'd be able to embed in a normal Web page. To get this application, search on the Facebook App Directory for Static FBML, or go to http://tinyurl.com/fbmlapp and click the first link under the profile picture: Add to My Page.

TurboTax, the popular tax-preparation software from Intuit, has done a great job integrating innovative custom apps into its Facebook Page. The case study that follows shares Intuit's strategy for marketing TurboTax on Facebook and the results seen by the company.

Case Study: Custom Apps Enrich TurboTax's Facebook Page

The social Web is a persuasion engine for TurboTax and a key part of the brand's overall marketing mix as it meets the challenge of driving a billion dollars in revenue in just 100 days from January to April each year. Facebook is an important platform for the company: Over half of TurboTax Online customers in 2009 are also Facebook users, a number that is expected to continue growing.

Innovative custom apps have allowed TurboTax to educate customers on tax questions, engage customers in conversation around the brand, and provide helpful tools for customers in completing their taxes.

Some examples from tax season 2010 include these:

- TurboChat, a live streaming video Q&A session hosted on TurboTax's Facebook page. In several sessions throughout tax season, a TurboTax VP who is also a certified public accountant answered Facebook users' questions about TurboTax and tax law.

- Product integration with Facebook that enabled customers to celebrate being done with their tax filing and post directly to their Facebook news feeds.

- TaxCaster, a free calculator available via TurboTax's Facebook page that allowed Facebook users to forecast their tax refund or tax owed.

continues...

- Friends Like You, an online recommendation engine that integrates with Facebook for Websites to allow users to see their friends' reviews of TurboTax—both positive and negative.

Each of these was a key driver of TurboTax's great 2010 results, up 20% from the previous year.

Managing Your Pages

After you create your Page, accessing it may be nonintuitive. One option is to start typing the name of your Page in the search bar. Your Page should appear in a drop-down of options for you to click on. Another option is to go to http://facebook.com/pages/manage, which lists all the pages for which you are an admin. Finally, consider bookmarking your Page or creating a vanity URL (more on how to do this in the upcoming section "Advanced Best Practices").

To delete a Page, click Edit Settings under the Page profile picture. You will see a Delete Page link under the page name.

For a list of additional frequently asked questions on Facebook, you might want to visit or bookmark www.facebook.com/help.php?topic=pages.

Getting (and Keeping) Fans

Now that you have your Facebook Page, you need to get people to "like" it. I recommend inviting friends, employees, and trusted customers to "like" your Page before advertising or inviting customers you don't know as well. Seeding your page with some initial activity and fans will make it more attractive to strangers than an empty page. You can invite them via email or the Suggest to Friends link in Facebook that appears below your Page profile picture (see Figure 11.10).

Include a link to your Facebook Page in your email signature, Web site, and print mailings. Ask customers to "like" the Page. Be sure to tell people *why* they should "like" it (for example, "Like our business on Facebook and get access to real estate news and the latest condo listings in Chicago")—otherwise, they have no incentive.

You can also try advertising on Facebook to get more fans (see Figure 11.10). Again, make sure you clearly convey what they get out of "liking" your Page. You can use neat tricks, such as hypertargeting ads so that only people who are friends with your existing fans, group members, or application users see an ad. Chapter 12, "How To: Advertise and Promote on the Social Web," covers Facebook ads, so read that next if this is a route you want to explore.

Keep in mind, however, that it isn't just about how many fans you have—it's about how engaged they are. Your agenda has no added value if everyone "likes" your Page but hides all your updates because they aren't relevant or interesting.

Figure 11.10
Below your Page profile picture are two links to help you get more fans: Promote with an Ad and Suggest to Friends.

When to Post

Post regularly (at least once a day), but not so much that people are annoyed (no more than twice back-to-back and no more than five times a day). Respond to fan posts and comments. Mix it up between news, video, and personal messages. If your page seems dead, people will stop coming to it and eventually may "unlike" your page.

Consider creating Wall post drip campaigns for a sequence of calls to action. Campaign calendars are a great way to provide brand consistency and build trust while saving time. Instead of having to spend time thinking of a new post at various times each day, you can come up with several posts at once and then space them out across multiple days or times of day.

Vitrue did a study in 2009 of a random sampling of Facebook Pages and found that Facebook Wall posts made on Mondays, Tuesdays, and Wednesdays had the highest click-through rates (see Figure 11.11). Of course, this varies depending on your product. For example, if your business is a night club or popular restaurant for dinner, your ideal times to post might be nights and weekends. Test the same kinds of posts at different times and days of the week to optimize what's most interesting for your audience.

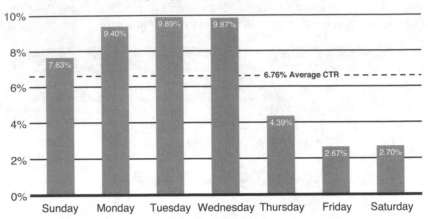

Figure 11.11
Vitrue study showing that, on average, Facebook Wall posts made on Mondays, Tuesdays, and Wednesdays yielded the highest click-through rates.

What to Post

You can post the same kinds of things to your Facebook Page as you do to your personal profile: photos, videos, links, status messages, and events. If you include a link, Facebook does a good job of fetching a link preview, which includes an image (if any), a title, and the first few lines of text.

A lot of people don't know this, but you can customize your post in two important ways. First, you can change what appears in the preview by toggling through all the different image thumbnails from the destination URL, as well as changing the title and preview text. Optimize for catchiness and click-through! Second, you can target the update by clicking just to the left of the Share button. (It defaults to Everyone.) Wall posts can be targeted to city/state/country and language (see Figure 11.12).

Figure 11.12

Two tricks you can do to increase the chances people will read and click through on your post are to customize the image and text previews and to target by geography and language. For example, you can do a separate post for the same content in Spanish, English, and Chinese.

A good rule of thumb is that you can talk about yourself or your product once in every five posts (or less). Facebook Pages are all about the soft sell. Overly self-promotional pages are a major turn-off. People should be able to figure out from your Page name, info tab, and blurb box what products and services you sell.

The best way to engage your fans is to offer something valuable on a consistent basis. Value can take different forms, including entertainment value, information, or financial value from special deals and coupons. Eight kinds of posts generate high engagement and response while contributing positively to your brand:

- **Be helpful.** Provide news and information people will appreciate. What you post should be relevant to your business and, most important, relevant to your fans (see Figure 11.13). Instead of going for the hard sell, Chicago-based Newman Realty posted about the federal tax credit for first-time home buyers. By being helpful, Newman Realty is building credibility, authority, and trust so that when people are in the market to buy, they will know who to call.

Reprinted by permission

Figure 11.13

The Page for Newman Realty focuses on providing valuable information and advice for first-time home buyers instead of going for the hard sell.

- **Be funny and entertaining.** Share jokes, stories, or musings that reflect your personality, and people will thank you for brightening their day. For example, Saint Louis real estate agent John Jackson has built quite a loyal following with his sense of humor. Each day, he posts a "Horrible MLS Photo of the Day" (see Figure 11.14).

> **John Jackson & Associates of RE/MAX Suburban**
>
> **This Real Estate Life: Horrible MLS Photo of the Day**
> thisrealestatelife.blogspot.com
> This one just seems so creepy, I thought it was worth sharing!! Guess I'm just not a huge fan of showering in a zip lock. Thoughts???

Reprinted by permission

Figure 11.14
Real estate agent John Jackson makes his fans laugh by posting a "Horrible MLS Photo of the Day" on his Facebook Page.

- **Love your fans.** Periodically recognize your fans. If someone just bought a car or a house, thank and congratulate them. Encourage your fans to post content such as pictures, videos, links, and musings. Your Facebook Page should be all about your fans (see Figure 11.15).

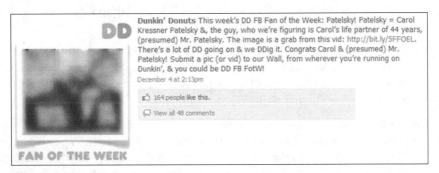

> **Dunkin' Donuts** This week's DD FB Fan of the Week: Patelsky! Patelsky = Carol Kressner Patelsky &, the guy, who we're figuring is Carol's life partner of 44 years, (presumed) Mr. Patelsky. The image is a grab from this vid: http://bit.ly/5FFOEL. There's a lot of DD going on & we DDig it. Congrats Carol & (presumed) Mr. Patelsky! Submit a pic (or vid) to our Wall, from wherever you're running on Dunkin', & you could be DD FB FotW!
> December 4 at 2:13pm
>
> 164 people like this.
>
> View all 48 comments

© 2010. DD IP Holder LLC. Used with permission.

Figure 11.15
Dunkin' Donuts runs an ongoing "Fan of the Week" contest in which fans submit photos of themselves with the brand. Each week, the winning photo is used as the Facebook Page profile picture for all one million fans to see.

- **Invite fans to your events.** Click the Calendar icon under the status message box to create an event. Fans will be able to RSVP and share with their friends. For example, Mercedes Benz Manhattan on Park Avenue promotes special events at the dealership to his Facebook fans, who appreciate connecting online with a traditionally offline brand.

- **Announce new products.** Share new product announcements. Ideally, link to a page on your Web site with more information and a picture. For instance, Ford drummed up excitement for its new 2011 Ford Fiesta by posting videos from the Los Angeles Auto Show featuring the new model (see Figure 11.16).

Reprinted by permission

Figure 11.16
Ford got fans excited about the 2011 Ford Fiesta by letting them preview photos and videos from the L.A. Auto Show.

- **Announce new locations.** Celebrate new offices, franchises, and locations by sharing with fans using geography targeting. For example, Chipotle has unveiled new locations such as one in Buffalo, New York, with Wall posts and special grand opening events.

- **Provide special offers.** Give your fans early or exclusive access to deals, offers, discounts, special events, free gift with purchase, or free gift for referrals to thank them.

- **Ask fans to weigh in.** Engage your fans and let them know that you value their opinion by periodically asking questions, either via a poll or survey application or simply by posting a question on your Page Wall.

- **Get personal.** Let your personality and office culture shine through. Share tidbits of personal information that help build trust and let people know you are really someone who care. Businesses can establish a genuine connection with customers by letting the personalities of their staff shine through on Facebook Pages through photos, holiday greetings, and other forms of authentic sharing.

Dealing with Negative Posts and Comments

The occasional fan complaint or negative comment is inevitable. The question is, what should you do in response, if anything? It depends on the situation. Consider a few different scenarios and how to handle each:

- **Complaints about a one-off bad experience**—Apologize and ask for more information so that you can investigate the situation. If it's something small, try to take it offline as soon as possible with private direct messages (DMs) on Twitter and Facebook messages instead of @reply and Facebook comments so that you aren't flooding everyone else's feeds with this one issue.

- **Multiple complaints about the same issue**—The customers are probably on to something. Hear them out and ask them to help you come up with a solution. Then really try to do something about it. Apologize publicly and let everyone know when you've fixed the issue.

- **Factually incorrect statement about your product or company**—Politely reply with the correction and encourage other customers to weigh in from their experience with your company.

- **Negative opinions about your brand**—It's hard to refute subjective statements other than to say, "I'm sorry you feel that way." If you come across consistently negative sentiment regarding your company or product, it may be time to launch a brand overhaul. You may need to influence how people think of your brand not only through social channels, but also through other online marketing channels, radio, TV, and print.

The following guest expert sidebar features some additional tips on effective Twitter for marketing from Sarah Milstein, coauthor of *The Twitter Book* (O'Reilly, 2009).

Five Tips on Effective Twitter for Marketing

Sarah Milstein

Twitter can be a game-changing tool for sparking positive connections with your customers, both current and potential. It can also be a time-sink—or, worse, an embarrassing channel for tone-deaf corporate communications. These five tips will help your company make the most of the medium:

- **Integrate it with your bigger communications strategy.** Twitter isn't an unfathomable new Web site just for geeks and other aliens. It's a communications channel, a lot like email, chat, phone calls, and other tools your company already uses. Companies that find the site most valuable figure first how Twitter fits with existing goals.

- **Before you speak up, listen in.** Here are just two great reasons to do a listening tour. First, conversation on Twitter involves a handful of oddball phrases and symbols. It's best to understand these so you can tweet like a native speaker instead of a tourist. Second, people are likely already talking about your company, your brand, and your competitors. Know what they're saying so you can join these conversations with confidence. Twitter search is free and public, so you can eavesdrop without an account: http://search.twitter.com. (Don't miss the powerful but under-used Advanced Search feature on the site.)

- **Post great messages.** Here's the secret to popularity on Twitter: Be interesting and share valuable stuff, like what we've already covered in this chapter.

- **Engage in conversation.** What's the biggest mistake companies make when they hit Twitter? They treat it like a broadcast channel. But Twitter is a *conversation* channel, and people already there will likely expect you to join in. Although you don't need to respond to every message to or about you, you should at least be aware of them. Messages that start with @your_account_name are addressed directly to you. From your Twitter home page, you can find a list of those messages by clicking the @your_account_name link on the right side of the screen.

- **Embrace customer support.** If you're in marketing and people on Twitter are sending you customer support questions, you can't ignore them and still expect good results from your account. Indeed, a mantra of the Web these days, "Customer service is the new marketing," is an important idea to understand. Twitter can spur great word-of-mouth for your company, or it can contribute to a reputation for unresponsiveness. Make sure you've got internal processes in place to fully support anybody tweeting out complaints or questions.

Sarah Milstein (@SarahM) is the coauthor of The Twitter Book *and the general manager and cochair of Web 2.0 Expo.*

Whatever you do, you must tread carefully and respect the autonomy, tacit rules, and culture of the community that has been created. The community might be around your product, but social Web communities are beyond your control. If anything, you should take what you learn from these less-than-positive conversations to improve your products and services—as we talked about in Chapter 5, "Customer Service in the Facebook Era," honest feedback is the only way we get better.

Advanced Best Practices

The remaining sections are tips and tricks for more advanced Facebook marketers, including best practices on segmenting audiences with multiple Pages, creating an emotional connection with persona marketing, improving conversions with special offers, and integrating with your existing online initiatives.

Offering an Easy URL to Your Page

By default, Facebook creates a very long and ugly URL to your Page, such as www. facebook.com/pages/Arlington-VA/Joe-Pasta-House/1234576891. This is challenging for people to type into a browser, especially if you are promoting your Page offline (such as with a billboard or sign in your store), because they can't just click on the link.

As a Page admin, once you reach 25 fans, you will see an option to create a unique username that allows your Page to be housed at http://facebook.com/*username*. For example, the username for this book's Facebook Page is thefacebookera, so the URL is http://facebook.com/thefacebookera. It's also not a bad idea to create a custom shortened URL through sites such as http://bit.ly or http://tinyurl.com that link to your Page so that it's even easier to tweet and share. For this book, I have set http://bit.ly/fbera to point to the Facebook Page.

Creating Different Pages for Different Audiences

Just as you can create different microsites in traditional Web marketing, consider creating multiple Facebook Pages to tailor products and messages to specific audiences. There's certainly a cost to maintaining multiple Pages, so don't do it unless you have truly distinct audiences and offerings. If you do decide to support multiple Pages, keep in mind that you can reuse elements across Pages, such as streaming blog updates, video, and applications, so that you aren't doing double or triple the work.

One of my favorite examples of well-orchestrated audience segmentation on Facebook is Sears Holdings Company, which owns Sears, Kmart, Land's End, and a handful of other major household brands. Not only is each brand encouraged to create its own presence and voice on Facebook and Twitter, but the Sears brand segments among its audience with different Pages, including Sears Portrait Studio, Sears Auto Center, and Craftsman Tools (see Figure 11.17). The company makes sure that all the brand and sub-brand Pages point to each other so that it's easy to navigate and taps into the full power of the entire portfolio.

Reprinted by permission

Figure 11.17
Sears Holdings Company has done a good job of creating different Facebook Pages and experiences for different audiences across its brands and product offerings. The main Sears Page (http://facebook.com/sears) has "favorited" all the other portfolio Pages for easy navigation and cross-referencing.

National Franchises: Thinking Globally, Acting Locally

Along these same lines of creating multiple Pages to connect better with audiences, national franchises have a huge opportunity to improve audience engagement by having local branches, agencies, and stores establish their own Facebook and Twitter presence. Having a corporate Page helps engage customers in your brand. It is extremely powerful to complement this with local Pages to engage customers in the day-to-day experience of interacting with your store, staff, products, and services.

As you saw in Figure 11.6, Newbury Comics is a good example of a company with a national following (more than 40,000 fans) that is now building out Pages for its 30 or so stores across the United States. The same store manager, product, or local event they see in the store is now also available to them on Facebook. Some customers "like" both the Newbury Comics corporate Page and their local store Page. Other customers choose one or the other. The key is to offer both options and let customers decide which they prefer to identify with, or perhaps both.

Hearsay Labs offers applications for corporate marketing to push out content (wall posts) to local stores', agents', and reps' Pages, as well as to monitor any content that gets posted otherwise, for regulatory and brand compliance.

Multinational Brands: Catering to Different Markets and Languages

An even greater management and coordination challenge arises when you are dealing with multinational markets, each with their distinct language, preferences, and customs. Multinational brands have three options on Facebook when deciding how best to communicate with the right audience in the right language with market-appropriate content:

- **Limit Page access and visibility by country**—One option is to create separate Facebook Pages for each country (or for certain countries), and edit the Page settings to limit Page access to people who live in the country.

- **Make your Page fully international**—For some companies, their global reach is an important part of the brand itself. In this case, you might want to allow posts in different languages to coexist on the same Page.

- **Target Wall posts and messages by language and region**—The last option is to have a single Facebook Page for multiple markets, but send targeted updates in each language, as we discussed in the earlier section "What to Post."

In the following guest expert sidebar, Ferrero new media director Guillaume du Gardier shares his experience in and insights about managing across multiple regional markets.

Engaging Fans in 25 Countries

Guillaume du Gardier

Ferrero has an amazing story on Facebook.

As of today, more than 23 million fans around the world have joined the various Facebook Pages of our brands. Nutella is the most popular, with 3.7 million fans, followed by Ferrero Rocher, with 2.5 million fans. In fact, we have more than 500 pages representing our brands. The astonishing thing is that the vast majority of these Pages are not official, but grassroots, created and maintained by fans.

After witnessing such tremendous passion for our products from fans, we decided to create some of our own official Facebook Pages, starting with Kinder France in September 2009. Today we directly manage five such Pages. Facebook has become *the* place for online conversation with our customers, so much that we are questioning the future of our brand Web sites. Does it really make sense to invest in an expensive branded Web site when we can directly connect with millions of fans who are already on Facebook? I expect that our Facebook Pages will only continue to grow in importance, perhaps to organize events, solicit feedback, announce new products, and so on. The possibilities seem endless.

continues…

One challenge for Ferrero is that we are a large multinational company that serves numerous global markets with distinct languages and preferences. We are continuing to learn as we go, but here are a few things we did that have helped us successfully cater to each unique market.

- **We have consolidated individual products under brands.** Instead of creating separate Facebook Pages for Kinder Surprise, Kinder Bueno, Kinder Chocolate, and so on, we created a single Page for the mother brand, Kinder. This reduced the number of Pages we need to maintain for every region. Any product-related posts are cleared with the specific product manager before going live.

- **We are creating separate Pages for each language.** To increase audience engagement, we decided to create separate Facebook Pages for different languages. For example, Kinder France is for the French market and Cioccolato Kinder is for the Italian market.

- **We are starting in the markets with greatest social media adoption.** Instead of rushing to create 25 or more Pages at once for each of the markets we sell to, we looked at data comparing Facebook adoption across different countries and are starting with the markets with the highest adoption rates. We get support from local digital agencies to ensure that any content we post is a good fit for the local market's culture and preferences.

- **For the remaining markets, we are in listening mode.** While we are focusing our development efforts on the key early markets, we are carefully monitoring the conversations taking place on our unofficial communities. We want to stay engaged and in the loop in case someday we want to expand our official presence to include these markets. Today we are testing the waters not only for audience reactions, but also for our own ability to execute in this constantly changing environment.

Guillaume du Gardier (@gdugardier) is the new digital media manager at Ferrero.

Persona Marketing: Creating an Emotional Connection

Persona marketing has been around for awhile but is taken to a new level in the Facebook Era, because customers can actually "friend" and interact with brand personas. Impersonal mass communications is giving way to personal, social, emotional dialogue.

Because identity and sharing are such a large part of the Facebook experience, companies have a unique opportunity to create an emotional connection with their customers. Allowing the personalities of your employees and executives to shine through can humanize even the largest and most bureaucratic organizations. The use of fictional character personas can make otherwise dull brands seem cool and fun. When you create a persona that feels genuine and authentic (even if it's made up!), people will remember and will be loyal.

Perhaps my favorite example comes from national fast food chain Jack in the Box. Instead of creating a Facebook Page about the restaurant (which might not be that exciting), company marketers created a funny, sarcastic biography and voice for their persona, Jack

Box, that includes factual statements about the restaurant (see Figure 11.18). For example, Jack's hometown is San Diego, because that's where the chain started.

Reprinted by permission

Figure 11.18
The Jack in the Box fast food chain has successfully created a persona around its brand: fictional CEO Jack Box. Jack Box stars in TV, radio, and print ads, and now has his own Facebook Page, with more than 40,000 fans, at http://facebook.com/jackbox.

The persona serves as a proxy for the restaurant, using humor and storytelling to bring the brand to life. It fits perfectly with the friending metaphor on Facebook that lets people connect with Jack just like they connect with other brands and friends. People love Jack. They post and comment on his Wall, write poetry, and send messages.

Other popular uses of personas include the Travelocity Roaming Gnome (http://facebook.com/travelocity), Nestle Nesquik Bunny (http://twitter.com/nestlenesquik), and Frank Eliason, senior director of Customer Service at Comcast (http://twitter.com/comcastcares). Especially in a customer service scenario where tensions and frustration levels are high, it has made all the difference at Comcast to make Frank the face of customer care. In the past, it was easy for people to hate and rant about Comcast—it was a big, faceless company just out to make a profit. Disliking Frank is much harder—as you read in his inset in Chapter 5, he is caring, friendly, and personable. Frank has good days and bad days, just like you and me. He has humanized the Comcast brand.

In the following guest expert sidebar, agency executive Rohit Bhargava from Ogilvy talks about the importance of having a personality in your social Web presence and provides a few tips on how to do so authentically, credibly, and collaboratively.

Personality Marketing on the Social Web

Rohit Bhargava

One of the biggest stumbling blocks for companies comes when they need to adjust the voice they're used to using for the new rules of the social Web. For one thing, companies have a lot less space to say something. For another, copying and pasting any kind of marketing lingo or even special offers into Facebook or Twitter just doesn't work. To succeed, companies need to have a personality.

To help, here are some surefire tips for building a great personality for your business on Facebook and Twitter:

- **Talk like a human—be authentic.** This may seem obvious, but even though it is easy to talk like a real person, it is surprisingly difficult to *write* like a real person. We are taught in school to remove the individual voice from our writing, yet without this voice, we do not sound authentic. Here's an easy trick: Read out loud whatever you are about to post, and listen to yourself. If it doesn't sound like something you would say verbally, don't post it.

- **Share proactively—earn credibility points.** It's easy to respond to posts that take place on your Facebook Page and are all about your brand, but where you really earn credibility points is in sharing links that have little to do with your brand and participating in conversations that happen elsewhere. These are the points that you cash in when you do post something specific about your brand, to keep fans from feeling like you are constantly pushing your own marketing messages.

- **Spread responsibility—make it a team effort.** Have multiple admins and individuals representing your brand voice. Establish parameters for team members in terms of what they can talk about, and create expectations for their ongoing contributions. The side benefit of this approach is that, by not leaving your entire social engagement in the hands of one person, you won't be left with a problem if any one team member decides to move on.

Rohit Bhargava (@rohitbhargava) is senior vice president of marketing at Ogilvy and author of Personality Not Included.

What personalities and personas make sense for your brand? What is their voice? What do they blog about? What story would you tell about them using biography, photos, and video? How do they interact with friends and fans? If you've never done persona marketing, social networking sites provide a good forum for trying it out.

Providing Special Offers and Deals

It's easy to generate interest from your fan base because this group of people has already elected to receive communications from your business. You can drive product awareness and sales with limited-time offers and coupons, and ensure relevance by using the targeting capability on fan messages and Wall posts.

The call to action could be a special deal or coupon, but you might also want to just invest in growing your marketing funnel with more fans. Thanks to profiles and social graphs, companies can now capture customer relationships online. That means the end game shouldn't be selling an item—it's about the longer-term view across multiple purchases in a customer's lifetime.

Similar to the Safeway giveaway, Papa John's Pizza experimented with promoting a free pizza offer through Facebook ads and added more than 125,000 fans in one day.

But how much is a fan worth? Well, a lot of it depends on your business, product price, purchase frequency, and more. One study published in the *Harvard Business Review* conducted an experiment with customers of Dessert Gallery, a Houston-based cafe and bakery chain. Results suggest that Facebook seems to positively influence purchase behavior. On average, people who "liked" the company's Page spent roughly the same amount per visit, but they increased the number of store visits per month and were more active word-of-mouth marketers, with an average Net Promoter Score of 75, compared with 53 for Facebook users who had not "liked" the Page and 66 for customers not on Facebook. As the authors of the study acknowledge, some self-selection likely occurred in terms of who chose to "like" the company's Facebook Page in the first place, so the results probably have elements of correlation. Still, even these early results are good validation for marketers that investing in customer relationships and loyalty will pay dividends in the long run.

Fans are valuable not only for what they purchase, but also for how they influence their friends. Some of the most successful campaigns on Facebook have been about rallying fans around word-of-mouth. As part of launching its branded line of ice cream in summer 2009, Starbucks gave 20,000 coupons to Facebook users to give to a friend (see Figure 11.19). This is a perfect example of marketing *between people*, not just *to people*.

Reprinted by permission

Figure 11.19
Starbucks launched its branded ice cream line with a Facebook application that let users send friends a coupon for a free pint of Starbucks ice cream. Nearly 20,000 coupons were redeemed over an 11-day period.

On the Twitter front, companies such as Dunkin' Donuts are finding creative ways to derive value from fans while providing value to fans. The company has a successful on going "Win Free Coffee for a Year" offer on Twitter that drives sign-ups for its "DD Perks" loyalty program and allows the company to gather valuable customer information.

Reusing Creative Assets and Integrating with Existing Web Efforts

The biggest challenge of your Facebook Page is keeping it dynamic. But this may be easier than you think, especially if you are already investing in periodically building new interactive content for an existing Web site. I highly recommend reusing some existing creative assets on your Facebook Page, not only because it will save you time and money, but also because it reinforces consistent branding and messaging. Different people prefer to access and interact with your business through different channels—and whichever channel they choose (and also if they choose multiple channels), they should have a consistent and cohesive experience.

To start, it's pretty easy to integrate an external blog into your Facebook Page by using Facebook's Notes application, which is installed by default when you first create a Page. (You should see it in the list of applications when you click Edit Page.) After you go through the one-time setup process of specifying the URL for your blog's RSS feed, the application autoposts any new blog entries onto your Facebook Page Wall. Sixty-two percent of Fortune 500 companies report that they have at least one customer-facing blog, so this is readily available content that you can funnel through an additional channel. Many company bloggers have found a much steadier and more engaged readership after bringing their blog to Facebook than they had when they expected people to come to their external blog site.

As for creative assets, the Gap Inc. brands do a good job balancing creative reuse with exclusive Facebook-only campaigns, as Old Navy did in Figure 11.20. This especially matters for industries such as clothing and retail, in which the inventory you are promoting is highly seasonal and constantly changing.

Figure 11.20
Instead of reinventing the wheel on every weekly ad, Old Navy wisely reuses elements from its Web site http://oldnavy.com on its Facebook Page, http://facebook.com/OldNavy.

The Gap's Facebook Page does an excellent job of weaving in existing video and other content, and it also links to Gap's Twitter and YouTube presence (see Figure 11.21).

Figure 11.21
The Gap's Facebook Page is laid out differently than on its Web site, but it actually reuses a lot of the same elements, including videos and photos, and links to The Gap's Web site, Twitter, and YouTube.

The Best of Twitter and Facebook Pages

When I speak at conferences, often one of the most popular requests during the Q&A is for me to walk through the "best" examples of corporate Facebook Pages and Twitter accounts. Of course, different Twitter accounts and Facebook Pages do different things well, and certain tactics that work well for one brand might be a poor fit for another.

That said, I next showcase some of what I think are the best, most innovative company presences on Facebook and Twitter based on audience engagement, creativity, and business fit. I encourage you to browse these Twitter handles and Facebook Pages to see what lessons you can apply to your own efforts. I also invite you to submit your company's Facebook Page or Twitter handle for these lists, which I'll update once a quarter.

The Facebook Era Top 15: Brands

I was on the panel of judges last year for The Big Money Facebook 50, a ranking of brands that currently make the best use of Facebook. For this, I did an in-depth analysis of nearly 100 brand Pages.

For *The Facebook Era* Top 15, I am also including brands on Twitter. Here are 15 of the best among the big brands (in no particular order):

- **iTunes** (www.facebook.com/itunes)—Does a wonderful job conveying Apple branding and incorporating offers and podcasts. Very active Wall indicates high levels of fan engagement.

- **Coca-Cola** (www.facebook.com/cocacola)—Gorgeous and memorable creative assets and great use of contests that encourage participation. Also a great story of how a brand worked with grassroots Page owners to come up with something that really works for both the brand and the community.

- **Victoria's Secret** (www.facebook.com/victoriassecret)—Great use of photos, videos, contests, and events to keep fans engaged. The Page owner is responsive and proactive about posting frequently, and each post gets thousands of likes and comments.

- **Disney** (www.facebook.com/disney)—Very nicely done page. I like how the Exclusives tab features special events and screenings—this really helps tie the social media angle back to Disney's offline motion picture business.

- **Red Bull** (www.facebook.com/redbull)—Solidly done Page incorporating contests, polls, videos, and promotions. I like the reuse of creative assets and branding from other Web properties, such as tying in Red Bull athletes on Twitter, to streamline efforts and provide a consistent brand experience.

- **McDonald's** (www.facebook.com/mcdonalds)—Fantastic Page that really captures McDonald's global, family-friendly brand while clearly engaging fans, as evidenced by the high numbers of likes and comments.

- **Ford** (www.twitter.com/scottmonty)—Like Frank at Comcast, Scott has really humanized the Ford brand on the social Web. His tweets are helpful, responsive, and funny.

- **Ben & Jerry's Homemade, Inc.** (www.facebook.com/benjerry)—Does a great job capturing the spirit of Ben & Jerry's, using applications and contests, and conveying an authentic grassroots feel through event photos. That's hard to do for many big brands, so kudos!

- **Luxor Hotel and Casino** (www.twitter.com/LuxorLV)—Genuine and lively Twitter account chock-full of exclusive promotions and giveaways, such as the CRISS ANGEL Believe gala party. Also personally responsive to individual tweets and @replies.

- **Chicago Bulls** (www.twitter.com/chicagobulls)—Real-time information is the perfect fit for sports fans trying to follow a game. Fans are highly engaged, often @replying with their game observations and complaints about the referees!

- **American Red Cross** (www.twitter.com/redcross)—Extremely vibrant community, with more than 110,000 followers and real-time updates on Red Cross initiatives, as well as helpful information for people in crisis-stricken sites.

- **Porsche—The Official Page** (www.facebook.com/porsche)—Very interactive Page, with a clever custom application that appeals to the core customers: sports car enthusiasts.

- **Forever 21** (www.facebook.com/forever21)—Great incorporation of a custom app that lets people shop within the Facebook environment.

- **Wachovia** (www.twitter.com/wachovia)—Helpful finance and banking tips—extremely responsive to fan tweets. Great outlet for promoting financial literacy Webinars and other content.

- **T.G.I. Friday** (www.facebook.com/fanwoody)—Has incredible personality and the highest fan engagement I've seen for any page with a similar fan count. It is a perfect example of persona marketing on Facebook.

The Facebook Era Top 15—Small Business

Big brands that are already well known and have a substantial offline following can more easily establish a big community on Facebook. For small businesses, it's a different story.

More than a million small businesses are on Facebook and Twitter. Obviously, I didn't have a chance to look at them all, but here are 15 great examples I came across:

- **Musicians Toy Store in New Bern, North Carolina** (www.tinyurl.com/fbmusicstore)—This vibrant community has high fan engagement on this local music store's Facebook Page. Staff members share photos and videos showcasing instruments and equipment, and post events, store hours, music lessons information, discounts, and more.

- **Venezia Day Spa in Lynnfield, Massachusetts** (www.facebook.com/VeneziaDaySpa)—This is a great example of a small business owner connecting with her clients and getting support from friends in the community via Facebook. I like the addition of the Reviews tab. (Everyone has been giving this place five stars so far!)

- **Moussy's Bistro in San Francisco, California** (www.tinyurl.com/fbmoussy)—Moussy's makes perfect use of its Facebook Page to announce its weekly Sunday movie showings, happy hour specials, and latest menu additions.

- **Resnicks Hardware Store in Bayonne, New Jersey** (www.tinyurl.com/fbhardware)—A historic neighborhood hardware store has a great online presence. Viewing photos and reminiscing helps bring back nostalgia, while new product announcements and discounts help drive business.

- **The Treats Truck in New York, New York** (www.twitter.com/TheTreatsTruck)—Fun homemade cookies, brownies, bars, and crispy treats are sold out of this truck. Its whereabouts are tweeted out to nearly 3,500 fans in Manhattan.

- **Plush Boutique in Atlanta, Georgia** (www.tinyurl.com/fbplush)—A boutique retail store in downtown Atlanta uses this Facebook Page to connect with shoppers, showcase its latest merchandise, and spread the word about sales and special promotions.

- **Busch Chiropractic in Fort Wayne, Indiana** (www.twitter.com/buschchiro)—Dr. Richard E. Busch, a chiropractor in Fort Wayne, tweets inspirational thoughts and information about back and neck pain. His Twitter profile background features his headshot and bio with a link to his Web site, which has additional information.

- **U-Save Moving in Detroit, Michigan** (www.twitter.com/USaveMoving)—A moving company owner based in Detroit shares his up-to-date whereabouts, random musings, favorite YouTube videos, holiday wishes, and @replies to people who ask about moving cost estimates.

- **Think! Graphic and Printing in Tempe, Arizona** (www.tinyurl.com/fbthink)—This well-designed Page shows examples of past work and lets you request a quote for flyers, screen print, and Web design jobs right from Facebook.

- **Fletcher Dentistry in Modesto, California** (www.facebook.com/fletcherdentistry)—A loyal customer base posts testimonials and gratitude. The dentist office posts favorite youth patient drawings, dental facts (such as explaining what causes bad breath), and birthday and congratulatory wishes to newlyweds and new babies.

- **Luke Zilli, Personal Trainer in Udine, Italy** (www.tinyurl.com/fbtrainer)—A personal trainer in Italy has drawn nearly 1,000 fans through sharing tips on nutrition, exercise, and bodybuilding, and by posting "before and after" photos of past and current clients.

- **416-Florist in Toronto, Canada** (www.twitter.com/416florist)—A local florist tweets floral care tips and updates on what flowers are in season. Not surprisingly, their Twitter profile background has a photo of gorgeous flowers.

- **Gardner's Used Books in Tulsa, Oklahoma** (www.twitter.com/GardnersBooks)—This very active Twitter account updates fans on the latest books available for sale, author readings and other events, and special promotions and sales.

- **Master Kleen Dry Cleaners in Columbus, Georgia** (www.tinyurl.com/fbcleaners)—A local business shares promotions, holiday wishes, and community event sponsorships on its Facebook Page.

- **Brooke Peters Master Plumber, Inc. in Omaha, Nebraska** (www.tinyurl.com/fbplumber)—This is a simple but effective Page for a local plumber, with a telephone number and opening hours.

Congratulations to everyone who made it on the list!

Submit Your Business for the Top 15

If you think others could benefit from seeing your company's Twitter handle or Facebook Page, submit it for *The Facebook Era* Top 15 at http://thefacebookera.com/top15contest.php.

The best submissions will receive public kudos on *The Facebook Era* Facebook Page, Twitter account, and blog!

< < < TAKEAWAYS

✓ The three most popular ways to build your company presence on Facebook are Facebook Pages, Facebook ads, and Facebook applications. I recommend starting with a Facebook Page because it's quick and free to get going.

✓ Facebook Pages are like Facebook profiles for your business. A growing number of small businesses that have struggled to drive traffic to their Web sites are beginning to ditch these Web sites in favor of a Facebook Page.

✓ For larger companies that already have an established Web presence and good Web traffic, Facebook for Websites might be a good way to bring features of Facebook to your Web site. Having a Facebook Page in addition can be a great way to drive additional traffic and improve your SEO.

✓ Persona marketing is extremely effective on social networks because of profiles and fan relationships. Either fictitious personas or employee personas can humanize your brand, help tell a more authentic story, and create an emotional connection with customers.

✓ Special offers on Facebook Pages are the best way to attract and engage fans—but remember to optimize for the long-term fan relationship rather than a one-time click or sale.

> > > TIPS and TO DO's

❏ Build your Facebook Page in stages and continue increasing investment if your efforts are well received. Start with a basic Page, then start posting more frequently, and then consider adding some apps.

❏ Seed your Facebook Page with friends, employees, and loyal customers so that when others visit for the first time, it is already lively and bustling.

❏ Brand your Page and offer something of value—this could be discounts, helpful news, education, or entertainment value, as long as you're consistent.

❏ Track your progress via Facebook Page Analytics and try to figure out which days of the week and times of day yield the highest number of impressions and click-throughs from your fan base.

❏ Reuse creative assets from your Web site, YouTube, email marketing campaigns, and other initiatives instead of reinventing the wheel. You can always supplement with original Facebook-exclusive content.

12

How To: Advertise and Promote on the Social Web

As I introduced in Chapter 6, "Marketing in the Facebook Era," marketers are now able to truly tailor the messages and experiences they provide for customers and prospects. Using the rich information on social network profiles, companies can make customer interactions more personalized and, thereby, improve relevance and conversions. Hypertargeting techniques can also tailor custom campaigns to make ads feel more relevant and personal to the people viewing them. Passive word-of-mouth broadcasts that occur across friend groups via Facebook News Feed further multiply the reach of these campaigns. This chapter walks through how to set up hypertargeted ad campaigns on Facebook and LinkedIn. It also touches on innovative new "engagement ad units" Facebook has been rolling out.

First, let's talk about what you're trying to accomplish. The ideal advertising campaign has 100% click-throughs and conversion. That's what would happen if every ad was perfectly targeted with the right content to the right person at the right time. After all, if an ad is targeted and relevant, then it is valuable to both viewer and advertiser.

Of course, perfect targeting is not possible. But we are getting close. As you can see in Table 12.1, as more activity has moved online, advertisers have drastically increased their capability to target based on activity by and information about individuals. Before the Facebook Era, online advertising was largely behavior driven, based on explicit actions such as searching on a keyword or visiting a Web site. With social networking sites, we can layer on an important personal identity component about people who view ads so that we can target not only based on what people are *doing,* but also what they say and how they identify themselves.

Table 12.1 The Evolution of Ad Targeting

Type of Targeting	What It Is and How It Emerged	Example
Contextual	Starting in the late 1990s, Overture and later Google pioneered ad targeting based on search terms and other contextual content. Context advertising includes paid search—that is, search engine marketing (SEM)—as well as organic search engine optimization (SEO).	Cynthia does a Google search for digital cameras, and targeted ads for digital cameras appear to the right and top of organic search results.
Behavioral	Information collected on an individual's Web surfing and shopping behavior is used to target ads. Early pioneers include Boomerang, Tacoda Systems (acquired by AOL), FrontPorch, and Phorm.	Ryan reads an article about new golf technology on Forbes.com. When he surfs the Web the next day, targeted ads for golf clubs appear on a different Web site belonging to the same ad network.
Retargeting	Retargeting is a specific instance of behavioral targeting. An ad is shown for an item that someone was looking at previously but didn't end up buying. Retargeted ads are like reminders to people who just left a site or abandoned their shopping cart to reconsider. Advertisers can even define sequenced ads in which they offer progressively steeper discounts until the person buys. Leaders in this space include Fetchback, Dapper, and Google.	Clayton lingers on the online product page for a pair of shoes, even selecting the shoe size, but does not end up going through with the purchase. Later, when Clayton is on a different website, he sees an ad for the same shoes.
Profile hypertargeting	Demographic information and personal preferences on social network profiles are used to hypertarget ads to specific audience segments. Early pioneers were MySpace, Facebook, and LinkedIn.	Steve writes on his Facebook profile that he is an Iron Man triathlete. Advertisers hypertarget triathlon equipment and competitions to him.

Building Your LinkedIn DirectAds Campaign

First, let's walk through LinkedIn's hypertargeted ad offering, DirectAds. LinkedIn's advantage over Facebook is that it tends to have more career-related information about people, as well as more structured data (a taxonomy) about industries. The disadvantage is that noncareer-related information about people is quite lacking, so DirectAds generally is a better fit for B2B than B2C scenarios.

Building your LinkedIn campaign involves three steps: 1) create the ad, 2) target the ad, and 3) specify your payment model and budget. First, go to www.linkedin.com/directads/create.

Step 1: Create Your Ad.

Your ad consists of an image, a headline, body text, and a destination link.

- **Image**—You can choose any PNG, JPEG, or GIF image file. The optimal dimensions are 50 by 50 pixels. Although the image is important, LinkedIn will sometimes strips out the image for cost-per-click (CPC) ads and shows a text-only ad. If the image is crucial to your ad, choose the cost-per-thousand impressions (CPM) model in step 3 or work directly with LinkedIn on your ad placement.

- **Headline**—As with search ads, your headline is key in grabbing people's attention (especially if your ad gets shown as text only). A good tip here is to choose a headline that relates to the target audience you define in step 2. For example, if you are targeting marketers, your headline might reference "The Perfect Tool for Marketers."

- **Body text**—You have two lines to communicate the key benefit of your product or service and a call to action. Most often ads fail because the call to action is weak or non-existent.

- **Destination link**—Just as you would for Google ads, create a custom URL so that you can track traffic and conversions back to this ad campaign.

Step 2: Select Targeting Criteria.

LinkedIn DirectAds allow hypertargeting on seven profile attributes: company size, job function, industry, seniority, gender, age, and geography:

- **Company size**—(See Figure 12.1.) This can be useful for prospecting to your ideal customer segments and is an example of data that Facebook does not have about employers. As in Facebook ads, the LinkedIn ad wizard dynamically updates the count of how many users match your criteria as you refine your targeting.

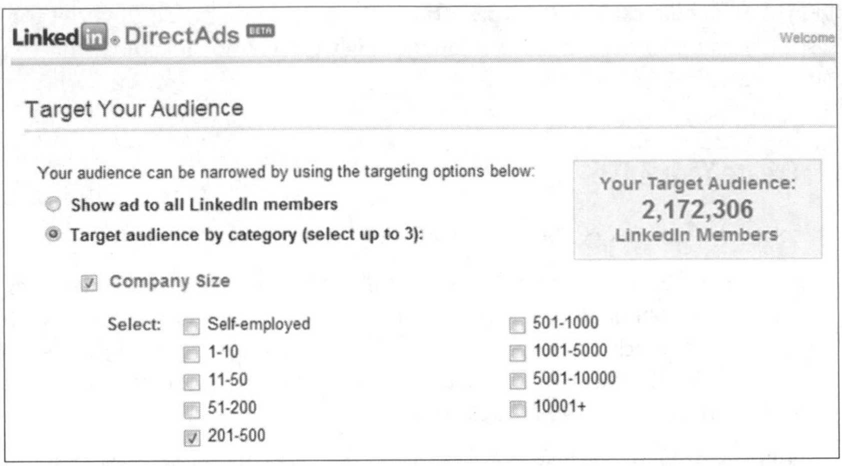

Figure 12.1
LinkedIn DirectAds allow hypertargeting based on the size of the company where someone is currently employed. Here you can see that more than two million LinkedIn members work at companies that have between 201 and 500 employees.

- **Job function**—(See Figure 12.2.) This can be useful for recruiting certain types of roles or to reach strategic decision makers in a sales cycle. You can select up to ten job functions from a structured list provided by LinkedIn. Facebook also lists job function, but it is free form rather than structured as it is here.

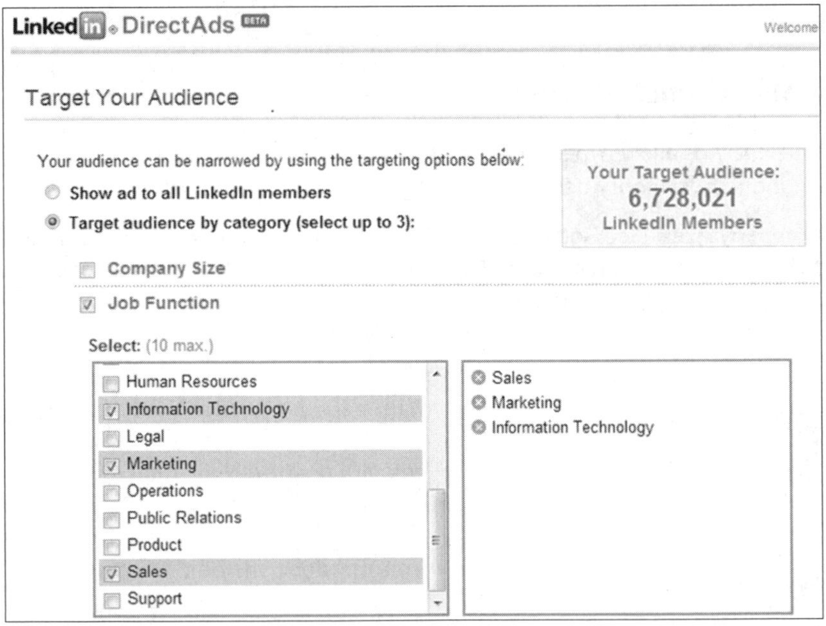

Figure 12.2
LinkedIn DirectAds allow hypertargeting based on someone's current or past job function. You can target up to ten job functions per ad campaign.

- **Industry**—Again, this can be useful for recruiting certain types of roles or to reach strategic decision makers in a sales cycle. You can select up to ten industries from a structured list provided by LinkedIn, and the targeting applies to both current and past industries. In comparison, Facebook does not have industry data on employers.

- **Seniority**—(See Figure 12.3.) This is another piece of useful information for recruiting certain types of roles or to reach strategic decision makers in a sales cycle. You can select from six different categories of seniority: individual contributor, manager, director, vice president, CXO, and owner.

Figure 12.3

LinkedIn DirectAds allow hypertargeting based on the someone's seniority level. Here you can see that more than 2.3 million CXO level executives are on LinkedIn.

- **Gender**—This should be pretty self-explanatory. LinkedIn claims to have gender information for 70% of its members.

- **Age**—Again, this is pretty self-explanatory. LinkedIn has age information for fewer than 40% of its members, so this might not be a great targeting dimension to use if you want to maximize your reach.

- **Geography**—(See Figure 12.4.) Facebook allows targeting by country, state, or city and includes radius targeting. LinkedIn's geography targeting is pretty limited, by comparison. There are only six countries to choose from, no state-level targeting, and city targeting only for select metro areas in the United States. LinkedIn's largest audience is the United States, with more than 30 million members (more than half of all LinkedIn users). Next is India (nearly 5 million members) followed by the United Kingdom (3.7 million), Canada (2.2 million), the Netherlands (1.7 million), and Australia (1.1 million).

Figure 12.4
Because LinkedIn does not have a huge membership base outside the United States and a handful of countries, geography targeting for ads is limited to 6 countries and 40 U.S. metro areas.

Step 3: Specify Your Budget.

As with Google AdWords, you can choose to pay per click (CPC) or per 1,000 impressions (CPM). The minimum bid is $2 for CPC and $3 for CPM, and the minimum daily budget is $10. You can run your campaign continuously as soon as it's approved or specify an end date.

Many advertisers find CPC appealing because they are paying for performance only. When ads are not clicked on, the advertiser essentially gets a brand impression for free. On the other hand, CPM can deliver impressions more cheaply when click-throughs don't matter. Without the pressure of having to generate a click, CPM ads might also tend to be flashier and contain more information.

What to Expect with LinkedIn Ads

Before you start your campaign, think about a few considerations unique to LinkedIn hypertargeted ads.

- You will notice less targeting on LinkedIn than on Facebook. For example, instead of defining your desired age bracket as you do with Facebook ads, LinkedIn lets you pick from four predefined age brackets.

- LinkedIn limits targeting on, at most, three of the seven criteria per campaign.

- You have the option to show ads on LinkedIn.com only or include LinkedIn's ad network partners. The trade-off is achieving a greater reach versus knowing what to expect. This matters less if you opt for CPC pricing, because then you pay only for performance.

Depending on whether you choose to pay by CPC or CPM, your ad might appear in different places. Figure 12.5 shows both. CPC ads often appear as text-only link ads (with the image omitted) at the top of the LinkedIn home page or profile pages. They might be appended with a link in gray to the LinkedIn profile of the person or company that created the ad. (You can configure this under profile preferences.) Most CPM ads that appear in the middle of the home page or profile pages are custom Flash-based ads. I recommend contacting a LinkedIn ad sales rep for these.

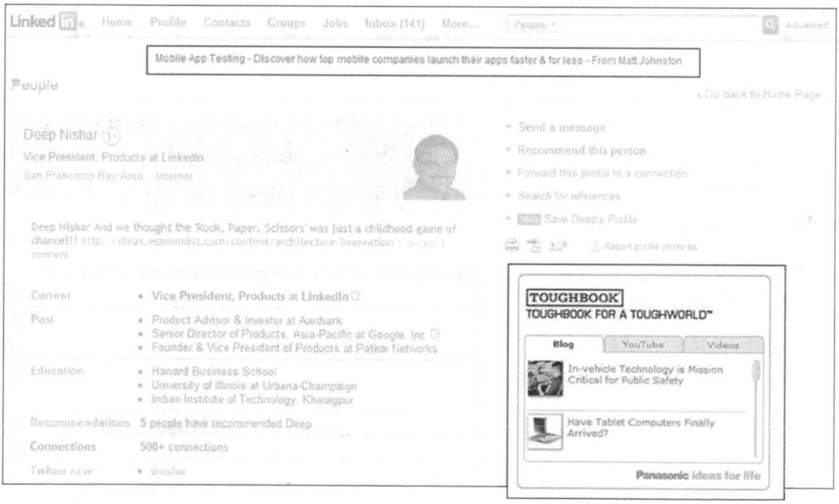

Figure 12.5
This is a text-only CPC ad appearing at the top of the LinkedIn home page. After the ad text is a link to the LinkedIn profile of the individual who created the ad. On the right is a Flash-based CPM ad.

One aspect of LinkedIn DirectAds that many people find hard to get used to is that there is no keyword matching. Ads are shown only by targeting the audience attributes described earlier.

It's early for social network ads in general, but especially so for LinkedIn ads. We ran nearly identical campaigns (to the extent possible, given the differences in the two ad systems) for the first edition of this book on both Facebook and LinkedIn. Facebook ads had more than twice as many click-throughs and conversions, and were a fraction of the cost. LinkedIn has an even bigger problem with a lack of purchase intent when people are on the site, as most people log in for the sole purpose of accepting or making a connection request, or searching for and viewing a specific set of profiles.

With the exception of recruiters, the companies I interviewed similarly struggled to see substantial results with LinkedIn ads—but if you have a success story, please share with me on whichever social network you prefer!

- **Twitter**—@clarashih #linkedin #ads
- **Facebook**—http://facebook.com/thefacebookera
- **LinkedIn**—www.linkedin.com/in/clarashih

Creating Your Facebook Ad Campaign

Facebook is an order of magnitude bigger than LinkedIn, so a lot more people might be interested in what your business has to offer. Of course, a lot more people also might not be a good fit for your products or services, so hypertargeting is even more important on Facebook.

Facebook has richer profile information about its members, which corresponds to more targeting criteria available to advertisers. Facebook lets you hypertarget against as many criteria as you'd like, which means you can define really narrow audiences to message to if that's what you want to do.

To get started, go to http://facebook.com/ads.

Step 1: Create Your Ad.

Similar to LinkedIn ads, Facebook ads consist of an image, a headline, body text, and a destination link.

Based on the audience you have identified and will target in step 2, customize your ad copy to appeal to the unique needs and preferences of that audience. What's important to this particular segment? What do you know about them (that is, what have you selected for) that you can use to make the message more personal? What have they bought in the past? What are they likely to want to buy in the future? Keep the ad text simple and be specific. Avoid compound sentences. Use simple language and good grammar. Especially if your objective is brand recognition, you should include your company or product name in the ad title or body.

As in any ad, the most important step is to provide a compelling call-to-action that encourages users to click on your ad. Users should clearly see in your ad copy exactly what you expect them to do and how they will benefit from going to your landing page. Use strong action-oriented phrases such as *buy, sell, see, order, register,* and *win.* Improve customer engagement and likeliness to click by making messages feel more personal and meant for them specifically.

Uploading an image is optional but highly recommended. Facebook's data shows that ads with an image perform much better than ads without one. The optimal image size is 110 pixels wide by 80 pixels tall, so you create or resize your ad image accordingly. Without special consideration, text in images, in particular, can sometimes become distorted and hard to read.

Step 2: Hypertarget Your Ad.

When you have your ad, you can target your audience along 11 different profile dimensions:

- **Location**—(See Figure 12.6.) Facebook lets you target by country, state, or city. Each ad can target up to 25 countries at a time. A powerful tool for local businesses such as restaurants, spas, and insurance agents is radius targeting, which shows ads to everyone within 10, 25, or 50 miles of a city. Behind the scenes, Facebook does the targeting based on the user's IP address and address, if the user has entered them.

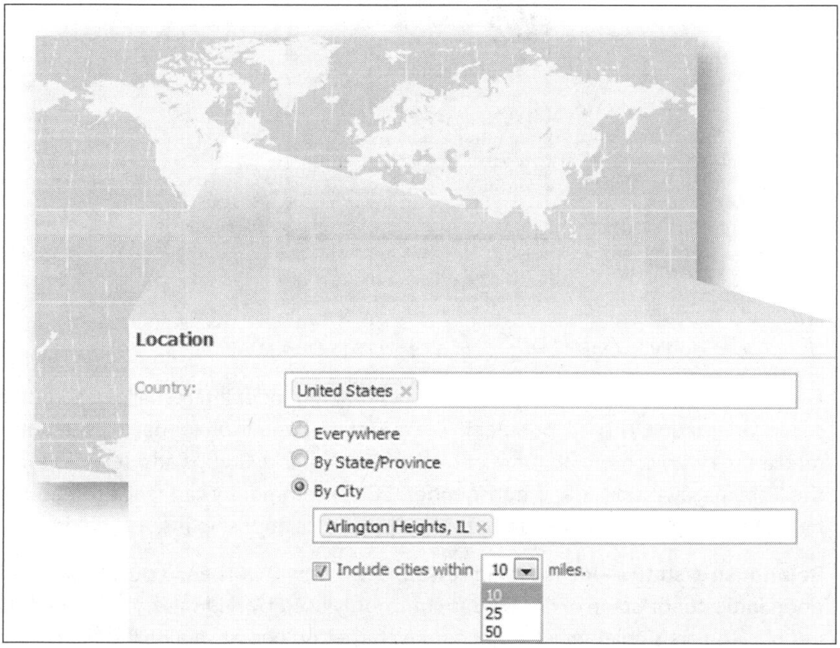

Figure 12.6
Location targeting on Facebook ads enables you to specify country, state, and/or city, as well as surrounding areas within a certain radius of a city.

- **Age**—You can specify an age range to target, from 13 (the minimum age to join Facebook) to 64. If you don't specify an age range, Facebook targets all users 18 and older. The college and recent graduate group is still the largest demographic on Facebook (29% of users), but older folks are catching up. More than half of Facebook users have been out of college for four or more years, and the fastest-growing demographic on Facebook is 35–49. Note that you can also choose to target people on their birthdays here, which a lot of businesses have found to be pretty effective—who doesn't appreciate a special wish or free gift on their birthday? More than a million birthdays pop up each day on Facebook!

- **Gender**—Nearly 95% of Facebook users have specified their gender, so this is a fairly reliable hypertargeting dimension. The U.S. Facebook population skews slightly female (55%). The optimal ad copy and image you select for your campaigns might differ greatly based on gender even if you are selling the same product. Gender is especially important in retail ads. If your product is meant for a specific gender, such as women, you might want to consider using two ad segments: ads appealing to women about your product and ads targeting men that talk about your product as a great gift for women. Figure 12.7 is an example of a gender-specific ad.

Give the gift of family

California Cryobank is seeking anonymous donors. Earn $100 per donation. Locations in Los Angeles, Boston and Palo Alto.

Reprinted by permission

Figure 12.7
This ad is applicable only to males (perhaps in a certain age range).

- **Gender interest**—The combination of gender and gender interest allows targeting for sexual orientation. This is a popular hypertargeting dimension for dating sites and media sites with content about relationships and dating. Groups and services targeting the lesbian, gay, bisexual, and transgender (LGBT) community can reach this audience by selecting the same gender in both the Sex and Relationship Interest fields.

- **Relationship status**—Relationship status, together with age and education level, is a good indicator of "stage of life." This is commonly used by dating services (targeting people who are single), jewelry companies (targeting people in a relationship, as in Figure 12.8), and the wedding industry (targeting people who are engaged).

Relationship status is also highly correlated with lifestyle, and certain lifestyles might be more amenable to your product or service. For example, a married person might be more likely than a single person to be interested in ads about purchasing life insurance or buying a home.

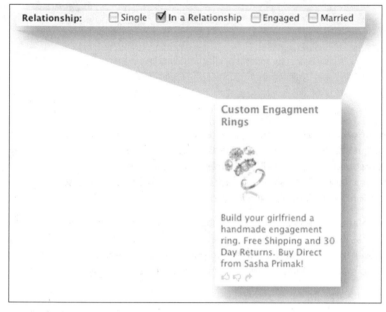

Reprinted by permission

Figure 12.8
An ad like this would likely be shown to a male who has specified that he is in a relationship but not yet engaged or married. (No pressure, guys!)

- **Languages**—Language targeting is extremely powerful for any multicultural initiatives your company might want to do. For example, you might want to run a custom campaign in Spanish for Spanish-language users in the United States. This is an important tool for media companies and agencies working on behalf of language-specific brands or subbrands.

- **Likes and interests (keywords)**—Keyword targeting is probably the most important hypertargeting dimension because it encompasses most of what's on a profile, including favorite movies, books, and music, groups and Pages they have connected to, religion, political views, and job title. A popular tactic is for advertisers to target based on competitors' brands or related products and services, as shown in Figure 12.9.

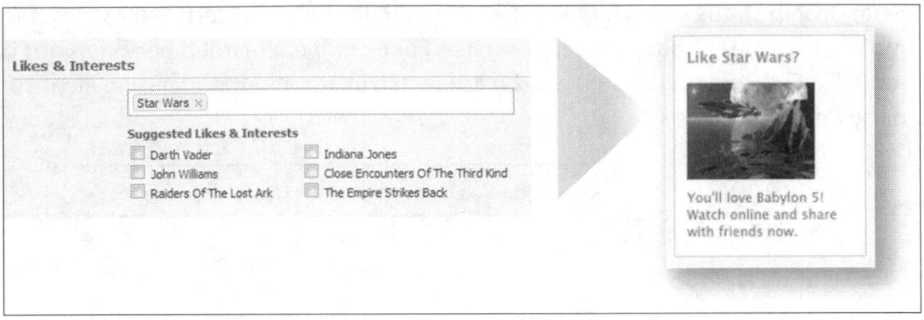

Figure 12.9
This ad for an American science fiction TV series targets Star Wars fans.

- **Education level and school**—Here's another stage-of-life proxy. *Tip:* Once you choose to target "In College" or "College Grads," Facebook gives an option to target by major and graduation year as well. This dimension is ideal for college recruiters, tutors, GMAT test prep services, and similar services. Alumni associations can also use this feature to reach former students who have graduated.

- **Workplace**—Workplace targeting enables you to reach employees in specific company networks and is most similar to the targeting on LinkedIn DirectAds. Unlike LinkedIn, however, there is no metadata on companies such as company size and industry—you have to manually enter company names. This is ideal for B2B sales and recruiting.

- **Connections**—This is an easy way to target existing fans, attendees, members, and users of your Facebook Page, Event, Group, or application. You can also choose to specifically target people who *aren't* fans, attendees, members, or users. I used connection targeting to promote this book to people who use my Faceconnector application and aren't already fans of the book, as shown in Figure 12.10. This resulted in much better conversions than my other ad campaigns because this group of individuals is highly qualified—these people are interested in using Facebook for business and trust me enough to use my application.

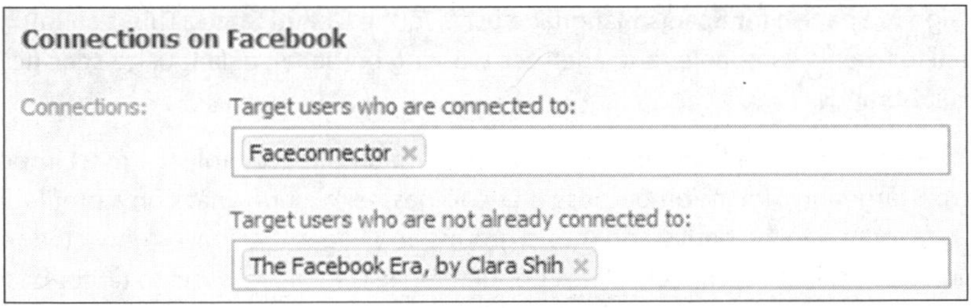

Figure 12.10
To reach a highly qualified group of individuals with ads for my book, I targeted people who had installed or were fans of the Faceconnector application I developed but who hadn't yet "liked" my book's Facebook Page.

- **Friends of connection**—Another great way to take advantage of connection targeting is to show ads to *friends of* fans, attendees, members, and users of your Facebook Page, Event, Group, or application. As shown in Figure 12.11, people viewing the ad will see which of their friends are already connected with your Page, Event, Group, or application, and the transitive trust and word-of-mouth concepts we discussed in Chapter 6 will hopefully kick in.

Figure 12.11
Friend-of-connection targeting yields social ads such as this one and can help companies build more immediate credibility by tapping into trust and social capital between friends. Because Chris likes my book and Chris's friends trust Chris, they are more likely to be transitively interested in my book. Recommendations and referrals from friends are the most powerful influencer of purchase decisions.

Step 3: Specify Your Budget.

As with search ads and LinkedIn DirectAds, you can choose to pay per click (CPC) or pay per 1,000 impressions (CPM). The minimum bid is 1¢ for CPC and 2¢ for CPM, and the minimum daily budget is $1, costs that are a lot lower than on LinkedIn. You can run your campaign continuously as soon as it's approved or specify both start and end dates and times.

I really like the Facebook ad tool because it takes a lot of the guesswork out of creating your campaign. Not only does it show a suggested bid range, but Facebook also lets you know roughly how many impressions or clicks you should expect per day based on the bid entered.

What to Expect with Facebook Ads

Facebook ads tend to have low click-through rate compared to AdWords, but higher conversions (see Table 12.2). A few reasons likely account for this:

- **Lack of purchase intent**—Search marketing is so effective because ads are targeted to people at the moment they are looking to buy something. On Facebook, people are generally in a different mindset. Most often they are browsing pictures and news about friends, or playing games. So Facebook ads are less about clicks today and more about seeding interest for tomorrow. Companies have a good opportunity to reach likely buyers earlier in the purchasing cycle.

- **A lot of ad inventory**—Facebook is the most highly trafficked Web site in the world, even beating Google. The huge number of page views creates a lot of ad inventory, which drives down click-through rates. But this isn't necessarily a bad thing, because price gets driven down at the same time.

- **People hate leaving Facebook**—The numbers are very telling. People spend an average of an hour per day on Facebook. More than half of those under age 30 are on Facebook more than 90% of the time they are online. Not surprisingly, ads that drive people to Pages, applications, groups, and events on Facebook benefit from a much higher click-through rate than ads that drive people to an external Web site.

Table 12.2   Comparing Average Performance for Different Ad Types

Ad Type	Click-Through Rate (CTR)	Conversion
Google AdWords	1–2%	1%
Email campaigns	2–3%	4–5%
Banner ads	0.17–0.30%	2.8% (higher if behaviorally targeted)
Facebook ads	0.05–0.5%	6–7%
Tweets	2–4%	7–8%

Sources: *Marketing Today*, Emarket2, and test campaigns

For the most part, people don't really search for products and services on Facebook, although this could change as the Facebook application ecosystem grows or if Facebook decides to create an ad network out of Facebook for Websites partners. Without clear purchase intent on Facebook, it's unfair to compare Facebook ads to search marketing. Compared to traditional banner advertising, Facebook is as good or better.

Note that Table 12.2 is a gross generalization of performance across different channels. Both click-through rate (CTR) and conversions are highly dependent on industry, brand equity, ad copy and placement, and offer or call to action. The goal of showing these high-level numbers is to highlight the very different nature of social network ads.

For example, Twitter could theoretically yield higher than 100% CTR if you get retweeted, which would basically never happen with AdWords. On Facebook, certain ads also are shown repeatedly to the same individuals, even if they have already clicked on the ad (and, for all we know, performed the call to action). This is especially likely to happen if you set the hypertargeting criteria so narrowly that only a small number of audience members qualify to view the ad. In this case, click-through rate and conversion *per person* might be really high, but because there are a large number of impressions shown to each person, the click-through *per impression* appears low.

We already talked about how CTR goes up when a Facebook ad points to something on Facebook instead of an external site because people hate leaving Facebook. For some businesses, it makes sense to count new fans, comments, and "likes" as conversions instead of trying to force traditional offers and email signups as the call to action.

Most people just don't have very much experience with hypertargeted or social ads. We talked earlier about how ads optimized for search marketing aren't generally optimal for social networks. One reason for poor performance could just be that we aren't yet good at social network advertising. But if you elect to pay per click, who cares about low CTR? You are just getting extra impressions for free. As marketers, we are still getting used to all of these nuances.

For additional help, we can get some advice on optimizing Facebook ads from the guy at Facebook who is in charge of them. In the following guest expert sidebar, Tim Kendall of Facebook shares a few tips for advertising on the social Web.

Four Tips for Successful Facebook Ad Campaigns

Tim Kendall

Facebook ads let you reach your exact audience and connect real customers to your business. Here are a few tips on how to optimize your campaigns, based on our experience working with advertisers across different industries and geographies:

- **Target people precisely.**   Reach people predisposed to your product or service by selecting relevant targeting parameters. Selling trendy, high-end handbags in New York? Target your Facebook ad to women in New York between the ages of 25 and 45 who are interested in "fashion" and like "handbags. As you develop your target group, Facebook autosuggests up to three additional parameters that are most common among the group of people you have already selected in the targeting tool. Adding these suggestions to your target set will increase the size of your ad's potential audience while ensuring that you still reach people with relevant interests.

- **Speak to each one of your customers.** Test a variety of images, experiment with different calls to action, and consider varying the creative based on the group of people you are targeting. The most effective salespeople often tailor their message based on the client's background, profile, and motivations. If you would describe your product or service differently to a female, twenty-something college student than you would to a forty-something male professional, develop specific creative that maps to each customer segment you intend to target.

- **Engage the user.**   Facebook ads allow people to engage with ads in the same way they interact with other content on the site and without leaving the page they're viewing. For example, potential customers can directly engage with your business by clicking on the Like This Page link or the RSVP to This Event link. This lightweight and common action automatically posts to the person's profile page and on their friends' home page, generating additional (and free) distribution.

continues…

- **Make it social.** People use Facebook to learn about their world through the lens of their friends. So it doesn't surprise us that ads with information about people's friends perform up to 50% better in terms of CTR, conversion rate, and BrandLift (a Nielsen offering that gauges ad effectiveness—we talk about this later in this chapter). Adding this friend information (or "social context") to your Facebook ads is simple. First, promote your page or event to build a base of people who "like" your page or RSVP to your event. Second, leverage "friends-of-connection" targeting to develop an ad campaign that targets the friends of people who "like" your page or have RSVP'd to your event. This ensures that every ad you run will include social context because you are constraining your campaign footprint to only the friends of the people who "like" your page or have RSVP'd to your event.

Tim Kendall (@tkendall) is the director of monetization at Facebook.

Which Attributes Should You Hypertarget On?

The hardest but most important aspect of Facebook ads is choosing the optimal attributes to target. The number of possible attribute combinations can be overwhelming for new advertisers. You select a particular attribute for two reasons:

1. **Your product has no relevance to people who have a certain attribute.** For example, an ad for women's shoes should generally be hypertargeted at females only. Unlike other items a woman might own (like jewelry or lingerie), shoes are not generally something that males purchase for women, so you would not be losing reach to likely buyers. You are simply not wasting ads on a group of people (men) who are not likely to be interested in your product. Women's shoes are not relevant to people whose gender is male.

2. **The way you message the same product differs greatly depending on this attribute.** For example, a heterosexual dating site might want to advertise to both men and women, but the ideal ad shown to males would differ greatly from the ideal ad shown to females.

It's easy to get carried away and overtarget. We have to weigh the extra hassle of creating a greater number of more narrowly focused campaigns against the benefits of higher CTR and conversion.

The trick is to find a small number of criteria that matter most about your product. These criteria vary by product. For example, relationship status ("engaged") and gender ("female") might be most important in ads for wedding planning services, but they have no bearing on ads for digital cameras. Over time, as you discover more about the audiences interested in your product, your targeting effectiveness should improve.

I always recommend starting a campaign with a broader audience and then honing in on narrower segments as you gain more insights from the ad analytics into what profiles of people are clicking the most. I learned this lesson firsthand when marketing the first edition of this book. Originally, I thought this book would appeal mainly to business professionals in sales and marketing, so those were the profiles we targeted. As an experiment one time, we decided to remove all the targeting criteria for one of our campaigns and were pleasantly surprised to discover that, besides our expected audience, there was also strong demand from the nonprofit and academic business school markets for this book. Once we discovered these new segments, we subsequently created different campaigns and bid different CPCs based on the combination of Facebook's suggested bid and our expected CTR for that particular segment. Specifically, my CPC for sales professionals has been an average of 79¢, and my CPC for the business school audience has been 61¢. Creating separate campaigns for each allows me to both tailor my message (which improves CTR and conversion) and avoid overbidding for the business school audience.

In traditional marketing, we likely might not ever have had the opportunity to challenge our prematurely drawn conclusions about which audience would be interested in this book. With Facebook, we have found two immense markets that I almost overlooked! (And by the way, it's thanks to Facebook that this edition of the book has a new chapter dedicated to nonprofits and political campaigns!) The ad analytics Facebook provides are a treasure trove of market insights—you might be surprised (as I was) by what you didn't know about your customers and prospects.

Selecting Your Ad Creative and Call to Action

The biggest distinction about Facebook ads is that instead of driving clicks to an external landing page, you can send people to your Page, application, group, or event on Facebook—and often it is better to do so. People don't like to leave the Facebook environment, so linking back within the same environment generally increases click-through rates.

Using the Static FBML application described in the previous chapter, you can create and link to a custom landing tab on your Facebook Page, as I did for this book's Facebook Page (see Figure 12.12). Static FBML lets you embed images, Flash, video, buttons, forms, and other HTML elements on your custom tab so that you can create a compelling experience and call to action in the split-second you have someone's attention after they click on an ad. Besides driving ad clicks to custom tabs, you can also specify the default tab for when anyone visits your Page. (Do this under Page Settings.)

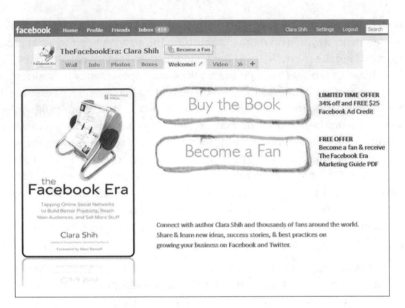

Figure 12.12
This is a custom landing tab with clear calls to action from this book's Facebook Page, at http://facebook.com/thefacebookera. Using Facebook Markup Language (FBML), you can code it so that different calls to action appear to people based on whether they have "liked" your Page.

As you get more sophisticated, you can even create multiple landing tabs for multiple campaigns to try new things, compare performance, or tailor to different audiences.

As for ad copy, don't just tell people to "like" Your Facebook Page. Tell them *why* they should. Give them a great offer, such as a discount, a free sample, or even helpful information. Better yet, provide incentives for people to share your offer with friends, as companies such as Groupon are doing. Some companies have found it effective to target ads at existing fans to improve engagement, build loyalty, and encourage sharing.

For your first few campaigns, start small. Tweak and test your campaigns with different hypertargeting criteria and values. Compare your cost-to-performance ratios for CPM versus CPC. Be creative. Try different messages. Run ads for two weeks, and then assess their effectiveness. What was the click-through rate? What was the conversion into sales? Which hypersegments performed the best? Learn from your tests and keep trying new things.

Tying Back to Your Goals

Of course, anything you do should be tied back to your social networking strategy developed in Chapter 8, "Recruiting in the Facebook Era." Work backward from your goals. Is your primary focus new customer acquisition? Or do you have plenty of customers but need to up-sell and cross-sell them on new products? Here are some goals for which hypertargeting works particularly well:

- Reach new audience segments, such as a new age group, region, interests, or college attended.

- Test new messages and see what resonates.

- Think globally, act locally—similar to how Bonobos, Inc., has global sales and operations but tailors its campaigns to each school and hometown sports team fans to make its products feel more personal and relevant.

- Up-sell or cross-sell existing customers on additional products and services.

- Learn about your customer base and what factors most heavily influence interest and purchase decisions.

If your campaigns aren't performing to your expectations, try using different copy or altering your hypertargeting strategy. Table 12.3 highlights common issues advertisers face with hypertargeting and offers suggested ways to address them.

Table 12.3   Common Issues with Hypertargeted Ad Campaigns and Suggestions on How to Resolve Them

If You Have This Problem ...	... Then Consider Doing This
Not enough impressions	Try adjusting your targeting to be less restrictive by reducing the number of dimensions or increasing the range of acceptable values.
Low click-through rate	Make ads more personal and specific based on what you know about the audience. Test different images and calls to action.
Low sales conversion	Make sure your landing page is consistent with your ad and similarly customized for the audience segment. Try using limited-time offers to create a sense of urgency.
Worsening campaign performance	Refresh campaigns with new ad copy and images. Your ads are probably stale.
Consistent low performance in a particular audience segment compared or with others	Consider cutting this audience segment altogether and focusing your efforts on more responsive segments, just bid less for this segment.

In the following guest expert sidebar, entrepreneur Auren Hoffman shares additional tips on how to run a social marketing campaign.

How to Run a Social Marketing Campaign

Auren Hoffman

Running a social media campaign has become a right of passage for every major marketer at large brands, retailers, banks, airlines, hotels, nonprofits, and more. Consider these six tips on what to do and what not to do:

- **Do tie in email marketing.** Email is the most important communication medium. I'll say that again: There is no more important communication medium than email—there's not even a close second. Until you do a great job on email, it's not worth investing in social campaigns.

  Every one of your customers has an email account, and most of them read their email ten times per day (or more). When you have email working and churning, you can drive people to Facebook, Twitter, YouTube videos, and more. Do this by creating short, targeted emails that people respond to and that they forward to others.

- **Don't expect immediate results.** Great social marketing campaigns take time. This is not the job of a single person: Successful campaigns require efforts by all departments. Try different things and experiment—successful campaigns require lots of iterations.

- **Do track and measure responses.** Data is the only way to know how effective campaigns are. Make sure you track clicks, opens, retweets, growth of fans, coupon codes redeemed, number of mentions, and more.

- **Don't treat everyone the same.** Make sure you identify your influencers and then make sure you reward them. Give influencers higher-priority customer service, special promotions, and exclusive invitations. Set up systems to automatically flag these special accounts.

- **Do get as much customer data as possible.** Supplement gaps in knowledge by asking for user information or using third-party data services. Learning about customer demographics, interests, social network behavior, and more can help you increase campaign effectiveness.

- **Don't hesitate to engage me.** I look forward to continuing the conversation: http://blog.summation.net.

Auren Hoffman (@auren) is CEO of Rapleaf.

Engagement Ads

In addition to click ads, Facebook is exploring what it calls engagement ads. Engagement ads were designed to offer advertisers minimally invasive ways of inserting their brands into everyday Facebook interactions. The thought is that if there are opportunities for people to engage with brands without disrupting their primary mission on social networking sites—that is, expressing themselves and socializing with others—then they will be much more likely to take advantage of these opportunities. Targeted ads, in contrast, are disruptive in the Facebook member's experience. Clicking on an ad drives users away from what they were previously doing without giving them a chance to socially engage.

Facebook has developed several models of incorporating advertising into social behavior that people are already doing on Facebook. These are innovative social ad units for people on Facebook to comment on videos, send sponsored virtual gifts, "like" your Page, RSVP for events, request free samples, and respond to polls without having to leave the Web page they are on.

Video commenting combines the viral nature of entertaining videos popularized by YouTube with the friend graph and feed stories (see Figure 12.13). For example, MTV purchased a video ad on Facebook of Britney Spears opening the Video Music Awards. Users could view and comment on the video completely in-line, without clicking to another page. This generated awareness and participation while offering members an opportunity to engage with friends.

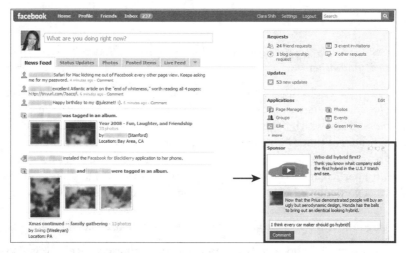

Figure 12.13
Video commenting ads are ideal for promoting popular media such as music videos, movie trailers, and TV shows. They encourage viral marketing by offering people a way to react and engage with their friends on the video.

Sponsored virtual gifts are a second engagement ad model. Virtual gifts have become a popular way for Facebook users to exchange social capital, express affection, and build rapport, such as for birthdays, special achievements, and other milestones. Brands now have the opportunity to sponsor virtual gifts so that instead of costing the sender $1, they are free. The brand benefits not only from the sender and recipient engaging with the brand, but also from the resulting social feed stories that get propagated to both sender and recipient's networks. For example, Wendy's, a popular fast-food restaurant, sponsored a branded virtual gift to spread the word about its new "flavor dipped" sandwiches (see Figure 12.14). Sponsored virtual gifts can be a fun, visual, and memorable form of word-of-mouth awareness for your product or brand.

Figure 12.14

Wendy's, a fast-food chain, sponsored a virtual gift to virally spread the word about its new line of "flavor dipped" sandwiches.

Facebook also offers polls that not only engage users but can also collect valuable audience data for advertisers. For certain polls, Facebook has partnered with Nielsen on a new tool called Brand Lift, which helps measure the impact of branded advertising on Facebook. The idea is that a large number of polls are used to measure audience sentiment and purchase intent (see Figure 12.15). Half the polls are shown to users who have been shown a particular ad. The other half of the polls are shown to users who have not been shown a particular ad but have otherwise identical profile attributes. The logic is that any substantive differences in purchase intent can be attributed to the advertising campaign. Currently, this tool is available only to existing Nielsen customers.

For consumer packaged goods and food and beverage products, Facebook is also offering "engagement sampling ads," which allow advertisers to make free physical samples available to certain audiences on Facebook (see Figure 12.16). Audience members see the sampling ad on their home screen and can enter their address to receive the free product sample. With this initiative, Facebook is starting to collect the physical mailing addresses of its users, although it's important to note that advertisers have rights to the address information for the purpose of mailing samples only, not to use or resell them as a list after the campaign.

Figure 12.15
Polls have been a great way for advertisers on Facebook to not only engage audiences, but also collect valuable data. Polls such as this one are part of Facebook and Nielsen's new Brand Lift initiative, which aims to measure the impact of branded ad campaigns on Facebook.

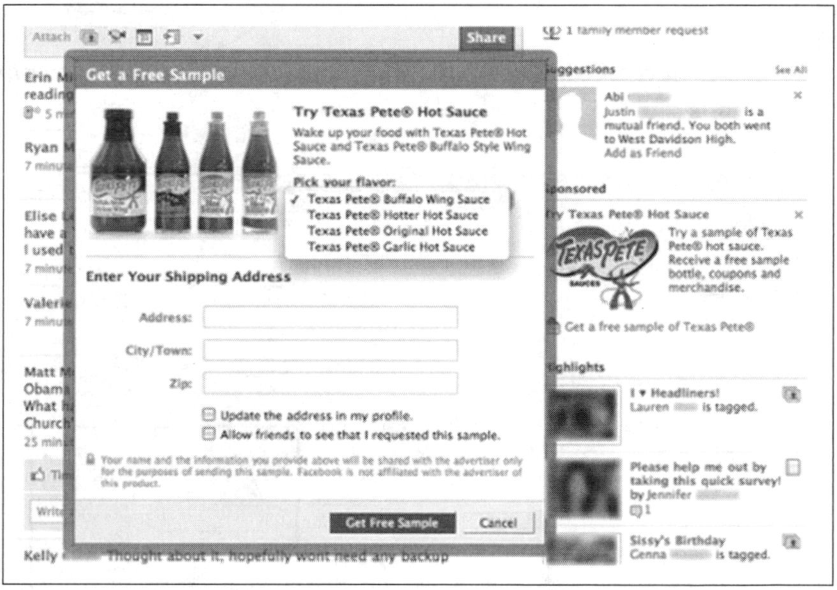

Figure 12.16
Facebook recently launched engagement sampling ads that allow advertisers to make free physical samples of their products available to Facebook users. For example, this sampling ad for Texas Pete hot sauce generated 5,000 signups for samples in two days.

The remaining engagement ad types are the in-line event RSVP and "likes" for your Page. The rationale for these is that people are much more likely to participate if it's easy for them to do so. Being able to RSVP or "like" a Page in-line without clicking to another page minimizes the amount of effort required by the user to engage (see Figures 12.17 and 12.18).

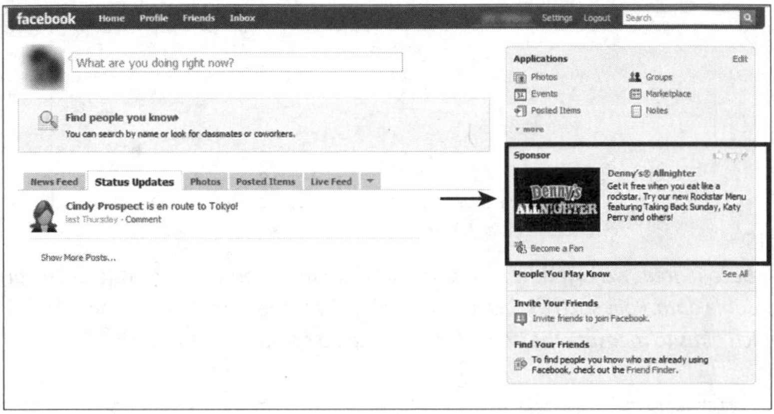

Figure 12.17
Engagement ads on Facebook allow users to "like" a Facebook Page with one click, without leaving the page they're on.

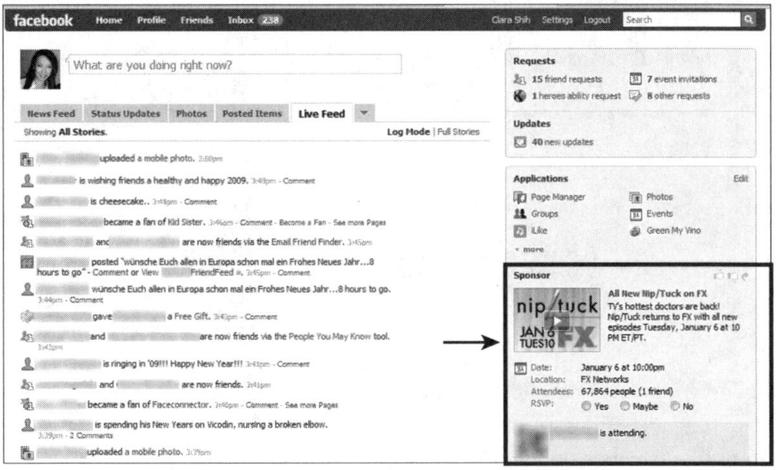

Figure 12.18
Engagement ads on Facebook also allow users to RSVP and leave notes for advertiser-sponsored events in-line without leaving the page they're on.

Engagement ads are geared more toward brand advertisers with deeper pockets. Home page campaigns start at $50,000. Unlike Facebook ads, which can be purchased self-service with a credit card, engagement ads require going through the Facebook ad sales team at www.facebook.com/business/contact.php.

Twitter's Promoted Tweets

Advertising on Twitter is quite different from advertising on either Facebook or LinkedIn. Twitter recently launched "promoted tweets," a form of search advertising that allows businesses and organizations to pay for placement at the top of Twitter search results (shown in Figure 12.19). Promoted tweets are can be @replied to, retweeted, and favorited just like regular tweets, which can help companies tap into the social sharing and engagements aspects of Twitter. This is a relatively new feature, so there aren't yet great stats on the effectiveness of promoted tweets.

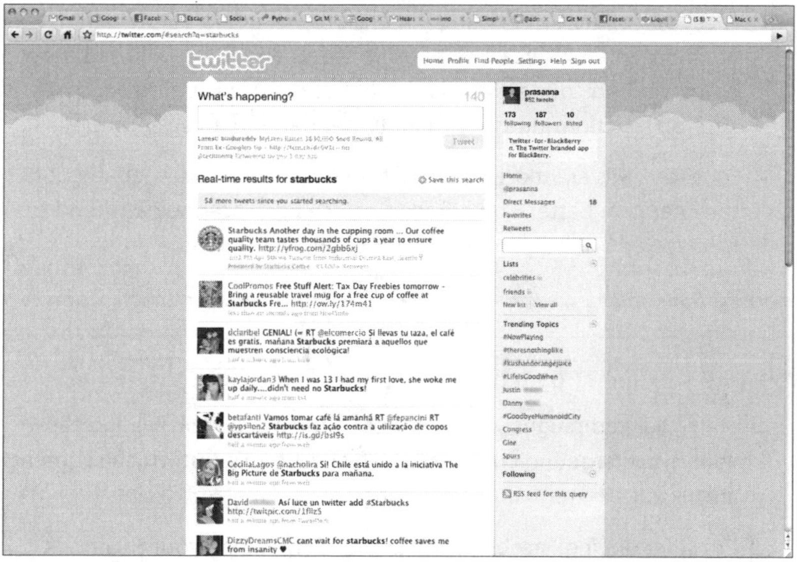

Figure 12.19
Promoted tweets on Twitter are paid corporate messages that appear at the top of search results.

< < < T A K E A W A Y S

✓ Regardless of whether you want to advertise on Facebook or LinkedIn, you can use their free ad targeting tools to determine whether your target audience is on those sites. As you update your ad targeting criteria, both Facebook and LinkedIn's ad creation wizard updates in real time the approximate number of audience members that fit the criteria you have specified.

✓ Because LinkedIn has more career information and industry metadata, LinkedIn DirectAds might be a better fit for B2B companies and recruiters who want to advertise.

✓ Be careful with CPC ads on LinkedIn. Often the image you uploaded isn't shown because LinkedIn displays your ad in the text-only slot at the top center of the home page and profile pages.

✓ Facebook offers 11 targeting dimensions, including age, location, gender, gender interest, relationship status and interest, likes, school, employer, and connections. LinkedIn has seven, including company size, job function, industry, seniority, gender, age, and geography.

✓ Facebook ads are most similar to traditional online banner ads, but they perform better. Compared to search ads, Facebook ads tend to have lower CTR but higher landing page conversions.

> > > T I P S and T O D O's

❑ Start your campaigns with a broader audience and slowly increase your hypertargeting criteria as you learn more about which segments are clicking through and converting.

❑ Consider driving Facebook ads to a landing tab on your Facebook Page.

❑ Create a clear call to action for your ads.

❑ Don't just tell people to "like" your Page; tell them *why* they should "like" it.

❑ Try and test new things with your LinkedIn and Facebook ad campaigns, to find the right formula that works for your product and audience.

IV

Social Networking Strategy

13

Advice for Small Business

Some of the tactics and strategies we've covered in this book aren't realistic if you're a small business owner. You don't have the time, the budget, or perhaps the need. Many small businesses, especially sole proprietorships, don't have a dedicated online marketing person, much less the luxury of a dedicated social media manager. I don't recommend that most small companies invest in building fancy applications or Facebook for Websites integrations unless it's absolutely core to your business. It's easy for brands to justify heavy investment in custom apps and creative because they are guaranteed millions of customer impressions and interactions. It's harder to justify that expense when your customer base is substantially smaller, and you have few resources and many competing priorities.

This chapter is a set of ten quick tips on how to do a lot with a little on the social Web.

1. Start Small

One of the great things about Facebook, Twitter, and LinkedIn is that you can start small and gradually ramp up your investment. They are all free to get started—the biggest cost is your time. Take ten minutes to create a basic profile. If you decide this is where you want to connect with customers and prospects, try to post something on a regular basis. It doesn't have to be every day—your customers realize that you have a business to run and will respect as little or as much commitment you can make, as long as you are consistent.

In the following guest expert sidebar, we hear from small business owner Amanda Cey on how a small time investment on her part in building out her social network presence has transformed her San Francisco-based event planning and production company.

How I Bootstrapped My Small Business with Social Tools

Amanda Cey

My company, ABCey Events, is an event planning firm serving the San Francisco Bay area. We have produced events for clients including Adobe, Michael Moore, and Razorfish. Every day, we leverage connections across social networks to provide highly targeted direct promotion for clients.

When I first started my business in 2007, all of my sales leads began with a phone call. Finding leads involved calling blindly until I uncovered an opportunity. My introduction to social media was born out of my dissatisfaction with traditional sales methods.

At the time, companies were downsizing, not throwing lavish events. Here I was with limited resources myself, trying to convince others to spend their money. I needed a way to keep my business alive during the economic downturn and an effective yet somewhat less outwardly aggressive strategy.

I decided to grow my presence and visibility utilizing the three key social networks: Facebook, Twitter, and LinkedIn. Through the Social Web, my network has expanded exponentially with each new friend or follower, requiring little traditional marketing work and at no cost! Social media networking has since become our #1 business tool and source of the majority of our leads.

We use Twitter as an interaction tool (see Figure 13.1). We respond even more than we post to show that we are a real-time resource for potential clients. LinkedIn also helps us reach out to professional clientele.

Reprinted by permission

Figure 13.1
Social networking sites like Twitter have become a valuable source of leads and referrals for ABCey Event Production Company.

Our blog content draws in and retains fans and followers. Blog articles are short, smart, and edgy. We have just a few lines to grab the readers' attention and to show that we are savvy of popular culture and the clear experts in event planning. The blog leads the reader to our social media sites. Facebook is a repository for everything about our company, from event pictures to the live comment feed.

But success in our industry does not come solely from behind a keyboard. Active fieldwork, such as attending networking events or arranging face-to-face meetings, is vital to our social media campaigns. Together, we can make a powerful human connection with clients and distinguish ourselves from everyone else.

Amanda Cey (@abceyevents) is owner and founder of ABCey Events Company in San Francisco, California.

2. Consider Using Your Personal Profile Instead of a Facebook Page

Facebook Pages are a good way to create a boundary between your business and personal life, but they also introduce overhead by needing to maintain a separate presence and set of contacts. You could easily double the amount of time and effort when you have a Facebook Page instead of only a personal profile. It might make more sense to stick with only a personal profile in these situations:

- You are a one-man or one-woman show who has deeply personal relationships with your customers.

- You are still on the fence about Facebook and want to test the waters before committing more resources.

- It feels strange to ask your friends and customers to "like" your Page.

- Many of the people who would "like" your Facebook Page are already friends with your personal profile.

- You don't have anything on your personal profile that is unprofessional or uncomfortable to share.

Figure 13.2 shows a wonderful example from Scott Newman, a top-producing residential real estate agent in Chicago. From Scott's perspective, he has nothing to hide and wants his clients and prospects to get to know his full personality. Using his profile for his business makes his Facebook presence and client interactions highly personal. Technically, Facebook's terms of service frown on business activity on personal profiles, but for certain kinds of small business (such as sole proprietorships), as long as you are being authentic to your personality and your friends don't complain, this setup works well.

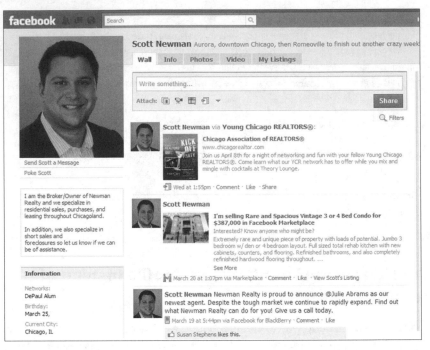

Reprinted by permission

Figure 13.2
Scott Newman, broker and owner of Newman Realty in Chicago, Illinois, uses his personal profile to also represent his business. Scott uses a combination of Hearsay 360 to manage client relationships and Oodle Pro to display new listings as a custom tab on his profile.

3. Take Advantage of Location Targeting and Geolocation

If you are a brick-and-mortar business, you should definitely consider location-targeted ads on Facebook that let you reach audiences within a certain city or a 10-, 25-, or 50-mile radius. Not surprisingly, nearly three-quarters of Facebook's ad revenue last year came from local advertisers. This is perfect for retail stores, salons, spas, restaurants, bars, and other local businesses. If you provide local business-to-business (B2B) services, you can use the geography targeting on LinkedIn DirectAds.

If you are a mobile business, such as a food truck or cart vendor, check out the geolocation features on Twitter, Loopt, Gowalla, and Foursquare that enable you to share your real-time location, or just tweet your location. This is how Los Angeles–based Kogi BBQ has grown to a following of more than 60,000 loyal fans. Fans track the real-time location of Kogi's Korean–Mexican taco trucks so they know where to pick up their next meal of spicy pork tacos, kimchi quesadillas, and short rib sliders.

4. Build Community

Especially if you decide to create a Facebook Page, use it as an opportunity to build community. Don't make your Page about you—make it about fans. Extend the face-to-face community you have in your stores to Facebook so that you can forge even stronger customer relationships. Publicize events, seminars, and even little league baseball games that your business is sponsoring via Facebook Events. Afterward, post photos and videos from events on your Page Wall to re-create the experience for anyone who visits your Facebook Page. As we mentioned earlier, it might feel awkward to ask friends and customers to publicly "like" your personal profile. This is another reason to create a Page about your company or community.

The team at Synthesis.net, an indie blog based in Chico, California, has figured this out. They created a Facebook Page, "Life in San Francisco," about all things San Francisco that has drawn nearly 15,000 fans (see Figure 13.3). In comparison, Synthesis.net's own Facebook Page has less than 1,000 fans. By making the first Facebook Page about San Francisco, the team is able to engage a much bigger audience while still guiding the conversation on the Page.

Figure 13.3
Synthesis.net's Facebook Page "Life in San Francisco" has little company branding. This Page has been extremely successful as a grassroots initiative, attracting nearly 15,000 fans and high levels of daily engagement.

5. Build Your Sphere of Influence

For many small businesses, you can't necessarily dictate when people should buy your product or service—but when they are in the market to buy, you want to make sure that they think of you first. It's the art of the soft sell, and it's equally true whether you're a real estate agent, an insurance agent, a veterinarian, or an auto mechanic. Sometimes you can help stimulate demand by encouraging people to do something that they have been delaying (such as a car repair) with reminders or discounts, but even then a hard sell rarely works.

The power of the social Web is that it enables small business owners to efficiently and effectively build a sphere of influence about their business. By offering valuable knowledge and advice and being genuine, you will slowly build trust and authority as the go-to person for whatever set of products and services you provide. One of my favorite examples of providing helpful information while being genuine and personal is from the Jimmy Smart Allstate insurance agency in Columbus, Georgia (see Figure 13.4).

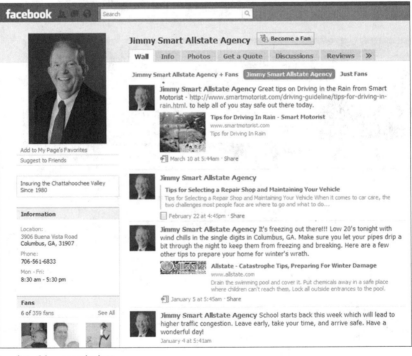

Reprinted by permission

Figure 13.4
Although the Jimmy Smart Agency offers promotions for submitting referrals and requesting an insurance quote, the majority of posts are focused on providing valuable information to customers and prospects, such as tips on car maintenance and how to drive in bad weather conditions.

In the following guest expert sidebar, Jonathan Smart of the Jimmy Smart Agency shares his experience and advice from the front lines as a small business owner.

Growing Our Business on Facebook

Jonathan Smart

In 2008, I began searching for new and innovative ways to advertise my business and reach an untapped audience. I found Facebook and started a Fan Page for our business, Jimmy Smart Allstate Agency, and my own personal profile. I then began using both tools in an effort to not only bring in new clients, but also nurture and retain current clients.

Facebook communications do not (and should not) be only business related. In fact, Facebook is different from other forms of customer outreach because it fuses personal relationships and business relationships in a way that can really benefit small businesses, in particular.

For example, friendly happy birthday messages to clients through Facebook can make people feel a stronger personal connection to your company, and comments on people's profiles about some shared experience (without being too personal or unprofessional) can help show you really care about their personal well-being.

On the business side, you want to make sure that you don't overdo it and push your potential clients away. Try not to sound too "salesy." For example, we promote our referral program and post helpful tips and useful information that would benefit our fans. We want to build a sphere of influence, awareness, and credibility so that anyone in the Columbus area in need of insurance will know to come to us. We use software from Hearsay Labs to help manage this and make sure that we are providing the best care, service, and outreach to clients and potential clients who are on Facebook, Twitter, or any other social media site.

We look at social media, especially Facebook, as the way of the future for businesses such as ours that are about reputation and relationships. Whatever business you're in, Facebook can be a very important and valuable channel for you. More than 100 million people in the United States use Facebook, and of those 100 million people, the average person spends more time on Facebook than any other Web site.

Have fun with your Facebook Page and use it wisely, and I promise that you will see results.

Jonathan Smart (@urinsured) is an Allstate insurance agent in Columbus, Georgia.

6. Consider Ditching Your Web Site

Take a look at your Web analytics. How many people visited your Web site last week? Last month? If the numbers are grim, and especially if it's expensive to maintain your Web site each month, you might want to ditch it. A growing number of small businesses, especially sole proprietors, are refocusing their efforts and dollars away from traditional Web sites in favor of Facebook Pages.

Keep in mind these important considerations:

- **Where is your audience?**—Are your customers and prospects on Facebook? If they aren't, you shouldn't invest in creating a Facebook Page, much less replace your existing Web site. If you don't know, survey your customers. You can also go to the Facebook Ad tool at http://facebook.com/ads/create, scroll down to the targeting section, enter the criteria of your current and ideal customer profile, and see the numbers as Facebook updates in real time to tell you how many Facebook users fit the criteria you have specified. If it's a very high number, especially compared to the number of Web site visitors you have, strongly consider focusing your efforts on your Facebook Page.

- **Are you comfortable with Facebook owning your Web presence?**—Facebook's terms of service clearly states that Facebook owns all content and interactions on the site, including on Facebook Pages. Do you feel confident in Facebook's longevity, and do you trust the company to treat Page owners fairly? I think we are probably safe because it's in Facebook's best interest to create a win–win situation for companies, but you should consider this as part of your due diligence.

- **How much traffic do you generate?**—Facebook generates a remarkable amount of Web traffic, recently surpassing even Google as the most trafficked site in the United States (more than 7% of weekly Web visits), according to analytics firm Hitwise. Your customers are likely on Facebook, so you should be there, too, instead of asking them to come to you. Your company also receives a boost in traffic when fans "like" or comment on a post because that gets shared to their networks. It really works. On *The Facebook Era*'s Facebook Page, a typical post gets roughly 8,000 impressions (see Figure 13.5). In comparison, we get 1,400–2,500 weekly visits to the Web site at http://thefacebook-era.com. Not only is Facebook's reach greater, but it's also more consistent because fans are logging in to Facebook on a consistent basis.

Figure 13.5
Facebook admins can see in real time the number of impressions for each Wall post.

- **How good are you at search engine optimization (SEO)?**—What about when some-one searches for your business or services on Google or another search engine? If you have a Web site today that has meaningful levels of traffic, you are probably investing a nontrivial amount of money on SEO (and search engine marketing). Because Facebook is so heavily trafficked, Facebook Pages benefit from very high SEO. For example, when I type "Clara Shih" into a search engine, my Facebook, Twitter, and LinkedIn pages are all within the top four results.

- **How much time and money does it cost you to update your Web site?**—Many small business owners who have traditional Web sites find them hard to update and main-tain. Every time you want to make a change, you need to ask a Web developer to help. In contrast, Facebook Pages and Twitter updates are as easy as writing on your Wall or tweeting. This means that you can share updates more frequently and create a more dynamic experience for customers and prospects. You also have the added benefit of being able to create targeted posts by location or language. For example, if part of your business targets Spanish speakers, you can create Spanish-language posts that are shown to Spanish-speaking fans only, and create the same post in English and show it to English-speakers only. I recently did an interview with Dutch magazine *EMERCE* and posted the link to *The Facebook Era*'s Facebook Page targeted to people who speak Dutch (see Figure 13.6).

The Facebook Era, by Clara Shih Clara' s gesprek in populair
Nederlands tijdschrift EMERCE http://www.emerce.nl/nieuws.jsp?
id=3001038 #Facebook

Emerce - Homepage: Amerikaanse pioniers over 2010 (1): Clara Shih
www.emerce.nl
Na een inktzwart jaar zien Amerikaanse online visionairs weer licht. De markt is weer gezond
genoeg om te denken aan winst en expansie. Social media moeten de grote beloftes voor 2010
gaan inlossen.

47 Impressions · 0% Feedback
March 22 at 5:00pm · Comment · Like · Share

Figure 13.6
Wall post targeted to Dutch-language speakers on The Facebook Era *Page at*
http://facebook.com/thefacebookera.

- **How much customer interaction occurs on your Web site?**—Perhaps the most important reason to have a Facebook Page (whether you decide to also have a Web site) is the opportunity for customer interaction. Facebook and, to a lesser extent, Twitter and LinkedIn are designed for easy sharing and interaction through likes, com-ments, retweets, and so on. This is much harder to accomplish on a traditional Web site. Even if you have blogging software installed that has a feature for commenting, it is often a hassle for people to register for a login and authenticate before they can comment.

7. Have a Personality

Create and convey a personality for your business, and also let the personalities of you and your staff shine through. Are you friendly, cheesy, knowledgeable, or funny? You can be any of these—just don't be boring. Review the examples and section on persona marketing from Chapter 11, "How To: Engage Customers with Facebook Pages and Twitter," that apply to companies of any size:

- Post pictures of you, your staff, your family, and your customers.

- Post a holiday card.

- Run a photo contest for "best-looking pet" or "best baby photo" to create an emotional connection with your fans.

- Post a funny joke, video, or photo and ask people to weigh in.

- Don't be so formal in your tone, and always respond to fan posts.

8. Do Some Networking

Imagine that—networking on social networks. Facebook, LinkedIn, and Twitter are all ideal opportunities to network with potential partners, customers, and vendors. Periodically peruse your network to discover new people, events, and groups.

Join groups to find and learn from likeminded individuals and prospective business partners. You'll likely find groups specific to your industry or geography, such as this one in Figure 13.7. If a group doesn't exist, maybe you should create one.

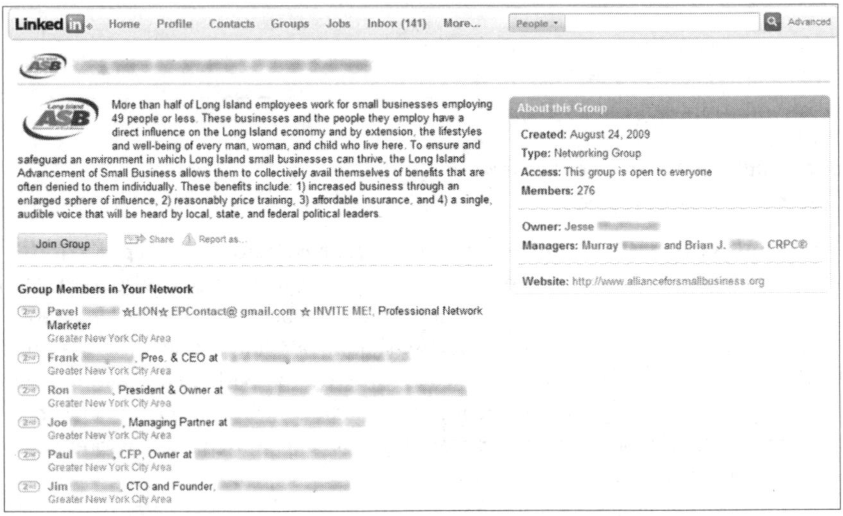

Figure 13.7
LinkedIn has thousands of groups that you can browse and join to get access to likeminded individuals, events, news, best practices, and other resources. The Long Island Advancement of Small Business alliance created this small business group in New York.

9. Be Smart About Your Time

Many small business owners find themselves trying to put out fires all day. What's more important to a real estate agent—showing a home to an interested buyer or posting on your Facebook Page? Certainly, the home showing is more *urgent,* especially if someone has contacted you. But seeding interest for the next 50 home showings on Facebook might actually be more *strategic and important.* It takes discipline and careful planning to move past reactionary business management and make time for strategic initiatives such as Facebook marketing.

You can be smart about your time in these ways:

- **Don't feel pressure to post every day.** Plenty of small businesses post just once or a few times a week, and they're still successful in engaging customers and building community.

- **Come up with material for several posts at a time (such as once a week), and post each one a few days apart.** You don't need to think of new material every few days.

- **Link your accounts.** You can set it up so that anything you post on Facebook automatically goes out to Twitter (under Facebook Page Settings), and anything you tweet automatically goes to your LinkedIn profile (under LinkedIn Profile Settings).

- **Answer frequently asked questions on Facebook.** If you're seeing a lot of the same questions come through via phone or email, consider preempting these by addressing the topic on Facebook so that it's available to everyone at once.

- **Use social media monitoring and management tools.** As mentioned earlier in the book, a number of Twitter stream-management tools exist, such as Seesmic and TweetDeck. Hearsay Labs has developed a small business solution that centralizes all your customer activity from Facebook, Twitter, LinkedIn, and Yelp so that you can efficiently track customer interactions, post content, and respond from one place (see Figure 13.8).

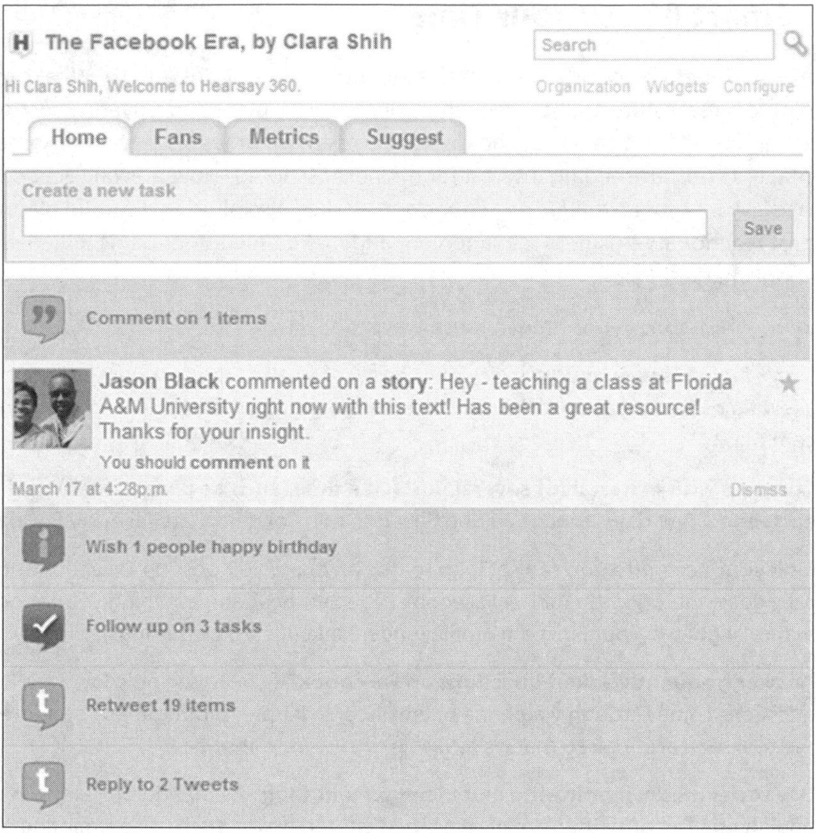

Figure 13.8
Hearsay 360 is a social media management tool for small businesses to capture leads, track customer interactions, post content, and respond across Facebook, Twitter, LinkedIn, and Yelp. To learn more, go to http://hearsaylabs.com/smb-signup.

10. Get Help

Finally, don't ever feel as if you have to do it alone. Many small business owners I know have an intern, an assistant, or a teenage son or daughter helping them with their Facebook and Twitter initiatives. You probably don't need a full-time person on staff to help you with social media, but it's nice to have someone help out for a few hours each week.

A number of digital agencies also cater to small businesses, including Chicago-based Fetch+ (http://twitter.com/fetchplus), New York–based theKbuzz (http://facebook.com/thekbuzz), and Salt Lake City–based Buzz Booster (http://twitter.com/buzzbooster). Find these and others at *The Facebook Era* Page (http: //facebook.com/thefacebookera).

Even if you decide to seek support for your social Web initiatives, make sure you aren't too far removed. Facebook and Twitter are both great places to be in the trenches with customers, live and breathe their issues, and adapt your business to address their goals. One way you could offload some of the work while staying in the loop is to ask for a summary of tweets and posts every week. You might even want to circulate it around the office. Another idea is to interleave posts by an intern or an agency with your own posts. However you approach it, find a way to stay connected, even during your busiest weeks. Nothing is more important than the voice of the customer.

< < < TAKEAWAYS

✓ Most small business owners find the greatest success with social initiatives when they start small and iterate incrementally.

✓ Build your sphere of influence by sharing valuable tips and advice with fans. Promoting your products and services too heavily on Twitter or Facebook is a huge turn-off.

✓ One advantage of Twitter and Facebook Pages is search engine optimization (because they are such popular Web sites). This means Twitter profiles and Facebook Pages tend to show up near the top in search results on Google, Yahoo!, and other search engines.

✓ Lists, groups, and hashtags on Facebook, LinkedIn, and Twitter are excellent ways to network with business professionals and find potential partners, distributors, and clients.

✓ To save time, some sole proprietorships simply use their personal profile for some business use instead of creating a separate Facebook Page. This approach has advantages (such as less redundancy and time required) and disadvantages (such as no separation between personal and professional information).

> > > TIPS and TO DO's

❑ If you don't have a Web site, or you have one with virtually no traffic, you might want to consider refocusing your efforts to a Facebook Page. A growing number of small businesses are using their Facebook Page instead of a Web site because it's easier to update and reach more people.

❑ Local brick-and-mortar services or retail stores should definitely take advantage of location targeting (including radius targeting) and geolocation applications, such as Loopt, to generate more business.

❑ Build community on your Facebook Page by making it about your fans and the things that matter most to them.

❑ Make sure to create a memorable personality for your business that people will remember and gravitate to, and let it shine on your Facebook and Twitter presence.

❑ Take advantage of time savers such as batching the post-creation process, linking your Facebook/LinkedIn to Twitter account, and using social marketing automation tools like Hearsay (http://hearsaylabs. com/smb-signup).

14

Advice for Nonprofits, Healthcare, Education, and Political Campaigns

This chapter synthesizes many of the earlier concepts and talks about how we can apply them specifically to nonbusiness settings. Instead of repeating what we have already covered in previous chapters, we focus on real case studies and expert perspectives on how the social Web has been used in education, healthcare, nonprofit, and political campaigns. In these situations—in which the stakes are not money, but instead social return, and people are even more swayed by each other's opinions—Facebook and Twitter are potentially more important channels for influencing and organizing.

We focus less on LinkedIn in this chapter because these public-sector initiatives most closely resemble business-to-consumer (B2C) marketing, although some situations (such as executive headhunting) are certainly similar to the business-to-business (B2B) instances, in which our earlier discussions on LinkedIn would apply.

Nonprofits

Nonprofit organizations can use Facebook and Twitter to manage different stakeholder groups, such as to mobilize donors and volunteers. As with any "product" that you are trying to sell, a combination of Twitter, Facebook Pages, ads, and events can be effective in seeding interest, engaging audiences, and facilitating word-of-mouth.

First, create a Facebook Page that represents your cause. Include photos and video. Tell a story that will cause people to form an emotional connection and feel a sense of urgency to help. With so many worthwhile causes competing for the same pool of charity dollars, even the most results-oriented donors end up contributing to the causes that resonate with their personal morals and emotions. Create a memorable and compelling experience for these individuals so that they can grasp the full impact of helping your organization and your clients and rise to the occasion, as Doctors Without Borders has done with its Facebook Page (shown in Figure 14.1).

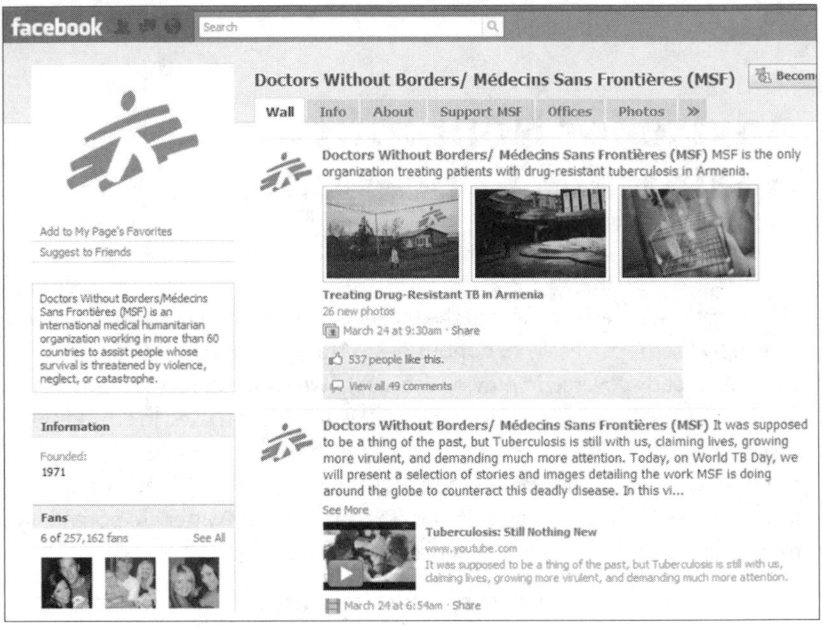

Reprinted by permission

Figure 14.1
Doctors Without Borders has amassed more than 250,000 followers on Facebook through up-to-the-minute news, photos, and video of its healthcare initiatives around the world.

To seed interest, you can explore using Facebook ads targeted at your ideal audience profile. If you are an education nonprofit, target people who are passionate about education. If your nonprofit is dedicated to animal rescue, target people who love dogs and cats. You can also target by stage of life—for example, college students might not have much disposable income to make donations, but they could potentially devote significant amounts of time to volunteering.

The team at Camp Amelia (now SearchLit.org), a nonprofit that I helped found in 2003 (I now serve on the board), has run Facebook ads for the last few years looking for donors and volunteers. We find a nine times or better response rate when we target ads at individuals who are college graduates and live within a 10-mile radius of the low-income neighborhoods we serve with our after-school and summer programs for children.

When people show interest and "like" your Facebook Page, keep them engaged with a stream of updates from the field. Don't just tell them—*show them*—how their dollars are making a difference. In the nonprofit world, people donate because they believe in the cause and think it's the right thing to do. Help them feel more emotionally connected to the cause, and you will get repeat donors who also tell their friends to get involved.

As the 2008 Barack Obama presidential campaign taught us, people are wary of being asked for money outright. They are open to a nonmonetary call to action first, such as signing a petition or volunteering, especially if it includes a social element. When you get people involved with taking action, not only are they more likely to donate, but they will also rally their friends around the cause because they feel more invested. Facebook Events are a good way to bridge your offline and online efforts with events, fundraisers, and volunteer meetings, and to encourage people to invite friends.

When you have set up a Facebook Page, the most popular applications for nonprofits on Facebook are My Merch Store, CafePress Listings, and Causes. Both My Merch Store (powered by Zazzle) and CafePress Listings let you and your community create and sell customized T-shirts, cards, posters, mugs, hats, and so on to promote your cause (see Figure 14.2). Especially if you have great designs that people will be proud to wear and use, these product stores can be a great way to generate revenue while building your organization's brand and buzz.

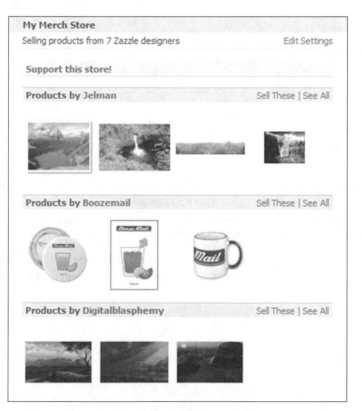

Figure 14.2
My Merch Store lets you create, display, and sell custom products promoting your nonprofit on your Facebook Page. You can add the application at http://apps.facebook.com/merchstore.

Causes enables Facebook users to create a cause about something they feel passionately about. Nearly 25 million people have installed Causes, which helps them set goals and tasks, spread awareness, facilitate dialogue, sign petitions, recruit friends, and raise money on behalf of any U.S.-registered 501(c)(3) nonprofit or Canadian registered charity. The application tracks and recognizes individuals who create causes, recruit others, and successfully take action for the cause (shown in Figure 14.3).

Figure 14.3
Causes is a popular application on Facebook for nonprofits and political campaigns that enables individuals to rally friends toward a particular cause in one of ten areas: animals, arts and culture, education, the environment, healthcare, human services, international issues, political campaigns, public advocacy, or religion. You can add the application at http://facebook.com/causes.

The following guest expert sidebar features practical advice from Causes cofounder Joe Green and nonprofit director Matt Mahan on how nonprofits can best take advantage of Facebook.

Five Tips for How Nonprofits Can Use Facebook

Joe Green and Matt Mahan

Nonprofits use Facebook for a variety of reasons, ranging from building community and listening to supporters, to cultivating donors and advocating their cause. Although the social media terrain is new and rapidly changing, effective nonprofits use time-tested organizing strategies to be successful:

1. **Be accessible**—Most nonprofits use Facebook because it's "where people are." But to join the conversation, you must integrate Facebook into what you do. Start by using Causes and Facebook Pages, Groups, Events, and ads to achieve some of your existing goals. Communicating with your employees and core supporters through Facebook makes it easier for them to activate their friend networks on your organization's behalf. When talking about what you do and why, craft a message that helps people personally connect with your organization, and don't be afraid to let your brand recede to the background. Remember that people don't join Facebook to interact with an institution, as much as they join to interact with friends, ideas, and resources.

2. **Tell stories**—Contextualize your message by couching it within a broader narrative about what's happening in our world and how your organization is taking action. What is your theory of change? Enable your supporters to play a role in producing the happy ending you work toward each day. Remember that stories have a beginning, middle, and end: Convey your mission, talk about your campaigns and projects, and explain the real impact of that work. Post photos, videos, and links to tell a fuller and more compelling story.

3. **Focus on impact**—At the end of the day, supporters and donors want to understand what their time and money are making possible and how it translates into social good. How do you define success? How do you know that you are succeeding? What does the "human face" of success look like? Use rich media and consistent messaging to convey these answers to your supporters. Enable the beneficiaries of your work to speak to your impact through Facebook's various communication media, such as Causes and Pages.

4. **Solicit broad participation**—Being accessible helps, but you also need to explicitly ask people to get involved. Remember that your supporters come to you from a variety of starting points. Some want to learn more, and others want to have a direct impact. Some want to help from a computer, and others want to volunteer in person. Use your public posts and events to offer diverse and concrete opportunities for supporting your organization. Aim to slowly move people from lower-impact actions (such as commenting on a post or viewing a media item) to higher-impact actions (such as volunteering, signing a petition, or donating money).

5. **Empower core supporters**—Organizations of all sizes have passionate supporters who want to share their time, relationships, and ideas. Although your paid-staff time is finite, you can use Facebook to identify and share certain responsibilities with avid supporters. Many of our nonprofit partners regularly communicate with supporters who manage "local chapter" causes, share and comment on media items, and promote fundraising and advocacy campaigns. Come up with creative titles, assign useful tasks, and recognize your online volunteers' work.

Joe Green (@causes) is the cofounder and Matt Mahan (@matthewmahan) is the nonprofit director at Causes.

To complement these tactics from the Causes team, Jennifer Aaker, the General Atlantic professor of marketing at the Stanford Graduate School of Business, has developed a useful model for thinking about how organizations can apply the social Web to social good. She shares four steps for getting your cause off the ground.

The Dragonfly Effect: Four Ways to Use Social Media to Change the World

Jennifer Aaker

The Dragonfly Effect is a model that emanated from "The Power of Social Technology," a class I teach at the Stanford School of Business. The framework—focus your goal, grab attention, engage others, and take action—taps social media and consumer psychological insights to create change. Named for the only insect that is able to move in any direction when its four wings are working in concert, the Dragonfly Model has four "wings" that work together to use social media to achieve unprecedented social good and customer loyalty (see Figure 14.4).

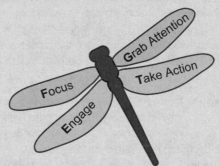

Reprinted by permission

Figure 14.4
Stanford Graduate School of Business professor Jennifer Aaker's Dragonfly Model illustrates using social media for social good.

Consider these four tips on how to get your goal off the ground:

- **Wing 1: Focus**—How you identify a single concrete measurable goal. (Quick tip: Make it small, concrete, and measurable.)

- **Wing 2: Grab attention**—How to catch someone's eye; it's similar to standing in the middle of a busy street, activating your target's fight-or-flight survival-based neurons. (Think of it as, "Made you look!")

- **Wing 3: Engage**—How to create a personal connection by accessing higher emotions, compassion, empathy, and happiness. It's about empowering the audience to care enough to want to do something themselves—and then actually do it. (Think of it as forging a connection that's deep and real.)

- **Wing 4: Take action**—Enable and empower others to take action. It's about creating, deploying, and continuously tweaking tools and programs designed to take audience members from customers to team members, furthering the cause beyond themselves. (Think of it as enlisting and enabling an army of evangelists.)

Onward and upward! To succeed in a sustainable way, we need to make it a group effort. Al Gore, the former vice president and master viral message maker (and possible inventor of the Internet), once said, "If you want to go quickly, go alone. If you want to go far, go together." Small acts create big change, and working in concert maximizes our capability to go farther faster in any direction that we choose. So enlist your friends, empower your followers, and get started.

Jennifer Aaker (@aaker) is the General Atlantic professor of marketing at the Stanford Graduate School of Business and coauthor of The Dragonfly Effect: Quick, Effective, and Powerful Ways to Use Social Media to Drive Social Change *(Jossey-Bass, September 2010).*

Healthcare

Perhaps one of the most obvious applications of social networking sites is in health epidemics, which is where we got the notion of "viral" in the first place. In the previous section, we talked about how organizations can use the social Web to reach and influence donors and volunteers. In healthcare especially, Facebook and Twitter have proven to be extremely effective in reaching and influencing *clients*.

The following case study showcases how an AIDS awareness campaign sponsored by the Kaiser Family Foundation has gained a strong grassroots following and is successfully spreading knowledge and social acceptance for victims of the disease in Latin America.

Case Study: Pasión por la Vida

Pasión por la Vida, or Passion for Life, is an HIV/AIDS awareness campaign across Latin America sponsored by the Kaiser Family Foundation and Fundación Huesped. Every day, more than 150 people die from AIDS-related diseases in the region. However, stigma and discrimination have kept people from talking openly about the issue in their communities.

To promote personal action in response to the epidemic, Pasión por la Vida has developed a successful Facebook Page (shown in Figure 14.5). The Page features 13 real testimonies of people living with HIV describing their passions and how they deal with the disease. The campaign Wall is updated frequently with related videos, photos, testimonies, news, tasks, and discussions from the community. The Page advances the idea that each one of us has a role to play in the fight against HIV/AIDS.

continues...

Figure 14.5

The Pasión por la Vida campaign's Facebook Page is a success story in the making of how nonprofit and grassroots initiatives can tap into the social nature of Facebook to connect people with knowledge, information, and one another. The Page URL is www.facebook.com/pasionporlavida.

Within four months, the Page had 9,000 fans representing every country in Latin America. These fans were remarkably all interacting openly about a traditionally taboo topic. The campaign used these steps:

- **Cross-promotion**—The campaign's Web site permanently and prominently links to Facebook from every page. Pasión por la Vida´s blog also promotes the Facebook Page and imports directly into the Facebook feed.

- **Targeted recruiting**—The campaign personally messages HIV/AIDS activists in countries with low participation. The campaign also runs Facebook Ads targeting friends of fans in those countries where penetration is low.

- **Redefining fans**—The Page refers to active fans as "2.0 volunteers." Deeming fans 2.0 volunteers catapulted the total number of fans from 1,500 to 3,000 in just 3 days. The title elevated fans from passive commentators to proactive advocates for HIV/AIDS awareness.

- **Calls to action**—The campaign poses interactive tasks for 2.0 volunteers. For International Women's Day, as an example, fans were encouraged to upload videos about their passions and HIV. Breaking the silence about HIV/AIDS, 40 women shared their story.

- **Active participation**—The 13 individuals featured in the campaign and the campaign staff keep the Facebook Page present and personal. They continually update the Page, delivering engaging and pertinent content.

The Page has become a community hub for all things related to HIV and AIDS. Users come to the Page to ask basic questions or share life stories. Facebook is the perfect platform for building this community—placing this conversation in a public space and enabling real people to do their part to fight HIV/AIDS.

Wall post: *Thank you for fighting for me ....I do not live in fear or with shame. I live with PASSION!*

Despite the tremendous potential utility of the social Web for healthcare applications, we first need to answer important questions regarding patient privacy and confidentiality, and the accuracy of health-related information. In the following guest expert sidebar, healthcare industry veteran Daniel Chao walks us through some of the biggest challenges currently preventing drug and medical device companies from investing in Facebook and Twitter initiatives.

Drug Companies and Social Networking—The Next Frontier

Daniel S. Chao, M.D., M.S.

The pharmaceutical industry spends $4 billion to $5 billion per year on direct-to-consumer marketing, yet it has been relatively absent from the world of social media and all the advantages discussed in this book.

Why? The answer lies in industry regulation (or lack thereof). The promotion of healthcare products is highly regulated, and regulatory violations by drug companies have resulted in massive fines. Last year, Pfizer was fined a record $1.19 billion for the improper promotion of Bextra, a pain medication used to treat arthritis. Not only was this a hit to Pfizer financially, but it also has contributed to growing public distrust of the healthcare industry.

The Food and Drug Administration (FDA) has largely remained silent on the topic of drug companies using social media. Most companies have decided to play it safe until the rules are clear, given the possible risks with patient confidentiality, healthcare misinformation, and so on.

In November 2009, the FDA convened public hearings on social media to give experts and the public a chance to shape the regulatory landscape. Two main issues came to the forefront:

continues...

- **Off-label promotion**—When the FDA approves drugs and devices, they are approved for a specific "indication." It is legal for physicians to prescribe a drug for use that is not part of the drug's official indication—this is known as **off-label use**. However, drug and device manufacturers are *not* allowed to actively promote off-label use.

  However, if a patient or physician specifically asks the company for information about an off-label use, certain company representatives—typically those not tied to sales or other commercial functions—are allowed to respond. But what happens when a patient asks the company about an off-label use on Facebook? Is the company allowed to respond? Are other patients and physicians allowed to respond?

- **Managing information**—Say a patient posts a question on a drug company's Facebook Page. A doctor responds, as does another patient. Neither of the responses is exactly correct. One of the responses contains information that is potentially dangerous. What does the company do? Delete the thread, or respond with accurate information? How quickly is the company expected to react to such a situation? Who is liable if others provide inaccurate information that results in harm?

It's widely anticipated that sometime in the coming months, the FDA will issue guidelines on how companies can use social media for their products, finally addressing questions such as these. When this happens, expect a wave of activity from drug companies expanding onto Facebook, Twitter, and other social networking sites to communicate with their customers.

Daniel Chao, M.D., M.S., is an entrepreneur in the San Francisco Bay area.

Education

Given Facebook's origins in college dorm rooms across the country and the social nature of school environments, another logical application for the social Web is in education. A number of educational institutions are already using Facebook and, to a lesser extent, Twitter, for a wide range of applications:

- **Student groups and sports teams**—Facebook is ideal for rallying students, parents, teachers, staff, and alumni around fundraising efforts, events, photos, and announcements for student groups and sports teams (see Figure 14.6).

- **Incoming freshmen**—At a growing number of schools, including Stanford, incoming freshmen are encouraged to join a Facebook Page or Group to receive official announcements, discover what the school has to offer, and meet their classmates before even setting foot on campus in the fall.

- **Alumni**—Facebook has long been a popular place for people to reconnect with their old friends and classmates. Alumni associations are also using it in a more official capacity to organize reunions and fundraising campaigns (see Figure 14.7).

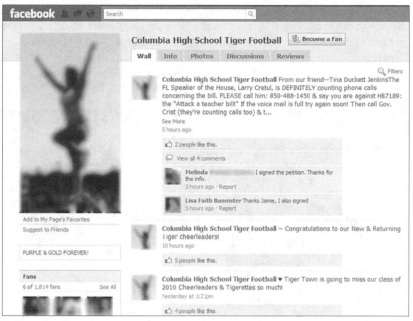

Figure 14.6
This Facebook Page belongs to the Columbia High School football team in Lake City, Florida, where sports are a clear priority and matter of pride.

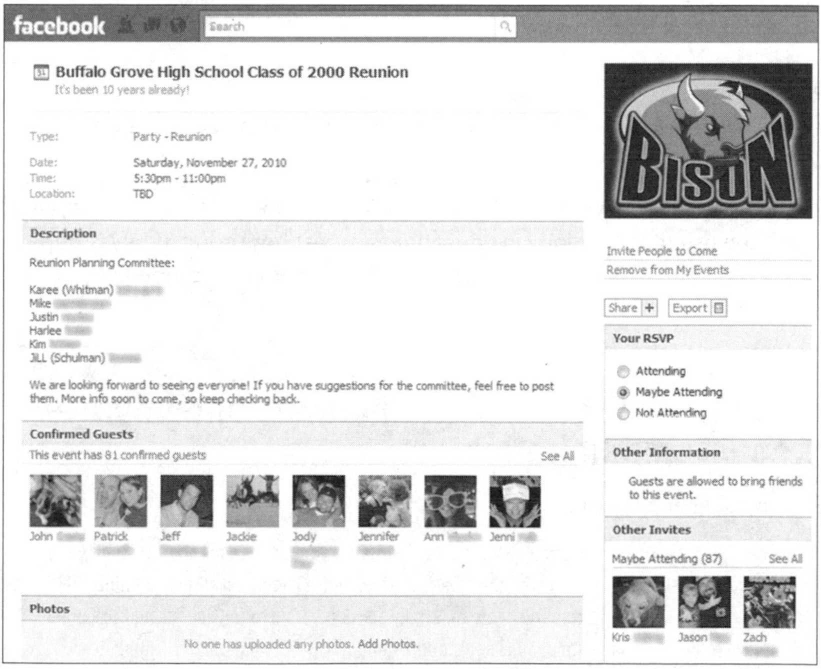

Figure 14.7
This Facebook event was created for the Buffalo Grove High School Class of 2000's ten-year reunion.

- **Courses, departments, and majors**—At the university level, departments, majors, and even courses are creating their own Facebook Pages and Groups to organize students and faculty. The University of Washington Computer Science and Engineering Department has done a great job on its Facebook Page, which has more than 1,000 fans and features announcements, a semiannual newsletter, videos of students and faculty talking about the department, and research updates (see Figure 14.8).

Figure 14.8
This Facebook Page belongs to The University of Washington Computer Science and Engineering Department.

Social science teacher Daryll Johnson and high school principal Shawn Roner, who have a blog about the use of technology in education, suggest how educational groups can use Facebook to build a sense of community and improve communication in primary and secondary schools.

Using Facebook to Build Community and Improve School Communication

Shawn Roner and Daryll Johnson

Facebook has become an essential tool for people to stay in contact with friends and family, and to create a sense of community with their peers. With effective communication increasingly difficult in today's noisy world, it makes sense for school administrators to consider using Facebook to improve communication with parents and students, and to create an interactive experience for the entire school community.

From an educator's perspective, the ability for users to participate and help create a vibrant online community makes Web 2.0 technologies appealing. Facebook is an effective tool for school administrators because most parents and students already have accounts and log in on a regular basis. This means school administrators have a powerful communication tool at their fingertips that they can use to share all kinds of information—event updates, safety information, sports team scores, announcements, photographs, and videos.

Creating a Facebook Page or Group provides parents and students with an easy way to quickly get information, see new announcements, and connect with one another. Creating Facebook Events associated with a Page or Group enables school administrators to invite and remind people of important meetings, school functions, and other events (see Figure 14.10). For administrators who have the time, the Facebook Notes feature can provide periodic blog updates on important issues and events that give valuable information to parents. As students have long discovered, Facebook presents an exciting opportunity to improve the way we communicate—now educators and administrators just need to catch up.

Figure 14.9

This Facebook Page belongs to Richland High School in North Richland Hills, Texas. It's a great example of using Facebook to build community and improve school communication with parents, students, teachers, alumni, and others.

continues...

It should be noted again that the minimum age to use Facebook is 13 (generally seventh grade and up), so primary school communications for grades K–6 have to be limited to parents only. Teachers and school administrators who are on Facebook should also take extra care to configure their privacy settings so that students, parents, and colleagues have an appropriate level of access (see Chapter 10, "How To: Build and Manage Relationships on the Social Web," for how to do this).

Shawn Roner (@shawnroner) is a high school principal and Daryll Johnson (@darylljohnson) is a middle school social science teacher. They are coeditors of EDBuzz.org, a blog about using technology in education.

Political Campaigns

As in nonprofit campaigns, constituent marketing for political candidates is a perfect example of hypertargeting on the social Web. In *Applebee's America* (Simon & Schuster, 2007), authors Ron Fournier, Douglas Sosnik, and Matthew Dowd make the compelling case that George W. Bush won the 2004 presidential election in large part because of his team's marketing savvy and knowledge of "the customer." The Bush team conducted the most extensive demographics and market research in campaign history, segmented different constituents of voters, and targeted each group with messages and promises that resonated with their "gut values." And that was when Facebook had eight million users, before anyone had ever heard of hypertargeted ads.

The Obama 2008 team understood this and did an even better job of targeting voters— aided in no small part by Facebook cofounder Chris Hughes, who took a sabbatical at the company to work for Obama's presidential campaign. The following case study walks through how the 2008 McCain and Obama campaigns differed in their use of social media.

Case Study: 2008 U.S. Presidential Campaign

Ray Valdes

When first hearing about social networking sites such as Facebook or Twitter, many people remark, "Social networking seems like light-hearted fun-and-games— which is all well and good, but what is the tangible business value? What real-world impact can result from these mostly trivial online interactions?"

One can respond to this question by pointing to the 2008 U.S. presidential election as a case study in effective use of social media. In that campaign, social networking and social media techniques played a major role in determining the outcome. It's hard to find an event in our society that has greater impact on business and finance than the outcome of this election, no matter what country you live in. And a pragmatic footnote is to point out that not just the votes, without obvious world-historical impact, but also $700 million in political contributions directly resulted from social media—a number that surely gets the attention of any businessperson.

This is not to assert that a hugely complex and multidimensional phenomenon such as the presidential election was determined by a single factor. Without getting into detailed political analysis (which is always subject to debate), it's clear that a large set of diverse factors played a role: highly entangled issues—such as the economy, the war, political parties, and interest groups—and the complex interplay of candidates' responses to events.

Having said that, take a moment to tune out the labyrinth of factors, set aside your political leaning, and look at the valuable lessons for business—in terms of both defensive maneuvers and aggressive offense.

Table 14.1 is a social media scoreboard for the two campaigns, McCain versus Obama in 2008.

Table 14.1   Social Media Activity—2008 McCain Versus Obama Campaigns

Category	Metric	McCain Campaign	Obama Campaign
Facebook	Members in group	620,000	2,300,000
MySpace	"Friends"	217,000	830,000
YouTube	Videos in channel	320	1700
Campaign Web site	Monthly visitors	4.1 million	8.6 million
Election results	Electoral votes	173	365
	Popular vote (%)	45.7%	52.9%
	Popular vote (M)	59.9 million	65.4 million

As you can see, Obama outpaced McCain in every metric relating to social media by anywhere from 2:1 to as much as 6:1. This led to a decisive victory in terms of state-by-state electoral votes and a healthy margin in terms of popular votes.

It's fair to ask the chicken-and-egg question: Aren't these social media metrics a mere reflection of broad public sentiment? What makes you think they're a driving factor?

In the 2008 campaign, it's clear that the participation in social media was both a leading indicator of later shifts in public opinion and a driving force in raising money and moving people to act. The Obama campaign was able to get 100,000 people to show up at a rally in St. Louis by getting the word out through inexpensive and fast social media channels. In the course of the campaign, it amassed a list of eight million supporter names and mobile phone numbers, and sent them emails, text messages, Twitter status messages, and Facebook updates.

One benefit of social media has been to lend visibility to campaigns at critical times. For example, the Facebook Group for the Obama campaign was very helpful when the campaign was getting started. Months later, the independently produced "Obama Girl" music video spread virally on YouTube and broadened the scope of the campaign's visibility. Finally, the well-crafted My.BarackObama.com portal (based, in part, on the MovableType blogging platform) proved effective in mobilizing supporters for get-out-the-vote efforts on an unprecedented geographic scale. More than visibility, a key factor was the capability to solicit funds: Obama's campaign reportedly raised $638 million from more than three million individual donors, with an average donation of less than $200.

The campaign social toolbox not only included a Facebook Group and Twitter account, but also an iPhone app that provided up-to-the-minute news and event information. As the political stakes get higher, campaigns rely on skilled staff and specialist contractors who have innovated their own proprietary techniques. For example, MoveOn.org released an effective get-out-the-vote message that integrated email, Web, and highly personalized video to create a compelling experience for the targeted recipient (see www.cnnbcvideo.com).

Ray Valdes (@rayval) is the vice president of research at Gartner Group.

Other political campaigns are starting to take notice. Last year, political rookie Patrick Mara used Facebook hypertargeting to defeat 16-year incumbent Carol Schwartz in a Washington, DC, city council primary. He used this targeting strategy:

- **Gays and lesbians**—Mara's team pushed information about his stance supporting gay marriage to everyone on Facebook who listed their sexual orientation as gay.

- **Parents**—Mara's team pushed ads about the public school system and education reform to everyone on Facebook with kids.

- **Republicans**—Mara's ads to self-identified Republicans on Facebook were about tax cuts, school vouchers, and other conservative darlings.

- **Location**—All of Mara's ads were location-targeted to people in the Washington, DC, area.

By directing specific messages that hit home with each of his voting constituents, Mara was able to establish the "gut values" connection that Fournier and his colleagues describe to defy all odds and win the election. Not only did Mara succeed in winning votes, but his hypertargeted messages helped recruit volunteers and grassroots donations.

In the following guest expert sidebar, Ray Valdes from Gartner Group explains why political campaigns are the ultimate marketing and branding exercise.

Political Candidates: The Ultimate "Considered Purchase"

Ray Valdes

Strong similarities exist between promoting a candidate and promoting a brand or product. In political campaigns, the candidate is being sold—the "product" that is being marketed to voters. This is a transaction whose economics are based not on money, but instead on the currency of trust, perception, and reference.

You can view the election of a president as the ultimate "considered purchase," in which prospective buyers invest a lot of time and effort in weighing alternatives before choosing. The presidential campaign process spans a multiyear time frame and, for 2008, consumed $2.5 billion in aggregate spending, ultimately resulting in a single "transaction"—actually, 130 million individual transactions (votes) executed on a single day.

As with any considered purchase, prospective buyers go through these decision phases:

- Awareness
- Consideration
- Transaction
- Fulfillment
- Loyalty
- Evangelism

The political sphere is unique because after an individual voter makes the purchase decision, no feedback loop is available about the outcome of that purchase to others considering the same item. This is different than a consumer decision to go to a movie, for example. In that scenario, the past experience of others with the same product provides valuable feedback for those who haven't yet made the choice. In the case of presidential elections, such post-sale feedback is not available, so the decision process must be based on *perception* instead of *reality*.

Therefore, political campaigns place an inordinate emphasis on less tangible aspects, such as branding, competitive positioning, and endorsements by trustworthy authorities. Successful candidates establish a distinctive brand, position it favorably, and also attempt to reposition their competitors in an unfavorable light. They use a wide range of media—paid media, "earned media" (conventional mainstream news), and social media—to communicate both factual information and content that works at the emotional level. In the presale phase, social media can be tremendously effective in shaping perception because of aspects that are personalized, participatory, peer-to-peer, and authentic.

Social sites and services enable campaigns to directly communicate in a personalized manner to an audience, and also enable "unofficial" communications (peer-to-peer instead of brand-to-consumer) that are often perceived to be more relevant, authentic, and credible than the official sources—and, therefore, are more effective in communicating the brand.

Ray Valdes (@rayval) is the vice president of research at Gartner Group.

Not only is the social Web valuable during the campaign process, but also elected offi-
cials such as President Obama are continuing to use Facebook and Twitter post-election
to stay connected to voters. Nearly 8 million people "like" Obama's Facebook Page and 3.5
million people follow him on Twitter (both managed by Organizing for America, a grassroots organization for Obama's agenda), and he uses these as important channels to provide policy updates; rally support for bills; encourage people to vote in city, state, House,
and Senate elections; share videos of speeches; and highlight issues that are personally
important to him (see Figure 14.10).

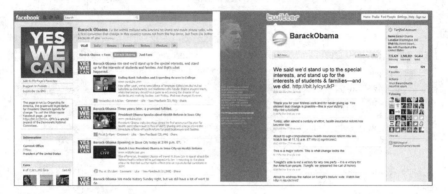

Figure 14.10
*President Obama has continued to use social media channels such as Facebook and Twitter while
in office to communicate and connect with his constituents.*

15

Corporate Governance, Strategy, and Implementation

We've covered a lot of ground thus far in terms of how to use the social Web on a product or brand level. But if you're a larger company with multiple departments, and especially if you're in a highly regulated industry, it's critical to address corporate governance and implementation across your organization. This chapter discusses the three aspects of corporate governance for social media: culture, policy, and tools.

Social Media Culture

As anyone who has tried introducing new technologies to an organization knows, tools and tactics are easy. Getting people to believe and adopt is hard. It requires organizations to change their culture, and where there is change, there will almost always be resistance.

It is doubly challenging when an organization tries to adopt Facebook, Twitter, and LinkedIn more generally because these sites are all about openness, transparency, and individual empowerment, which is not always aligned with enterprise culture. Yet a more open culture is needed for social initiatives to take root in the first place and to succeed, and the customer voice exposed by social media also forces organizations to change and become more open. The following sections provide a few examples and tips on what it takes to influence company culture to support corporate social initiatives.

Getting an Executive Sponsor

Most social initiatives start bottom-up by an individual or group of individuals who interface with customers or are familiar with Facebook and Twitter from their personal lives. But for these initiatives to succeed, they need to be blessed at the highest levels. Executives need to be aware of these initiatives—and, ideally, involved in and contributing to them—to set the right culture, signal support, and allocate resources.

In fact, the leaders of some of the most innovative organizations in recent years have also been some of the earliest adopters of Twitter and Facebook, including Warren Buffet, Marc Benioff (CEO of Salesforce.com), John Stumpf (Group EVP of Community Banking at Wells Fargo), and U.S. President Barack Obama.

Executives who embrace social media are also evolving their leadership style to become more open. Consider some thoughts from Charlene Li on some of the benefits of giving up control.

The Benefits of Giving Up Control

Charlene Li

The annals of business literature proclaim the wisdom of flat organizations and hierarchies. But if you look at the organizational charts of most companies, you'll see one person at the top and multiple layers. This isn't an org chart; it's a *control* chart. The reality is, most people want and need to be in control, because that's the only way they can be sure things will get done.

I believe that leaders need to learn how to give up control while still being in command. It seems like a contradiction, but let's take a closer look at what leaders actually do. Ultimately, they need to inspire people to band together and accomplish a specific goal. Giving up control can be a very effective way to reach that goal. That's because being open, in terms of information sharing and decision making, has very real benefits, including these:

- **Removing friction**—Moving information up and down a hierarchy is inefficient and, in some cases, becomes such a barrier that people just don't bother. Collaboration and social technologies make it much easier to share information, thus removing much of the friction. Want to know who the internal experts are on behavioral targeting? Do a search to see who has written a post or worked on a project in this area. Removing barriers to information and people improves access to information and lowers the time and cost of getting things done.

- **Scaling efforts**—Instead of having just one person focused on a problem, what if you could have your entire department working to solve the problem? Or even your entire employee base providing customer service? Best Buy enables any of its employees to answer customer questions at www.twitter.com/twelpforce; to date, more than 2,200 employees have signed up to do exactly that. So if you're worried about the time and resources needed to engage in social media, turn to your customers and employees to scale for you—of course, this can happen only if you're willing to give up control.

- **Enabling fast response**—If something happens on the front lines, who's empowered to fix it? At the State Bank of India, Chairman Om Bhatt transformed the culture of its 200,000 local banks so that customer service problems were addressed by the people best able to solve them: the bank window teller. Instead of having to wait for information to go up and a decision to come back down a hierarchy, bank branch employees were given the training—and, more important, the permission—to make decisions at their discretion. The result was a marked improvement in customer service marks.

- **Gaining commitment**—Something amazing happens when you give people power: They commit themselves, heart and soul. When customers realize that they can tell a company what they really think about a product and know that the company will take it to heart, many will provide detailed ideas on what they would like to see improved. Employees who understand the responsibility that comes with power begin to act like owners, taking the small actions that cumulatively can move markets.

Giving up control isn't easy or natural, but if you can understand the benefits that come with it, you'll be on your way to putting in place the guidelines, parameters, and training that act as the guardrails to keep people pointed and pulling in the same direction.

Charlene Li (@charleneli) is the founding partner of Altimeter Group, author of Open Leadership *(Jossey-Bass, 2010), and co-author of* Groundswell *(Harvard Business Press, 2008).*

Creating a Cross-Functional Social Media Council

Often social networking projects fail because of competing functional agendas, organizational politics, or some compliance issue that was overlooked because legal or IT never had a chance to weigh in. Companies such as DeVry and Prudential have successfully achieved collaborative buy-in across the organization by creating a cross-functional social media council or task force. Some of the council's responsibilities include these:

- Creating and communicating a simple set of social media guidelines for employees on appropriate use and conduct on social networking sites.

- Reviewing and auditing social media assets at least quarterly so that the appropriate action can be taken if, say, someone creates a Facebook Page for the company but stops posting to it on a regular basis (it essentially becomes a dead asset).

- Developing a succession plan for Twitter accounts and Facebook Pages when the employees who created them move on to a different job within the company or to a new employer.

- Establishing a process for handing off certain customer requests or complaints that appear on social networking sites to the appropriate internal departments and closing the loop with the customer. (Most companies are doing this via email today. If you want to get fancy, you can try to integrate Twitter with a CRM system.)

- Making sure all the disparate social media initiatives link back to one another when and where appropriate. For instance, a Facebook Page can "favorite" other Facebook Pages and, of course, Twitter accounts can follow other Twitter accounts. Pepsi has its main Facebook favorite the Facebook Pages of its subbrands, affiliates, and spokespeople, including Pepsi Canada, Gatorade, and athlete Clint Dempsey.

- Determining what aspects of Facebook or Twitter to in-house versus outsource to an agency.

- Standardizing on tools and negotiating a company-wide license or discount.

Having everyone who wants to be involved on board increases the chances that functional agendas can give way to the customer agenda. Social media can be one of those high-profile, high-stakes, high-reward initiatives, so it's better to have everyone win together and learn together.

At the same time, you don't want to create more bureaucracy and hinder creativity within your organizations. A few best practices for social media councils are to limit the time and duration of meetings to only what's absolutely necessary and to limit the number of individuals from each department. (In most cases, one representative is sufficient.)

Partnering with IT, Legal, and Compliance

Make sure you include representatives from IT, legal, and compliance on your cross-functional council. The challenge is that these departments are, by design, typically averse to change. From their perspective, social media is scary because it exposes your organization to new technology, legal, and compliance risk—and if something goes wrong, they're on the hook.

Yet business environments change quickly, and it's important for those teams in your company to recognize that those risks are already at play because your customers and employees are on Facebook and Twitter talking about your company. The most important thing you can do is get buy-in from top-level executives around your social initiatives and ask them to help rally IT, legal, and compliance resources and support around business objectives. People managing the social accounts need to spend time understanding and staying up-to-date with the terms of service on Facebook, Twitter, LinkedIn, and anywhere else the company has a presence. Together you will best be able to identify the risks that are the greatest threat to your business and come up with the set of policies and plan to mitigate them.

Communicating Business Value

Another challenge for social media is how to make and keep it a priority. Ultimately, this hinges on your ability to tie your Facebook, LinkedIn, and Twitter efforts back to important business objectives (as we talked about in Chapter 10, "How To: Build and Manage Relationships on the Social Web") and be able to measure the value in dollars, NetPromoter score, renewal rate, or whatever you are optimizing for.

As with your company's other marketing initiatives, this is where reports and dashboards come in handy to provide qualitative and quantitative results justifying your social media investment (see Figure 15.1).

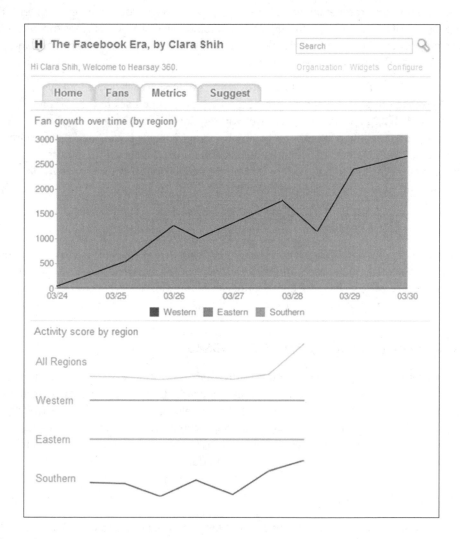

Figure 15.1
Analytics and reporting such as this one from Hearsay Labs help visually and clearly communicate the business value of Facebook, Twitter, and LinkedIn initiatives.

Educating and Inspiring

People are often most afraid of what is unknown, so training and educating your employees on not only the value of the social Web but also how to achieve their personal and department goals using social tools will reduce the amount of resistance to change. Companies such as Zappos, Coldwell Banker, and the State of Utah now incorporate Twitter and Facebook training as part of new-hire orientation, as well as provide ongoing tutorials and support for employees. Other companies have encouraged "reverse mentorship" on social media topics, with Gen-Y hires helping teach older employees the ins and outs of Facebook. Many employees and executives also just ask their teenage sons and daughters or nieces and nephews for help.

A number of popular conferences that provide an immersive experience for key employees to quickly learn and absorb best practices to bring back to the company, including Web 2.0 Expo and the Social Networking Conference. (Register at www. socialnetworkingconference.com/clarashih.php to get $75 off.) If you have a large number of employees or company-confidential information and scenarios to discuss, it may be more cost-effective to host your own mini-conference to facilitate companywide learning and support for social Web projects.

Hiring the Right People

Companies are also hiring for social media savvy. Bring in new employees who tweet and use Facebook on a regular basis, and they will help spread social media knowledge and culture. Just as you'd think twice about hiring someone who doesn't know how to use email, basic social media skills are becoming an important job skill to seek or train for.

Social Media Policy and Processes

To help create and support a corporate culture that accepts social media, it helps to have clear guidelines and processes in place to steer individuals and departments in the right direction. The point of introducing policy isn't to stifle innovative grassroots efforts, but rather to align the organization's goals and ensure compliance with company brand-level objectives and industry regulation. The first step is to identify key risks for your organization, and then to craft a social media policy that addresses those risks.

Identifying Key Risk Areas

Enterprise social networking requires a certain degree of openness to work and to succeed, but this introduces new risks around privacy and security, intellectual property, and misrepresentation by employees. An important first step in instituting proper corporate governance is to honestly assess where the key risks might be. At the end of the day, it is more important to be aware of and manage risk than try to avoid risk altogether because that is costly, frustrating, and impossible. The optimal level of risk is not zero; it's just something you need to acknowledge, mitigate, and manage.

- **Privacy and security**—The biggest security risks around enterprise social networking are generally not related to technology. They involve identity and privacy. A wealth of personal information about individuals is available on social networking sites. To establish their identity and build rapport with their friend connections, people are very forthcoming with personal data such as date of birth, education, employment history, and the like. But especially without the right privacy settings in place, members of online social networking sites could become easy targets for identity theft. Seemingly harmless pieces of information such as your hometown or your pet's name are often the same kinds of security questions that other sites, such as banking sites, use to verify your identity.

- **Intellectual property and confidentiality**—The second big risk area for businesses is safeguarding intellectual property and confidentiality against competitive or malicious threats. Sites such as Facebook and LinkedIn remove a lot of barriers to interacting with customers and others in the community-at-large for productive activities such as marketing, sales, product innovation, and recruiting, but they also expose your business to the risk that data will be shared with the wrong people.

- **Data ownership**—An important issue to keep in mind is ownership of data and content related to your brand generated on Twitter or Facebook Pages. At least in the Facebook terms of service, Facebook owns this data. Facebook has always maintained open access to this data for brands and Page owners, but from a legal perspective, it's important to recognize this technicality. For this reason, any content or information that requires clear ownership and confidentiality that you do choose to publish to social networking sites should appear via a platform application that you commission for this purpose rather than through the out-of-the-box mechanisms the site provides. (Popular custom application developers include Context Optional and Buddy Media.)

- **Employee productivity**—One risk of encouraging Facebook is that your employees waste all their time on nonbusiness-related activities such as socializing with friends, uploading pictures, and playing Farmville or Mafia Wars. Businesses can mitigate this risk by restricting access to certain parts of Facebook from the company network or by developing and communicating clear social media guidelines for employees, as we discuss shortly.

- **Brand misrepresentation**—Last, but not least, the openness of social media may increase the opportunities for your employees to speak out of turn and potentially misrepresent your brand to customers, partners, and the public-at-large, either purposefully or inadvertently. For the former, you could imagine, for example, that a disgruntled former employee who was fired might attempt to retaliate by saying negative things about your company on public forums in Facebook. For the latter, a common example involves employees who carelessly or unknowingly post inappropriate public photos on their Facebook profile, which then reflects badly on your company. As we discuss in the next section, it's very important to develop a social media policy and make sure that employees and others receive the proper training *before* they are allowed to participate.

Table 15.1 calls out the top issues to consider *before* you embark on corporate social initiatives.

Table 15.1   Confidentiality Pitfalls of Enterprise Social Networking

Business Area	Major Threat	How to Mitigate
Sales	Sales reps at competitor vendors target your contacts.	Accept friend requests only from people you know and trust. Adjust privacy controls to hide the visibility of your friend connections.
Marketing	Negative buzz in your social community gets publicized by competitors.	This is unavoidable and exists to a lesser degree on pre–Facebook era sites. If there are consistent instigators of negative feedback on your social communities, spend time investigating who these people are. Maybe they are competitors you should kick out.
Human resources	Your organizational structure is revealed to company outsiders; top executives are easily targeted by headhunters.	Although some HR departments have tried to institute corporate policies to limit what company-related information employees disclose on their profile, this is difficult to justify and enforce on employees' personal profiles.
Product innovation	Product plans and ideas put forth are visible to competitors.	Limit participation to a select group of trusted individuals instead of making it an open free-for-all.

Crafting a Social Media Policy

If your business is like most, company policy should be in place governing offline activities and likely online activities such as sending email, instant messaging, and surfing the Web. Companies should also develop policies governing suggested and permissible use of social networking technologies by employees, specifically to mitigate the risks identified.

Certain things you don't ever want employees to say (such as profanity), and it's good to communicate a clear stance on those. This also helps your employees internalize the policy if you can talk about the implications of their participation and include real-world examples of when employee use of social media has gone wrong, such as in the Domino's Pizza video on YouTube that we mentioned in Chapter 5, "Customer Service in the Facebook Era." A lot of what ends up in your social media policy may feel like common sense, but formalizing it in writing is often a good wakeup call for employees to "think before they tweet." It also provides grounds for termination or other disciplinary action if employees do abuse social media privileges.

Beyond communicating clearly unacceptable use, it's a good idea to offer guidance rather than requirements, allow for flexibility, and encourage employees' creativity and unique personalities to come across, within limits. Otherwise, if your PR team is scripting every tweet, what's the point of letting employees participate in the first place?

Every company might end up with a different social media policy that reflects its unique culture and business, but it can be helpful to use other organizations' social media policy or guidelines as a starting point. Your organization might want to incorporate a few common elements into its social media policy:

- **Communicate trust and goals**—Acknowledge that the company is entrusting its employees with its brand, trade secrets, and legal compliance. In turn, the company expects employees to use Facebook, Twitter, and other social technologies in responsible and productive ways that contribute to the goals of the company.

- **Provide helpful reminders and suggestions**—Remind employees that they are representing your brand in their posts and responses. You might want to suggest which kinds of content to post, which content to respond to, and which issues to defer to a different department to resolve, such as a customer service team.

- **Establish rules for moderating public discussion**—Part of your social media guidelines should also include your organization's outward-facing policy, including when it is acceptable for employees to delete a post (for example, if it contains profanity, contains messages of hate, or is otherwise irrelevant to the purpose of the Facebook Page or online community). Communicate this both to the public on your Web site or Facebook Page and to employees so that they know how and when to moderate.

- **Clearly articulate compliance requirements**—If you are in a regulated industry, such as financial services, certain statements and personal information cannot be discussed on a public forum such as Facebook or Twitter. Make sure your employees are aware that these blacklisted conversations apply also to social media, and consider using a tool that helps monitor and flag any situations in which these requirements may have been compromised. Don't give your employees legalese—try to explain it in clear and simple terms.

- **Limit use to business-related activities**—Especially if you have nonsalaried workers being paid by the hour, it might be a good idea to clearly articulate that the time they are at work needs to be focused on business-related activities (both online and offline). If it's a serious problem for your organization, you might want to consider getting IT involved to block certain URLs (such as to any Facebook games).

- **Develop a transition plan**—Employees and even entire teams or departments can come and go. It's important to create a transition plan to ensure seamless and continued ownership for assets such as Facebook Pages and Twitter accounts.

The State of Utah's Department of Technology Services has done an excellent job incorporating many of these elements in formulating a social media policy for state employees. The state's chief technology officer, Dave Fletcher, realized that Facebook and Twitter are valuable channels for state agencies to reach, engage, and provide information for residents. Here is an excerpt from its policy. (The full version can be accessed at http://tinyurl.com/utahsocialguide.)

State of Utah Social Media Guidelines (Excerpt)

The purpose of this document is to provide guidelines for use of social media at the State of Utah. Agencies may utilize these guidelines as a component of agency policy development for sanctioned participation using Social Media services, or simply as employee guidelines. If you are a State employee or contractor creating or contributing to blogs, microblogs, wikis, social networks, virtual worlds, or any other kind of social media both on and off the utah.gov domain, these guidelines are applicable. The State expects all who participate in social media on behalf of the State, to understand and to follow these guidelines. These guidelines will evolve as new technologies and social networking tools emerge.

Engagement

- Emerging platforms for online collaboration are changing the way we work, and offer new ways to engage with customers, colleagues, and the world at large. It is a new model for interaction and social computing that can help employees to build stronger, more successful citizen and agency business relationships. It is a way for State employees to take part in national and global conversations related to the work we are doing at the State.

- If you participate in social media, follow these guiding principles:

  - Ensure that your agency sanctions official participation and representation on social media sites.

  - Stick to your area of expertise and provide unique, individual perspectives on what is going on at the State, and in other larger contexts.

  - Post meaningful, respectful comments, no spam, and no remarks that are off-topic or offensive.

  - Pause and think before posting. Reply to comments in a timely manner, when a response is appropriate.

  - Respect proprietary information, content, and confidentiality.

  - When disagreeing with others' opinions, keep it appropriate and polite.

  - Ensure that your participation is consistent with the provisions of Utah Administrative Rule R477-9. Employee Conduct.

  - Participation must comply with the posted Privacy Policy of the State.

  - Know and follow the State's Acceptable Use Policy, Information Protection 5000-1700, and Confidential Information 5000-1701 policies.

  - Use social media collaboration tools explicitly authorized in the State's Internet based Collaboration Tool Standard 4300-0012.

  - Follow applicable agency social media policies.

Rules of Engagement

- **Transparency**—Your honesty will be quickly noticed in the social media environment. If you are blogging about your work at the State, use your real name, identify that you work for the State of Utah, and be clear about your role. If you have a vested interest in something you are discussing, be the first to point it out.

- **Judicious**—Make sure your efforts to be transparent do not violate the State's privacy, confidentiality, and any applicable legal guidelines for external communication. Get permission to publish or report on conversations that are meant to be private or internal to the State. All statements must be true and not misleading and all claims must be substantiated and approved. Never comment on anything related to legal matters, litigation, or any parties the State may be in litigation with without the appropriate approval. If you want to write about other government entities, make sure you know what you are talking about and that you have any needed permissions. Be smart about protecting yourself, your privacy, and any sensitive, restricted, or confidential information. What is published is widely accessible, not easily retractable, and will be around for a long time, so consider the content carefully.

- **Knowledgeable**—Make sure you write and post about your areas of expertise, especially as related to the State and your assignments. If you are writing about a topic that the State is involved with but you are not the State expert on the topic, you should make this clear to your readers. Write in the first person. If you publish to a Website outside the State, please use a disclaimer something like this: "The postings on this site are my own and do not necessarily represent the State of Utah's positions, strategies, or opinions." Respect brand, trademark, copyright, fair use, disclosure of processes and methodologies, confidentiality, and financial disclosure laws. If you have any questions about these, see your agency legal representative. Remember, you are personally responsible for your content.

- **Perception**—In online social networks, the lines between public and private, personal and professional are blurred. By identifying yourself as a State employee, you are creating perceptions about your expertise and about the State by legislative stakeholders, customers, business partners, and the general public, and perceptions about you by your colleagues and managers. Be sure that all content associated with you is consistent with your work and with the State's values and professional standards.

continues...

- **Conversational**—Talk to your readers like you would talk to people in professional situations. Avoid overly "composed" language. Bring in your own personality and say what is on your mind. Consider content that is open-ended and invites response. Encourage comments. Broaden the conversation by citing others who are commenting about the same topic and allowing your content to be shared or syndicated.

- **Excitement**—The State of Utah is making important contributions to the State and nation, to the future of government, and to public dialogue on a broad range of issues. Our activities are focused on providing services and on government innovation that benefits citizens and stakeholders. Share with the participants the things we are learning and doing, and open up social media channels to learn from others.

- **Value**—There is a lot of written content in the social media environment. The best way to get yours read is to write things that people will value. Social communication from the State should help citizens, partners, and co-workers. It should be thought-provoking and build a sense of community. If it helps people improve knowledge or skills, build their businesses, do their jobs, solve problems, or understand the State better, then it is adding value.

- **Leadership**—There can be a fine line between healthy debate and incendiary reaction. Do not denigrate others or the State. It is not necessary to respond to every criticism or barb. Frame what you write to invite differing points of view without inflaming others. Some topics, like politics, slide easily into sensitive territory. Be careful and considerate. Once the words are out there, you cannot get them back. Once an inflammatory discussion gets going, it is hard to stop.

- **Responsibility**—What you write is ultimately your responsibility. Participation in social computing on behalf of the State is not a right but a privilege.

- **Pause**—If you are about to publish something that makes you even the slightest bit uncomfortable, do not post the statement. Take a minute to review these guidelines and try to figure out what is bothering you, then fix it. If you are still unsure, you might want to discuss it with your manager or agency legal representative. Ultimately, what you publish is yours, as is the responsibility, and any possible repercussions.

- **Mistakes**—If you make a mistake, admit it. Be upfront and be quick with your correction. If you are posting to a blog, you may choose to modify an earlier post. Make it clear that you have done so.

October 12, 2009

One area where it gets tricky is what employees do in their own time with their personal social networking profiles—the line blurs between what affects your brand and business, and what is none of your business. Especially if you have nonsalaried employees who get paid by the hour, anything they do on Facebook, Twitter, or LinkedIn related to your business after hours technically counts as overtime. If this is desirable, you need a way to track this time spent. If this is not desirable, make sure you include in your policy that such employees are not allowed to do any company business on social networking sites except during business hours.

Of course, having a social media policy is pointless if your employees don't know about it. Training and education are an important part of corporate governance. As we talked about earlier, update your new-hire orientation curriculum to include mention of both the advantages and risks of social networking. Give a short presentation about best practices and risks of social tools at your next company all-hands meeting.

Communicating a Policy to Fans

Except for minors and country restrictions, basically anyone can view and "like" any Facebook Page. And any Page fan can post on the Wall. This lowered barrier to sharing is great for engaging the community but also poses certain legal and compliance risks, especially for certain industries. Although there is no way to avoid these risks altogether (even if you're not on Facebook, customers or employees could still be creating situations in which your business might be liable), there are ways of mitigating these risks on your Facebook Page.

The first approach is to establish ground rules for your community of fans and let them know you hold them in good faith. If it's your policy to remove inappropriate comments, it might not be a bad idea to be transparent about that fact. A wonderful example of this comes from Dunkin' Donuts, which created a section on "DD Facebook Etiquette" on its Facebook Page (see Figure 15.2).

Figure 15.2
Dunkin' Donuts displays its ground rules for the community on its Facebook Page.

From the looks of it, this seems to work pretty well for the Dunkin' Donuts Page. But Dunkin' Donuts is a well-loved brand. For other businesses, especially those in highly regulated industries such as financial services, insurance, and medicine, extra care needs to be taken to ensure that the openness of the social Web doesn't come at the expense of compliance with government and industry regulation. At Hearsay Labs, we have worked with many customers across these industries to monitor and react in real time to these situations (see Figure 15.3).

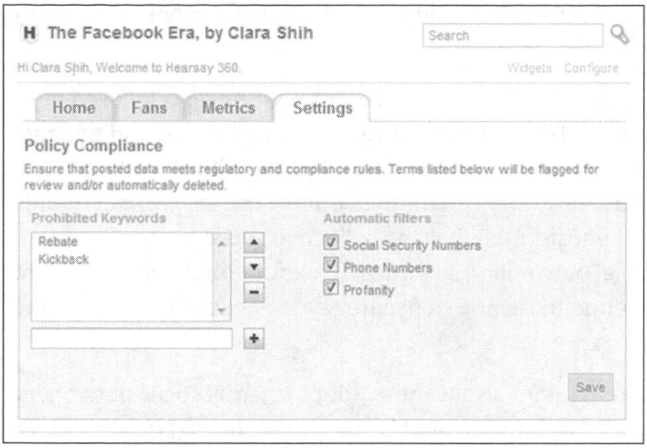

Figure 15.3
Hearsay 360 monitoring and keyword-filtering tools enable corporate admins to quickly customize discussion blacklists and protect the company brand and protocol across all company Facebook Pages and Twitter accounts.

Social Systems and Technologies

With the right culture and policy in place, we are ready to talk about the technology. In this section, we cover open versus custom networks, standards, integration, and popular business tools.

Choosing the Right Network Model

Companies have two technology options for how they want to run their customers networks: create communities on open networks such as Facebook or create custom invite-only networks using services such as Ning or Lithium (see Table 15.2).

Table 15.2   Open Networks and Custom Networks for Business

Open Networks	Custom Networks
Facebook	Ning
Twitter	Lithium
LinkedIn	Jive
Yelp	Leverage
MySpace	INgage Networks
	Drupal

Each approach has pros and cons. Open networks benefit from better user adoption because customers, partners, and employees are already using many of these online social networking services in their personal lives. Instead of asking customers to come to you, you are going to them. But going this route also presents risks surrounding privacy, security, and intellectual property.

Closed networks, on the other hand, offer more control and focused interaction among community members, but at the expense of lower adoption and engagement. For many chief information officers (CIOs), in particular, going with closed networks might be tempting, but in doing so, they might miss out on the very aspect of online social networking that is so transformational: the collective social graph. Metcalfe's Law tells us that the value of a social networking site goes up exponentially with the number of members. Indeed, the reach, openness, and transparency of Facebook, LinkedIn, and Twitter make them so compelling.

Although companies might also want to adopt internal social networking and collaboration tools such as Thoughtfarmer and Lotus Connections (both introduced in Chapter 7, "Innovation and Collaboration in the Facebook Era"), these should be in addition to, not in place of, the greater opportunity of plugging into sites where employees can access and cross-pollinate ideas with customers, partners, and others outside the company.

What does this mean for companies? Legal and IT will to accept the new realities of the social Web and take extra precautions to address issues around compliance, security, and governance, as mentioned already. Social network technology providers need to continue rising to the challenge with more and better features that address enterprise requirements. A great example of this is how Facebook has partnered with companies such as Hearsay Labs to bring a trusted corporate standard for security, privacy, reliability, availability, and compliance to a traditionally consumer model. The partnership is helping make strides in addressing valid IT concerns and giving CIOs peace of mind about implementing social technologies for the enterprise.

Industry Standards and Portability

With the hundreds of social networking services and platforms that have emerged in the last few years, businesses that want to adopt these technologies face another difficult challenge around data portability. Many in the industry are calling for standards around social data to accommodate the large number of these heterogeneous open networks. OpenSocial was developed (originally by Google) as a set of open source APIs that extends functionality across any social networking site or other Web site. Having a standard set of APIs would theoretically enable developers to write an application once and have it work on any OpenSocial site. OpenSocial has since spun off from Google as its own independent nonprofit organization and is supported by an industry consortium of social networking sites, including MySpace, LinkedIn, Hi5, Orkut, and Ning. More than 7,500 applications were developed on OpenSocial in its first year.

The goal of OpenSocial is to allow social applications and data to transcend the boundaries of different Web sites and particular social networking sites. It is an interesting idea with a large number of participating vendors, but it will work only if steps are taken to define the data visibility and security rules across applications on each site.

A separate initiative, OpenID, is an open and decentralized standard for user authentication that enables users to log in to different Web sites with a single digital identity. Instead of having to create a separate user name and password for each site, users can create an OpenID once and have single sign-on to sites that support the system.

Integration

Although Facebook actually supports OpenID as an alternate way to log into the site when you already have an account, it is also trying to create a proprietary single sign-on system around Facebook for Websites (which, as we discussed in Chapter 1, "The Fourth Revolution," is a way for Web sites to let users log in with their Facebook credentials). As the dominant players in this space, it is not in the best interest of companies such as Facebook, Twitter, and LinkedIn to fully standardize their functionality. Instead, they (and just about every social networking site) have invested heavily in building out rich platforms and APIs to make it easy for external Web sites to integrate with their services.

To get started, you (or your IT staff) can review the API documentation here:

- **Facebook**—http://developers.facebook.com
- **LinkedIn**—http://developer.linkedin.com
- **Twitter**—http://apiwiki.twitter.com

Perhaps because of its simplicity, Twitter has been the most aggressive about opening its API for integration and encouraging outside parties to build applications on top of its real-time stream "plumbing." Here are some thoughts from Ray Valdes of Gartner Group on how Twitter is like an "information bus" for the Web.

Twitter as an "Information Bus" for the Web

Ray Valdes

Twitter provides an API or programming interface that makes it easy for other social sites to integrate with. Because the Twitter notion of identity and relationships is not as rich and robust as Facebook, there are different scenarios and modes of use. Twitter makes it really use to use it as a broadcast medium and share information with the world. For example, Plancast is a social site that centers on events, calendars, and plans (in some ways, It's a next generation of sites such as Eventful and Upcoming). Users of Plancast create calendar entries with public events that they will be attending, such as an industry conference. When you join or create an event on Plancast, you can optionally publish this event to Facebook and Twitter.

Twitter can be viewed as the "information bus" for the social Web, and the simplicity of its programming interface makes it easy to broadcast information to this channel. A large crop of location-oriented ventures, such as Gowalla, BrightKite, Loopt, FourSquare, and ZoomInfo, uses Twitter (and Facebook) as a content broadcast or content syndication mechanisms.

Ray Valdes (@rayval) is the vice president of research at Gartner Group.

Popular Tools

If you're short on resources (and even if you're not), there's no reason to reinvent the wheel: Thousands of social media applications have emerged to tackle different common business areas. Table 15.3 is by no means an exhaustive list, but it covers some of the most popular tools companies are using today.

Table 15.3   Popular Social Tools for Business

Key Areas Addressed on the Social Web	Leading Tools	Department
Listening and monitoring	Radian6, Scout Labs, Visible Technologies, TweetBeep	PR and brand management
Fan base construction and management of client relationships on Facebook and Twitter	Hearsay Labs	Marketing and sales
Twitter stream management	Seesmic, TweetDeck, Brizzly, TwitHive, Hootsuite, CoTweet (acquired by ExactTarget)	Depends on use cases
Sales intelligence	Gist, Xobni, InsideView	Sales
Branded sweepstakes and contests	Votigo, Wildfire	Marketing and agency
E-commerce	SocialAmp, Wishpot, Payvment	Online sales ops
Social ad networks	Cubics (acquired by AdKnowledge), RockYou!, Appvert, AdChap, VideoEgg	Marketing and agency
Responses to customer issues	Lithium, Helpstream, RightNow, Salesforce	Customer service

< < < T A K E A W A Y S

✓ Enterprise adoption of social tools requires culture change before anything else, followed by process and policy, and then technology.

✓ Although it's important to have an executive sponsor, the most successful corporate initiatives are collaborative across multiple departments, including IT.

✓ The leaders of today and tomorrow are learning to give up "control" and are instead inspiring and listening to their employees and customers.

✓ Companies have a choice of cultivating communities on public networks such as Facebook and Twitter, or developing their own custom networks on Ning, Lithium, Jive, or other vendor systems. Even in the latter case, companies should be monitoring and tying back public discussions on Facebook and Twitter to these private forums.

✓ All the popular social networking sites, including Facebook, LinkedIn, and Twitter, offer APIs that allow for custom development and integration.

> > > T I P S   a n d   T O   D O's

❑ Form a cross-functional social media council with representatives from marketing, IT, legal/compliance, individual brands' business units, and others.

❑ Always tie social efforts back to established business priorities, to rally support as well as align vision and expectations.

❑ Identify and honestly communicate social media's risks to your business, such as privacy and security, intellectual property, and employee productivity. Use these to drive your social media guidelines.

❑ As part of your social media policy, make sure you come up with a transition plan in case certain employees leave the company or a team decides to abandon its Facebook Page.

❑ Consider developing a social media policy for fans and communicating that on your company's social network presence, similar to what Dunkin' Donuts has done on its Facebook Page.

16

The Future of Social Business

Online social networking for business is still a nascent and rapidly changing field. Even in the short amount of time between the last edition of this book and this one, new vendors, user interfaces, and jargon have sprung up—along with new possibilities. Indeed, vendors and technologies might come and go—Six Degrees, for one, is long gone but left an important legacy. And many new players almost certainly will emerge in this space.

What's critical isn't the specific technologies of today, but rather the general shift in mind-set toward an increasingly socially networked world. To adequately prepare, we must rethink and evolve our relationships, interactions, and business strategies to account for a social Web. Just as the Internet fundamentally changed nearly every aspect of our personal and professional lives, the social graph represents a radical step that is already beginning to permeate many important areas of our lives.

Social media is a major disruption for how businesses market, sell, and innovate. The social Web is transforming how organizations and individuals learn, adapt, and evolve. Expectations and norms have changed regarding customer participation and how companies are organized. Companies today have no choice but to become transparent, responsive, and collaborative, or else risk going out of business.

With the Facebook Era, we move closer than ever before to becoming people-centric instead of technology-centric. Companies can get closer than ever before to their customers. Organizational strategies and decisions can be developed based on relationships and business goals instead of on technological limitations. Indeed, the online social graph at its best becomes invisible, fully ingrained in our online and offline tasks, transactions, and interactions. It makes our Web interactions and experiences emotional, interesting, and trusted.

Social, Personalized, and Real Time

Four themes will continue to grow in importance and dominate the customer experience in the Facebook Era: social, personalized, and mobile/real time.

Social

Companies are finally realizing the importance of social influence on purchase decisions and brand perception and are catering to these dynamics through their Web sites, email campaigns, Twitter accounts, and Facebook Pages. Within organizations, traditional enterprise applications that contributed to isolated functional silos are giving way to open, transparent systems that recognize that most business workflow takes place between individuals (that is, it is social).

Personalized

The ideal experience for a customer is one that delivers the right content to the right person at the right time. Over time, we have slowly gotten better at this, first with Google keyword search targeting and more recently with behavioral targeting based on past purchases and page views. Our social network profiles provide a key missing piece of our digital identities—who we are, where we're from, and what we like. These elements combined are powerful for businesses to use in determining not only who is a likely customer, but also how best to approach and message to this individual.

Mobile/Real Time

A number of startups, led by Loopt, Foursquare, Gowalla, Booyah!, and newcomer Burbn, have built popular geolocation applications to let users share their real-time location with friends. Facebook, Twitter, Yelp, and social gaming companies such as Zynga and SGN are also rapidly adding mobile and geolocation features. These mobile, real-time apps provide users with proactive real-world recommendations and incorporate game-like dynamics, such as awarding virtual goods, property, and status for "checking in" to certain places.

For example, users on Foursquare receive a "bender" badge for bar-hopping four nights in a row or a "gym rat" badge for checking in to ten "gym" locations within 30 days. Checking in at a certain location more times than anyone else earns you the title of "mayor," and some businesses now offer free drinks or snacks to the Foursquare mayor of their location. Gowalla is similar to Foursquare, but with fewer badges and more "items" to pick up and drop off in places (in other words, more gaming, less status). It is the second mover, but many people believe it has a better code base and product design. MyTown is GPS-enabled Monopoly with real physical places. Users can buy places and collect rent from others who check in to those places. Both Loopt and Foursquare are exploring geotargeted coupons. (For example, Loopt has partnered with Jack in the Box to serve up coupons when users are in the vicinity of a restaurant.)

Especially for local hangouts such as bars and restaurants where people like to socialize with friends, geolocation applications hold a lot of promise.

The ROI of the Social Web

Understandably, a large number of you are focused on return on investment (ROI) and might feel frustrated that no "magic bullet" answer can quantify the ROI of corporate social networking initiatives. The best parallel I can draw here is to rewind ten years to the early days of the Internet. It was as hard, if not harder, then to calculate the ROI of having email and a company Web page. The Internet was changing rapidly. (Of course, it is still changing!) Many businesses then chose to wait before going online. This was a mistake, especially for small businesses. Across almost every industry, new players emerged with more efficient, lower-cost models driven by the Web. Their competitive advantage was magnified as these new companies shaped and innovated new online models for their respective industries. Those who waited lost.

So what is the ROI of the social graph for business? What is the ROI of the Internet for business? This is the wrong question to ask because is too broad to adequately answer. The ROI depends on your business objectives and *how you are using* social networking to achieve them. The ROI in the sales context could be based on how many business contacts a rep can maintain, an increased close rate on deals, and a heightened capability to up-sell and cross-sell. For marketing, ROI might be measured via click-throughs and views, as is common today in advertising—or maybe a new metric of engagement is more appropriate.

As social networking technologies continue to evolve and our capability to tie social initiatives back to impact improves these next few years, ROI will become much more quantifiable and standardized. I encourage you to review the "Define Your Metrics" section in Chapter 9, "How To: Develop Your Facebook Era Plan and Metrics," in developing your organization's own social ROI model. Of course, if you need a starting point, you're welcome to use the social customer lifetime value formula I conceptualized.

Trends in the Social Web

So what does the future hold? Only time will tell, of course, but important trends are already taking shape. Fewer new social networking sites are emerging. The online social graph is becoming better integrated with other emerging technologies, such as video and mobile.

First, social networking services appear to be consolidating. This is partly because of standards initiatives, such as OpenSocial, but it is also the result of the network effects governing online social sites—large sites get larger and small sites get smaller much more quickly. Therefore, we should expect that clear winners and losers will emerge in the coming years even more than they have already.

Second, an increasing breadth of applications has become integrated with the social Web. Facebook started largely with profiles, photos, and events but is growing to include games, commerce, and even customer relationship management (CRM). The future will bring the power of the online social graph to the cutting edge in information and communication technology, such as real-time interactions and tighter integration with mobile devices. Already we are seeing applications such as Loopt and Foursquare use GPS technology to let people check into their favorite places and see where friends are in real time. Another area that might benefit greatly from enterprise social networking services is videoconferencing and Web conferencing. What if, in real time, people on a video or Web conference could see one another's profiles and mutual contacts? This might help establish greater rapport, especially among groups of people who are geographically dispersed and might not have met face-to-face. If efforts such as Facebook for Websites are successful, a few years from now we will think of Facebook less as a Web site and more as a social identity layer over other Web sites, covering perhaps a large portion of the Internet.

Third, as enterprise social networking and general social networking become the norm, we will see a sociological shift in people's behavior toward relationships and interactions. More value will be placed on social capital. People who are well connected will be disproportionately favored. They will be more empowered than ever to accumulate and exercise social capital. This is true both within organizations and on the Web, where product "influencers" (such as people who get retweeted a lot) will be worth more to advertisers and may even be asked to become affiliates for certain brands.

Fourth, IT departments and technology vendors will have no choice but to incorporate social technologies into the applications they provide. Employees will demand that their business tools have the same user interfaces and experiences that they utilize in their personal lives. As discussed in the previous chapter, CIOs will need to balance the benefits of plugging into the online social graph with the risks of not having complete control.

Finally, social networks and advertisers will need to address unanswered issues regarding user privacy, especially when it comes to behavioral targeting. For example, some progress has been made so far with the Network Advertising Initiative, an industry cooperative of online marketing and analytics companies (that is, ad networks and behavioral data companies) to introduce checks and balances for responsible privacy and data management.

Final Remarks

We are very lucky. Not only do we get to witness one of history's most profound technology and cultural revolutions, but we also get to shape it and directly experience it every day in numerous ways across our personal and professional lives. What exactly the future holds is anyone's guess, but where we are now with online social networking is similar to where we were in the 1990s with the Internet. We don't know specifics, but we do know that it will be big, whatever your company size or industry and regardless of whether you are in sales, marketing, product development, recruiting, or another business function.

Just as then, both extremes exist—the naysayers who believe this is a passing fad, and the yea-sayers who are eagerly jumping on the bandwagon and committing substantial resources without thinking through their business strategy and objectives. This book was meant to appeal to the vast majority of us who are in between, to help real companies with real customers understand the transformation that is underway and determine how they might adopt specific online social networking strategies to run a better business and please their customers.

Remember, this book is all about *you*. Please stay in touch and join the conversation as together we learn and invent the rules and possibilities of this new era:

- **Facebook**—www.facebook.com/thefacebookera
- **Facebook for Websites**—http://thefacebookera.com
- **Twitter**—http://twitter.com/clarashih

Good luck, and see you on the social Web!

Index

P